Southern Legal Studies

All for Civil Rights

All for Civil Rights

AFRICAN AMERICAN LAWYERS IN SOUTH CAROLINA, 1868–1968

W. Lewis Burke

The University of Georgia Press
ATHENS

A Sarah Mills Hodge Fund Publication
This publication is made possible in part through a grant from the Hodge Foundation in memory of its founder, Sarah Mills Hodge, who devoted her life to the relief and education of African Americans in Savannah, Georgia.

Athens, Georgia 30602
www.ugapress.org

Set in 10.25/13.5 Minion Pro by Graphic Composition, Inc., Bogart, GA

Most University of Georgia Press titles are available from popular e-book vendors.

Printed digitally

Library of Congress Cataloging-in-Publication Data

Names: Burke, William Lewis, author.
Title: All for civil rights : African American lawyers in South Carolina, 1868–1968 / W. Lewis Burke.
Other titles: Southern legal studies
Description: Athens : The University of Georgia Press, [2017] | Series: Southern legal studies
Identifiers: LCCN 2016051437 | ISBN 9780820350981 (hardback : alk. paper) | ISBN 9780820350998 (ebook)
Subjects: LCSH: African American lawyers—South Carolina—Biography. | African American lawyers—South Carolina—History. | African American lawyers—South Carolina—Registers.
Classification: LCC KF354.S6 B87 2017 | DDC 340.092/3960730757—dc23 LC record available at https://lccn.loc.gov/2016051437

CONTENTS

ACKNOWLEDGMENTS

No book can be written by one person alone. For me to thank everyone who has helped with this project is certainly appropriate but also a challenge. I have to start with the late Dr. George Rogers, who gave me Dr. John Oldfield's article on black lawyers in nineteenth-century South Carolina. Naturally, John's work and friendship have been invaluable. J. Clay Smith became an inspiration and my friend, and his work, my encyclopedia. Dr. Michael Mounter has been friend, colleague, and "my researcher." Although this book may have some errors, it will not be because Michael Mounter did not do everything possible to prevent them. There is no thanks sufficient enough for Michael. Lisa Davis has helped with innumerable tasks, including careful editing. Such eminent historians as Eric Foner, Joel Williamson, Patricia Sullivan, Leon Litwack, Lou Falkner Williams, Chris Waldrep, Dan Carter, Bill Hine, Darlene Clark Hine, Bobby Donaldson, and Jack Bass have offered words of encouragement and advice. My law school colleagues James L. Underwood, Herb Johnson, Ken Gaines, Vance Cowden, Bill McAninch, Dennis Nolan, Rebekah Maxwell, Terrye Conroy, David Lehmann, Karen Taylor, Danielle Holley Walker, John Montgomery, Rob Wilcox, Burnele Powell, and Jack Pratt have helped in more ways than I can count. I owe Keith McGraw, Cecil Williams, Beth Bilderback, Natalie Williams, and Megan Brown great thanks for their help with the photographs. For a project that has taken years, I have had innumerable students assist with research and a myriad of other tasks. Chief among these have been Romona Keith, Steve Bates, Justin Werner, Katherine Frankstone, Jack Cohoon, Shanaya L. Thompson, Melissa Garcia, Amanda Turner, Mark Williams, Hamp Markel, Constance Holloway, Amanda Barnhart, Allison Bullard, and Jessica Harrington. And if Judy Curry and Chris Coates had not provided me with a great place to eat and sleep in Alexandria, Virginia, I never would have gotten to spend so much time in the treasure trove of archives in Washington, D.C. My wife Anne and our daughters have been loving and supportive, and without Anne's editing this book would never have been finished. The University of Georgia Press is owed much, including Nancy Grayson, Walter Biggins, Paul Finkleman, and Tim Huebner.

Of course, I also must thank the black lawyers of South Carolina. Although this book covers more than a hundred years, I have been fortunate to have actually known and worked with some of these lawyers. Both Matthew Perry and Ernest Finney gave generously of their time in furtherance of this project. Harold Boulware advised and coached me in my early years as a lawyer in his courtroom, but I never took the opportunity to interview him. While William Whipper died forty years before I was born, I feel like I knew him also. So this book is dedicated to Matthew Perry, Ernest Finney, Harold Boulware, and William Whipper.

ABBREVIATIONS

AMA	American Missionary Association
CORE	Congress of Racial Equality
HUD	Department of Housing and Urban Development
MSBC	Minutes of the State Board of Canvassers of the State of South Carolina
NAACP	National Association for the Advancement of Colored People
SCDAH	South Carolina Department of Archives and History, Columbia, South Carolina
SCL	South Caroliniana Library, University of South Carolina
SCLC	Southern Christian Leadership Conference
SCSU	Historical Collection, South Carolina State University
SNCC	Student Nonviolent Coordinating Committee
USC	University of South Carolina

All for Civil Rights

INTRODUCTION

The history of the black lawyer in South Carolina is one of the most significant untold stories of the long and troubled struggle for equal rights in the state. From the Reconstruction period and continuing to the modern civil rights era, 170 black lawyers shaped both the political and legal lives of all the citizens of the state.

No other state's black bar has been studied over such an extended period of time. Other studies have been shorter in both time and treatment. Irvin Mollison's 1930 article "Negro Lawyers in Mississippi" covered thirty-one lawyers admitted to the bar between 1873 and 1912 and was the first such state study done.[1] Also in the 1930s, Charles Houston's "The Need for Negro Lawyers" in the *Journal of Negro Education*, and Fitzhugh Lee Styles's *The Negro Professional Man His Community* and *Negroes and the Law* examined a small subset of lawyers.[2] Judith Kilpatrick's 2000 study on Arkansas's black lawyers covers a longer period of time, but only at article length.[3] Another modern study of South Carolina's black lawyers, John Oldfield's "The African American Bar in South Carolina, 1877–1915," offers another snapshot of a relatively short period of time and focuses primarily on Charleston's black lawyers.[4] Other modern studies have focused on subsets of lawyers, such as women or NAACP lawyers, in a particular state.[5] The most significant study of America's black lawyers was J. Clay Smith's *Emancipation: The Making of the Black Lawyer, 1844–1944*, which is important for three reasons.[6] First, it is the encyclopedia on black lawyers of the United States over the century from 1844 to 1944. No one else has come close to achieving a more comprehensive longitudinal study of the changes that the profession has experienced as it grew, declined, and recovered. Second, Smith painstakingly identified the first black lawyer admitted in each state, as well as other significant lawyers in each state's legal history. Third, he wrote a short history of the struggle of these early black lawyers in each state. While Smith's treatments in his encyclopedia are by necessity brief, he laid the groundwork on which studies such as this one can build.

Why a state study of South Carolina? Although a small state in size and population, South Carolina is not small in the history of the black lawyer. It had the largest black population by percentage of any state until 1930. The state's population was 60 percent black from 1870 to 1890 and 58 percent in 1900, and it remained majority black through 1920. The state had one of the largest black bars in the Deep South before 1900. More significantly, South Carolina's bar also had the highest percentage of black lawyers of any southern state from 1880 to 1900.[7] In addition, South Carolina had the longest period of Reconstruction government—from 1863 to 1877, according to historian Eric Foner.[8] During that time, hundreds of blacks, including a number of lawyers, moved to the state seeking a place where they would be able to control their destiny. In fact, the first three black lawyers admitted to the bar in South Carolina were not natives. One came as a soldier from the Midwest; one came as a missionary society teacher from Pennsylvania; and the third came from New England planning to be a newspaperman. Two of them had had previous legal training and were soon actively practicing. Other black lawyers came from such diverse places as Maryland, Vermont, Massachusetts, Indiana, Ohio, Georgia, Barbados, and the West Indies.[9] Of course, Reconstruction also produced black lawyers who were natives of the state, including some who were former slaves.

In 1868 the majority of delegates elected to the state's constitutional convention were black, and black lawyers led the convention. In the following months, African Americans won a majority of seats in the state legislature, as well as other offices across the state. The leadership of the new legislature was

TABLE 1. Racial Breakdown of Population in Hundred Thousands According to South Carolina Census

Year	*Black*	*White*	*Total*	*%Black*
1870	416	290	706	59
1880	606	391	995	61
1890	699	462	1161	60
1900	782	558	1340	58
1910	836	764	1600	52
1920	865	819	1684	51
1930	794	944	1738	46
1940	814	1084	1898	42

TABLE 2. Number of Black Lawyers in Old Confederate States, 1880–1940

	1880	1890	1900	1910	1920	1930	1940
Alabama	4	13	6	12	11	4	4
Arkansas	5	30	27	20	26	16	8
Florida	8	13	13	14	13	10	10
Georgia	6	17	33	18	27	14	8
Louisiana	7	30	15	13	8	8	6
Mississippi	12	26	24	21	14	6	3
North Carolina	6	14	25	19	27	27	27
South Carolina	22 (15)	23	29	17	14	13	5
Tennessee	15	35	73	43	33	26	16
Texas	5	12	28	33	31	20	22
Virginia	18	38	53	37	52	57	48
TOTAL	108	251	326	247	256	201	157

composed primarily of black lawyers. Soon they were writing the statutes of the state. In 1870 a black lawyer was elected to the state supreme court, and for the first time in American history a state's laws were being definitively interpreted by a black appellate judge. Other black lawyers held major state executive and legislative offices. Freedom was defended and refined by black lawyers in courtrooms across the state. Some of these lawyers were the first black members of the bar to have graduated from the newly desegregated University of South Carolina School of Law. Two black lawyers were even elected to Congress.

These Reconstruction lawyers were in many ways the first black civil rights lawyers in America. Their primary role in the courts was as criminal defense counsel. Freedom was under constant challenge by the state's white population. Some blacks were prosecuted for simply being black, others for not working as the white man demanded. Some were assaulted and killed for exercising their political rights. Any black defense lawyer was a civil rights lawyer, whether in a simple assault case or in a challenge to racial discrimination in public accommodations. The prominent role these lawyers played in politics also made them leaders in the civil rights revolution that was Reconstruction. In a society where the majority of its citizens were illiterate, the speeches given by these black lawyers were the chief means of educating the populace about their political rights. Through their orations, these lawyers became both advocates and educators. When Reconstruction ended through political subterfuge and physical violence, black lawyers lost their role in shaping the laws in the legislature, but their continued advocacy and mere presence laid the cornerstone for the modern civil rights revolution.

That struggle continued for more than a hundred years and in many ways still goes on today. The battle for civil rights included grassroots organizing, sit-ins, demonstrations, marches, petitions, voter registration, campaigning, and resistance in many forms. But of course, much of the struggle took place in more formal settings—for at least ninety years after Reconstruction, it was fought and won in the courts. This book will attempt to tell the story of the legal struggle in South Carolina through the lives of the state's black lawyers, beginning in Reconstruction and continuing into the 1960s. Some of that story will take place in the courtrooms and in the legislative halls, but the history must include who these lawyers were, how they were educated, and how they earned a living. In fact, the effort to educate black lawyers may have had more impact than the legislative work did.

Following the end of Reconstruction, black lawyers did not simply surrender. Some remained active in politics, and a few served in office. Some became astute courtroom advocates, others were successful in business, and still others helped educate new lawyers. In fact, the black bar continued to grow in the state. According to the 1900 U.S. Census, South Carolina had 29 black lawyers, a higher percentage of the bar than in any other southern state. As the twentieth century dawned, however, the black lawyer faced the rapid growth of Jim Crow. With each decade the number of black lawyers in the state declined, a situation not unique to South Carolina. In seven of the eleven former Confederate states, the number of black lawyers decreased in each decade between 1900 and 1940, and by 1940 all eleven of these states had seen a decrease. In 1900 the region had 326 black lawyers, but by 1940 there were only 157. South Carolina had 5 black lawyers in 1940. Only Alabama and Mississippi had fewer. (See table 2.)

Despite the declining numbers in South Carolina, lawyers such as Jacob Moorer and Nathaniel J. Frederick continued to advocate for equal rights. In 1940, when he returned home from Howard University Law School, Harold Boulware became the state's first person formally trained as a civil rights lawyer. He became the local counsel for the NAACP and co-counsel to NAACP Legal Defense Fund's Thurgood Marshall. The confluence of Boulware and Marshall reversed the course of oppression for African Americans in South Carolina and in the nation. The great victories in *Briggs v. Elliott* and *Brown v. Board of Education* and the creation of the law school at South Carolina State College shattered Jim Crow and segregation. It is my belief that this revolution in South Carolina would not have happened without the foundation laid by the black lawyers who had been struggling for equal rights since the 1860s.

To tell the story of all these lawyers is one of my chief objectives, but it is not a simple task. I have identified 167 men and 3 women who were admitted to the practice of law in South Carolina between 1868 and 1968. The number of black lawyers admitted by historical period shows an interesting pattern.

During Reconstruction 49 men were admitted to the bar. From 1877 to 1900 46 more were admitted. But from 1901 until 1924, only 11 were admitted, and none between 1925 and 1939. Beginning in 1940, the growth started slowly and then accelerated to 10 in the 1940s and 29 in the 1950s. These admissions show the dramatic effect of Reconstruction on black bar membership, the serious decline after 1900, and the rise after World War II.

Because the struggle for freedom has been so long and arduous, the complex story of these lawyers and their careers is not neatly recorded. During Reconstruction, the numerous black lawyers in the state included many who were in positions of political power, so records from this era are substantial. Immediately after Reconstruction, the number of black lawyers remained relatively high, but as their power declined their story faded from the record since they were no longer writing the laws. However, as they struggled to combat Jim Crow, they began to handle cases that generated appellate and congressional records, making their legal activities again more transparent. After 1895, when Jim Crow was formalized in a new state constitution, the number of black lawyers declined precipitously, but the few that practiced law became even stronger advocates for civil liberties. As the civil rights movement became more active across the country and the NAACP launched a major civil rights litigation campaign, South Carolina's black lawyers played a major role.

CHAPTER 1

The Coming of Freedom

For the first three hundred years of its history, South Carolina had no black lawyers and no advocacy within the state for the rights of blacks. Virtually all blacks were slaves. As a colony and later as a state, South Carolina relied on slaves as its dominant economic asset. Not only was its plantation economy dependent on slavery, South Carolina's slave merchants were among the largest importers of slaves in America. The first slave rebellion in North America occurred in 1526 in the Spanish settlement on Saint Helena Island in what is now South Carolina. Later, the English colony faced multiple slave revolts in the 1600s and 1700s. This resistance persisted after the American Revolution and establishment of the republic. To maintain the slave economy, the white minority developed a legal system that ensured suppression of blacks and deprivation of all freedoms.

From colonial times forward, "all negroes" were presumed to be slaves, and slaves had no civil rights.[1] A slave could not contract, marry, assemble, be taught to read and write, own property, testify against a white person, take an oath, wear clothing that the law considered finer or of greater value than "negro cloth," travel without white escort, or possess a gun.[2] Blacks who had managed to acquire the designation of "free negro" had some rights, including the right to own property, to contract, and to sue and be sued, but freedom for them was also constrained. They could never strike a white person even in self-defense, and they could not testify in court against a white person.[3] South Carolina's whites so feared freedom for their African American population that slave owners had to have legislative consent to emancipate one of their slaves.[4] Such fear also caused the legislature to prohibit the migration of emancipated blacks into the state.[5]

The criminal laws were even more egregious in their application to slaves. Whipping was a common punishment. For shooting a deer, twenty lashes were imposed. Thirty-nine lashes was the penalty for nighttime hunting, and fifty lashes were imposed for branding livestock. The death penalty was imposed for the third offense of striking a white person, for the burning of crops, and for grievously wounding, maiming, or bruising a white person.[6] It was also imposed for the crime of insurrection. In 1822 Denmark Vesey, a freedman, and as many as thirty slaves were tried in a secret court, convicted of insurrection, and hanged. In an appeal from another insurrection conviction, Judge Elihu H. Bay rejected the claim that the rules of evidence and procedure had been improperly applied to the defendants, who were slaves. Judge Bay opined as to slaves that "they have no rights, other than those which their masters or owners may give them. They are the property of their masters or owners, and are considered in this State, in law, as goods and chattels, and not as persons entitled to the benefits of freemen."[7]

Despite the laws that restricted black freedom in order to maintain white supremacy, African Americans, whether slave or free, still resisted. Insurrections and fears of blacks continued in South Carolina through the Civil War. Simple forms of resistance such as work slowdowns and feigned illness were common, and more serious measures such as violence against masters and even suicide were not unheard of. The greatest form of resistance was escape. In fact, runaways were so common that South Carolina required every white male above the age of eighteen to serve in the "militia beat company" or slave patrol.[8]

Across the country the abolitionist movement grew as slavery became the nation's greatest moral and political issue. But abolitionist views were not welcome in South Carolina, and the few abolitionists born there were compelled to leave. South Carolina and its leaders, such as John C. Calhoun, were the dominant defenders of the "peculiar institution," as well as the interrelated issues of nullification and states' rights. South Carolina led the nullification movement in 1832, and its governor even called men to arms against the national government.[9] In 1860 South Carolina was the leader of another southern movement, but unlike in 1832, this crisis was not averted. South Carolina became the first state to secede from the United States, leading the South into a losing war to save slavery. At the time of secession, South Carolina's population was 58 percent black, the highest percentage of any state.

The long and bloody war that followed resulted in freedom for blacks in stages. In late 1861 the Union navy and army took control of the Sea Islands, including the town of Beaufort. Whites abandoned the area, and their slaves acquired a kind of "quasi freedom." The Emancipation Proclamation was announced a year later, in September 1862, but freedom was still not a legal reality for all of South Carolina's 400,000 enslaved people. There would be a long and arduous struggle for a full realization of equal rights. The coming of black lawyers was a natural response to the imminent struggle. The first one probably arrived before the surrender at Appomattox Courthouse. The Thirteenth Amendment was ratified in December 1865, but its legal definition of freedom had yet to be established. By the beginning of Reconstruction in 1866, several of the first black lawyers in America were practicing law in South Carolina. The coastal area, known as the Low Country, and the Midlands, with its large cotton plantations, were dominated by the newly freed people. These areas became the places where black lawyers played a significant role.

The Arrival of the Black Lawyer

The first record of a black lawyer appearing in a court in South Carolina is from the summer of 1866. On July 20 the *Charleston Daily News* reported that "by far the most important case before the Court to-day was that of the United States v. Poinsett Simmons, Alick Murphy, and James Richardson (colored) for vagrancy."[10] According to the newspaper, trial attorney William J. Whipper had been practicing in the court for some time; despite his efforts, the military court convicted the three men. The next month, a black lawyer appeared before the provost court suing a local merchant for violation of the federal civil rights law by refusing service to a black soldier. Again, the lawyer was unsuccessful.[11] It seems quite likely that Whipper was that lawyer.

Another early case was handled by Jonathan Jasper Wright. In April 1867 Wright petitioned the military governor of South Carolina to obtain title to a rowboat for Kit Christopher, a freedman from Beaufort County. For Christopher, owning a rowboat meant he could navigate the numerous creeks and rivers of the coastal community and catch fish, net shrimp, and gather oysters to feed his family and to sell in town. When Christopher won title to that rowboat, Wright helped his client obtain civil rights that he would have been denied prior to the Civil War.[12]

The journey by which lawyers such as William Whipper and Jonathan Jasper Wright came to represent clients had many intertwining origins. The major one was, of course, that moment when white South Carolinians began shelling Fort Sumter in Charleston in April 1861, the start of the Civil War. By November of that year, the Union navy sailed into Port Royal Sound in Beaufort County and bombarded the Confederate forts. When the Union troops came ashore on the Sea Islands of Beaufort County, freedom had come to people such as Kit Christopher. Despite Gen. William Tecumseh Sherman's promise that he would not interfere with the institution of slavery, virtually every white person evacuated, and an overwhelming majority of the slaves refused to join the whites in their flight.[13] Disregarding the rumors spread by whites that the Union army would re-enslave blacks, the slaves of Beaufort and other coastal communities welcomed the Union troops. The Union army occupied other parts of the South Carolina coast at various times over the next three years, and by 1863 the black soldiers of the Fifty-Fourth Massachusetts helped lay siege to the harbor of Charleston. Within two months, the harbor was under Union control. In Beaufort the Union Army employed Harriet Tubman to travel by boat in the bays, rivers, and creeks of the coastal country to penetrate the Confederate lines. In one dramatic operation, she led Union soldiers in boats up the Combahee River to free more than seven hundred slaves.[14] Tubman's experience in South Carolina caused one member of her family to move to the state and help the newly freed people. James A. Bowley, Tubman's nephew, came to Georgetown County as a Freedmen's Bureau agent and then became a lawyer and legislator. Encouraged by Tubman, the Emancipation Proclamation, and the presence of the Union army, more than thirty thousand former slaves from the South Carolina coastal area fled to freedom in the occupied areas during the war.[15]

In this new world, freedom was more an emotion than a reality. Nonetheless, thousands of black men and women were insisting on a revolution, aided at first by Union army soldiers and then by northern missionaries.[16] Of course, not all white northerners were sympathetic to the newly freed peoples. Instances of racial prejudice by white missionaries and Union soldiers were not uncommon. On the other hand, black missionaries became advocates for the rights of the former slaves. Their advocacy was dramatically furthered by such figures as Harriet Tubman and the presence of the United States Colored Troops who were both sent to and recruited from South Carolina. These black soldiers were naturally more sympathetic to the former slaves' vision of freedom.

William Whipper and Jonathan Jasper Wright arrived within the ranks of the army and the missionaries. Whipper, a soldier, and Wright, a missionary, would both become major political leaders in the state. The world in which these two northern men and their clients had to seek justice had been formed in antebellum South Carolina and then turned on its head by the Civil War. The former slaves and their legal advocates faced a world of unknowns. What was certain was that freedom would be different than slavery, and that the new freedom would not be welcomed by most whites. In fact, while black South

Carolinians believed freedom had come, whites simply refused to accept it as a fact. Moreover, since immediately after the Civil War the native whites still controlled the civil government, they had the ability to formally resist. And resist they did.

The Black Codes

Despite the surrender of the Confederacy and emancipation of the slaves by the Thirteenth Amendment to the U.S. Constitution, white South Carolinians for the most part disregarded these new realities. In September 1865 a convention composed solely of white male delegates met in Columbia and promulgated a new state constitution.[17] This convention was called by provisional governor Benjamin F. Perry, who had been appointed by President Andrew Johnson to lead the state back into the Union. Perry knew that to comply with the requirement of the president's plan for Reconstruction, the convention had to declare secession "null and void" and adopt a constitution that recognized the abolition of slavery. However, though the convention did agree to repeal the articles of secession, it refused to declare them "null and void." Likewise, the convention only grudgingly abolished slavery.[18] Historian Walter Edgar describes the wording of the abolition clause as an "omen."[19] With some dissenting votes, the convention acknowledged that "the United States authorities" had emancipated the slaves.[20] The purpose of the new constitution was supposed to have been to gain approval for the state's congressional delegation to return to the U.S. Congress.[21] However, in its defiantly racist mind-set, the convention adopted a new constitution that allowed only free white men twenty-one and older to vote or hold elective office.[22] In addition, a Black Code was proposed that would have virtually re-enslaved the state's black population. While the codes were not made part of the state constitution, the all-white constitutional convention authorized the governor to appoint two commissioners to draft a code that would regulate "the Colored Population" of the state.[23]

In late November 1865, at the Colored People's Convention in Charleston, the black citizens of South Carolina voiced their opposition to this new constitution.[24] Beginning on November 20, representatives gathered from twelve districts in the state. Among these men were Jonathan Jasper Wright, representing the Beaufort District as the convention's only lawyer, and future lawyers Robert DeLarge, William F. Myers, and Francis L. Cardozo. Wright was elected a vice president and appointed to the rules and business committees on the first day. The next day he reported out the rules for the convention. After their adoption, the business committee presented the first substantive matter taken up by the meeting, a resolution that began "Whereas, 'Knowledge is power,'" and then implored the state legislature to establish schools for "our children." Resolutions were approved that the convention held "no hatred or malice" toward former slaveholders and that the "Negroes" of the state were law-abiding citizens.[25] But by the fifth day of the convention, the tenor of the resolutions changed. Wright's committee proposed that the federal government be asked to continue the Freedmen's Bureau and reject the state constitution's restriction of the franchise to white voters. On the sixth day, the convention condemned the proposed "negro code" as unjust and urged the legislature not to enact such laws.[26]

These black delegates exhorted the white legislature to disregard race in its enactment of *any* laws. Their final speeches and resolutions called on the state legislature to recognize the famous words of the Declaration of Independence, "that all men are created equal"; to end the "surges of despotism"; and to extend to blacks those rights of citizenship that had been denied by the new constitution. The convention also adopted a "Declaration of Rights and Wrongs." In this declaration, "rights" meant that a man had the right to own and dispose of rightfully earned property but, more importantly, to "own his body and mind." In the closing letter to the General Assembly, the convention said, "We, the colored people . . . , do hereby appeal to you for justice . . . [and] the right of suffrage and the right to testify in court."[27] So in the end, education, voting, justice, and equality in the courts were the crucial goals of the convention. Wright delivered one of the final addresses of the convention, and all of the final goals certainly reflected Wright's view and his work in the convention. As a former teacher, he had introduced the resolution on education. With the emphasis in the final address on justice and the right to testify in court, one has to assume that Wright the lawyer was quite pleased.

Wright was the very first black lawyer in South Carolina history. The missionary teacher had been trained in the law in Pennsylvania but was denied admission to that state's bar because of his race. So, in the fall of 1865, Wright obtained employment with the American Missionary Association to teach black Union soldiers in South Carolina to read and write.[28] His first post was in the Paris Island school in Beaufort County, where he reported that all of his forty-two students had learned to read. In addition, he lectured the troops on their legal rights, and by December he was interacting with the new free people of South Carolina and playing a major role in the Charleston convention. While in Charleston, Wright also visited Francis Cardozo's school for free people.[29] Cardozo would later become a lawyer and one of the most powerful men in the state. They joined each other in advocating for civil rights during the convention. Afterward, in January 1866, Wright reported that he was spending his time among the local people and teaching them three nights a week about "business." Since the primary business activity of the newly freed people was negotiating labor contracts with white plantation owners, it seems clear that this "teaching about business" was Wright's first legal work with the civilian population in South Carolina.[30] For his advice some freedmen even offered him small payments. It is possible that Wright's work was the first civil rights work done by a black lawyer not only in South Carolina but in the entire South. Unfortunately, Wright felt that his fellow missionaries did not approve of his legal work because it was not true "missionary work."[31] Suffering from health problems and the disapproval of these white missionaries, Wright returned to Pennsylvania.

In the meantime, the all-white legislature had convened in December 1865 and totally ignored the request for civil rights made by the Colored People's Convention. Almost to spite the black citizens' call for justice, the legislature enacted the infamous Black Codes.[32] Although the 1865 constitution acknowledged the abolition of slavery, the Black Codes were modeled after the old slave codes and were a veiled attempt to re-enslave African Americans.[33] The Black Codes denied social and political equality and freedom of movement to any "person of color." Black servants were not permitted to be absent from the farms where they worked "without the permission of the master."[34] The 1865 constitution denied blacks the right to vote. The Black Codes went even farther, relegating all black litigants and black criminal defendants to a separate court system, and permitting blacks to testify as witnesses only in cases involving disputes between blacks. They were even limited in how they could earn a living. The Black Codes provided that "no person of color shall pursue or practice the art, trade or business of an artisan, mechanic or shopkeeper, or any other trade, employment or business (besides that of husbandry or that of a servant under a contract for service or labor) on his own account and for his own benefit, or in partnership with a white person, or as agent or servant of any person, until he shall have obtained a license therefore from the Judge of the District Court."[35]

Following the enactment of the Black Codes, the federal government wrangled with the white legislature over these laws.[36] Gen. Daniel Sickles, the federal military commander of South Carolina, issued an order on January 1, 1866, abrogating the Black Codes. On June 13, 1866, the U.S. Congress proposed the Fourteenth Amendment to the Constitution. On September 21, 1866, the South Carolina legislature, in a half-hearted attempt to appease the federal authority, enacted a law that granted some civil rights to African Americans, though not the right to vote.[37] It was clear to Congress that "no legal State governments or adequate protection for life or property" existed in South Carolina.[38] On March 2, 1867, in order to establish "peace and good order" in the southern states, Congress passed "an Act to provide for the more efficient Government of the Rebel States," which divided them into military districts. North and South Carolina comprised the second military district.[39]

Freedmen's Bureau and the Emergence of the Civil Rights Lawyer

In addition to the creation of a military government, in March 1865 Congress established within the War Department the Bureau of Refugees, Freedmen and Abandoned Lands. More popularly known as the Freedmen's Bureau, this agency supervised all relief and educational activities in the old Confederate states. Although it was under the auspices of the War Department, the bureau operated somewhat outside the military and was more of an adjunct to the military government. Its agents were often civilian employees. In fact, one of those civilians sent to South Carolina was Jonathan Jasper Wright, the state's first black lawyer.

Wright had finally gained admission to the Pennsylvania bar, but law practice there was not to his liking. In late 1866 he traveled to Washington, D.C., searching for work as a lawyer. He must have been delighted to be offered a position with the Freedmen's Bureau to assist "free people in legal affairs" in Beaufort, South Carolina.[40] However, he faced many challenges; for example, simply obtaining law books was nearly impossible. Stone reported he could not purchase a copy of the South Carolina law in Charleston in March 1866 and settled for a copy of Blackstone. Even more daunting was the bureau's broad charge to him and other agents. All bureau agents were governed by the orders and circulars issued by the military and the agency. They were charged with everything from distributing rations, accounting for government property, and establishing schools to reviewing all of the labor contracts between white planters and the newly freed slaves.[41] Of course, this last charge was critical in preventing white planters from taking advantage of black workers. In addition, agents were to encourage voter registration and "to inform the freed people of all the rights and privileges conferred upon them by government."[42] Wright shaped the civil rights of the people of the state through his legal counseling and advocacy, and by working in the Freedmen's Bureau courts and the military courts. In one case, as a legal adviser to the bureau, Wright was asked to render an opinion to the revenue commissioner about a tax sale. Wright gave the opinion that while the tax sale should be voided because of fraud by the initial purchaser, the subsequent good-faith purchaser should be given title.[43]

In the case previously mentioned, Wright's advocacy secured for Kit Christopher title to his rowboat.[44]

The most significant task of bureau agents was resolving disputes. Initially, the Freedmen's Bureau had operated courts throughout the state. However, in late 1866 such courts were discontinued and replaced by the state courts and the military's various tribunals. The state's district court system applied the law as if the Black Codes were still operable, and there is little evidence to suggest that these courts, run by local whites, ever dispensed anything but injustice to blacks. In fact, in 1866 General Sickles reported that the state courts essentially ignored offenses by whites against black citizens. He noted further, "When arrests are made by military authority and the parties are turned over to the civil tribunals, the accused are generally admitted to easy bail. . . . It became necessary, therefore, to authorize commanding officers to treat these outlaws as guerrillas and punish them summarily."[45] When blacks did not obey the wishes of whites, the white planters reacted with anger. Much to the consternation of these planters, however, the military courts intervened. One planter complained to South Carolina governor B. F. Perry that his son had been convicted by the U.S. Army provost court for shooting a black man who had disobeyed his order.[46] Other whites physically assaulted blacks who took their complaints to the provost courts.[47] Because the Black Codes prohibited blacks from being witnesses in state court, the military had issued an order in June 1866 granting exclusive jurisdiction over the newly freed people to the military courts. Despite assurances by the governor that the rights of black citizens would be protected by civil authorities, General Sickles pointed out that magistrates, constables, and sheriffs were in fact failing to do so. To illustrate, he cited a case from Beaufort in which perpetrators of a homicide were members of the coroner's jury. Naturally they came to the verdict that the death was "by means unknown to the jury."[48]

In addition to the provost courts, military commissions, courts-martial, and field officers' courts were held across the state. Because the state remained under military control, the provost courts and the military commissions heard cases involving civilians. For example, eight white and ten black civilians were tried by military commissions in the state between October 1866 and March 1867. Moreover, the military was so distrustful of South Carolina white justice that in 1867, when state court judge A. P. Aldrich tried to hold court in Barnwell, the new military governor of the state, Brevet Major General E. R. S. Canby, suspended Aldrich for refusing to allow blacks to serve on juries and ordered that he "not hold any courts in his circuit."[49] Some whites had hoped that Canby was not going to be as "radical" as his predecessor, General Sickles, but Canby's dispute with Judge Aldrich demonstrated that he was prepared to enforce the civil rights of blacks in the state. The presence of black jurors and lawyers, along with the exercise of judicial power by black officials such as Wright, was revolutionary.

Of course, the military courts served as an important bridge to the realization of civil rights in the state. These courts were seen by the military as contributing largely to "the restoration of peace and order." While outrages by whites against blacks were the motivating factor behind the application of military judicial authority over the civilian population, the courts often served as a means to restoring simple normalcy to life.[50] These courts heard many cases involving minor offenses. For example, a June 1866 term of the provost court in Sumter heard minor criminal matters that resulted in fines as small as 6¼ cents and as high as thirty dollars.[51] The U.S. Army established the provost courts primarily to hear minor criminal cases with fines up to $100 and sentences of up to two years; the military commissions were to hear felonies. But in South Carolina these military courts exercised jurisdiction over both civil and criminal matters. In addition, when a bureau agent could not resolve a dispute, he referred it to the provost courts.[52] Because they had such wide authority, these courts have been described by one scholar as providing the "greatest degree of sophistication obtained" when compared to the state courts.[53]

However, these courts were presided over by white military officers who often were prejudiced and could not necessarily be relied on to rule impartially. Historian Thomas D. Morris has concluded that the bureau and the U.S. Army officers shared an "infectious prejudice" against blacks in South Carolina.[54] Moreover, these officers viewed their chief role as requiring blacks to work on the plantations. Without slavery, labor contracts were creating a new system of agricultural labor. Naturally, the courts saw many disputes about such agreements. Morris found that the military courts routinely ruled against blacks in contract disputes and often imposed harsh criminal penalties for violations of the contracts.

This was not the case in Beaufort County. The Freedmen's Bureau agents were assigned to assist the military courts, and in that county, Jonathan Jasper Wright was that agent. He served remarkably in the provost court on the Sea Islands throughout 1867, appearing to have been adviser to both the court and the parties. At times it appears as if he was in fact holding court himself.[55]

The magnitude of Wright's work as an agent in the provost courts can be found in his Freedmen's Bureau monthly reports.[56] He participated in more than two hundred cases in ten months. In his report dated February 16, 1867, Wright recorded some of the following decisions made by the court: "Frank

Wineglass complains that he bought a cow and it died shortly after and the original owner would not pay him back." Wright noted that it was ordered that the original owner "does not have to pay back the money unless the cow was sick when he sold it." When "Isaac Fields complained that George W. Woodman is indebted to him in sum of $16," Woodman was ordered to pay. In another case, Philip Brown claimed that he should be paid more than two dollars for a coffin he had built that was rejected. In another, "Solomon Psalms com[plained] that Abram Mack borrowed a boat of his in 1866 and had not returned it. Ordered that he should return it or pay for it." P. E. Ezekil made the complaint that Byas Middleton was indebted to him for $24.96, and Middleton was ordered to pay.

Similar claims decided in February included disputes over wages with white planters, a dispute between two women over a wardrobe, and another involving the killing of a dog. In March Wright reported on thirty cases that ranged from a dollar claim about some clothes to the wages due a man who had constructed two houses for another. In the case of Smart Washington, it was ruled that Mr. Halls did not have to refund the five dollars he had charged Washington for fixing his watch when the watch quit running after three weeks. At court on Saint Helena Island, Jack Green was ordered to return Sampson Green's mule, and William Davis was ordered to return William Alston's beehives. The court ruled that Ables Simmons should pay three dollars to Edward Hays for keeping an infant for a month. Since cotton was the major money crop grown on the island, stealing cotton was a major problem for the planters as well as the farm workers.[57] The case of Nelly Hayes involved "seed cotton," unginned cotton that was usually stolen.[58] Hayes claimed that Able Simmons owed her 107 pounds of seed cotton, but Simmons successfully argued that the cotton was stolen and he had returned it to its rightful owner.

A similar pattern followed in the April cases. For example, someone threatened to shoot a farmer's hogs and cows. The farmer complained, and the court enjoined the aggressor from shooting or trespassing on the farmer's property. Ned Jones was reprimanded for abusing his wife, Dafney. Disputes over farm labor issues grew. In one case, a foreman named B. T. Sellers was reprimanded for not providing rations to Jackson Jenkins, and in other cases, the court ordered payments for work performed. But when one woman who had contracted to work for four weeks but only worked two complained that she had not been paid, the court refused to award her any wages.

Wright's May report is quite different from his others. It begins with a narrative of his travels and observations about the people of Beaufort County. He found substantial unrest and unwillingness to work among blacks and laid the blame at the feet of the white planters. He investigated "two cases of actual beatings of Freedmen by planters." Having found the claims meritorious, Wright obtained promises from the planters not to commit this offense again. He praised a group of freed people who were jointly farming 150 acres in potatoes, corn, and cotton. Wright opined that if left alone they would "do exceedingly well," noting with pride that they refused to work for any of the neighboring planters. Overall, he found conditions poor for both whites and blacks in the district. Although he was sympathetic to poor whites, he was displeased with some white planters who were trying to undermine his authority by telling the freed people not to take their disputes to him.

When Wright reported on his twenty-eight cases in May, B. T. Sellers was again before the military court. Sellers, as foreman for a plantation owned by William Middleton of Charleston, was accused of beating workers, running them off without cause, and not paying their wages. Each of the workers on the Middleton plantation had signed contracts to be paid half their wages at the beginning of the month and the remaining half a month after the crops were gathered. However, none of the contracts was signed by either Sellers or Middleton, and Sellers refused to explain why. Wright discovered that Sellers was paying the workers with postdated scrip only redeemable seven months later at Sellers's store. This dispute continued into May and then into June. Sellers also denied that he beat any workers, saying that he was trying to drive off only those who would not work. Wright's investigation found that even white witnesses disputed Sellers's version of events. Ultimately, despite Sellers's denials, William Middleton accepted responsibility and paid the workers. The heavy caseload continued in July, August, September, October, and November. Wright participated in approximately 145 cases in those months.

The impact of Wright's legal work in Beaufort requires more than simply a report of these cases. Within the Freedmen's Bureau, views differed as to what assistance, if any, the former slaves needed. Gen. Rufus Saxton, who was in charge of the bureau in South Carolina, believed very firmly in the need to educate and protect the rights of the black citizens of the state.[59] One white observer quoted a freed person as saying, "I am going to Gen[eral] Saxton for justice."[60] In Beaufort the freed people could say they were going to lawyer Wright for justice. Land, labor, and freedom of movement were their initial needs. The land issue was the "40 acres and a mule" myth. Saxton and other bureau officials tried to make it a reality, but as few as 1,500 former slaves in the state received title to land through the federal government.[61] As an alternative, the bureau encouraged the use of labor contracts between the landless freedmen and their former owners. Here bureau agents such as Wright provided legal assistance by reviewing the contracts and even seizing crops to protect the rights of the freedmen.[62] Clearly a black lawyer serving as a bureau agent made a huge difference to the new citizens of Beaufort County. One study of the Freedmen's Bureau concluded that in the South Carolina towns of Barnwell, Darlington, and Moncks Corner, the bureau had favored white parties against black parties.[63] While the provost court under Wright's advisement appears to have been very strict with workers who failed to live up to their contracts, when the case was made that the work had been done or the worker had been mistreated, the workers prevailed. In fact, the workers seem to have prevailed in 27 out of the 33 cases on which Wright reported. Moreover, Wright's tenacity in obtaining wages and improving conditions for workers under the supervision of B. T. Sellers demonstrated the lengths to which he would go on their behalf.

Debt disputes constituted more than 33 percent of the cases heard, and labor cases made up more than 15 percent. The majority of the cases involved what might seem minor matters but which were in reality basic civil rights issues, such as the right to own property—issues that were critical to the survival of the freed people. For example, twenty-five cases involved livestock, and ten resolved title to crops. A myriad of other cases decided ownership of shoes, clothes, furniture, and guns. Wright appears to have assisted twelve freedmen who came before the provost court to recover their boats. Freedom gradually became a daily reality for the Sea Islands' freedmen whom Wright assisted.

It was in this military court system that Wright and William J. Whipper appeared as trial lawyers. Whipper, a former Union soldier, was, like Wright, a native of Pennsylvania. He was also the nephew of a prominent abolitionist. Whipper had studied law in Detroit and may have practiced both there and in Cleveland.[64] Whipper was proud of his service in the army and defended his fellow black veterans from attacks on their motives for moving to the state.[65] He had been discharged from the army in November 1865 and settled in Charleston with his wife and child. He was soon practicing in the provost courts in that city, as well as in the coastal counties of Beaufort, Charleston, and Georgetown.[66]

In November 1866 Whipper filed a complaint with Gen. Robert K. Scott asserting that some black citizens were being improperly treated in the provost court on Saint Helena Island in Beaufort County.[67] Significantly, Whipper was joined by Jonathan Jasper Wright when a legal action was filed three months later. Two historians have opined that the joint efforts of Wright and Whipper in the case of *United States v. William T. Bennett* in February 1867 may be the first recorded instance of black attorneys practicing before a legal tribunal in South Carolina.[68] Wright appeared as "Solicitor of the Bureau."[69] William

Whipper served as counsel for the victims and assisted Wright in seeking to have Bennett prosecuted. They asserted that Bennett, a brevet brigadier general who had commanded colored troops during the war, had shot two black men and should be charged with intent to kill. Bennett, who was the chief judge of the provost court, asserted that the two men were trying to kill him.[70] There is no record of the disposition of the case.

While Wright and Whipper were certainly the first black lawyers in the state, it is possible that other black men may have appeared as advocates in the bureau courts or the provost courts. We do know that a group of men who would become lawyers were bureau agents. These men were Stephen A. Swails, Robert DeLarge, James A. Bowley, Thaddeus K. Sasportas, Landon S. Langley, William A. Hayne, and Henry J. Maxwell.[71] Edwin T. Belcher, who was admitted to the South Carolina bar in 1872, served as a Freedmen's Bureau agent in Georgia.[72] Even if these agents of the bureau did not appear in the provost courts, they often had to provide "legal" assistance to black South Carolinians. As agents, they had to negotiate labor contracts with white planters, resolve disputes between blacks, and serve as educators of the civil rights of the freed people.[73]

During these early years of Reconstruction, black lawyers came forward to challenge the Black Codes and protect the civil rights of black citizens. Before the Civil War, it would have been inconceivable to whites in South Carolina that a black lawyer could advocate for equal rights for his clients. By 1866, not only had the first black lawyers advised clients, they were opening law offices and trying cases in the courts. As the appearance of these black lawyers shows, the newly freed people of the state were not going to accept dominance by the white minority without a struggle. Black lawyers have played an integral role in that struggle ever since.

CHAPTER 2

Reconstruction and the Birth of a New Kind of Lawyer

The first few years after the Civil War were the era known as Presidential Reconstruction. President Andrew Johnson's concept of reuniting the nation after the war was so conciliatory toward the ex-Confederates that it was doomed to failure. Johnson encouraged southern whites to believe that the country would return to the antebellum system, albeit without legalized slavery. In reaction Congress asserted its leadership by enacting the first Reconstruction Acts in 1867. As a prelude to returning power to the former Confederate states, these acts set up military governments in the South. With them came the military legal system to administer justice, and it was in these military courts that black lawyers first practiced. To accomplish a restoration of civil governments in the South, the acts set the conditions under which the "Rebel States" would be "declared entitled to representation in Congress." Those states, South Carolina included, had to draft and promulgate constitutions that conformed with the U.S. Constitution in all respects. In addition, these new constitutions had to be adopted by a convention of delegates elected by the male citizens of those states, twenty-one years old and upward, of whatever race, color, or previous condition of servitude, who had resided in that state for one year before the day of such election. Even more revolutionary, Congress required that these new state constitutions be ratified by "a majority of the state's registered voters" and approved by Congress. The states were also required to adopt the Fourteenth Amendment to the Constitution.[1]

Under this mandate, more than 125,000 people in South Carolina registered to vote in a referendum on the question of whether to call a constitutional convention.[2] When eighty thousand African Americans registered to vote, for the first time in the history of the state, a majority of potential voters were black.[3]

Recognizing that the black majority would approve the call for a convention, whites decided to boycott the election in hopes that the black vote would be low enough not to constitute the "majority of registered voters" requirement imposed by Congress. However, when the polls were opened on November 19 and 20, 1867, more than 71,000 people voted, of whom 68,768 cast their ballot to approve the constitutional convention.[4] In fact, 85 percent or more of registered blacks voted in this historic election, the first ever in South Carolina history in which blacks were allowed to vote. To obtain such a turnout from a largely illiterate and oppressed population was extraordinary. In their desire to prevent the drafting of a constitution, 95 percent of whites had either cast negative votes or boycotted the election.[5] A mere 5 percent of white voters, 2,350 persons, accepted the idea that the Confederacy had been defeated and that freedom had come to the majority population of the state.

The Constitutional Convention of 1868

On January 14, 1868, black and white delegates from across South Carolina assembled in Charleston to draft the new constitution. The majority of the delegates were black. Estimates on the numbers range from 71 to 76 out of 124.[6] Among these black delegates were three men with legal training: Jonathan Jasper Wright, William Whipper, and Robert Brown Elliott.[7] The delegates also included six other men who would later become lawyers. Stephen Swails and Robert DeLarge were former Freedmen's Bureau agents. George Lee, from Massachusetts, had come south to farm.[8] W. H. Jones Jr., originally from Philadelphia, came to teach, Benjamin Byas was a farmer from the West Indies, and Francis L. Cardozo was an American Missionary Association teacher. Of these particular delegates, only Cardozo and DeLarge were natives of the state.

On the very first day of the convention, DeLarge, Cardozo, Whipper, and Byas took an active role in the proceedings, and they remained active throughout.[9] Often when business bogged down, it was the leadership of these black "lawyers" who kept the convention running smoothly. They understood the purpose of a constitutional convention. In his role as chair of the Committee on Rules and Regulations, Swails worked to keep the body focused and organized (91). Whipper, Wright, and Cardozo also demonstrated a strong influence on the body and helped the delegates avoid arguing over minutiae or matters that should more appropriately be left to the legislature (102–3ff).

However, as one of the earliest debates demonstrates, these delegates did not speak with one voice. When a local newspaper ran racist stories about the convention, Wright moved to censor the newspaper. Whipper quickly opposed the motion on the grounds that free speech must be allowed (27–29). Despite the newspaper's direct attack on Cardozo, he joined in the successful move to table Wright's motion.[10]

In postwar South Carolina, many people were destitute, including a number of large landowners. Some of these property owners were being sued for debts owed for the sale and purchase of slaves. When a delegate proposed a resolution requesting that the military governor impose a moratorium or "stay" on the collection of judgments, Wright and Cardozo both opposed the measure. When Wright was accused by one delegate of advocating against the resolution because it would affect his law practice, Cardozo came to Wright's defense. Cardozo favored the conservative position and argued that a moratorium would constitute an impairment of the obligation of contracts in contravention of the U.S. Constitution (42–43). Cardozo saw another benefit in allowing the execution of judgments. Executions would force the partition and sale of large plantations, thereby undercutting the plantation economy that had been built on slavery (115–18).[11]

In contrast, William Whipper, who might have shared Cardozo's ultimate objective, viewed the issue differently. He feared that allowing execution of judgments would give the land to northern speculators and not benefit working people. Whipper also supported the stay as a conciliatory measure for the destitute white property owners. He characterized the execution of judgments as an attempt to seek vengeance on former slave owners. While admitting that when he left the army, he had wanted all the leaders of the rebellion hung, Whipper now saw vengeance as "wrong, cruel, and unjust" (130). Whipper appropriately pointed out that whether judgment executions were stayed or allowed, either result would be morally questionable. The obvious point to Whipper was that these contracts were between two culpable parties. One sold slaves, and the other bought slaves.

When the convention was informed that the state's military governor was going to exempt personal property and $2,000 worth of land from execution, debate shifted to how much property should be exempted by the constitution. Therefore, in the next day's proceedings, as the stay law debate resumed, J. J. Wright moved that the constitution exempt from execution homesteads up to a hundred acres. He argued that it was critical to protect farms rather than plantations and that a hundred acres of land were necessary for a person to be able to produce sufficient crops to support a family (136). Whipper and Wright agreed on the acreage question, but Cardozo disagreed and unsuccessfully attempted to reduce the homestead to fifty acres (161–62). The matter was referred to a committee of which Whipper was a member (460–66). When the committee reported back, the biggest supporters of the proposal were Cardozo, Wright, and Whipper. The new proposal called for protection of a hundred acres or $2,000 in a homestead and $500 in furniture, but in the end the convention could not agree on how much property should be exempt and simply established a right to a homestead exemption, directing the legislature to enact "a reasonable amount."[12] This would become the first homestead exemption in the history of the state. More importantly, the homestead was adopted as part of the "Declaration of Rights" in the new constitution.[13] In the end, however, the state legislature proved more conservative than Wright, Whipper, or Cardozo and exempted only $500 for a homestead.[14]

The approval of the homestead did not end the debate on the vexing issue of whether to enforce contracts for monies owed for the sale of slaves. The delegates understood that no matter how they decided the issue, either the seller or the purchaser of humans would be rewarded. A small minority saw the right to contract as a necessary constitutional command that overcame the immorality of such contracts. In the end, the convention declared null and void all contracts where the consideration was human beings. Of the lawyers and the lawyers-to-be, only Francis L. Cardozo voted against the resolution (248–49). But on the next-to-last day of the convention, the body returned to the issue. Ironically, both Whipper and Wright argued against the provision on the grounds that it should be left to the legislature, but the convention remained firm and incorporated the ban as Section 34 of the Judicial article (918). The convention was more unified on related contract and debt matters. Cardozo's concerns were encompassed by a provision prohibiting any law that impaired the obligation of contract (325–26). In addition, Wright, Cardozo, and Robert Brown Elliott successfully supported the passage of a ban on debtors' prison (318–25).

Probably the most important issue for the state's newest citizens was the promise of forty acres and a mule. This famous pledge of General Sherman had been thwarted in Washington, but some delegates to the convention were determined to somehow make it a reality. No greater civil right was at stake to the newly freed people than the right to own land. When a resolution was introduced petitioning Congress to appropriate a million dollars to purchase land for the former slaves, it was criticized on the grounds that it was a meaningless gesture, since there was no chance Congress would appropriate the money (389). Not swayed by such arguments, Elliott urged adoption of the resolution because there could "be no possible harm, while it may result in great good" (396). On the other side, Whipper opposed it, asserting that a million dollars was not sufficient to help even a fourth of the people of the state (400–401).

Whipper's opposition was also influenced by the strong belief that the resolution was nothing more than a political gesture. He wanted nothing to do with a proposal that would offer another false promise to people who had already suffered enough; he argued that laborers needed opportunities to work, not handouts. Cardozo questioned Whipper's motives, pointing out that Whipper had sought relief for planters and accusing him of being "the tool of the rebels" (404). In the end, the resolution passed with only five delegates voting in the negative. Both William Whipper and Stephen Swails voted no (439).

The administration of justice was of great import to the lawyers in the convention. The delegate who demonstrated the deepest concern for civil rights was Francis L. Cardozo, who, though eight years away from earning his law degree, already demonstrated a very perceptive and practical legal mind. When a delegate introduced a resolution to abolish the district courts of the state because of the injustices these courts inflicted on the people, there was much debate about the authority of the convention to pass such a resolution. Cardozo moved quickly to the heart of the matter. While the proposed constitution could abolish these particular courts, Cardozo argued, it did not matter what court system they adopted. What mattered was who presided as judges in the courts (78). The district courts were abolished by the new constitution. On a similar point, Cardozo pointed out the importance of maintaining juries as a safeguard for justice. Therefore, on the question of whether the constitution should include a provision requiring grand juries, Cardozo observed that while both grand and petit juries might have deficiencies, juries "have not one-fifth the tendency to evil results . . . of a bad or corrupt Judge" (307).

Legally trained delegates such as William J. Whipper and J. J. Wright (who served as chair of the Committee on the Judiciary [98]) strongly advocated the inclusion of many protections from the tyranny of the state. Not only did they support the grand jury, they favored granting to the petit jury the exclusive power to decide the facts in a case. This was quite a modern advance over the English system that still prevailed in South Carolina at the time, which allowed the trial judge to charge the jury as to what facts to believe or not (284, 305, 306). Wright and Whipper also demonstrated a high level of legal sophistication in the debate on whether the state constitution should contain a clause defining treason against the state. The two lawyers spoke against such a provision, using legal authorities such as Chancellor Kent, the constitutions of other states, and the U.S. Constitution. They asked what the consequences would be of establishing a crime of treason against South Carolina. In their view, it was treason against the United States, not against the individual state, that had brought on the Civil War. Clearly these black lawyers did not trust any provision that granted "nation-like" status to the former Confederate state of South Carolina. Their position persuaded the convention to reject the proposed treason proviso (326–28).

Wright's role on the judiciary committee meant he also helped shape the court system. His committee proposed a legislatively elected supreme court with six-year terms. Some delegates strongly disagreed with the legislative election as well as time-limited appointments. These delegates argued for the federal model with executive appointment subject to consent of the senate and lifetime appointments (597–602). However, Wright's position on these two points prevailed. Two years later, Wright himself was elected to the state supreme court, becoming the first black person in the nation's history to serve on an appellate court. As to circuit or trial court judges, Wright advocated for popular election, and the committee recommended as such. However, the convention decided to give that power to the legislature (617).

The historic import of the constitution was quite evident in the debates on the education section, which included four radical features. First, it required the establishment of a public school system. Second, it compelled attendance for twenty-four months. Third, it contemplated a free and open school system. Fourth, the section required the establishment of a "State Normal School," or teachers college, that was to be open to all persons. When this section was attacked for requiring integrated classes, Cardozo deftly denied that it would be mandatory, but he did state "that if any colored child wishes to go to a white school, it shall have the privilege to do so" (706).[15] DeLarge, Cardozo, Wright, and Elliott were very active participants in the debates on these sections. Elliott gave a strong speech favoring compulsory education, while Wright gave an equally long speech opposing it (694–700). As proof of the volatility of the issue, the section on opening schools to all races did not come back for final consideration until the last three days of the convention. Finally, after Cardozo, DeLarge, and Wright made forceful arguments on behalf of the section, the convention approved it on Monday, March 16, 1868 (893, 899–901).

The black lawyers' aim was to draft a constitution that made the civil liberties of the people paramount instead of the sovereignty of the state. This constitution even recognized the rights of conscientious objectors. When some protested, the supporters responded that they must not forget the great contributions made by Quakers to the abolitionist movement (349). Another issue that occupied considerable time was the gubernatorial eligibility clause. While there was much maneuvering over the residency requirement, the sticking point for Jonathan Jasper Wright was the proviso that the governor must recognize the existence of a supreme being. Wright argued that such a provision was in violation of the U.S. Constitution's First Amendment, but his view was rejected (560–61).[16]

Individual liberties were important, but protection against tyranny by the white minority over the black majority was the true aim of the convention. Francis L. Cardozo probably summarized this best when he said: "It is a patent fact that, as colored men, we have been cheated out of our rights for two centuries, and now that we have the opportunity, I want to fix them in the Constitution in such a way that no lawyer, however cunning or astute, can possibly misinterpret the meaning. If we do not do so, we deserve to be, and will be cheated again. Nearly all the white inhabitants of the State are ready at any moment to deprive us of these rights, and not a loop-hole should be left that would permit them to do it constitutionally" (354). Hence, as Professor James L. Underwood has shown in his multiple works on the constitutions of the state, the 1868 constitutional convention drew its "sharpest contrast" with any other South Carolina constitutional convention in the "area of political equality."[17] The linchpin of their vision of equality was the right to vote. The Reconstruction Acts required the new constitution to grant the vote to black men. Beyond that, some of the lawyers displayed both legal and political astuteness as they maneuvered to assure that the right to vote would be protected as broadly as possible. When the Committee on Franchise and Elections introduced its proposed section on voting rights, the provision immediately drew opposition from Robert Brown Elliott because it contained a provision for a poll tax (711). He opposed the tax because it could be used as a bar to the franchise. Always the conservative, Jonathan J. Wright was vociferous in his support of barring from voting any man who had not paid his poll tax (724–25). While much was heard on the need for the tax, Elliott rejoined, "I would rather lose the fine and the dollar . . . than cause a man to lose his vote" (730). After some debate the poll tax survived, but the convention approved Elliott's amendment providing that a man could not be barred from voting for nonpayment of the poll tax (720, 737–38).

Later, when the committee proposed an educational qualification on the right to vote, Elliott moved to strike it (824–25). The proposal would have required that after 1875, no elector except the physically disabled could vote unless he could read and write. Francis L. Cardozo supported Elliott's motion. Relying on his experience as a teacher, Cardozo argued that it would be decades before there were enough public schools to teach the people to read and write (825–26). Committee member Robert DeLarge first spoke in favor of amending the proviso to be applicable after 1890, but then he capitulated, as did nearly the whole body, including all of the black lawyers, by approving Elliott's amendment that eliminated any literacy requirement for voting (831–35).

As the convention finished its debates on the wording of the franchise section, William J. Whipper made a motion that the word "male" be stricken and the phrase "every citizen" be substituted (836). Whipper then gave a short but forceful speech on behalf of granting women the right to vote (838). He later married Frances Rollin, whose sisters Charlotte and Kate became some of the first suffragettes in the state. Whipper was quite serious, but it is clear from his speech that some of his fellow delegates were interrupting with "frivolous" remarks. Unfortunately, the convention reporter failed to record any of the comments. The report simply ends with the notation that Mr. Whipper's motion was "decided in the negative."[18]

After two months of debate, the convention approved the final draft on March 17. The 1868 South Carolina State Constitution was a remarkable document written by a group of remarkable men—the most egalitarian legal instrument in the state's history. Universal public education was established. While the poll tax was preserved, nonpayment no longer disqualified a voter, and the tax system was modernized by placing a greater emphasis on funding government with the property tax. The property-holding qualification for public office was eliminated. The popular election of presidential electors took power away from the legislative branch and transferred it to the citizenry. The General Assembly was to be apportioned on the basis of population, and the old district system was replaced by counties, which set in motion a greater emphasis on local control of government. The list of franchise-disqualifying crimes was shortened and debtors' prison abolished. A land commission was established to try to meet the need for land ownership by the former slaves. Many of the more significant sections on civil rights were the direct result of the work of the black lawyers and lawyers-to-be. The most important section was Article VIII, which provided that every male citizen twenty-one years of age or older, "without distinction of race, color, or former condition," was entitled to vote.[19] For the first time, a South Carolina constitution allowed an African American man to vote. This set the stage for the real revolution that followed: Reconstruction under black majority rule.

Government by the Majority

This new constitution, already a radical document, next faced another equally radical hurdle. For the first time in South Carolina history, a constitution had to be approved by the voters.[20] The vote for ratification, held in April 1868, coincided with an election for local offices, the state house of representatives, the state senate, and state offices. In 1860, when the nation had teetered on the edge of the Civil War, few would have imagined, much less predicted, what South Carolina would be like fewer than eight years later. The state that had led the South into the war was now seeing former slaves and other black candidates running for and being elected to public office. A black majority was elected to the state house of representatives.[21] Twelve of these men elected to the state legislature in 1868 were lawyers or would become lawyers: Representatives Joseph Boston, James A. Bowley, Laurence Cain, Robert DeLarge, Robert Brown Elliott, W. H. Jones, George Lee, Samuel J. Lee, and William Whipper, and Senators Henry Maxwell, Stephen Swails, and Jonathan J. Wright.[22] Francis L. Cardozo was elected secretary of state, becoming the first African American elected to any statewide office in the nation.[23]

Not only was the political landscape transformed, the legal and judicial system was also substantially changed. The new state court system established by the 1868 constitution made it possible for black clients, black jurors, black lawyers, and even black judges to play significant and, at times, dominant roles in the administration of justice.

On June 28, 1868, the U.S. Congress approved the South Carolina constitution and allowed the state's congressmen to take their seats. This specific statute for the seating of the congressmen required that South Carolina's constitution never be amended "to deprive any citizen or class of citizens of the United States of the right to vote in said State, who are entitled to vote by the constitution thereof herein recognized, except as a punishment for such crime as now are felonies at common law."[24] In effect, this Reconstruction statute became the first federal voting rights act. By 1870, the statute had led to the first black from South Carolina being sent to Congress. These first black congressmen from the state included two lawyers, Robert Brown Elliott and Robert DeLarge. J. H. Rainey joined the two lawyers as the third African American in the state's congressional delegation.

Despite the congressional protections for African American voters, whites were not without their friends in Washington. President Andrew Johnson issued the Amnesty Proclamation of December 25, 1868, which restored all civil rights, including that of suffrage, to the vast majority of the men who had fought for the Confederacy.[25] Encouraged by their expanded rights, whites began considering how to limit black electoral activity. Whites had discovered in the constitutional convention referendum that boycotting elections was not the answer. However, since the majority of the voting population was black, voting in a fair election would not necessarily prove to be the whites' solution, either. More aggressive tactics had to be employed. Many white planters threatened and intimidated black laborers in their employ. Other planters formed clubs and pressured their peers into keeping their black workers out of politics.[26] Both as an outgrowth of the tradition of slave patrols and in response to the black victory in the constitutional convention election, the Ku Klux Klan soon organized across the state.[27] The KKK became America's most infamous terrorist organization as its night riders and assassins roamed across the state aiming to overthrow the black majority and restore white rule.[28]

As Legislators

African Americans constituted a majority of the state's general assembly, and black lawyers were a small but powerful subgroup of that majority. At one point in 1868, a newspaper opined that eight men controlled the legislature, and of the four black men named in the article, three were the lawyers Elliott, Whipper, and DeLarge.[29] Others played leading roles as well, however. R. H. Gleaves of Beaufort, first a probate judge, later served as lieutenant governor from 1872 to 1877. Samuel J. Lee from Aiken served six years as speaker of the house, and then a term as a local solicitor (prosecutor). Stephen Swails from Williamsburg County served as a state senator and the senate's president pro tempore for six years. In his work on the Reconstruction legislature, *Black over White*, Thomas Holt described lawyers George Lee, William Whipper, and Robert Brown Elliott as members of the most radical coalition in the legislature.[30] Elliott served as speaker of the house, Whipper served as chair of the judiciary committee, and Lee was elected by the General Assembly to a judgeship.

Holt concluded that Reconstruction failed in South Carolina because of socioeconomic differences among black leaders. According to Holt, this factor created an atmosphere in which the Republican Party could not come to a "unifying ideology or legislative program." In particular, Holt found their lack of unity on labor issues to be a significant failure. He further explained that this factor may have been the result of "an underlying failure of purposefulness, a failure of perception, a lack of urgency in acting." These factors were doubtless present among black lawyers. However, Holt concluded that within the context in which they had the most impact, that of civil rights, there was less class distinction than in any other category of legislation.[31] These lawyer-legislators were some of the first pro–civil rights legislators in the South. The very first state civil rights law was passed by the South Carolina General Assembly.[32]

Who were these legislators? The senate had 32 seats in 1868 and the house of representatives 121; in 1872 the seats increased to 33 and 125, respectively. Six black lawyers served in the senate during Reconstruction, and fourteen in the house.[33] As noted above, these men held the leadership positions in both houses in all the sessions of the legislature during Reconstruction except the first session of the state senate in 1868–70.

Service in the legislature was not without peril, and white resistance to black activism led to violence. During the 1868 fall campaign, at least four black politicians and one white Republican were murdered in the Third Congressional District. A resident of the district, Robert Brown Elliott, was selected to serve on a legislative committee to investigate the crimes. Jonathan J. Wright was also elected to the committee. The investigation revealed that the Ku Klux Klan was operating in the state and was trying to kill Republican leaders or "drive them from the state." As a result, the legislature created a state militia to which Elliott was named assistant adjutant general.[34]

However, the South Carolina legislative response was not sufficient to quell the Klan's activities. In reaction, Congress passed three Enforcement Acts.[35] With the new statutes, the federal government prosecuted Klan members for their campaign of violence. Former Confederate general Wade Hampton recruited some of the best lawyers in the country to defend the Klansmen. Reverdy Johnson of Maryland and Henry Stanberry of Ohio were both former U.S. attorneys general. Despite the efforts of these two renowned lawyers, the federal prosecutors obtained "an enviable conviction record."[36] Successful prosecutions in 1871 and 1872 managed to break up the Klan as an organization. However, Klansmen remained active in less organized ways, and their influence remained constant both during and after Reconstruction.[37]

Within the halls of the statehouse, the legislature wanted to appropriately remember the lives of two legislators who had been murdered, state representative James Martin of Abbeville and state senator B. F. Randolph of Orangeburg. The resolution to memorialize them was accompanied by supportive, emotion-laden speeches, the two most impassioned by Robert Brown Elliott and William J. Whipper. If Whipper and Elliott had not made their mark before, they certainly made it that day. Their careers as "radicals" were firmly established, because they made it clear that they did not stand in awe of whites and their superior attitude. Whipper began his eulogy, "Their names have been stricken from our roll and added to the list of martyrs offered at the shrine of American diabolism, . . . immortalized by John Brown of Ossawatomie."[38] After praising the fallen legislators, Whipper used his rhetorical skills to condemn those responsible for the murders:

> I do not charge any particular individual with complicity in these crimes, as I know not the foul hands which perpetuated them, but I do arraign the Democratic party of South Carolina, and charge it with responsibility of these heinous outrages. I am reminded of a dream once related of a celebrated warrior, in which arose before him an army reduced to skin and bones, pointing their bony fingers at him, they said "thou art the cause." And could the shades of the departed Martin and Randolph stalk forth from their bloody tombs, they would point their gory fingers at the Democracy and say, "you are the cause."[39]

Whipper called not for revenge but enforcement of the law. He lamented that "so much of the wealth and culture are on the side of the mob." He asserted to the nation that the white leaders seemed to "bear the olive branch abroad" but were in fact protecting the murderers. He also added a personal note about even "the minor outrages which daily pain our ears," attesting to the pain that a black person had to endure in the state.[40]

To Elliott, the matter was personal. He reminded all the Republicans that before they entered politics, they must have asked, "Will it be I? and . . . wondered whether he should be the first martyr to the cause of truth, justice and liberty." Elliott invoked words similar to Abraham Lincoln's as he spoke of the career of Martin: "it is indeed true that in the midst of life we are in death. We can do no more now than pay a fitting tribute to his memory. Let us dedicate our lives to the carrying out of those principles which he maintained. Let us in the presence of God, resolve that, though we may suffer, we will never recede from them." In conclusion, he called for justice and bluntly pointed out that "the intelligent portion of the people of this State are, at least, indirectly responsible for these diabolical acts."[41]

Two white Democrats took umbrage at the attacks of Whipper and Elliott. John B. Moore of Anderson replied, "Sir, I hurl back the charges with scorn and contempt upon any man, or set of men, either in this legislature or elsewhere who dare to charge me, either directly or indirectly, with murder." While Whipper and Elliott's laying the blame for the murders at the feet of all Democrats was quite sweeping, the truth may have hit too close to home for Moore. His election was under challenge on the grounds that he had used fraud, bribery, and intimidation against black voters in his campaign.[42] Claude Turner of Spartanburg also responded. Moore and Turner were among seven Democrats who refused to vote for the memorial, citing the condemnations by Whipper and Elliott as their excuse.[43]

Despite the violence, the depressed economic conditions, and the divisions within the Republican Party, the black legislators had an enormous impact on the law. Blacks held a majority of the seats in the statehouse; they won seven congressional elections and numerous statewide elections for lieutenant governor, secretary of state, state treasurer, and adjutant general.[44] They helped transform the state. In the first legislative session in 1868, these men wrote and enacted the first civil rights bill in the state's history, with Elliott as one of its most vocal proponents.[45] However, the legislature was not united in its support. Whipper accused white Republicans of hiding outside to avoid voting on the bill.[46] The *Orangeburg News* reported that when the house passed the bill, 8 white legislators and 53 blacks voted "yes," while 19 whites and 5 blacks voted "no."[47] At the same time the legislature ratified the Fifteenth Amendment.[48] They also modernized the criminal laws of the state and abolished capital punishment except for willful murder.[49]

The state legislature remained concerned with civil rights. In 1870 they passed another civil rights bill that was more symbolic than necessary, declaring that the state courts were open to all people regardless of race.[50] In addition, the legislature passed an act that made it unlawful for common carriers or businesses licensed by the state to discriminate based on race or color. The act established various monetary and incarceration penalties for violators of the act. It specifically prohibited passenger train cars and theaters from favoring one race over another in accommodations. Enforcement power was given to solicitors, or failing action by the local solicitor, to the state attorney general.[51]

In an additional response to the political murders, William Whipper introduced legislation to compensate the widows and orphans of victims of political crimes.[52] Although his bill died, a similar bill passed in March 1872 after "the South Carolina Klan in its fury committed some of the most heinous crimes in the history of the United States."[53] The Klan's night riders whipped and murdered Republicans for the simple act of voting. The 1872 bill limited compensation to those victims of political murders committed in the nine upstate counties where President Ulysses S. Grant had suspended the writ of habeas corpus. Whipper supported the 1872 bill and reported it favorably out of committee to the full house.[54]

Out of concern for education, the legislature insisted that state schools and incorporated private schools be nondiscriminatory in their admission policies.[55] Other bills ranged from pure civil rights bills to welfare and prison reform legislation.[56] The legislature also modernized the legal system in the state. William Whipper served as one of the three commissioners charged with revamping the code.[57] Senator Jonathan Jasper Wright introduced a bill that would have compensated appointed counsel in criminal cases: $50 for capital cases, $20 for arson and rape cases, $15 for manslaughter and burglary, and $10 for all other types of cases.[58] This proposal failed, and Wright soon left to serve on the state supreme court.

The Black Judiciary

Jonathan Jasper Wright served on the supreme court of South Carolina from 1870 to 1877. His career on the state's highest court has been thoroughly examined by J. Clay Smith in his essay "The Reconstruction of Justice Jonathan Jasper Wright" in *At Freedom's Door*.[59] Professor Smith's major conclusions bear repeating. Wright was one of three justices on the court, but during his tenure, he wrote only 21 percent of the opinions issued by the court. Smith proposed that Wright's assignment to write so few decisions might have been because of his race. There is no direct evidence to support such a belief except the reality that whites generally believed in their own racial superiority; therefore, there is no reason to suspect Wright would have been treated any better by his peers on the court. Newspaper accounts at the time of his election claimed that Chief Justice Franklin J. Moses and Associate Justice A. J. Willard did not want to serve with "a colored judge" and predicted that one of them might resign.[60]

Smith's second conclusion was critical of Wright. In Smith's opinion, Wright was a "formalist" and, consequently, too conservative as a justice. He cites the case of *Russell v. Cantwell* to demonstrate the effect of Wright's rigid jurisprudence. In that case, Russell, a former slave, brought a malicious prosecution suit against a white man who had charged him with a crime during the Civil War. Wright concluded that Russell had no rights when he was a slave, meaning that no cause of action could be enforced against the white man, Cantwell. Russell's current status as a free man was irrelevant to Wright. Smith suggests that this decision may have prompted one of Wright's contemporary critics to express the opinion that Wright was of some ability but "of little or no moral courage."[61]

Two other black lawyers held important judicial positions during Reconstruction, a fact largely overlooked by historians.[62] This may be because the two judges were black and the court in which they served was so short lived. On March 13, 1872, the criminal court of Charleston County was created by the legislature, and on the same day, George H. Lee was elected over Macon B. Allen by the body to be judge of the new court.[63] A native of Salem, Massachusetts, Lee was thirty years of age. In January 1866 he had come to South Carolina and tried life as a cotton planter before entering the world of politics. Elected a member of the constitutional convention of 1868, he then served two terms in the legislature. Governor Scott appointed him a trial justice for Summerville before his elevation to the Charleston court bench.[64] When Judge Lee died in

February 1873, Macon B. Allen was elected to succeed him.[65] But Allen was not elected without opposition. His former law partner, William J. Whipper, ran against him. Whipper carried the senate, but Allen carried the house by a large margin and won the election.[66] Allen served as criminal court judge until 1875.[67] Allen continued his judicial career with his election in 1876 as probate judge for Charleston County, defeating the incumbent white Democrat, George Buist, by a vote of 14,924 to 8,853. He held that position through 1878 and did not seek reelection.[68]

The Charleston court was granted "exclusive" jurisdiction in all criminal cases arising in Charleston County, except capital cases. Because the death penalty applied only in murder cases, the court was to hear the overwhelming majority of criminal matters in the most populous county in the state from April 1872 to January 1875. The court was abolished by the legislature effective at the end of January 1875, based on complaints that it was redundant and too costly.[69] Since the court with its black judge had usurped the role of the circuit court and its white judges, there is reason to believe that race played a role in the abolition. However, the county's Republicans were so factionalized that the court could likely have been a victim of political infighting.

But the court was a remarkable one, despite its short tenure. Its two judges—the state's only black trial judges—displaced the Court of General Sessions and its white judges.[70] The court tried numerous black defendants before predominately black juries. The criminal court was the major trial court where black lawyers regularly appeared in Charleston County. When it sat in Charleston, the Court of Common Pleas, the civil side of the court, seldom saw a black lawyer, as was true across the whole state except in Aiken County.[71] Obviously the poverty of the black clientele would mean that they would have fewer civil disputes and less money to spend on lawyers in such disputes. Another factor in Charleston was that the leading Republican white lawyers in Charleston County held all of the lucrative government legal jobs.[72] The only time that a black lawyer served as a government counsel in Charleston during Reconstruction was when Judge George H. Lee appointed W. J. Whipper "acting solicitor" for at least three terms of court in the Charleston criminal court because Solicitor Seabrook was prosecuting cases in another county.[73] Thus for the most part, black lawyers could not share in the largesse of local government and had to earn their way by attracting clients and appearing in court. Consequently, a criminal court presided over by a black judge would be the ideal forum in which black lawyers could attract clients as well as appear before both a sympathetic judge and jury.

A few black lawyers served as judges in other minor courts across the state, chiefly the probate and the trial justice courts. W. H. Jones Jr. of Georgetown was a trial justice; Richard Gleaves was elected both probate judge and trial justice in Beaufort from 1870 to 1872; James A. Bowley served a term as probate judge in Georgetown; Thaddeus K. Sasportas was appointed as a magistrate in Orangeburg County; William Hannibal Thomas was appointed, dismissed, and reappointed as a trial justice in Newberry County; Walter R. Jones was elected probate judge of Richland County in 1876 but died before assuming office; Samuel Dickerson served as a trial justice in Charleston; and Macon B. Allen was elected to the probate judgeship for Charleston County in 1876 and served until 1878.[74] One can assume that black lawyers appeared in numerous cases in the trial justice courts because these courts heard minor criminal matters and small claims civil cases. Also since all estates were administered through the probate courts, black clients had to appear in these courts on a regular basis as well. We may assume that when black judges presided in these courts, black litigants would have wanted black lawyers. But records for these courts generally do not include names of lawyers making appearances; therefore, these assumptions about these minor courts must remain merely assumptions.

In part, the paucity of black judges in the state can be explained by the failed election of William J. Whipper to the circuit court bench. Initially, the white Republican leadership in the state had worked to elect only whites to major judicial offices, and for a time they even supported the election of white Democrats. The leadership's aim was to curry favor with native whites. Many blacks went along with the election of white judges, but Whipper opposed the plan.[75] Soon others joined his opposition, and in 1870 the General Assembly elected the conservative Jonathan Jasper Wright as a supreme court justice. The Republican party also nominated, and the people elected, three black U.S. congressmen. In 1872 half of the statewide constitutional offices were filled by blacks, but no black circuit court judges had yet been elected.

William J. Whipper had served as the first chair of the judiciary committee in the Reconstruction house. However, he was replaced by a white Democrat in 1870, and thereafter the post was so assigned "as a gesture of nonpartisanship."[76] When Wright was elected to the supreme court, Whipper had been an unsuccessful challenger. Whipper also failed in his election bids for the criminal court of Charleston and the circuit bench in 1874.[77] In December 1875 Whipper resigned from his house seat, and with the strong support of Speaker of the House Robert Brown Elliott, he won a circuit court judgeship. Although Whipper faced five opponents, he was elected by a comfortable margin of 83 to 59 by the General Assembly. With Whipper's and Elliott's endorsements, the other circuit court candidates were elected by substantial margins, except for former governor Franklin J. Moses Jr., who was elected by a one-vote margin, 70 to 69.[78]

While an adverse reaction to Moses's election could be expected because he was easily the most dishonest of the candidates, a firestorm erupted against the election of Whipper. The *Charleston News and Courier* roared that the Republican legislature's "plan is to Africanize the state and to put the white man under the splay foot of the negro and hold him there." Republican governor D. H. Chamberlain proclaimed that "civilization . . . [was] in peril" and asserted that Whipper was just as corrupt as Moses.[79] To prevent Whipper from assuming the judgeship, the governor refused to sign his commission.[80] While the governor was ostensibly trying to prevent corruption and to reform state government, he was in fact trying to win reelection in 1876. His assertions that Moses was corrupt were no doubt true; however, his accusation that Whipper was corrupt was at best a contrived political reaction and at worst a racist appeal to the white voters of the state. As historian Hyman Rubin III has observed, "It is difficult to resist the judgement made by Elliott that the main objection to Whipper was racial."[81]

No doubt, Whipper was a flamboyant figure. He had wagered large sums in horse races and led an elegant lifestyle. Even Whipper's granddaughter accused him of gambling and drinking too much. But corrupt he was not. As a legislator he was outspoken in his condemnations of corruption and supported the impeachment of a Republican governor whom he accused of accepting bribes.[82] For example, the most infamous event in the Reconstruction "corruption" narrative was the election of Republican John J. Patterson to the U.S. Senate in December 1872. Without question, "Honest John" Patterson bought the votes of the South Carolina legislature and consequently was elected to the Senate.[83] However, Whipper was not even a member of the legislature in 1872 and obviously could not have been bribed to vote for Patterson.[84] The other major corruption scheme was the exorbitant state printing budget. This scheme lasted through much of the Reconstruction era. The chief recipient of the printing business was the Republican Printing Company, which was owned by the clerks of the house and senate. When the post-Reconstruction legislature held hearings on corruption, both testified extensively about whom they had bribed. Clerk of the House A. O. Jones never mentioned Whipper. When Josephus Woodruff, the clerk of the senate, testified, he presented a large number of checks to prove whom he had bribed. Included in these checks was one made payable to Whipper in the amount of $200, but it was not endorsed and presumably never cashed. In addition, the legislative committee issued a

1,700-page report after the hearings. Included was a twenty-seven-page list of the bribery checks supposedly endorsed by members of the legislature, and Whipper's name was not on the list. Ironically, Governor Chamberlain's law firm received $10,000 from the Republican Printing Company, presumably for helping obtain passage of a printing appropriation of $250,000.[85]

Whipper lacked Chamberlain's support for many reasons. To a Harvard-educated elitist such as Chamberlain, Whipper's attitude must have been galling. Whipper had little use for the governor and other "elite" whites; in fact, he did not even try to ingratiate himself with whites. When whites opposed legislation that might benefit blacks by asserting that such legislation was class warfare, Whipper responded to the hypocrisy by pointing out that "the white race have had the benefits of class legislation ever since the foundation of our government."[86] Moreover, Chamberlain was a politician trying to win reelection by currying favor with whites, and radical black men such as Whipper stood in his way.[87] Whipper was ahead of his times in his attitude, which made him a victim of Chamberlain's race, class, and ambition. Ironically, after Reconstruction, Chamberlain fled the state, while Whipper remained and finally achieved his ambition when he was elected probate judge in Beaufort County in 1882.

In Congress

Robert Brown Elliott and Robert DeLarge were elected to the U.S. House of Representatives in 1871 and both sworn in on March 4, 1871.[88] They were the first black lawyers to serve in the U.S. Congress.[89] Their congressional services and careers were quite different; in fact, they were neither political allies nor friends.[90] Elliott's service in Congress was quite notable, while DeLarge's service was unremarkable.

Elliott had been elected to the same congressional district that Preston Brooks had represented before the Civil War. Brooks had been a strong supporter of slavery and is best known for his vicious caning of Massachusetts senator Charles Sumner on the Senate floor.[91] Fittingly, the twenty-nine-year-old Elliott became a strong voice for the civil rights of his constituents. Only ten days after being sworn in, he made his first speech to Congress. He addressed the body in the debate on an amnesty bill for the former Confederates. Elliott asserted that the ex-Confederates were encouraging the Klan in South Carolina, which had killed more than six hundred in the state. The bill failed, and his speech attracted much attention. On March 23 he gave another major speech, again arguing for civil rights. His advocacy for President Grant's proposed Ku

Klux Klan bill helped persuade Congress to pass legislation that helped protect the black citizens of South Carolina.[92]

However, the Klan outrages had continued in South Carolina. On October 12, 1871, President Grant suspended habeas corpus in nine counties because of Klan violence. The next day, when Elliott was making arrangements to return home, he wrote his wife a letter that was to become his will. It ended "because life is uncertain . . . I hereby constitute you my sole heir. . . . If anything happens send for Whipper." Elliott survived and returned to Congress. His stature had risen so high in Washington that he was invited to deliver the principal speech at the District of Columbia tenth anniversary celebration of the emancipation of slaves in the district. He concluded that speech: "Citizenship and a participation in the government are guaranteed to us—let us now go faithfully forward. . . . Let us lift ourselves to the height of our responsibilities . . . and fear no danger. . . . So living and so acting we shall be worthy of the high privileges we possess, worthy to perform our part in preserving the temple of liberty, and in perpetuating our Republican institutions."[93]

But Elliott's greatest triumph was his speech in January 1874 in support of Senator Charles Sumner's civil rights bill. This far-reaching bill, in keeping with both Sumner's and Elliott's views, was designed to ban discrimination in public inns, public transportation, and public education. The debate on the bill on January 5, 1874, created one of those truly dramatic moments in American history as a former Confederate official and a black congressman debated the question of civil rights. Georgia congressman Alexander Stephens, former vice president of the Confederacy, was granted an hour to speak against the bill, and through "some parliamentary maneuvering" Elliott was granted equal time to respond in support of the bill. Elliott eloquently demonstrated a command of constitutional law as he argued with Stephens and other southern congressmen. Elliott's biographer, Peggy Lamson, described the speech as "an overwhelming success" with prominent coverage by the national press.[94] The bill eventually became law as the Civil Rights Act of 1875, but it was declared unconstitutional by the U.S. Supreme Court.[95]

Robert Carlos DeLarge's experience was quite different from that of Elliott.[96] He served less than one term because his election was contested. DeLarge also differed in his political views. In what may have been his only speech in Congress, DeLarge also spoke on the subject of Ku Klux Klan violence in the state, but the South Carolina native spoke against the civil rights bill. He argued that his state's Republicans were in part responsible for the violence because of their poor performance in office.[97]

Civil Rights Educators

The political lives and influence of black politicians in Reconstruction South Carolina have been thoroughly studied by historians. The best two studies are without question Joel Williamson's *After Slavery* and Thomas Holt's *Black over White*. These thorough histories notwithstanding, the unique contributions of the black bar of the state have not been closely examined. A prime example of their uniqueness was their role as educators. The state's forty-nine black lawyers were influential in teaching their fellow citizens about civil rights.

The educational function was both a necessity and part of the oral tradition of the culture.[98] During slavery it had been illegal in South Carolina to teach a slave to read and write.[99] Not surprisingly, much of the population was illiterate. Consequently, one of the best methods of communicating the message of civil rights was through political organizations and speeches by black politicians. One of the most effective organizations was the Union League, which was both a political and a quasi-civic/labor organization. The national organization's objective was to register voters and to encourage them to vote Republican. But at the local level these organizations were formed by freedmen to aid freedmen. The local leagues served as political debating clubs as well as civic clubs that performed community projects. Some chapters in South Carolina even led strikes for higher wages and better working conditions. Historian Eric Foner said that "virtually every black voter in the South had enrolled in the Union League or some equivalent local organization."[100] While the league was often led by northerners, in South Carolina the president was a lawyer and a native, Francis L. Cardozo, who was elected as secretary of state and state treasurer. Robert Brown Elliott also began his political career as a Union League official, organizing for the league in the backcountry.[101] Elliott was observed in action by an army officer and praised for his effective speeches.[102] After being elected to the South Carolina House of Representatives in 1868 and the U.S. Congress in 1870 and 1872, Elliott presided over virtually every statewide Republican gathering throughout Reconstruction.[103]

These men rose to power with the votes of the freedmen who had been educated about their civil rights through the activities of the Union League. All Union League chapters had copies of the Declaration of Independence and the U.S. Constitution, and part of their membership's initiation included reading from those documents. In one local league meeting, the Black Codes were read to the members to warn them of the injustices whites would impose on them. Other chapters encouraged jury service, which led to a greater confidence in the legal system and, as will be seen below, to successes by black lawyers in court.[104]

Outside the Union League meetings, various political and community gatherings featured speeches by lawyers. A perusal of the political speeches of black lawyers in Beaufort County during Reconstruction reveals that W. J. Whipper, R. B. Elliott, Robert DeLarge, S. J. Bampfield, R. H. Gleaves, Thomas Miller, L. S. Langley, Samuel Dickerson, F. D. J. Lawrence, Thomas Wheeler, and even Justice Jonathan J. Wright were so active as to occupy many lines of newsprint with their political orations.[105] Similar activity is found in every county where there was a Republican newspaper that covered the political activities of these men. In Richland County, the chief speakers mentioned were Professor Richard T. Greener, Walter R. Jones, Thomas McCants Stewart, T. J. Minton, Paris Simkins, and, of course, Francis L. Cardozo.[106] In Orangeburg, it was Elliott, Whipper, Benjamin Byas, T. K. Sasportas, Jonathan J. Wright, John L. Humbert, and Samuel Dickerson.[107] These lawyers not only campaigned for themselves and the Republican tickets but often gave speeches on the issues of the day and on important occasions. For example, Benjamin Byas spoke to a mass meeting against the Klan in Orangeburg in 1871.[108] Charleston lawyer John M. Freeman organized an event at Claflin College in 1875 to celebrate the first anniversary of the emancipation of the slaves in the West Indies, with speakers including T. K. Sasportas, R. B. Elliott, W. J. Whipper, and West Indies native Benjamin Byas.[109] Justice Wright was invited to lecture students and give graduation speeches.[110] Walter Raleigh Jones was the featured orator at Columbia's Fourth of July celebration in 1876.[111]

In Charleston, public officials such as Whipper were often invited to deliver an address.[112] But non-office-holding lawyers were invited too. Lewis J. Taylor spoke at Emancipation Day and Independence Day rallies or picnics.[113] In Aiken on July 4, 1874, both Samuel J. Lee and A. A. Bradley spoke and then waited with the audience of eight hundred for the arrival of Robert Brown Elliott, who spoke for more than an hour.[114] In Marlboro, John P. Green gave the Fourth of July address in 1871, and he substituted for Senator Henry Maxwell at some political meetings, even though like many Republican speakers, Green was threatened by the Klan.[115] William H. Thomas of Newberry spoke to political gatherings in Horry, Laurens, Greenwood, and Charleston as well as in Newberry County.[116]

The power of the spoken word of these black lawyers is probably best demonstrated by one of the strategies of the white Democrats in 1876. It is generally recognized that the Red Shirts were armed white horsemen who intimidated and sometimes inflicted violence on potential black voters. No doubt this strategy had an impact, but the chief public activity of the Red Shirts was to disrupt Republican rallies. At these gatherings the leading black lawyers such as Greener, Whipper, or Elliott would be speaking. When the Red Shirts arrived, they would demand equal time for Democratic speakers. Usually the intimidation of the armed horsemen was enough to compel the Republicans to retreat or to grant equal time to a Democratic speaker. Either way, the Democrats succeeded in interrupting the proceedings and, in many cases, ending the black speakers' attempts to advocate their position. The effect of these black lawyers' speeches had been so important to the freedmen and their rise in power that the white Democrats were determined to end them and thus destroy their influence.

CHAPTER 3

The Education of the New Lawyers

On September 23, 1868, the South Carolina Supreme Court, with Justices A. J. Willard and S. L. Hoge sitting, swore in the first black lawyers ever admitted to the state's bar. First, Jonathan Jasper Wright was admitted based on his previous admission in Pennsylvania. Then after an examination of 250 questions administered by the state's attorney general and a state senator, William James Whipper and Robert Brown Elliott were admitted.[1] This event was reported by at least three South Carolina newspapers.[2] In the most detailed article, the correspondent for the *Charleston Daily News* criticized the members of the supreme court who admitted the three new lawyers because the justices were not members of the state bar nor citizens of the state "except under the negro-carpet-bag constitution." The reporter also questioned the veracity of Wright's claim that he had been admitted in Pennsylvania, but he then conceded that Wright had an album with three hundred newspaper accounts of his admission. The report concluded by describing the three new lawyers as "full blooded negroes, with black skins, thick lips and wooly heads, yet, in justice to them, I must say that I believe they are as good lawyers as at least one of the judges who admitted them, and certainly any one of them can make a better speech than either of the judges."[3]

After that day, the rise of the black legal profession in South Carolina was remarkable. Between 1868 and 1877, forty-nine black men were admitted to law practice in the state.[4] The process by which these pioneering lawyers gained admission was no different than that for whites. Admission was either by the supreme court or by a circuit court judge. A majority of these black lawyers were admitted by the state supreme court and hence were licensed to practice in all the courts of the state. Eighteen lawyers were admitted by a circuit court judge, which allowed the lawyer to practice only in the circuit, probate, and trial justice courts. A few of this latter group subsequently sought and obtained admission by the supreme court. (See appendix A.)

State law allowed three means of qualifying for admission. Prior admittance in another jurisdiction was the easiest method. Such an applicant simply presented proof of admission in another state or in the federal courts and was sworn in by the court. Wright was admitted by this method.[5] Macon B. Allen was admitted by the same procedure. He had been admitted in 1844 in Maine and was the nation's first black lawyer.[6] Allen was admitted in the circuit court in Charleston by Judge R. B. Carpenter in November 1869 and the state supreme court in 1875.[7] The only other case of a black lawyer gaining admission by use of another jurisdiction's law license was Thomas H. Wheeler. An 1873 graduate of Howard University Law School, Wheeler had been admitted to the bar in the District of Columbia. On October 16, 1873, W. J. Whipper moved the circuit court for the admission of Wheeler on the basis of his membership in the bar of District of Columbia.[8] Wheeler was later admitted by the state supreme court.

The other two methods of qualifying for admission were reading law (apprenticing) for two years or graduating from "any recognized law school in the United States" and then passing an examination.[9] The bar examination was conducted the same way whether in the supreme court or the circuit court. A member of the bar moved the admission of the candidate, then a committee of two or three members of the bar was appointed by the court to orally examine the candidate in the presence of the judge or judges.[10] After the examination, if the committee approved, one member moved the admission. The record is unclear how vigorous the examination was, but certainly it must have varied. Commonly these black aspirants were examined by friendly black and white Republican lawyers.[11] But not all had Republican examiners. John Mardenborough said he was examined by three "Democratic lawyers, Norris, Abney, and Rainey."[12] On the day John Patterson Green sought admission, two white candidates were admitted by Judge J. M. Rutland, but a committee of three white lawyers was appointed to examine Green. Early the next morning he was required to appear before Judge Townsend for the examination. Green says he passed, and the committee reported that he was "well qualified."[13] Samuel R. Dickerson was examined by "leading members of the Charleston bar."[14] In 1872 some white lawyers apparently suspected an irregularity in the admission of two black lawyers because one of the examiners for one of the candidates was absent when the test was administered. However, one newspaper opined that the "irregularity" was the color of the two young lawyers.[15] The only record of anyone being denied admission after such an exam was in a June 1877 newspaper account of a circuit court judge who refused to admit some applicants because they had not read law for two years.[16] The unsuccessful applicants were not identified by the newspaper.

Prior to the Civil War, the vast majority of lawyers in the United States served an apprenticeship with a lawyer, "reading the law" to gain admission to the bar.[17] There were no law schools in antebellum South Carolina, so hardly any of the state's lawyers had attended one of the nation's few law schools. In the post–Civil War era, law schools proliferated in the nation; South Carolina would have three before the end of the nineteenth century. But during Reconstruction, the majority of South Carolina's lawyers still gained admission to the bar by reading law.

Reading Law

Of the forty-nine black men admitted during Reconstruction, thirty or more read law. At least six studied under a lawyer in the North before coming to South Carolina. Jonathan J. Wright apprenticed in Pennsylvania, first with a law firm and then with a judge.[18] William J. Whipper was tutored by lawyers in Ohio.[19] Robert Brown Elliott claimed to have read law in England, attended law school in Massachusetts, and learned the South Carolina code on his own for six months.[20] Macon Allen had read law with an abolitionist lawyer, Samuel Fessenden of Portland, Maine, and was admitted in 1844.[21] A. A. Bradley had been admitted in Maine and Massachusetts, but it is unclear with whom he studied law.[22] John Patterson Green read law in Ohio with Seymour F. Adams and Judge Jesse P. Bishop.[23]

At least nine read law in South Carolina under the tutelage of a black lawyer. George Lee, who practiced in Charleston, was mentored by Jonathan Jasper Wright while both men were in the state legislature.[24] Theophilus J. Minton, who would graduate from the University of South Carolina School of Law in 1876, was first admitted by the circuit court in November 1871 after studying law with Robert Brown Elliott.[25] James A. Bowley read law under Macon B. Allen; his examination committee consisted of Allen and two white Republicans, C. W. Buttz and John G. Mackey.[26] Lewis Taylor's motion to be admitted was made by Whipper, Elliott, and Allen, and Macon B. Allen served as one of his examiners.[27] A. W. Watson's admission was made by Whipper, Elliott, Allen, and Taylor.[28] Dempsher Powell, L. S. Langley, and A. H. Ezekiel were all examined by William Whipper, Samuel J. Lee, and a white Republican, Alfred Williams, and admitted on February 8, 1877, in Beaufort County. We know

Powell read law with Whipper.[29] Since Whipper was the senior member of the Beaufort bar, it seems likely that all three were tutored by him. George C. Clyde was admitted by the state supreme court in November 1874. Since he resided in Aiken at the time of his admission and immediately went into practice with Samuel J. Lee of Aiken, it is logical to assume he studied law with Lee.

A number of lawyers were mentored by white lawyers in the state. Thomas Miller attended the University of South Carolina but read law with white judge P. L. Wiggin.[30] John Mardenborough read law in New York and then with R. W. Seymour of Charleston.[31] It was the norm for the lawyer with whom an applicant studied to move his admission. Such was the case of F. D. J. Lawrence and Samuel R. Dickerson, whose admissions were moved by C. W. Buttz of Charleston.[32] John L. Humbert and T. K. Sasportas both apprenticed with T. H. Cooke of Orangeburg, who moved their admission before Judge Robert Graham on May 9, 1872. Wiggin, Seymour, Buttz, and Cooke were all white Republicans. Stephen J. Swails may have read law with Melvin J. Hirsch, a white Republican with whom he practiced law in Williamsburg County.[33] Benjamin Byas's examining committee included Buttz as well as two other white lawyers, both Republicans.[34] Other Republican lawyers serving on examining committees in Charleston included John G. Mackey and D. T. Corbin.[35] The only instance found in Charleston court records of white Democrats serving on an examining committee was at the admission of Dickerson.[36]

Of the others who became lawyers during Reconstruction, it simply cannot be confirmed how they qualified for admission. Eight were admitted by the supreme court and were prominent political figures. U.S. congressman Robert DeLarge, Speaker of the South Carolina House Samuel J. Lee, senate president pro tempore Stephen Swails, state senator Henry J. Maxwell, and Representative W. H. Jones Jr. were all admitted by the court on the same day in 1872.[37] William F. Myers was a senator, and Samuel J. Bampfield, William A. Hayne, and John M. Freeman Jr. were state representatives when they were admitted by the court in 1875. Based on their residence at the time of admission, age, and place of birth, it is likely that they read law with a South Carolina lawyer.[38] The exception among this group was William Hannibal Thomas, who gained admission shortly after moving to Newberry; it is logical to assume he was educated out of state.

There are no detailed records of the process of reading the law in South Carolina. The best account is that of John P. Green about his apprenticeship in Cleveland, Ohio. While Green graduated from a law school, he also read law. Green said he was invited by Judge Jesse P. Bishop "to occupy a desk in his office." Although he was invited by Bishop, Green's education was actually supervised by another lawyer, Seymour F. Adams. Green described Adams as "a gentleman and scholar." As a result Green says he "devoured Blackstone, Kent, Bishop, Byles, Stephen, Parsons and other great commentaries on the English and American law, during the ensuing four months, reading as I truly believe, day and night, well nigh as much as the average reader would cover in a year."[39]

Former slave F. D. J. Lawrence said he studied law for six years with a white lawyer, C. W. Buttz of Charleston, and was admitted by circuit judge J. P. Reed in February 1875.[40] Lawrence's long apprenticeship demonstrates the inconsistent training these lawyers received. In his work *The Rise of the Legal Profession*, Anton-Hermann Chroust concluded that reading law "was of widely varying thoroughness and quality, and that particularly in the lesser law offices much of it was of a purely mechanical type."[41] The recollections of white lawyer George B. Cromer further illustrate the varying experiences in South Carolina. In 1924, in his address as president of the South Carolina Bar Association, he reminisced about his experience reading the law. Cromer said he studied law for only eleven months with "James H. Rion of Winnsboro, one of the most distinguished lawyers in South Carolina." In addition to the short course of "reading," Cromer related that Rion never asked him a single question, although the busy lawyer did answer questions put to him by the young apprentice. In addition, every other week Cromer was allowed to farm to support his "widowed mother and sister."[42]

The apprenticeship method made it possible for thirty or more black men to become lawyers in Reconstruction South Carolina. It offered an avenue to a profession with economic, political, and social opportunities that were unheard of before the Civil War. It also meant that the black community had advocates prepared to help safeguard the rights gained by the Great War and its aftermath. But reading law had its drawbacks. With few black lawyers in the state, the opportunities for an apprenticeship were small. To undertake a mentorship, a lawyer often charged a fee, frequently a high one in South Carolina. The apprentice paid his mentor and was expected to perform uncompensated legal work for him.[43] In Lawrence's six-year apprenticeship, the process could be quite time consuming. Moreover, the instruction was uneven. Mentors were not required to provide any formal instruction, and their level of interaction with the students varied greatly. Often the apprentices simply had to read the law on their own. There were seldom any moots or other forensic opportunities. Reading law emphasized copying forms and had neither uniformity, skills instruction, nor academic rigor. The apprenticeship system also served as a gatekeeper for the profession, allowing admission to only those acceptable to the bar. Such a system would admit only a limited number of men from outside the ruling class. These criticisms were in part responsible for the quest for a more formal method of instruction.

Law School

After the Civil War the legal profession underwent great changes. As Kermit Hall observed, the "economic and social transformation" of the country dramatically affected the legal profession.[44] This transformation resulted in the rise of the law school. In his authoritative work, *Emancipation: The Making of the Black Lawyer, 1844–1944*, J. Clay Smith finds no evidence that any black student attended a law school in the United States before 1868.[45] Howard University Law School was founded in 1869 and graduated its first students in 1871. Three of Howard's first graduates came to South Carolina and were admitted by the state supreme court. Edwin T. Belcher, Eugene R. Belcher, and John F. Quarles were residents of Georgia. Quarles and Eugene Belcher practiced in South Carolina for no more than a year, and both listed Augusta, Georgia, as their hometown at their date of admission. Quarles and Edwin Belcher became active in Georgia politics.[46] Both Belcher brothers obtained federal jobs and remained in Georgia, but there is no record of their practicing law.[47] Another Howard graduate, D. A. Straker, did practice in South Carolina and played a significant role in the legal profession in the state until the 1880s (see chapter 6). Howard graduate Thomas Wheeler practiced in Beaufort until about 1890. Ohio Union Law School graduate John Patterson Green practiced briefly in Marlboro County.[48]

The increase in black political power eventually led to the desegregation of the University of South Carolina. The new era began on October 7, 1873, when the university admitted its first African American student, Henry E. Hayne, to the School of Medicine. Before the end of the month, five black students entered the law school. These men were Walter Raleigh Jones from Charleston, Joseph D. Boston from Newberry, C. M. Wilder from Columbia, and Laurence Cain and Paris Simkins from Edgefield. Not only had the university become the first institution of higher education in the South to admit African American students, but the law school was the nation's first state-supported law school to educate black law students.

The mere presence of African American students on campus outraged conservative, white South Carolinians. One newspaper, the *Charleston News and Courier*, pronounced, "The University is dead."[49] The *Edgefield Advertiser* described the university as "only a dreary and dirty sham."[50] The *Georgetown Times* issued this diatribe: "Let the sons of carpetbaggers, scalawags, and

African citizens go there and have a homogenous genetic mixture of elements in perfect accord."[51] As late as 1875 the Charleston newspaper was asserting that "the South Carolina University has been broken up by the admission of colored students and except in the matter of cost, has only a nominal existence."[52] The fact was, however, that before integration, the university had only 65 students, while in 1874 and 1875 the university had more than 150 students.[53] In response to the criticism, some Carolina students wrote to a local newspaper that "white and colored students are now pursuing their studies amicably together, and there is no war of races."[54]

Other derogatory claims were made about the university during Reconstruction. One of these was that the African American students were all Republican politicians who entered the school on pretense "to show the white people of South Carolina that the negroes intended to dominate in the state university and there enforce the social equality of the black with the white race."[55] Another newspaper described the university as "a political nursery."[56] While it is true that many students were Republicans, there is little to suggest that they entered simply to integrate the university, and much evidence that they were serious about obtaining an education. Of the nineteen African Americans who enrolled in the law school from 1873 to 1877, eleven got their degrees. Two of these, Lawrence Cain and Paris Simkins, were Republican legislators, but they managed to obtain their law degrees while fulfilling their official duties. Favoritism toward Republicans does not seem to have been a significant factor, since Thomas Miller, J. D. Boston, G. T. McIntyre, and W. F. Myers, all Republican legislators, never were awarded law degrees. On the other hand, Styles Linton Hutchins, a well-known black Democrat, did obtain his degree.

Another claim made against the school was that the "student body was composed almost entirely of boys and men of the black race."[57] This was inaccurate. Historian Daniel Hollis found that in June 1874 the student body was equally divided between the races.[58] In testimony before a congressional committee, Professor Richard Greener was asked about the composition of the student body and how the students tolerated persons of another race. Greener replied that a third of the students were white and that students of both races "recite together in recitation rooms and play together."[59] White professor Fisk Brewer observed that the white and black students "do not see why, if a black man and a white man can ride on the same seat in the market wagon or in the railroad car for the sake of convenience or economy without impropriety, why they may not sit on the same seat to hear about medicine and law and science and literature."[60]

Between 1868 and 1876 the law school had thirty-nine graduates.[61] Before the integration of the university in 1873, the law school had five graduating classes and a total of twenty graduates. All of these graduates were white, and most were probably natives of the state. By contrast, all the law school's graduating classes from 1873 to 1876 were integrated.[62] These three classes had nineteen graduates, eleven of whom were black. According to a Reconstruction-era student, C. C. Scott, by 1874–75 there were seventeen African Americans enrolled in the law school.[63] Of the eight black students who did not graduate, four went on to become lawyers.[64]

In 1873 the University of South Carolina School of Law resembled similar schools around the country.[65] There was one professor of law and a two-year curriculum that many students completed within a year, and its faculty complained about law students who came to class unprepared.[66] The professor of law in 1873 was C. D. Melton, a native South Carolinian and a Republican. Before the integration of the school, Melton had served as defense counsel for one of the Klansmen convicted in the Ku Klux Klan trials of 1871 and 1872.[67] Melton had graduated from South Carolina College in 1840.[68] He practiced law after his admission to the bar in 1844, and after the Civil War he had been in partnership in Columbia with Washington A. Clark.[69] He was appointed professor of law in 1869. In addition to Melton, university professors T. N. Roberts, Henry J. Fox, and Richard T. Greener also taught in the law school. Greener was the first African American on the university faculty. Roberts, a medical doctor, was the professor of history, political philosophy, and political economy. Fox was a minister who taught rhetoric, criticism, elocution, and English language and literature.[70]

The academic program was intended "to acquaint the student with the principles, and prepare him for the practice of his profession." The 1869 university catalog included in the "course of study" for the law school such readings as *Blackstone's Commentaries*, *Chitty on Contracts*, *Kent's Commentaries*, *Stephen's Pleadings*, *Greenleaf's Evidence*, *Bayley on Bills*, and *Russell on Crimes*.[71] The first-year curriculum consisted of common and statute law, history, English language, declamation and composition, contracts, and mercantile law. The second year included pleadings, code practice, evidence, political philosophy, elocution and composition, constitutional and international law, equity, rhetoric, logic, political economy, orations in the chapel, and moot courts twice a month.[72]

Professor Melton died in the summer of 1875. He was succeeded by Franklin J. Moses, chief justice of the South Carolina Supreme Court. Moses had been admitted to the bar in 1825 after reading law under James Louis Petigru, the leading lawyer in South Carolina at the time.[73] Moses was a native, a Jew, and a former slave owner.[74] He modified the curriculum to place a heavier emphasis on *Blackstone's Commentaries* and *Kent's Lectures*. In addition to moot courts, the students were expected to write essays on legal topics. Lectures were on Mondays, Wednesdays, and Fridays at 5:00 p.m. in Justice Moses's chambers at the supreme court.[75] In 1877 Styles Linton Hutchins, in testifying before a congressional committee, was asked how he came to be a lawyer. He replied that he had read law in the chambers of Chief Justice Moses.[76] However, Hutchins was enrolled as a law student in 1876, so his experience as a law student was such that he referred to it as "reading law."[77]

CLASS OF 1874

In 1874 the law school had five graduates, including its first black graduate, Walter Raleigh Jones, a native of Charleston.[78] Jones had attended Oberlin College in Ohio. He worked for the secretary of state, where he compiled a large report on corruption in the state land commission as well as an index of the state's laws. Before he graduated from law school, he had been elected city clerk of Columbia. Both ambitious and bright, Jones was someone of whom much was expected. However, he died in November 1876 of meningitis just a few days after he had been elected probate judge for Richland County.

CLASS OF 1875

In 1875 the class again had five graduates, three of whom were black.[79] Henry Barton Johnson was born in Charleston around 1850. He served as chief clerk to Secretary of State Henry E. Hayne, who had been the university's first black student. Johnson was active in Republican Party politics and drew the ire of the Democratic press for his activities. He was admitted to the South Carolina bar in November 1877. However, he soon left the state and his activities thereafter are unknown.

Another member of the class of 1875 did not fade from view so quickly. In 1874 a Columbia newspaper, reporting on a speech by a South Carolina student, remarked, "[If this student] does not write his name upon the annals of his country, it will be because justice is not done to the race which he represents."[80] The student was Thomas McCants. Stewart, born in Charleston, the son of free persons of color. After the Civil War he attended Avery Normal Institute and received a scholarship to Howard University, which he attended from 1869 to 1873. He enrolled at the University of South Carolina in January 1874.

As a student, Stewart was ever on the move; one month he was lecturing students in a rural school, and the next he was delivering the Fourth of July oration in Sumter or debating in the Clariosophic Society. His activities drew an admonishment by the faculty for "his gross neglect of his college duties." Nevertheless, he was chosen to give the valedictory address at his graduation. He received his AB and LLB in December 1875 and was admitted to practice by the supreme court in November 1875. He practiced briefly in Sumter, then he joined Robert Brown Elliott and D. A. Straker in a law firm in Orangeburg. He actively campaigned for the Republican ticket for the 1876 election.[81]

After getting married, Stewart took a teaching position at the State Agricultural and Mechanical College in Orangeburg.[82] In 1877 he was ordained as a minister. He resigned from the college in July 1878 and moved to New Jersey to accept a pastorate, where he attended Princeton Theological Seminary and later became pastor of a church in New York City. In 1883 he became a professor at Liberia College in Monrovia, but he returned in 1885 and practiced law. He also became a corresponding editor for the *New York Freeman*. In this position he returned to South Carolina, ever hoping that his home state might be welcoming, but while he reported promise in the state, he could not bring himself to move home.[83]

Until the late 1890s Stewart lectured, wrote, and practiced law in New York. Disillusioned with the Republican Party, he became a Democrat, a move that drew a sharp rebuke from Frederick Douglass. His association with the Democrats also led to an open and bitter dispute with his old professor, Richard Greener. Following *Plessy v. Ferguson*, Stewart again looked for a new promised land and moved to Hawaii, becoming the first African American admitted to the bar there. In 1905 he moved to London and then on to Liberia, where he renounced his U.S. citizenship. As a Liberian, he served as a diplomat, a deputy attorney general, and an associate justice of the Liberian supreme court. Following a dispute with the president of Liberia, Stewart returned to England in 1914. In 1921 he moved to the Virgin Islands and practiced law. He died there in 1923.[84]

The third black member of the class of 1875 was Joseph Henry Stuart, born in 1849. He graduated from law school a month after he was admitted to the bar. While a student, he had been thrown off a train in the middle of the night for refusing to leave a first-class car that the conductor claimed was for whites only. Stuart's protestation led to the arrest of the conductor. Stuart was an excellent law student who was selected to deliver one of the two student addresses at his graduation. Following his admission to the bar, he served briefly as principal of the Sumter Graded School but was soon practicing law in Camden. He moved to Kansas and was admitted to the Kansas bar in 1883. His law practice there included an unsuccessful suit to integrate the public schools. He then moved to Denver and was admitted to the Colorado bar in 1891. He served two terms in the Colorado House of Representatives and practiced law in Denver until his death in 1910.[85]

Graduating with Johnson, Stewart, and Stuart were two white men. Henry Austin Fox was the son of a university faculty member. Admitted to the bar in 1875, he served for a time as assistant principal of the preparatory school at the university. Mortimer A. Warren had been principal of the state normal school. He was never admitted to the bar in South Carolina but remained an educator and moved to Connecticut after Reconstruction.

THE CLASS OF 1876

The law school class of 1876 had nine graduates, seven of whom were African American.[86] One of the two white graduates was the son of a university faculty member. C. J. Babbitt served as Governor Chamberlain's private secretary after the death of Walter Jones and was practicing law in Columbia in 1879 and 1880. Thomas Meredith Canton, the other white graduate, was also a Republican. He had been appointed as a trial justice by Governor Chamberlain. The African American graduates included three elected officials, a university professor, and one of the few African American Democrats in the state.

One of those elected officials, Lawrence Cain, had been born a slave in Edgefield, South Carolina. After the Civil War, Cain tried both farming and teaching. As a teacher he drew the praise of local whites, but when he entered politics, the praise ended. In 1868 he was elected to represent Edgefield County in the South Carolina House of Representatives. He won reelection in 1870 and then was elected senator in 1872. Cain was an able legislator whose speeches and legislative proposals often drew comment from the press. Cain's ability to turn a phrase is demonstrated by this excerpt from one of his letters: "If the straws can indicate the wind's course, it seems to me that facts, undeniable and undenied, of so grave importance as these should throw some light upon the 'mutual distrust' entertained in my county between the races."[87] Cain entered the law school in 1873. Since he took three years to get his degree, he was a member of the last nineteenth-century class to include African Americans when he graduated in December 1876.

His law school graduation coincided with the end of his senatorial career. Cain's home county of Edgefield was one of the major battlegrounds in the election of 1876 to be marred by violence as white Democrats overthrew the black majority state government. In fact, the white Democratic campaign plan came to be known as the "Edgefield plan." Although the majority of Edgefield's voters were African American, Cain lost his senate seat to a white candidate by a margin of more than two to one. The white Democrat received 6,268 votes, just slightly less than the entire voter-eligible male population in the county. Cain testified that having received numerous threats, he was afraid to campaign and knew of hundreds of his supporters who were not allowed to vote. He remained active in public life, attending Republican conventions and serving as deputy director of the Internal Revenue Department. Senator Cain died of tuberculosis on March 28, 1884.[88]

On October 7, 1874, state treasurer Francis Lewis Cardozo enrolled in the law school. As noted previously, Cardozo was one of the leading and most influential delegates to the constitutional convention of 1868. He had begun his political career by attending the National Convention of Colored Men held in Syracuse, New York, in 1864, then he attended the Colored People's Convention held in Charleston to protest the 1865 constitution, which had failed to grant suffrage to African Americans. Many thought him the most powerful African American in South Carolina. Governor D. H. Chamberlain considered Cardozo his "ablest and wisest adviser."[89] Moreover, Cardozo had been mentor to most of the African American law students at the university. Critics of this early period of integration claimed that Cardozo entered just to inflate enrollment figures. But his keen insight and interest in legal issues at the 1868 constitutional convention would suggest that he wanted a legal education.

Cardozo was born January 1, 1836, in Charleston, South Carolina. His mother was a free woman of color, and his father was from a prominent Jewish family. He traveled to Scotland and attended the University of Glasgow from 1858 to 1861. He also studied at seminaries in Edinburgh and London. In 1864 he returned to the United States and was soon ordained a Congregational minister in Connecticut. In 1865 Cardozo was called to Charleston to teach for the American Missionary Association. He helped found Avery Normal Institute and became its first superintendent. As a delegate to the 1868 constitutional convention, he was chairman of the education committee. He subsequently was elected secretary of state and then state treasurer.

Cardozo resigned as South Carolina's secretary of state in 1871 to teach at Howard University. Of this decision, he wrote, "I did this under a profound conviction that I can be of more service in the great work of reconstruction in the South by occupying such a position, where I can prepare the rising generation, of my own race especially, for the honorable discharge of the important duties resting upon them as American Citizens."[90] After 1877, he taught in the public schools of Washington, D.C., until one month before his death in 1903. Francis L. Cardozo High School was named in his honor in 1928 and remains a high school in the city today.

Richard Greener was born in 1844 in Philadelphia.[91] He attended Oberlin

College Preparatory School in Ohio and Phillips Academy at Andover, Massachusetts, and in 1870 he became the first African American to graduate from Harvard College. After his graduation, Greener became vice principal at the Institute for Colored Youth in Philadelphia, and then principal of a high school in Washington, D.C. In 1873 he was appointed professor of mental and moral philosophy at the University of South Carolina. In addition to his professorship, he also taught in the law school and served as the university's librarian. On October 7, 1874, he enrolled in the law school and graduated in December 1876.

While at the university, Greener was in great demand. The community sought his attention, and the local press noted his activities. He was an active Republican, serving as a state representative to the Union League of America's National Executive Committee. His experiences in the 1876 campaign were recounted in his testimony before the congressional committee that held investigative hearings on the election violence.

Greener was admitted to the bar by the South Carolina Supreme Court on December 20, 1876. He resigned from the University of South Carolina in June 1877 and moved to Washington, D.C., where he worked at the Department of the Treasury. He was admitted to the bar in the District of Columbia on April 14, 1877, and from 1878 to 1880 he served on the faculty of Howard University School of Law, including one year as dean. While on the Howard faculty, he defended a black cadet from South Carolina who was being court-martialed by the U.S. Military Academy.

After 1880 Greener served in various government positions. In 1898 he was appointed as the first U.S. consul to Vladivostok, Russia, where he served seven years. This was a period of armed conflicts in Asia, including the Boxer Rebellion and the Russo-Japanese War. After 1906 he lived in Chicago, where he practiced law. He also wrote and lectured until his death on May 2, 1922.

Styles Linton Hutchins was born in 1852, in Lawrenceville, Georgia. The son of a prominent Atlanta barber, Hutchins graduated from Atlanta University and became a teacher and principal.[92] He testified before a congressional committee that he read law under a lawyer named Goss in Nashville and John A. Wempey in Atlanta.[93] Hutchins moved to South Carolina in 1873 and graduated from law school in December 1876. He was admitted to the South Carolina bar in November 1876. Despite political differences with his fellow students, Hutchins was elected class secretary. Unlike most of his classmates, he campaigned extensively for General Wade Hampton and other Democrats in the fall 1876 campaign. In fact, he was a featured speaker at Hampton rallies.[94] On one occasion, Hutchins was allowed to speak and debate classmate Richard Greener. When the U.S. Congress held hearings on the issue of 1876 election violence, Hutchins was called as a witness by the Democrats, and his classmate Greener was called as a witness by the Republicans.

After the election, Governor Hampton appointed Hutchins as a trial justice. But the legislature abolished his judgeship, forcing him to resign after only five weeks on the bench. Hutchins returned to Georgia and sought admission to the Georgia bar and by 1878 was practicing in Atlanta.[95]

In 1881 he moved on to Chattanooga, Tennessee, where he started a newspaper, entered Republican Party politics, and practiced law. He was elected as a Republican to the Tennessee House of Representatives in 1886 and served two terms. In 1909 Hutchins represented a client who was lynched while his appeal was pending before the U.S. Supreme Court. Because the lynch mob had violated a stay of execution, the U.S. Supreme Court held those who could be identified in contempt and jailed them. The jailing so angered the local whites that Hutchins and his family were forced to flee to Oklahoma.[96]

Theophilus J. Minton was born in Philadelphia and graduated from the Institute for Colored Youth in Philadelphia. He moved to South Carolina after the Civil War and was admitted to the bar in November 1871. For several years he worked as a bookkeeper in the office of the state treasurer. In 1875 he enrolled in law school and graduated in 1876. Minton was an active Republican who campaigned with Richard Greener in Laurens, a town notorious for the killing of Joe Crews, a Republican leader. Minton testified against another former classmate, Niles Parker, in his corruption trial. Minton also testified for the defense in the corruption trial of his former employer, Francis L. Cardozo. With the end of Reconstruction, Minton moved to Washington, D.C., to work in the Treasury Department. After the loss of his Treasury post, he was admitted to the Pennsylvania bar in 1880. He was became one of the best-known African American lawyers in Philadelphia and remained active in Republican politics until his death in 1909.[97]

Joseph White Morris was born a slave in Charleston in 1850. His parents, John B. Morris and Grace Morris, had two daughters and two sons. John Morris was a wheelwright and the owner of real estate valued at $1,700. In 1851 he purchased his wife, Grace, and his son, Joseph, from William Bee. In reality, however, John Morris could not free his wife and son because in 1820 the South Carolina General Assembly had prohibited the manumission of slaves except by act of the legislature. Therefore, Joseph Morris legally remained a slave, though he was raised free. Morris attended Simeon Beard's school in Charleston and then Avery Normal Institute. While at Avery he came under the tutelage of Cardozo, who helped procure a scholarship for Morris to attend Howard University. After graduating from Howard in 1875, he enrolled in the

University of South Carolina School of Law, graduating in December 1876. He was admitted to the bar by the supreme court in November 1876. He practiced law briefly and then became the principal of Payne Institute. When Payne Institute merged with Allen University in Columbia, Morris became a professor and later president of the university. He served two tenures as president of Allen University from 1881 to 1885 and from 1895 to 1897. During his first term, he oversaw the early years of Allen's law school. He continued to teach at Allen until his death in 1913.[98]

Paris Simkins was born a slave in 1849, in Edgefield, South Carolina. His mother was a slave, and his father was his owner, Arthur Augustus Simkins, publisher of the local newspaper. Although it was illegal, a fellow slave taught Simkins to read and write. When his master joined the Confederate army, Simkins accompanied him, working as a barber. After the war he returned home and opened a barbershop. He became involved in politics, religion, and civic affairs by serving as head of the local militia, a member of the jury commission, and a trial justice. Elected to the house of representatives of South Carolina in 1872, Simkins served as chair of the Ways and Means Committee, where his efforts to fight corruption drew the attention of even the opposition press as he led efforts to prosecute former state treasurer Niles Parker and to impeach a state court judge.[99] While in the legislature he attended law school and graduated in 1876.

Only thirteen days after Simkins graduated from law school, he was called to testify before a congressional committee on voter intimidation. He testified that he ran for reelection in 1876, but facing trumped-up criminal charges as well as a bounty on his head, he campaigned little and did not even vote. Once he was defeated the conspiracy charges disappeared. He also testified that of the Republicans who came out to vote, many were physically prevented from voting. After Reconstruction, Simkins remained active in church, civic, and political affairs. He was not admitted to the bar until 1886. He never tried cases, but he did draw up the legal papers for the Mutual Aid and Burial Society. He also served as postmaster in Edgefield, the position from which he retired. Simkins, the father of sixteen children, died on September 26, 1930.

THE DEMISE OF THE RADICAL LAW SCHOOL

When Chief Justice Moses died in June 1877, at least two African American students, Joseph D. Boston and William F. Myers, were still enrolled at the law school. Both had been admitted to the bar in 1875. In 1877, before either man could be awarded a degree, the university and the law school were closed.[100] The critics of the "radical" university and law school had been right in predicting destruction. That destruction, however, did not come about because African Americans studied in the halls of the university, but because white conservative South Carolinians used violence and fraud to overthrow the Republican government in South Carolina.[101] These white Democrats closed the school in 1877 to prevent African Americans from being educated at the university. Their excuses for the closing and their malicious criticisms of the "Radical University" are mostly answered now.

The careers of the African American men who graduated from the University of South Carolina in the 1870s add no weight to the claim that they enrolled only to produce some "homogenous genetic mixture."[102] These men were advocates for civil rights and equal treatment, as well as serious students who saw the value of a legal education. They sought equality and expected to be leaders. A legal education offered much, simply because of the promise of the law. The great American experiment in democracy was being opened up to their race for the first time. The Thirteenth and Fourteenth Amendments to the U.S. Constitution and the South Carolina Constitution of 1868 clearly provided for equality under the law for all men. These men believed in these promises and used their legal training from the University of South Carolina to further the cause of civil rights.

Joseph H. Stuart fought valiantly to prevent the fraudulent attempt to remove an African American judge in the dying hours of Reconstruction and brought one of the earliest lawsuits to integrate the schools in the country when he filed such a suit in Kansas. Richard Greener used his skills to try to undo the injustice done to an African American cadet at West Point. T. McCants Stewart used the legal system to challenge civil rights violations from the saloons of New York City to Hawaii and Africa. Styles Linton Hutchins fought for civil rights in the legislature of Tennessee and saw his legal career and his family's lives threatened because of his advocacy for a client. Just as lawyers had done for centuries, these men entered public service. They served as judges, lawyers, legislators, constitutional officers, diplomats, civil servants, ministers, college presidents, teachers, and in other positions of service to their communities. Their leadership was recognized throughout the African American community. Indeed, four of these graduates were included in William Simmons's *Men of Mark* as leading men of their race in America in 1887.[103]

One of the criticisms of the radical law school was that all of these men were Republicans who were exerting their political power by attending the university. It is true that if the Republicans had not been elected by a majority of the voters of the state, there would have been no radical law school. It is also true that most of these men were Republicans, but in fact, as the one Democrat among them, Styles Linton Hutchins, soon found out, no other political party would allow an African American to achieve any position of power or influence in the South. In the eyes of many whites in South Carolina, a Republican was black and a Democrat was white.[104] As the nineteenth century faded and the memories of Reconstruction dimmed, the desire for political acceptance for African Americans did not. Both T. McCants Stewart and F. L. Cardozo sought influence in the Democratic Party. Their sojourns were short lived, however, as they discovered their race constituted a barrier to any real future in American politics, Republican or Democrat.

Despite the dire predictions of the conservatives, between 1873 and 1877 the law school lived up to its mission of preparing students for their profession. Most of the graduates practiced law. Thomas McCants Stewart, Richard Greener, Styles Linton Hutchins, T. J. Minton, and Joseph Henry Stuart remained active in their profession until the turn of the century and beyond.

Three months after Thomas McCants Stewart enrolled at the university, he wrote, "The institution is calculated to do much good for South Carolina and the Negro race. If the time ever comes when the descendants of the Rutledges and the Marions shall believe in the unlimited brotherhood of man, the University of South Carolina will have a dwelling place in the breast of every Africo-American."[105] Stewart's hope for the future was not to be. The end of Reconstruction in the spring of 1877 signaled the end for the integrated school. Following the removal of federal troops from South Carolina, the Democrats "quickly acted to close down the Republican-dominated school" because it "represented everything its loyal native supporters detested."[106] When the university reopened in 1881, it was all white and remained so until the 1960s. Although the law school had opened in 1867, one modern historical sketch asserted that its "real beginning" came in 1883.[107] The centennial history of the university, published in 1905, relegated the period of Reconstruction to an appendix in the back of the book titled "The Negro in Possession, 1873–1877."[108] As the title and placement of the appendix suggest, the Reconstruction era of the university, including the law school, was not worthy of honor in Jim Crow South Carolina.

CHAPTER 4

Law Practice in Reconstruction

While the greatest contributions to civil liberties by South Carolina's black lawyers in the nineteenth century came through the political and legislative processes, many of these men were also effective courtroom advocates who advanced the cause of civil rights on a case-by-case basis. During Reconstruction, at least thirty black lawyers practiced in the state's courts. Just as Abraham Lincoln had done in Illinois, South Carolina's lawyers and judges traveled on circuit across the state. Criminal cases were tried in the Court of General Sessions, and civil cases were heard in the Court of Common Pleas. William Whipper and Robert Brown Elliott rode circuit, appearing almost exclusively in criminal courts in numerous black-majority counties. Other black lawyers also represented clients in sixteen majority-black counties; unfortunately, only nine of these counties have surviving court records.[1] Some counties such as Edgefield County had black lawyers in residence, but there is only one record of a black lawyer appearing in court.[2] In addition to official county records, newspapers and other secondary sources provide insight into law practice in a few other counties. What follows is a description with some analysis of the evidence from twelve counties.

Aiken County

Aiken County was the only county in which black lawyers had any significant civil trial practice.[3] Samuel J. Lee and George Clyde were the two prominent black lawyers in the county, and both had substantial civil and criminal caseloads. Lee was elected to the legislature in 1870 and became Speaker of the House. He was admitted to the bar in 1872 and left the legislature in

1874 to manage his growing law practice. In December 1873 he was joined in his practice by George C. Clyde, whose arrival was noted by the press thusly: "George C. Clyde, Esq., who has been residing in Aiken for some months past, during which he assisted the Clerk of Court in the discharge of his official duties, was examined before the Supreme Court of this State, in Columbia, last Wednesday, and admitted to the bar. He will practice his profession in Aiken, and will bring to it large intellectual attainments, an unblemished character and social qualifications of the highest order. We wish him abundant success."[4]

If caseload is any indication, success is what Lee and Clyde enjoyed. Between 1873 and early 1877, Lee had at least forty-three lawsuits on the civil trial calendars of the circuit court in the county. George Clyde was his co-counsel in most of those cases.[5] A few resulted in verdicts, but most were settled or discontinued. No proceedings are recorded where Lee's and Clyde's clients won a money verdict. The cases were suits for money, actions on notes, recovery of real property, and claim and deliveries. A number of cases cannot be classified because the dockets simply do not provide the necessary information, but nineteen cases were actions for "relief" against the county or a public official. In one case, Clyde represented Lee in a lawsuit against him for money, but there is no recorded resolution of the case. In two cases, Lee and Clyde represented the plaintiff in a divorce action.[6] Robert Brown Elliott joined them as co-counsel on one civil case.[7]

Lee and Clyde had an even larger criminal practice. During Reconstruction, Lee handled sixty criminal cases in the circuit court in Aiken County. Robert Brown Elliott was his co-counsel in six of those cases, and George Clyde co-counseled in forty. The results they obtained for their clients were impressive. Out of all of these cases, twenty-four clients were either found not guilty or had their cases dismissed. Two cases ended in mistrials, and only one client was found guilty. In the six trials in which Robert Brown Elliott teamed with Lee, their clients received not guilty verdicts, including two charged with murder. William Whipper joined Lee and Clyde in two cases. In a murder trial in May 1876, their client was found guilty.[8] The official misconduct trial of white Republican Henry Sparnick ended in a mistrial.[9]

In 1876 Lee returned briefly to the world of politics with a run for solicitor. Tensions were high in the county, and just a few days before the election, Lee and Clyde both signed a petition to the governor requesting federal troops to protect the Republican voters in Aiken.[10] Despite the strong white Democratic effort, Lee was elected solicitor as a Republican; however, he was forced to resign in 1877 in the face of allegations of corruption.[11] Lee was subsequently convicted but served only a short time in jail. (See discussion in chapter 5.)

Clyde never held elective office but was active in Republican politics, and in addition to his work in the clerk of court's office, he was a sergeant at arms of the South Carolina House of Representatives.[12] Lee and Elliott practiced law after Reconstruction, but not in Aiken. Clyde seems to have disappeared after 1876.

Barnwell County

Barnwell had no resident black lawyer. Although they lived in other counties, Macon B. Allen, William J. Whipper, and Robert Brown Elliott did appear in the Barnwell County courts. In August 1869 Whipper and Elliott were appointed as defense counsel in a murder trial in Barnwell. They not only obtained a not guilty verdict, but they also drew the attention of a Charleston newspaper, which reported on the "politeness and general good bearing" of the two lawyers.[13] Later in 1869, the law firm of Whipper, Elliott, and Allen was counsel for William Stuart, charged with stealing a mule. They obtained his release.[14] William Whipper often appeared without his partners in Barnwell. In a September 1873 trial, he was co-counsel with two white attorneys. The three lawyers were able to obtain not guilty verdicts on two serious charges of riot and assault and battery of a high and aggravated nature, but their clients were convicted on a lesser charge of assault and battery.[15] There is no record of black lawyers appearing in civil cases in Barnwell County.

Beaufort County

Beaufort County had a large contingent of black lawyers. One of the most prominent was R. H. Gleaves, who later became lieutenant governor. In Beaufort, Gleaves served as trial justice and probate judge but did not practice law. The elder statesman of these black lawyers actually practicing law was clearly William J. Whipper.

Records for Beaufort County Court reveal few appearances in the Court of Common Pleas by black lawyers.[16] The only civil case found was brought by Whipper to enjoin the county treasurer from accepting scrip instead of currency for land sold at tax sales.[17] However, it was in the criminal courts where Whipper was most active and successful. During one term in 1873, he won acquittals for clients charged with murder, rape, and assault and battery with intent to kill.[18] He took small cases and won those, too; one such example was the case of Niles Graham, charged with stealing ten dollars from a Dr. Randall and whose release Whipper obtained by habeas corpus.[19] He also represented both white and black defendants, and he was tenacious in fighting for his clients, even after a guilty verdict.[20] In February 1873 Whipper represented Thomas Wright on a murder charge and was disappointed when his client was found guilty of manslaughter. This prompted Whipper to seek a pardon from the governor for his client.[21] In another case, white murder defendant Richard Wickham hired Whipper and a Colonel Wiley from Savannah to defend him. Wickham was accused of killing Michael Burke on an excursion of the Irish Union Society in the waters of the Calibogue Sound on the steamer *Nick King*. The jury was out all night and failed to agree on a verdict. When the case was retried in June, Wickham was again represented by Whipper and Wiley and this time was found not guilty.

In 1873 Howard University Law School graduate Thomas Wheeler joined Whipper as another black member of the Beaufort bar.[22] By February 1876, black lawyers A. A. Bradley, F. D. J. Lawrence, and S. J. Bampfield had also arrived. Whipper often tried cases with these younger lawyers.[23] However, he remained the senior and most experienced lawyer in the group. When a term of court opened, Whipper would often be appointed in murder cases while the other lawyers handled more minor cases.[24] In one murder case, Whipper is said to have brought the jury to tears.[25] From 1873 to 1876, the Beaufort newspaper recorded six criminal cases tried by Whipper. All of his clients were found not guilty, including three who had been charged with murder.[26]

Thomas Wheeler persuaded juries to return not guilty verdicts in eight out of his nine trials.[27] Based on newspaper accounts, six black lawyers tried criminal cases in Beaufort during Reconstruction. In their trials, the juries returned twenty not guilty verdicts, six guilty verdicts, and one mistrial. Not all lawyers were successful, however. A. A. Bradley was criticized in court by one client, had a bloody encounter in court with F. D. J. Lawrence, and was jailed more than once.[28] F. D. J. Lawrence was a native of Beaufort who had read law in Charleston and moved back to Beaufort; he lost both cases he tried.[29]

Another young lawyer from Beaufort had been admitted to practice by the state supreme court in December 1875. Thomas Miller had studied at University of South Carolina Law School, but the university does not record him as graduating. He was to go on to a stellar career in both politics and education; however, as a young lawyer he had some rough going in his first days in practice in rural Beaufort County. In the most dramatic incident, he was nearly beaten to death after obtaining his client's acquittal in a case where the victim was white.[30]

The only other incident of violence and intimidation against a black lawyer also arose in Beaufort County and was against William Whipper. One of his cases was removed to Barnwell for trial because of local passions, but the victim's supporters and family went to Barnwell for the trial. Whipper obtained a not guilty verdict in the murder trial, but he faced threats of physical violence after his victory.[31] However, such incidents did not deter the black bar.

Whipper, Miller, and others continued to practice in the county even into the twentieth century. In fact, other black lawyers were attracted to the county. In 1877, as Reconstruction came to an end, three more lawyers were admitted by the circuit judge in Beaufort. William Whipper, Alfred Williams, and Solicitor Samuel J. Lee were appointed to examine six applicants for admission, and L. S. Langley, A. H. Ezekiel, and D. W. Powell, all African Americans, were admitted.[32]

Charleston County

In Charleston County, eight black lawyers practiced from the late 1860s through the end of Reconstruction. In February 1869 Whipper appeared in the circuit court in Charleston on behalf of a client charged with assault and battery. The *Charleston Daily News* reported this case as the first instance of a black lawyer appearing in a state court.[33] Whipper and Robert Brown Elliott were soon practicing together, and in 1869 they opened a law office with Macon B. Allen on Broad Street in Charleston.[34] While Whipper had practiced law in the city as early as 1866, he represented Beaufort in the constitutional convention in January 1868 and listed Beaufort as his home when he was admitted to the bar in that same year.[35] Similarly, Robert Brown Elliott lived in Charleston at the time of the constitutional convention of 1868, but he represented Edgefield in the convention and listed Aiken as his home at the time of his admission to the bar in 1868.[36]

While Whipper and Elliott practiced law across the state, only Macon B. Allen worked in Charleston throughout Reconstruction.[37] Allen maintained their law firm in Charleston until 1874, when he became a judge of the Charleston criminal court.[38] Politics and ambition caused conflicts among the three. Not only had Whipper run against Allen for the criminal court judgeship, he had also vied with Elliott for the Republican nomination for lieutenant governor in 1868. Whipper withdrew from that race and threw his support behind the eventual winner, a white candidate, Lemuel Boozer. Later in 1868, after both had been elected to the South Carolina House of Representatives, Whipper nominated Elliott to be Speaker of the House. Elliott did not win, and the two men continued to practice law together.

As in other counties, black lawyers seldom appeared in civil cases in the

Court of Common Pleas in Charleston. In 1869 Whipper, Elliott, and Allen were listed as counsel in only one civil case.[39] After that, no black lawyers appeared in Common Pleas until 1876, when Macon Allen and Lewis J. Taylor were co-counsel in an action by the administrator of an estate. Their opposing counsel included John H. Fordham, a black lawyer who had a white co-counsel. When the case appeared next on the calendar later in the year, Taylor had a white co-counsel while Fordham continued with his same white co-counsel.[40]

The civil courts in Charleston were dominated by white lawyers, including white Republicans.[41] The one appearance of Allen with Taylor as co-counsel and Fordham on the other side is unique. Even the black labor unions on the city's docks used a prominent white Democratic lawyer, C. H. Simonton.[42] White Republican lawyers held governmental legal positions such as U.S. attorney, circuit solicitor, county attorney, county treasurer's attorney, and city attorney, but no blacks held such positions.[43] Other white lawyers, such as D. H. Chamberlain, had flourishing private practices.[44]

Clearly being a Republican did not prevent a lawyer from practicing in Charleston, so one must assume that race played a role in the paucity of black lawyers maintaining offices and appearing in the civil courts. George Lee, who had read law with Jonathan Jasper Wright, was elected by the state legislature to be the criminal court judge for Charleston County in March 1872.[45] Sometime later in 1872, Judge Lee had a white Republican county councilman jailed for contempt. D. T. Corbin, a prominent white Republican lawyer, sought a writ of habeas corpus from Chief Justice Franklin Moses. Corbin was less than genteel in his attitude toward Lee; he called Lee's order "foolish" and the judge "very young at the bar" and condescendingly claimed to have been one of Lee's examiners when Lee was admitted to the bar "not more than a year ago."[46]

Despite animosity from the white bar, black lawyers continued to be admitted to practice, most often by the circuit court. On the motion of Whipper, Elliott, and Allen, Lewis J. Taylor was admitted by a circuit judge on June 11, 1872. As noted earlier, James A. Bowley was admitted by circuit judge R. F. Graham on the motion of Macon B. Allen on November 16, 1872.[47] A. W. Watson was admitted by the circuit court on November 8, 1872.[48] Benjamin Byas, who had represented Orangeburg in the state house of representatives, was admitted by the circuit court in Charleston on June 10, 1874.[49] He appeared as the attorney of record on one case in the Charleston criminal court in the July 1874 term.[50]

F. D. J. Lawrence had a Charleston city law office in 1876.[51] Lawrence, who had been born a slave, read law for six years with C. W. Buttz, a white Republican who practiced in Charleston.[52] Lawrence was admitted by a circuit judge on February 5, 1875.[53] He was also associated with Lewis Taylor and John H.

Fordham, who advertised themselves as a law firm in Orangeburg County.[54] Samuel R. Dickerson, who served as a trial justice in Charleston, was admitted to the bar by circuit Judge J. P. Reed on December 3, 1875.[55]

During Macon B. Allen's tenure as judge of the Charleston criminal court, black lawyers made frequent appearances.[56] These included the Charleston lawyer Lewis J. Taylor as well as the leading out-of-town black lawyers William J. Whipper of Beaufort, James A. Bowley of Georgetown, A. A. Bradley of Beaufort, and John H. Fordham of Orangeburg, as well as Benjamin Byas, who lived in Orangeburg but practiced law in Charleston.[57] These black lawyers had sixty-three cases in the criminal court between 1873 and 1875. Whipper had twenty-three, and Lewis Taylor had twenty-two. Whipper's record supports the conclusion that he was an able trial lawyer. He obtained six acquittals, two new trials ordered, four cases struck, and one quashed. Eight of his clients were found guilty. In the Charleston circuit court's General Sessions term, Whipper had two cases, and in both his clients were found not guilty.[58] Lewis Taylor was not so successful—only four of his clients were acquitted. He also had one mistrial, one *nolle prossed*, one new trial granted, and two cases struck. Handling less serious cases, A. A. Bradley had the best record with six not guilty verdicts, three guiltys, and one *nolle prossed*. James Bowley had two acquittals, five guilty verdicts, and two mistrials. Benjamin Byas lost his only trial, and John Fordham's only case was continued.

Colleton County

During Reconstruction, William F. Myers was the only black lawyer from Colleton County. He had served as the county auditor and was in constant conflict with Governor Franklin J. Moses Jr. Moses removed Myers from office in July 1874. Myers responded by running for and being elected the county's senator in 1874 and serving until 1878. After his election, he obtained admission to the bar in 1875 and opened a law office in Walterboro. There are no court records of appearances by Myers. Apparently, politics and local conditions did little to help Myers grow his law practice. By the spring of 1876, his constituents were starving because of the economic conditions and conflicts with white plantation owners. When the planters tried to impose a wage reduction for rice field workers, the destitute workers went on strike. Myers supported the "Combahee strikers," an action that placed him at loggerheads with establishment Republicans such as Republican governor D. H. Chamberlain. When Senator Myers attempted to have a trial justice removed from office because of the judge's attitude against the strikers, Chamberlain ignored Myers's request despite the support of a petition signed by three hundred Republicans.[59] After Reconstruction, Myers continued to live in Colleton County and remained active in politics.

Edgefield County

One of Robert Brown Elliott's first trials was assisting in the prosecution of a murder case in Edgefield County. While the defendant was found not guilty, Elliott's speech to the jury was described as "fluent," "temperate," and "a fair legal argument."[60] Otherwise there are no records of black attorneys appearing in the circuit courts in the county. John Mardenborough had read law with white Republican R. W. Seymour in Charleston and was admitted there by the circuit court in 1876, but he practiced in Edgefield. He testified before a U.S. congressional hearing in 1876 that he handled cases in Edgefield County before the trial justice court. In one case, Mardenborough sought to have a warrant issued against a white man who threatened to kill Mardenborough's client for complaining that he had not been paid for the cotton he raised.[61] A. W. Watson, who was admitted in Charleston in 1872, may have practiced in Edgefield.[62]

Georgetown County

Georgetown County had at least two resident black lawyers and three others who made appearances during Reconstruction. The first recorded appearance of a black lawyer in the county was that of William Whipper in June 1869 in the case of *Ham v. McArn*.[63] Although Whipper was probably living in Charleston at that time, it would not be his only trial in the courts of Georgetown. That same 1869 term of court, Whipper lost an assault and battery case.[64] Senator W. H. Jones had been admitted to the bar by the supreme court in November 1871, but the minimal records of Georgetown County do not reveal any litigation instituted or defended by Jones.

In 1872 James A. Bowley was the second black lawyer to appear in the courts of Georgetown. Bowley read law under Macon B. Allen in Charleston for two years, and in 1872 he passed the bar examination administered by Allen, John G. Mackey, and C. W. Buttz and was admitted by circuit judge R. F. Graham.[65] An advertisement for "Jas. A. Bowley, Attorney at Law, Georgetown, S.C." was published in the *Georgetown Planet* on May 31, 1873. Bowley was the nephew of Harriet Tubman. She had literally rescued him from the auction block and secreted him to freedom on the Underground Railroad. Bowley lived with Tubman after his escape, and she sent him to school.[66] Probably inspired by his aunt, Bowley came to Georgetown to work as a teacher for the Freedmen's Bureau on the Rice Hope Plantation. Bowley successfully defended his first client in a June 1874 battery trial.[67] That same term, he also represented a client charged with larceny. The case was continued for a year and then dismissed.[68] There is no other evidence of Bowley's law practice, although he was active in local politics and had returned to teaching in Georgetown by 1880.[69]

One of the biggest trials in the county's history occurred in June 1875. Christopher Columbus Bowen, sheriff of Charleston County, was the defendant in a murder trial. Bowen had been arrested in April and charged with causing the murder of a Confederate colonel eleven years earlier.[70] Bowen, a former congressman, had married Susan Petigru, daughter of South Carolina's most famous antebellum lawyer, James Louis Petigru. Despite his marriage into this respected family, white Democrats attacked him because he was the Republican boss of the county. In addition, Bowen's private and public lives constantly drew attention and attack. He had been previously convicted of bigamy and pardoned by President Grant. So it is not surprising that his alleged killing of a Confederate officer during the Civil War would result in criminal charges being brought a decade later. Bowen was accused of persuading another Confederate soldier to murder their commanding officer, who had had Bowen court-martialed for forgery. The officer had been killed in Georgetown County, so the trial was set there. For his defense, Bowen hired the best lawyers he could find: Robert Brown Elliott, William Whipper, Stephen Swails, and H. C. Hirsch, Swails's white law partner. When Bowen was acquitted the courtroom crowd reacted with enthusiasm.[71] The not guilty verdict obtained for Bowen was not unusual for Elliott and Whipper. The two would prove multiple times their prowess in serious criminal cases. In that same term of court in Georgetown, Elliott also represented two other clients charged with murder. One client was acquitted, and the other was convicted of the reduced charge of manslaughter.[72]

Marlboro County

Marlboro County had two black lawyers. John Patterson Green was born in North Carolina but at age twelve moved to Cleveland, Ohio. He studied law with the firm of Bishop and Adams in Cleveland, graduated from Ohio Union Law School in 1870, and was admitted to the Ohio bar. He then moved to South Carolina. Green had relatives in Bennettsville and had hopes of finding employment as a teacher or postal worker. To him, South Carolina was the land of opportunity. But there were no jobs, and when his wife had a baby, he opened a small store. Perversely, Green reported that his store was an immediate success because of crowds flocking to town to see the public hanging of a black man who had confessed to murdering his wife.[73] With some financial cushion, Green then sought admission to the bar and was admitted to practice in Bennettsville by circuit judge C. P. Townsend on September 20, 1870. Green does not appear in the civil court records for Marlboro County.[74] But his criminal practice was active for his short tenure. Two clients were found not guilty, and two were released when Green persuaded the court that his clients were being held without an indictment.[75] In the Irene McKay case, Green used "puerperal mania" (postpartum depression) as his defense, and the seventeen-year-old mother who had killed her baby was found not guilty.[76] He lost the murder trial of Franklin Cook, but before the death sentence was carried out, Green procured a commutation from Governor Robert Scott.[77] However, Green's talents could not prevent another client from receiving two years in prison for bigamy.[78] While Green was active in Republican politics, he and Republican county senator Henry Maxwell had conflicts, and Green did not feel he had a political future in the county.[79] Citing the "poisonous miasmata" as damaging the health of his family, Green pulled up stakes and returned to Ohio in 1872, where he became a prominent figure. Among his accomplishments were authoring two books and being elected to the Ohio legislature.[80]

But Marlboro was not without a black lawyer when Green departed. Senator Henry J. Maxwell was admitted to the bar by the state supreme court in March 1871.[81] Maxwell had been a free person in Charleston before the war. He moved north in the 1850s and was active in efforts to obtain the vote for blacks in Michigan. Once the Civil War began, he served as an army recruiter and later as a first sergeant in the Union army. After being mustered out of service, he returned to Charleston and was employed by the Freedmen's Bureau in Marlboro County. When elections were held in 1868, he won a seat as state senator and served until 1877. Shortly after his admission to the bar in March 1871, Maxwell was charged with perjury, but he was found not guilty on May 18, 1871.[82] His lawyer in that case was Duncan McColl, a local white lawyer who was his co-counsel in two criminal cases.[83] Over the next six years, Maxwell handled at least thirty criminal trials at various terms of the Court of General Sessions with mixed results. However, Maxwell's legal career seems to have come to an end when he was indicted for receiving money under false pretenses in September 1877. Since the charges were dismissed, it is likely that the indictment was part of the general pattern across the state of indicting Republican officeholders to force them to resign from public office. These indictments were highly suspect, and even the state attorney general who prosecuted some of the cases said they were politically motivated.[84] Maxwell lived until 1906, but by 1900 he had turned to brick masonry to earn a living.[85] However, his legacy includes his granddaughter Cassandra Maxwell, who became the first black woman lawyer in the state in 1941. (See discussion in chapter 11.)

Newberry County

Newberry County had two black lawyers. William H. Thomas and Joseph Boston appeared separately and jointly in more than twenty criminal cases. Court records reveal that between the two of them, they had had one guilty verdict, eight not guilty verdicts, five dismissals, and one mistrial. There was no record of the results of the other cases, and there are no records of any civil court appearances.[86] Joseph Boston represented the county in the legislature from 1868 to 1876 and attended the University of South Carolina Law School but never graduated. He was admitted to the bar in 1875.[87] Boston taught for a time and died in 1880.[88] William Hannibal Thomas moved to Newberry from Georgia in late fall of 1873 but was gone by May 1877. Within a short time, the Ohio native and army veteran was quite active in law and politics. Thomas claimed that he had studied law entirely on his own. He was admitted on January 30, 1874, by circuit judge Montgomery Moses after what he described as a rigorous exam by three white lawyers. He underwent another exam and was admitted by the state supreme court in the fall of 1876. Thomas was appointed a trial justice by the governor and was elected to the state house of representatives in 1876. John David Smith, his biographer, described Thomas's law practice as "varied but unexceptional." He served as a prosecutor on two occasions and then appeared in eleven criminal cases as defense counsel. Smith says Thomas won nine of these cases. Thomas's election to the legislature in 1876 threw him into the midst of the struggle for control of the state between Republicans and white Democrats, and he was forced out of the body. (See the discussion of election of 1876 and the Compromise of 1877 in chapter 5.) Thomas was indicted for stealing a bale of cotton in 1877 and left the state. According to his biographer, John David Smith, Thomas became one of the most reviled black men in America after his book *The American Negro* was published in 1901. Smith describes the book as one of the most antiblack books ever written. Thomas died in relative obscurity in 1935.[89]

Orangeburg County

Orangeburg County's population in the 1870s was more than two-thirds black.[90] At least three black firms were established in the county between 1874 and 1876, but few county court records and little secondary evidence of these law firms' practices survive. The first was Humbert and Fordham, established in the spring of 1874.[91] One year after his graduation from Claflin College in Orangeburg, John L. Humbert had been admitted to the bar by the circuit court in May 1872.[92] The second black law firm was Taylor, Fordham, and Lawrence, founded in March 1875. This firm advertised "special attention to the collection of claims." The Orangeburg newspaper commented that "the combination of legal talent and ability ought to attract many clients."[93] If their advertisement was meant to attract clients in the civil courts for debt collection work, it appears to have failed. None of the firm's lawyers appear in any newspaper accounts of legal proceedings in the county.

The first record of John H. Fordham's law practice was in a Court of Common Pleas case in October 1875.[94] Fordham also supplemented his income by serving as county coroner.[95] If Lewis Taylor practiced in Orangeburg County, no record of it has been found. The same is true for F. D. J. Lawrence. Robert Brown Elliott often came to town in his capacity as congressman, and he also unsuccessfully defended the lawyer John L. Humbert, who as county treasurer was charged with corruption.[96] T. K. Sasportas was admitted to the circuit court at the same time as Humbert.[97] There is no evidence that Sasportas practiced in the courts, but he too had income from his positions as postmaster and later as county treasurer.[98] In 1875 Elliott formed the third Orangeburg law firm with David A. Straker and T. McCants Stewart. Elliott's biographer says the firm flourished until the end of Reconstruction.[99] In April 1876 Straker was listed as counsel for the county of Orangeburg in a lawsuit brought by a property owner alleging damage to his land by road construction.[100]

Richland County

One might assume that as a majority black county and the home of the state capitol, Richland County would have had many black lawyers practicing in its courts during Reconstruction. However, there are no surviving court records for the county, and other sources such as city directories do not list any black lawyers. The newspaper reports reveal only a few accounts of a black lawyer appearing in court in the county. Robert Brown Elliott, who had practiced in Charleston and had represented Barnwell County in the legislature, purchased a home in Columbia in 1870 and resided there while in Congress. In 1875 Elliott formed a law firm in Columbia with James A. Dunbar, a young white lawyer, and Thomas McCants Stewart, a black lawyer and recent law school graduate.[101] Dunbar was the city attorney for Columbia, but his legal career was short lived as he died in January 1876.[102] After D. A. Straker was invited to join the firm, they also practiced in Orangeburg. There are no court records of the firm practicing in the Richland County courts. According to the *Columbia Union-Herald*, Elliott was actively practicing in the summer of 1876, handling a rape case, an arson case, and an assault case that took days to try.[103] In the assault case, Elliott successfully defended the son of the county's state senator, William Beverly Nash. There are no records of any other black lawyer practicing in the county.

Williamsburg County

Stephen A. Swails appears to have been the only black lawyer in practice in Reconstruction Williamsburg County. The former Union army lieutenant and decorated war hero had been elected to the state senate in 1868. He was admitted to practice in March 1872 by the supreme court. He practiced in Kingstree with M. J. Hirsch, a white Republican and Confederate veteran. Hirsch had practiced in the county before the war, served one term in the Reconstruction legislature, and was then elected solicitor.[104] The law partnership of Swails and Hirsch may have been the first multiracial law firm in the state's history and possibly the nation as well. Williamsburg County court records document that the law firm had one case on the civil trial calendar.[105] But like so many other black lawyers, Swails handled mostly criminal cases. He and Hirsch had eight criminal trials together, of which they won two, and Swails alone had seventeen criminal cases on the calendar, of which he won five and lost seven.[106] In addition to his litigation practice, he handled real estate transactions, as a few records from his papers show. Among them are at least two deeds prepared by Swails on behalf of Williamsburg County residents who had purchased land through the South Carolina Land Commission.[107] Swails also served as co-counsel with Whipper, Elliott, and Hirsch in the C. C. Bowen murder trial.[108] Swails served in the South Carolina Senate and as president pro tempore of that body from 1870 to 1876. His subsequent political and legal careers are discussed later in this volume.

~

Why were these black lawyers primarily engaged in criminal defense work? Because of the poverty of the black clientele, there would have been little legal work to undertake in the Circuit Court of Common Pleas. There are no records from the trial justice courts where smaller civil cases were heard. We do know that Samuel J. Lee and George Clyde had a substantial civil practice in the Court of Common Pleas in Aiken County, but even they handled more criminal than civil cases. The surviving records from the Reconstruction era demonstrate that black lawyers were criminal defense lawyers, perhaps because criminal cases were the area of practice that was open to them. However, it was also by choice. They were members of an oppressed race and a minority group in the profession. But they and their clients were part of the 60-percent-majority racial group in the state. In some counties, the percentage was much higher. The obvious consequence of this situation was that their clients would be judged by black jurors and often by majority black juries.[109] In addition, black (and even some white) clients would have every reason to believe that a black lawyer would be more persuasive to these juries than a white lawyer.

After Reconstruction, and as Jim Crow spread, one of the chief legal battles that would be fought across the South and in the U.S. Supreme Court was the exclusion of blacks from juries (discussed at length in later chapters). But this was certainly not an issue in Reconstruction South Carolina. There were no appeals brought by black lawyers on behalf of their black clients on the grounds of race discrimination in jury selection. Jury composition was not an issue because blacks served on juries and the black lawyers more often than not won their criminal jury trials. Consequently, few appeals were handled by black lawyers in this era. The majority of the citizens of South Carolina were newly freed people. While there had been promises of "40 acres and a mule" for the former slaves, it was an unfulfilled promise. These new citizens had little property or money over which they would have had contests in the civil courts. Small claims were handled in the magistrate's courts and, as noted earlier, in the Freedmen's Bureau courts. When these black citizens came into contact with the law, it was commonly because their freedom was under attack. Native white South Carolinians simply did not accept the concept of free and equal black citizens. In fact, whites tried every means to keep blacks subjugated and were highly motivated to re-enslave as many blacks as possible to maintain a cheap labor pool. In the criminal justice system, this was often seen in retaliatory prosecutions by white planters wanting to punish black farm laborers.[110] So the record is clear. By necessity and inclination, South Carolina's black lawyers during Reconstruction were criminal defense lawyers and, as a consequence, civil rights advocates.

CHAPTER 5

The End of Reconstruction

Purge, Exodus, and Demise

The 1876 presidential election and an armed rebellion by white Democrats led to the overthrow of Reconstruction government in the state. The Redeemer Democrats' use of terrorist tactics in the campaign of 1876 signaled that white Democrats would use any means necessary to terminate the civil rights of the state's black citizens. Once the gubernatorial election results came in, both the Democrat Wade Hampton and the Republican incumbent D. H. Chamberlain claimed victory. The contest was dependent on the returns from Edgefield County.[1]

Edgefield was home to two black legislators, Senator Lawrence Cain and Representative Paris Simkins. Both were law school graduates and had been leaders in the Reconstruction legislature, and both were incumbent candidates for the legislature in 1876. However, Cain and Simkins, as well as many other black citizens, were prevented from voting by threats and actual physical violence. In addition, whites stuffed the Edgefield ballot boxes and imported white voters from Georgia to vote for the Democrats. These efforts resulted in Democratic gubernatorial candidate Wade Hampton receiving more votes than the total number of registered voters in the county. Based on the margin in Edgefield, Hampton claimed victory in the statewide race. Lawrence Cain and Paris Simkins were also defeated.

Despite Hampton's claim of victory in the governor's race, nearly every election in the state was under challenge. Overcoming the terrorist campaign and the stuffed ballot boxes, many black Republicans won their elections, and the Republicans swept the state offices below governor and lieutenant governor. According to official reports, Robert Brown Elliott was elected the state's first black attorney general, and Francis L. Cardozo was reelected as state treasurer.[2]

Black lawyers such as Thomas Miller, D. A. Straker, W. H. Thomas, Henry Maxwell, W. F. Myers, and Stephen Swails were all elected to the legislature.[3]

However, the white Democrats were determined to overturn these Republican victories. For nearly six months the election remained disputed. Two separate bodies claimed to be the legitimate state house of representatives, and government came to a standstill. The Compromise of 1877 settled the Hayes-Tilden presidential election. The Republican Rutherford B. Hayes was awarded the electoral college vote of South Carolina, Florida, and Louisiana in exchange for a withdrawal of federal troops from the state. Under the agreement, the national Republicans abandoned the South to the white Democrats. Without the army, Republicans, especially black officeholders, had no one to protect them from violence and other illegal means that might be used to oust them from office. Thus, Wade Hampton and other white Democrats seized control of state government. When incumbent governor Daniel H. Chamberlain withdrew in April 1877, Hampton assumed the governorship. Though these events have been well chronicled by historians, the consequences for black lawyers in South Carolina have not been closely examined. With white Democrats in power, a systematic attack on black leaders, especially lawyers, began.

The white Democrat body known as the Wallace House designated itself as the state's house of representatives and began to banish a number of blacks who had clearly been elected. Two outspoken black lawyers had been elected to the house of representatives, D. A. Straker from Orangeburg County and Will Hannibal Thomas from Newberry County, but when the men tried to assume their duties, the new white Democrat legislature demanded that they resign their seats. When Straker and Thomas refused, they were expelled and denied their seats by a vote of the house, which cited the "gross contempt and defiant attitude" of the two lawyers.[4] Soon thereafter, Thomas left the state. Straker stayed and remained active in politics and as a lawyer. He ran for his house seat in 1878 against black Democrat Benjamin Glen Frederick and lost.[5] In the senate, Stephen Swails and Henry Maxwell resigned. Threats and intimidation probably caused Swails to capitulate, and Maxwell abdicated after being charged with bribery. After the compromise and the expulsions, only twenty-seven African Americans kept their legislative posts and served in that first session of the legislature. Of these, only two black lawyers remained in a legislature that was once dominated by such men. They were state senator W. F. Myers from Colleton County and Representative Thomas Miller from Beaufort County.

The decline continued in 1878. The elections that year were again marked by fraud, intimidation, and violence.[6] A U.S. marshal said of the Democrats in that campaign that they were "more defiant in expressing their determination to crush the Republican party out of existence by force if necessary."[7] A few black lawyers ran for office, others campaigned for Republican candidates, and some just tried to keep the Democrats honest. However, their efforts were often thwarted by threats and actual violence. In Charleston, John M. Freeman, serving as an elections supervisor, was physically assaulted when he tried to prevent voting fraud. Young lawyer Joseph Henry Stewart saw a black judge assaulted and kidnapped as well as black voters being intimidated by Red Shirts armed with a cannon. William J. Whipper campaigned in Beaufort and Hampton Counties and was threatened by Red Shirts brandishing pistols. State senator William F. Myers from Colleton County saw blacks intimidated by rifle clubs as well as wholesale voting fraud with the use of tissue ballots to overwhelm the legitimate black vote. However, one black lawyer, Benjamin Byas, testified before Congress that he saw no fraud, intimidation, or violence toward blacks in the 1878 election, nor had he ever seen any such tactics used from 1870 to 1878.[8] Whatever tactics were used by white Democrats, they had a devastating impact on the number of blacks in the legislature. After the election, there were no black lawyers in the state senate, and only one, Beaufort representative Thomas Miller, in the entire General Assembly. Over the next twenty years, Beaufort County voters elected three black lawyers to the legislature, Thomas E. Miller, Thomas J. Reynolds, and Julius I. Washington.[9] The only other black lawyer to serve in the legislature during this time was James A. Bowley from Georgetown County, who served in the house from 1890 to 1895. By 1878 the tactics of white Democrats had effectively eliminated the black lawyer legislator.

While most black Republican officials were threatened and forced from office, black lawyers and judges were a special target. In 1877 the new Democrat-controlled legislature launched an investigation of supreme court justice Jonathan Jasper Wright.[10] The legislature held secret hearings concerning Wright and then issued a report recommending that he be impeached for "drunkenness."[11] Representative Thomas Miller fought back, claiming that the committee chair had been bribed. But with so few black or Republican members left in the legislative body, Wright was impeached in the house on June 6, 1877, by a vote of 75 to 23. Before a trial could be conducted in the senate, Wright resigned effective December 1, 1877. Thus ended the service of the first black man on an appellate court in U.S. history. As historians Richard and Belinda Gergel have noted, the charges against Wright were no doubt false and intended to rid the state of Republican officials.[12]

On the same day that Wright was impeached, the house and senate passed resolutions authorizing a Joint Committee of Investigation to expose the public "corruption" that supposedly occurred during Reconstruction.[13] Previously, the legislature had asked President Hayes to grant clemency to all the white Democrats charged with election violence. Hayes refused and ordered the prosecution of three of the Democrats. After Hayes's reply, the state countered by launching its investigation of corruption. The joint committee served as the most important tool in the plan to dismantle Reconstruction and end any black power on a statewide basis. The committee called dozens of witnesses and released a series of reports amounting to nearly 1,800 pages. Despite the exhaustive investigation and the "Fraud Report," only three men were tried and convicted, and only one of the three served any significant time in jail. Democratic attorney general James Conner admitted that these indictments were intended to "politically guillotine" the Republican Party, and that the committee's work "would not stand test as legal evidence." The three men that were tried were former state treasurer Francis L. Cardozo, Congressman Robert Smalls, and former congressman L. Cass Carpenter. Of the three, only Carpenter was white.

The Chief Target

As a prominent Republican leader, Francis Cardozo was a prime target for white Democrats. Cardozo's trial and conviction demonstrated the lengths to which white Democrats would go to purge the state of prominent black figures. It is true that some Republicans in Reconstruction South Carolina were corrupt; the same is also true of some Democrats. Yet when the facts are closely examined, Cardozo's innocence seems apparent.[14]

Many thought Cardozo the most powerful African American in South Carolina. Throughout his political career, he had enjoyed a reputation for honesty. As state treasurer, Cardozo drew praise from conservative newspapers for his efforts to curtail corruption, chiefly through tight money management. His efforts caused corrupt Republican legislators to try to impeach him in 1875. That impeachment was defeated by a coalition of reform Republicans and Democrats.

However, in 1877 the newly empowered white Democrats now saw Cardozo as an enemy. Called before the committee in July and arrested two days later, Cardozo was charged with seven felonies and a misdemeanor.[15] The legally trained, astute politician Cardozo suffered either from the hubris of his former success in politics or the naïveté of a newly minted lawyer in his belief that justice would prevail. Unfortunately, Cardozo had made too many enemies. As a powerful Republican and black lawyer, he was the perfect choice for white Democrats to prove their assertion that Reconstruction was corrupt. To those indicted Republicans who had been the target of Cardozo's reform efforts, he was the perfect sacrifice to offer white Democrats. Not only could these Republicans avoid jail, they could have their revenge on him.

The charges were essentially the same as those brought by the corrupt Republicans in the 1875 impeachment. After posting bond, Cardozo moved his family to Washington, D.C. However, he did not try to avoid trial. He returned to Columbia in early October to prepare, but in a move that portended an atmosphere of hostility, Cardozo's bail was revoked, and he was jailed. Just two days prior to the trial, the attorney general announced that Cardozo would be tried on only one misdemeanor count. This count charged Cardozo of conspiring with former lieutenant governor Richard H. Gleaves, former Speaker of the House Samuel J. Lee, former house clerk A. O. Jones, and sitting senate clerk Josephus Woodruff to issue a fraudulent legislative pay certificate or check for $4,000, made payable to a fictitious person, C. L. Frankfort.

The trial was a major news event in the state. The local newspapers published almost verbatim transcripts each day. (By contrast, when Smalls and Carpenter were tried, they attracted little press coverage.) The team of prosecutors shows the importance of the Cardozo trial to white Democrats. Led by Attorney General James Conner, the prosecution had five lawyers, including one who also had been Cardozo's defense lawyer in his impeachment. Cardozo's lawyer, Samuel W. Melton, was quite able, but he had the disadvantage of working alone.

When jury selection began, the state struck the first two jurors called, both of whom were black. When Melton attempted to strike the next two jurors called, who happened to be white, the judge issued a bizarre ruling that the defense could not object to jurors substituted for those struck by the state. Then Melton challenged the entire jury panel as being improperly stacked by the Democrats. Again, he lost. Finally, a jury of six whites and six blacks was sworn. At the end of the first day, despite defense objections, the jury was sequestered. Hotel after hotel refused to house them. Finally, the judge persuaded a hotel to house the mixed jury in a billiard parlor under guard of the sheriff.

Once the trial began, the state called six witnesses. The first was black lawyer and former Speaker of the House Samuel J. Lee, who was also under indictment for issuing $29,000 in fraudulent pay certificates. Lee was no friend of Cardozo's. They had clashed repeatedly when Lee was speaker, and Lee had served as lead counsel in the house in the failed impeachment of Cardozo.[16]

In his testimony, Lee admitted signing the Frankfort certificate, but he offered conflicting testimony about how the conspiracy to issue the certificate had been designed. First, it was a plot proposed by Cardozo to steal a $4,000 surplus in legislative appropriations, then he testified it was a plot to steal surplus certificates of indebtedness. Appropriations and certificates of indebtedness were quite different. Legislative appropriations were paid by certificates that were, in essence, the checks issued by the legislature; certificates of indebtedness were issued by the treasurer to creditors of the state. The actual documents at issue in the trial were clearly issued by the legislature. On cross-examination, Lee admitted that Cardozo had warned him and other house officers that it was illegal to overissue pay certificates.

If anyone had a motive to get Cardozo convicted, it was the next witness. Josephus Woodruff was the sitting clerk of the state senate and co-owner of the Republican Printing Company. His company had been the official state printer, and the "Fraud Report" supposedly documented that his company had stolen hundreds of thousands of dollars from the state. Woodruff's reputation provoked a newspaper on the eve of the trial to proclaim, "Woodruff is still for sale, but who will buy him?"[17]

According to Woodruff, Lieutenant Governor Richard Gleaves told him that Cardozo directed him to prepare a $4,000 certificate, to be divided five ways, because of a $4,000 surplus in the appropriation for legislative expenses. Woodruff admitted he invented the name "C. L. Frankfort," and he contradicted many of Lee's details of the conspiracy. Woodruff said he prepared the fraudulent certificate and had it signed by all the officers of the house and senate, but he also said he gave Cardozo $2,400 in certificates of indebtedness from his printing company in exchange for the certificate.[18]

Over objection, Woodruff was allowed to testify from the books of his printing company and his diary. The company books recorded entries for $800 credits to Woodruff and Jones. This was offered as proof they had gotten their shares. Woodruff's diary was in a form of shorthand that he claimed to have invented. Over objection, he translated and read excerpts to the jury. These translations had been prepared for the legislative investigating committee, but the defense had been denied access to any of these records before trial. While the actual shorthand diary is now lost, some of the surviving portions of the translated version clearly document Woodruff's long-term animosity toward Cardozo.[19]

On cross-examination, Woodruff admitted that he had issued more than $100,000 in fraudulent legislative certificates during every legislative session since 1868. It was his job to inform Cardozo of legislative expenditures, and not once had he done so. Consequently, he conceded, there was no way for Cardozo to have known of a surplus.[20]

With a magnifying glass, Cardozo's lawyer showed that the $800 entries for

Woodruff and Jones in the printing company books had been altered by an erasure and a different handwriting. In another dramatic moment, Woodruff denied that he had tried to bribe Cardozo with a $5,000 certificate on behalf of the officers of the legislature. He denied "positively" that Cardozo had demanded that he write "cancelled" on the certificate and sign it. Then Melton dramatically produced the cancelled certificate, and Woodruff said, "I take it all back." Woodruff admitted that this rejected $5,000 bribe had been offered to Cardozo in December 1873.[21] The importance of this evidence, of course, was that it raised the question of why Cardozo would refuse a $5,000 bribe, then in the same month turn around and propose a conspiracy with four political foes to steal and divide $4,000. Woodruff also admitted that Cardozo had refused other bribes of the printing company, and that he had sued Cardozo for printing company appropriations and had never gotten his money.

Alleged coconspirator A. O. Jones, former clerk of the house, testified for the state but denied any knowledge of the Frankfort certificate conspiracy. A clerk in the Democratic treasurer's office was called to prove that there had been a specific $4,000 surplus that Cardozo could have planned to steal. But his testimony showed that there was an even larger surplus in the legislative accounts at the time of the alleged conspiracy.

The defense called only two witnesses. Cardozo denied any knowledge of the Frankfort certificate and supported his denial by using the records of the treasurer's office to contradict the two versions of surpluses presented by Lee and Woodruff. On cross, Cardozo denied that he had ever paid certificates he knew were fraudulent.

Former treasury department clerk T. J. Minton testified for the defense that the office practice was to pay certificates like the Frankfort certificate if they were endorsed by the appropriate officers of the legislature. In this case, the certificate had been signed by the appropriate officers, Lee, Gleaves, Jones, and Woodruff.

In rebuttal, the state recalled Josephus Woodruff, who claimed he had bribed Cardozo many times and that he "paid him . . . in currency." The attorney general asked, "You always paid him in currency?" He answered, "Yes, sir." When asked if he could prove it, Woodruff read his January 13, 1873, diary entry: "I paid Cardozo $3,000 in currency."[22] In fact, the translation of Woodruff's shorthand into English still exists. The January 13 entry records that Woodruff had a $3,000 check, not cash, for Cardozo.[23] Of course, this translation was denied to the defense.

The closing arguments began with C. R. Miles arguing for two hours. S. W. Melton argued for five hours, and Attorney General Conner closed in reply for two and a half hours. The only account of the closings describes them as being dominated by political accusations. In his closing, Melton brought his client to tears as he told the jury, "While I am paid to be here, I have a feeling of gratitude toward him when I remember how he stood by me in fighting the fraudulent claims against the State." Attorney General Conner concluded by attacking Melton for expressing his personal affection for Cardozo, saying, "I might as well tell you that you must find the defendant guilty because I believe him guilty."[24]

In his two-hour jury charge, Judge Townsend recounted the facts fully for the state, but he mentioned none of the discrepancies in the state's evidence. Instead, he attacked Cardozo's defense. He then added that a misdemeanor defendant could be tried in his absence, so there was no reason to think it remarkable that Cardozo had returned to face trial.

After twelve hours of deliberations, the jury returned a verdict of guilty. On hearing the verdict, Cardozo and Melton were visibly affected and "without a word . . . marched out of court."[25] Melton's greatest blunder came when he heard the verdict and did not request to have the jury polled. Later, Melton discovered that the jury had decided the case by a majority vote. But he had waived Cardozo's right to a unanimous jury verdict by not polling them before they were dismissed. Immediately after Cardozo's trial, Smalls and then Carpenter were tried and convicted.

In a scathing condemnation, Judge Townsend sentenced Cardozo to two years in jail and a $4,000 fine. Many historians assume that shortly after the trial, Cardozo was pardoned by Governor Wade Hampton. In fact, it was Carpenter, the white carpetbagger, who was pardoned by Hampton in February 1878. Cardozo and Smalls both refused pardons, hoping to win fair trials on appeal. Cardozo could not post an appeal bond. He spent six months in jail, a hostage to negotiations between President Hayes and Governor Hampton. In March 1878 Hampton asked Hayes to pardon three Klansmen. Within the next month, Cardozo was released on a reduced bond. In May 1878 Cardozo wrote President Hayes crediting Hampton for the reduced bond and he urged the president to pardon the Klansmen. By July 1878 Hayes had pardoned the Klansmen, but still Cardozo waited for his vindication. It did not come on appeal. Cardozo lost on November 29, 1878, in a two-to-one party-line decision by the state supreme court.

In the aftermath, Cardozo was threatened with arrest. He returned to South Carolina from Washington and was again jailed in March 1879. Soon a petition for pardon signed by many prominent citizens and ten of his twelve jurors was sent to the governor. After more clandestine negotiations, the white Democrats extracted more concessions from the federal government, and the U.S. attorney *nolle prossed* all of the pending election fraud cases against Democrats in South Carolina. Finally, on April 23, 1879, Governor W. D. Simpson pardoned Cardozo and Smalls.

After his release from jail, Cardozo was penniless. Property records and other documents also demonstrate that he had acquired no significant wealth during Reconstruction. Despite the Democrats' harangues about corrupt carpetbaggers and scalawags, not a single scalawag or prominent carpetbagger was brought to trial. The Democrats abandoned prosecutions of the other seventeen individuals indicted. But South Carolina whites convicted the honest treasurer, "proving" that all Republicans were corrupt. Just as importantly, they had the pawns needed to bargain with President Hayes. In the end, the Redeemers achieved Cardozo's conviction through jury manipulation, conflicts of interest, judicial bias, manufactured evidence, and perjured testimony, and just as they had in the election of 1876, they proved that their form of justice was only a means to a political and racist end.

Other Targets

Other black lawyers who had been active in Reconstruction politics suffered similar but less egregious fates. At least nine black lawyers were summoned to give testimony to the fraud committee. Paris Simkins described his arrest as follows: he was taken to Columbia under armed guard and told that if he did not implicate some Republican leaders, he would be sent to prison whether he had committed a crime or not. Simkins testified that under this duress he made up a story about accepting bribes to acquire his freedom.[26] Simkins returned to his home in Edgefield. He apparently maintained good relations with Governor John C. Sheppard of Edgefield, which gave him some protection from Red Shirt harassment.[27] Consequently, Simkins was able to remain active in his community and in the Republican Party on the state and national level.[28]

In some counties, even resignations of the Republican lawyer-legislator were not sufficient. A *New York Times* correspondent observed, "Every branch of the Government, all the courts are in [the whites'] hands, and still they are not satisfied."[29] Intimidation and violence were used to try to force black politicians to flee the state. After Williamsburg County's state senator, Stephen Swails, resigned in November 1877, the former senate president pro tempore discovered that the local Redeemer Democrats were determined to drive him from the county.[30] Unlike Simkins, Swails had no powerful white Democratic friends. Even his closest political allies were no longer to be trusted. Melvin J.

Hirsch was the Republican solicitor and a former legislator from Williamsburg County. More importantly, Hirsch and Swails had been law partners and copublishers of a newspaper. In May 1877 Hirsch abruptly dissolved their law practice, claiming that Swails had attacked him in the press.[31] Hirsch's abandonment of Swails was certainly influenced by the political winds. Being the local prosecutor, Hirsch should have tried to protect Swails and other black Republicans in the county, but he refused to help his former allies. As a white Republican house member, Hirsch had been lucky not to be named in the Fraud Report; however, some Democratic-leaning newspapers called for his head. Hirsch's public break with Swails worked to his benefit as Hirsch was never indicted. Hirsch switched parties in 1878.[32]

Although Swails resigned his senate seat, he was not willing to remain silent nor give up politics. In the spring of 1878 Swails let it be known that he was considering running again for his old seat. In response, white attorney Samuel W. Maurice urged Governor Wade Hampton to persuade the attorney general to indict Swails for bribery, because it was the only way to break down his political influence.[33] During the fall of 1878, Swails campaigned for Republican Party congressman Joseph H. Rainey and also ran his own campaign for his former state senate seat. On October 5, 1878, Swails addressed a Republican meeting in a rural Williamsburg community called White Oak.[34] His speech was interrupted by a Redeemer Democrat who demanded equal time. After he was escorted out, another white man demanded time to speak on behalf of Democrats. Soon it became apparent to the black Republicans at the meeting that they were outnumbered and were going to be continually harassed by the Democrats, many of whom were armed. This gang of about a hundred whites was dressed in the red shirts made infamous in the 1876 election campaign. The Republican leaders adjourned their meeting, and Swails and some of his supporters then mounted their horses and attempted to ride home to Kingstree. The contingent of Democrats rode in back, then a group of the armed men moved to the front so that Swails and his supporters were surrounded. The whites kept demanding that Swails separate from his party and join the white leaders of the Red Shirts. Swails refused and continued to ride toward the county seat, but as they neared the town of Kingstree, the leader of the militia, a Dr. Byrd, announced that Swails was under arrest. Swails and his party were then led to the county courthouse.

At the courthouse, one of Swails's supporters said he feared "that the Red Shirts intended to take them out and 'put them to sleep.'"[35] So he and some other friends wrested Swails from the militia and rushed him into the courthouse. In the melee two shots were fired, wounding one of the rescuers, Boston

Hanna. Shortly after the shooting, the county sheriff arrived and dispersed the mob.[36] On October 7 Swails wrote a letter of complaint to Governor Wade Hampton.[37] The next day, the Democratic executive committee of Williamsburg County issued a resolution demanding that Swails leave within ten days or forfeit his life.[38] John A. Kelly, a white lawyer, came to Swails's home and read the resolution. E. M. Pinckney, a black Republican, witnessed the reading and transcribed the demands as they were being read, verifying the details of the resolution. Fearing for his life, Swails left almost immediately, going first to Charleston and then to Washington, D.C.[39]

After the White Oak incident and the shooting of Boston Hanna, Swails wrote to Governor Hampton, describing the violence in the county and complaining how the local trial justice stood by and did nothing. The governor replied to Swails's letter that while he deplored violence, it was up to Swails to pursue his legal remedies by seeking indictments. After the incidents drew the attention of the national press, Hampton requested that Solicitor Hirsch investigate.[40]

Hirsch's report to the governor was a whitewash. Hirsch claimed there was no credence to the allegation that the Democrats had threatened Swails's life. The shooting was dismissed with the claim that the victim was satisfied with the system of justice in Williamsburg County. Moreover, Hirsch claimed that E. W. Pinckney, who had witnessed the reading of the death threat by the Democrats, was unavailable to talk with him. In January 1879 a U.S. Senate committee held hearings in Charleston concerning the elections of 1878 and in particular what had happened in Williamsburg County. The committee heard from both white and black citizens, both Republican and Democrat. Pinckney (who had according to Hirsch been unavailable to him) was the first witness to give testimony to the Senate committee. He verified the story about the White Oak incident, the shooting of Hanna, and numerous death threats. He and other witnesses testified about the subsequent efforts by the Redeemer Democrats to silence the black Republicans in Williamsburg County. Pinckney also testified that John Kelly warned him that if Swails returned to the county, he would be killed. On another occasion, Kelly assaulted Pinckney. Because Pinckney had given an affidavit to federal authorities about the threats against Swails's life, Pinckney was charged in state court with perjury and arrested.[41]

After fleeing Kingstree, Swails worked for the U.S. government in Washington, D.C., for nearly twenty years. However, his family remained in Kingstree, and he returned often for visits and also to participate in the state Republican Party activities.[42] He sought the party's nomination for congress in 1884 but was defeated by Robert Smalls.[43] In 1886 Swails was the presiding officer at the state Republican convention, which again nominated Smalls for Congress.[44] Swails's political activity did not go unnoticed by the state's Democrats. After the inauguration of Grover Cleveland as president in 1885, South Carolina's U.S. senators, Wade Hampton and Matthew Butler, engineered Swails's removal from his job at the U.S. Post Office because he was "offensive to the South Carolina Democrats."[45] In 1888 Swails participated in an abortive effort to revive the Republican Party on a statewide basis.[46] After the return of a Republican president, Benjamin Harrison, Swails regained his post office job in 1890.[47] He returned to the state in his final days, died in May 1900, and was buried in Charleston, South Carolina.[48]

The treatment of other black lawyers varied with the locale. Henry J. Maxwell of Marlboro County was arrested and charged with accepting a bribe from U.S. senator John Patterson. Maxwell resigned from the state senate in October 1877 and was never tried.[49]

In Sumter, young University of South Carolina Law School graduate Joseph Henry Stuart tried to practice law and teach school. In February 1879 he defended Sumter County probate judge Samuel Lee against charges of "misconduct in office." The facts of this case were so egregious that the young lawyer expected to see his client acquitted. The charge resulted from whites having threatened Lee's life and surrounding the courthouse to prevent the black judge from holding court. Using Lee's absence from the courthouse as a basis to charge him with malfeasance, the white Redeemers put the probate judge on trial. Despite Stuart's able defense, Lee was convicted of the charge and forced from office. Stuart saw no future in such a legal system and fled the state.

Samuel J. Lee, the former Speaker of the House, solicitor, and chief witness against Cardozo, was forced to leave Aiken County after local authorities tried and convicted him of corruption. However, he served only a few months of his two-year sentence and was released. There is no record of why he was released, no recorded pardon, and no indication that the state supreme court ever heard his appeal. Nonetheless, Lee simply moved to Charleston, where he became the most prominent and successful black lawyer in the state in the immediate post-Reconstruction era.[50]

After Reconstruction, Styles Linton Hutchins, the black Democrat, served very briefly as a trial justice in Richland County in the spring of 1877. Within weeks, however, the legislature abolished his post. He moved to Georgia but failed at his attempts to practice law there. He then relocated to Chattanooga, Tennessee, where he became a Republican and was elected to the state house of representatives.[51] Hutchins had an active law practice until he was run out of town in 1909 because of his advocacy against a mob that lynched one of his clients.[52] His final home was Illinois, where he worked as a barber and died at age 97 in 1950.[53]

Shortly after the close of Reconstruction, former lieutenant governor Richard Gleaves was appointed as a trial justice in Beaufort by Governor Wade Hampton.[54] However, he was forced from office after he was indicted for issuing fraudulent legislative pay certificates, and he fled the state. A few years later Gleaves returned by appointment as a customs inspector for the federal government. He was never tried. He died in Philadelphia in 1907.[55]

The purge of black officials continued well after Reconstruction. After the removal of Hutchins, Gleaves, and Lee, only two black judges, William Whipper and Zachariah Greene, would hold judicial office in the state in the remainder of the nineteenth century. Both men were probate judges, elected by popular vote. William Whipper had remained in Beaufort County, where he was active in law and politics. He became a bitter opponent of Robert Smalls. Despite his early defeats in his quest to be elected a judge by the legislature, Whipper persisted. He finally achieved his ambition by being elected probate judge in Beaufort County in 1882. He was reelected in 1884 and 1886, but he was defeated in 1888.[56] In his winning elections in 1882, 1884, and 1886, Whipper received 2,940, 2,012, and 1,364 votes, respectively. In 1888 the total recorded certified vote for both candidates was 1,465 with 852 for white candidate Thomas Talbird and 613 for Whipper. Whipper claimed he received 991 votes and his opponent 879. Whipper asserted that he was defeated by fraud. Without question, the decreasing number of votes demonstrates the impact of white Democratic efforts to suppress the black vote. Moreover, an action taken by the State Board of Canvassers supports Whipper's claim. The county canvassers had refused, without any justification, to count the votes from three Republican precincts. The State Board of Canvassers voted 3–2 to affirm the county canvassers' refusal to count the three precincts.[57]

Whipper refused to relinquish the office or the papers of the probate court. He was jailed on January 23, 1889, for contempt of court.[58] On January 29, 1889, the *New York Times* reported Whipper's incarceration. Unfortunately, the *Times* could not get its facts straight and reported that Whipper had been defeated by a "colored man." Moreover, the newspaper reported that Whipper hung onto the court's records because he feared prosecutions for malfeasance. The New York paper then quoted the *Charleston News and Courier* as calling Whipper a "Systematic robber."[59] The South Carolina Supreme Court denied his appeal on January 7, 1890.[60] After that final ruling and thirteen months in jail, Whipper relinquished the office and the probate court's records. Whipper had held on for principle. He believed that he had lost the election because of fraud. After Whipper lost his appeal and returned the court records, he was released, and no more talk of criminal prosecutions followed.

Zachariah Greene's short career illustrates the hope and false promise of justice in the legal system in South Carolina as the nineteenth century concluded. Born into slavery during the Civil War, Greene graduated from Allen University's law school in 1890. He practiced law in Georgetown and during one term of court succeeded in winning three criminal cases and obtaining a dismissal of murder charges against his client.[61] In the murder case, Greene served as local counsel for the more experienced lawyer, Samuel J. Lee.[62] The young lawyer became probate judge for Georgetown County in 1894. Greene was elected on what came to be known as a fusion ticket. Under this arrangement, blacks and whites split local offices in overwhelmingly black counties. But by the mid-1890s Georgetown County's whites were beginning to rebel against office sharing with blacks. In the summer of 1895, Greene played a prominent role in a meeting of black leaders beseeching the federal government to intervene and protect the rights of black voters in South Carolina.[63] Soon, Greene became a target of whites who wanted to rid the county of black officeholders. As had been done by the Redeemers after Reconstruction, Greene was accused by a circuit judge of "official misconduct."[64] His troubles stemmed from his failure to file reports with the circuit judge and to obtain the circuit judge's approval for investing money from an estate. Greene admitted that he had failed to file reports and kept poor records but denied he had committed a crime.[65] In 1897 Greene was indicted, convicted, and sentenced to six months in jail and fined $500 for each of the two offenses of misconduct.[66] Greene appealed to the state supreme court, which reversed his conviction and ordered that the indictment be quashed.[67] Greene left the state and moved to Florida, where he practiced law and was active in politics.[68]

Exodus

Other prominent lawyers also left the state. Robert Brown Elliott, who was facing a loss of political power and serious financial problems, sought a federal job instead of practicing law. He obtained a Treasury Department position, and according to his biographer, he was transferred to Louisiana because the Republican administration in Washington wanted the once-powerful leader out of South Carolina. Elliott was not happy with the transfer, but he moved to New Orleans in June 1881. In April 1882 he was terminated from the Treasury Department. He then returned to law practice, which his biographer described as "precarious."[69] While most of his practice was in the police courts, in late 1883 he was retained by white clients in three murder cases.[70] But he died of malaria the next year at age forty-two. His death was noted by contrasting obituaries. A South Carolina newspaper described him as a crook, while a New York paper praised his "brilliant achievements."[71]

After Richard T. Greener lost his job at the University of South Carolina, he moved to Washington, D.C., then to New York City, and eventually he even served in the foreign service in Vladivostok, Russia.[72] University of South Carolina Law School graduates T. J. Minton, Thomas McCants, and Henry Barton Johnson all moved north. Robert DeLarge and Walter R. Jones both died before the end of Reconstruction; Robert Brown Elliott, Laurence Cain, Joseph Boston, and Landon Langley all died by the early 1880s.[73]

~

In fewer than twenty years, the state's black lawyers experienced an incredible downfall. In 1877 black lawyers held leadership roles in the legislative, judicial, and executive branches of state government of South Carolina. In the election of 1876, three black congressmen were sent to Washington to represent the state, but in 1878 not a single black returned to Congress from the state. In 1880 Robert Smalls of Beaufort was again elected to Congress, but he was defeated by a white Democrat in 1886. Thomas Miller was the only black lawyer in the state's congressional delegation in the post-Reconstruction era, serving a partial term from 1890 to 1891. By 1897 not a single black lawyer held a position of power in state or county government anywhere in the state. In fact, only one black person held public office in the state. John W. Bolts of Georgetown County held onto his state legislative seat until 1902. No black would be elected to public office again until 1968.

CHAPTER 6

New Lawyers

After Reconstruction, the black community's struggle for equality and justice required new tactics and increased resistance. Critical to the struggle was the education of new lawyers for the continuation of the black bar. In his book *The New South*, D. A. Straker titled one of his chapters "The Necessity for a Broader and Higher Education in the South." While not specifically addressing the need for legal education, Straker made an impassioned case for the benefits of higher education. At one point, he stated that the South must answer "to the spirit of liberty and freedom and [march] to the tune of progress, law and equality."[1] As a lawyer and legal educator, Straker played one of the most important roles in the education of the black bar. He was the first dean of Allen University's law school in Columbia.

Reading Law

While law schools were becoming more common across the country by the 1880s, the traditional avenue to admission to the bar in South Carolina was still through reading law in an attorney's office.[2] The major advantage of the apprenticeship system for the student was the involvement in the dynamic day-to-day life of the lawyer.[3] It also offered a means of entry to the profession that assured acceptance and acclimation by fellow members. However, for the black law student, the apprenticeship system created a major roadblock. With whom were these young students going to read law? Since only a small number of black lawyers still practiced in the state, the legal aspirant had to find a lawyer with both the interest and sufficient law practice to offer an apprenticeship. Even more daunting was the prospect of finding a white lawyer willing to take on a black apprentice in his office. Based on the number of bar admissions of blacks in the early years of Jim Crow, it appears likely that a few white lawyers were still allowing some black aspirants to study in their offices. One black lawyer in Columbia said he read law with some of the most prominent men of the state's bar, but he did not reveal who they were.[4] But the practicing black bar still offered the best opportunity to study in a lawyer-mentor's office. The leading mentor for the black bar was William J. Whipper of Beaufort.

William Whipper, a well-known leading political figure and trial lawyer, would mentor a number of young lawyers. After Reconstruction, Whipper limited his law practice primarily to Beaufort. In February 1877 three new black lawyers were admitted in Beaufort by the circuit court. Whipper, solicitor Samuel J. Lee, and white Republican Alfred Williams had been appointed to examine six candidates for admission, and all were admitted. Three of them were African American: L. S. Langley, A. H. Ezekiel, and D. W. Powell.[5] Dempsher Powell was Whipper's adopted son and had "studied law" in his office.[6] Both Ezekiel and Langley were political allies of Whipper, and because Whipper was the senior black Beaufort lawyer, it is likely that he mentored them also. We know that Ezekiel practiced because he represented Whipper in one case.[7] London S. Langley was convicted of election fraud in 1870 and pardoned,[8] and there is no record of his ever practicing law.

After reading law with Whipper, state senator Thomas Reynolds was admitted by the supreme court in 1885.[9] William Still was admitted in 1887. He was from a prominent Pennsylvania abolitionist family, as was Whipper, and he probably came to Beaufort specifically to study with Whipper. Still never practiced in the state, returning instead to Philadelphia.[10] Julius I. Washington was also admitted in 1887. His obituary in 1938 noted that he had read law with Whipper.[11] The last lawyer admitted to the bar from Beaufort in the nineteenth century was Isaiah R. Reed, a political ally of Whipper's and, again, someone who probably also read law with Whipper.[12]

Other mentors for black lawyers were Samuel J. Lee, Jonathan Jasper Wright, and possibly John M. Freeman. William J. Bowen and Thaddeus St. Mark Sasportas read law with Lee.[13] Admitted in 1881, Bowen practiced with Lee for at least a decade, and on occasion he served as sole counsel in cases. Sasportas was admitted in 1895. He practiced across the Lowcountry, and by the time of his death in 1937, he was the only black lawyer still practicing in Charleston.[14] Robert C. Browne, admitted in 1886, read law with either Lee or John M. Freeman.[15] Browne had cases on both the Berkeley and Charleston dockets. He lived in Charleston until his death in 1915.[16]

New Law Schools

After Reconstruction, the road to bar admission for blacks was made even more difficult. In 1878 the state legislature eliminated admission by a circuit court judge.[17] Even more significantly, in that same year the state closed the University of South Carolina and its law school. When the law school reopened in 1880, black students were no longer accepted.[18] The black legal community responded by starting law schools at the two universities in South Carolina that were open to black students, Claflin University and Allen University. These two law schools had 23 graduates who were admitted to practice in South Carolina. While 49 men had been admitted to the bar during Reconstruction, the black bar had decreased to 22 in 1880. Because of these law schools, the black bar grew to 23 in 1890, and to 29 in 1900.[19]

The first black law school was affiliated with Claflin University in Orangeburg and was structured according to the mentor model. After he was forced off the South Carolina Supreme Court, Jonathan J. Wright opened a law office at 84 Queen Street, Charleston, which became the Claflin College Law Department.[20] Claflin was a natural institution to create the state's first black law school. It was a well-established church-supported institution that had enjoyed significant state support during Reconstruction.[21] However, after Reconstruction the relationship with the state and the white Democrats proved more burdensome, and the state would eventually sever its ties with Claflin.[22] Moreover, the college was in Orangeburg, more than fifty miles from Charleston, where Wright had chosen to live and practice law.

The former supreme court justice had seven students: George Marshall, Robert L. Smith, Thomas A. McLean, John Wragg, William F. Holmes, Joe McKnight, and Joseph C. Berry.[23] Johnson C. Whittaker was a possible eighth.[24] Apparently only Holmes was awarded a law degree by Claflin.[25] While these students had the first African American appellate court judge in America as their teacher, the quality of their instructor did not guarantee that they would have significant legal careers. Only Marshall, Holmes, Smith, and Whittaker were admitted to the South Carolina bar, and none had more than a limited legal career. With Wright's death in 1885, the Claflin College Law Department ceased to exist.

Allen University Law School had students and graduates from 1882 until 1898, and the university continued to list the law school on paper until 1912. Allen University was located in Columbia, the state capital. The law school was one of the first operational departments of the university. Allen was named for the African Methodist Episcopal Church's first bishop, Richard Allen. It opened on April 8, 1881, under the leadership of South Carolina AME bishop W. F. Dickerson, school president James C. Waters, and law school dean D. A. Straker.[26] As Straker proudly noted, it was a black school for black students.[27]

When the law school opened, it had eight students and three instructors.[28] It is ironic that the school held its first classes in a wooden mansion that had belonged to a "slaveholding aristocrat and democrat" but was now "consecrated to the mental training of negroes."[29] The university's first graduates were its law students.[30] Desire of the students and need of the community no doubt contributed to this boom in legal education.

Allen's law dean was a strong believer in the U.S. Constitution's equal protection clause. Even after leaving the South, D. A. Straker wrote, "Yes there *is* a tomorrow for the Negro in the South. . . . The day is near when . . . all race feeling will disappear."[31] Straker and his young students entered a world of dualities. They had a desire to see justice done, but they had a need to support themselves. They had a community that needed them, but one that could seldom pay them. But more problematic, they entered a legal system that promised colorblind justice but never practiced what it preached.

Despite the overwhelming racism of the era, the school had a remarkable record. It had more than thirty graduates, twenty of whom became licensed lawyers in South Carolina.[32] In the same era among black-led law schools in the South, only Shaw University in Raleigh, North Carolina, had more graduates.[33] Many of Allen's graduates practiced law in South Carolina, and two had legal careers in Georgia. The school's first dean was Straker, a graduate of Howard University Law School and a native of Barbados. Straker was well educated and articulate. Before migrating to the state, he was already a published author; he had served as secretary to General O. O. Howard, founder of Howard University; and he had been befriended by Senator Charles Sumner. After he moved to South Carolina in 1874, he formed a close relationship with Congressman Robert B. Elliott, which resulted in the formation of a short-lived law firm in 1876.

Straker was joined on the faculty by Joseph White Morris, a graduate of the University of South Carolina School of Law. Morris, who served as dean of Allen's law school for a time after the Straker era, practiced very little law. He is reported to have handled one "prominent" case and won it before entering higher education.[34] Morris also later became president of Allen.

The secretary of the interior's education report in 1892–93 stated that the school had a two-year curriculum. Like Howard University, Allen offered classes in the afternoons and evenings so students could work and still attend law school. Commonly the students worked as teachers, and some traveled long distances to attend school. Others left their families at home and boarded in Columbia during the term. The law school charged its law students forty dollars in tuition.[35] The first year's courses were quite traditional, including Blackstone, Kent, contracts, bills, and constitutional law. However, Allen also offered the more practice-oriented course of evidence in the first year. In the second year, the students took criminal law, state statutory law, equity, and procedure. The school reported that moot courts were held, but its reports give no indication of whether the moots were incorporated into the regular courses or a separate additional course.[36]

With Straker, an experienced practitioner, as dean, the school attracted a number of students. In 1883–84, Allen had five law students and graduated four in its first law class that spring. The four graduates were John B. Edwards, Talley R. Holmes, Peter F. Oliver, and Robert A. Stewart.[37] Dean Straker presented the four young men to the South Carolina Supreme Court for examination. "Having passed a creditable examination, as told by the court in open session, [they] were admitted to practice."[38] Edwards practiced law in Colleton County.[39] Stewart taught at the law school for a time and was offered the deanship but chose to practice law instead.[40] After Straker stepped down, Peter Flynn Oliver served two years as dean of the law school and then moved to Kansas in 1888.[41]

The class of 1886 had three graduates: E. J. Sawyer, E. C. C. Washington, and B. E. Watson. Sawyer had studied law at the University of South Carolina during Reconstruction and had been admitted to the bar in 1885.[42] He became a prosperous and prominent businessman (see chapter 7). In 1891 E. C. C. Washington and Benjamin E. Watson were living in Columbia.[43] Allen's 1910 catalog listed Washington as deceased. Benjamin E. Watson's name is only found in the Allen University bulletins, which listed him as living in Washington, D.C., in 1910.[44]

After the departure of Straker, the school continued to operate. The class of 1887 had three graduates. Thomas A. Saxon and Andrew E. Hampton were admitted to the state bar. A. J. Jamison was not admitted but became a lawyer in Arkansas.[45] Hampton never practiced law. For many years he attempted to organize a state fair but met with much opposition, criticism, and failure.[46] The third member of the class, Thomas Saxon, was made dean of Allen's law school in 1888. Both Peter Oliver and Saxon were young, inexperienced lawyers when named dean. Government reports reflect that after Oliver became dean, the school increased its faculty to two.[47] The next year, when Thomas A. Saxon was named dean, the school again reported it had two instructors.[48] The inexperienced deans may have affected enrollment, as there were no graduates in 1888 or 1889.

But between 1890 and 1893, the school flourished. It had twelve law graduates, more than had graduated during Straker's tenure. In the 1889–90 academic year, Allen had ten law students and four graduates, and twenty students and four graduates for the 1890–91 academic year. The 1890 graduates were Casper G. Garrett of Laurens, Butler W. Nance of Newberry, Zachariah D. Greene of Georgetown, and Walton W. Williams of Columbia. All four were admitted to the bar. Greene became probate judge in Georgetown (see chapter 5). He moved to Florida, taught school, and was admitted to the bar there in 1899.[49] Garrett, admitted to the bar in 1890, taught for twenty years as a professor at Allen University.[50] After Butler Nance's graduation, he taught in Fairfield County and then moved to Columbia to work as a mail clerk at the U.S. Post Office.[51] In 1915 Nance helped organize the state's first NAACP chapter (see chapter 10).[52] Walton W. Williams was admitted in 1890, but there is no record of his practicing law.[53]

In 1890 Joseph White Morris was named president of the university, and Saxon remained as the law school's one professor.[54] Under Morris, the university conducted special law school graduations that featured substantive addresses by the law graduates. These graduations were noteworthy enough to gain newspaper coverage. One article included a full report with the names and topics of each speaker.[55]

From the class of 1891, only T. T. Hilton was admitted to the state's bar. Nothing more is known about him, and very little is known about his fellow graduates. James L. Bumgardner became a teacher at Allen Normal School and later was a mathematics professor at Allen.[56] N. W. Edwards was listed as deceased in 1910, and Charles Brown was a teacher in Horatio, South Carolina.[57]

According to the *State* newspaper, the law school had nine students with two graduates in 1892, James W. Goudlock and Dock J. Jordan. In an article about their graduation, Saxon's teaching was praised as "thorough and painstaking."[58] In addition, the school's catalog for 1908–10 lists Eugene R. Hayne and S. Simmons as graduates in 1892.[59] Goudlock was never admitted to the bar. Dock Jordan was admitted in 1892 and became president of Kittrell College in North Carolina. Simmons, a minister in Charleston, was never admitted. Eugene R. Hayne was not admitted until 1897. He practiced in Charleston for a time, and he and Alonzo Twine had one case in Berkeley County in 1901 and 1902.[60]

In December 1892 Saxon and another university professor resigned because they had not been paid. However, the school's board of trustees, instead of accepting the resignations, dismissed the two professors in a fit of pique, asserting that their resignations damaged the school's reputation. In dismissing the professors, the board eliminated two of its four professorships, citing decreased university enrollment as its justification.[61] The U.S. secretary of the interior in his education report for 1892–93 records that Allen's entire law faculty was also the president of the university.[62] That person was the legally trained Joseph White Morris.[63] For that report, the school informed the Department of the Interior that over the past six years, five classes had graduated with "a majority of the members meeting with a great degree of success in life."[64] Morris stepped down as president in 1894 but continued on the faculty.[65] Law school classes continued for four more years. The school's 1899 catalog listed a full curriculum for each of the four terms, noting the courses, treatises, and number of lectures required for each class.[66] In addition, potential applicants were directed to apply to the dean.[67]

While the school's catalogs do not list him as a graduate, Julius Linoble Mitchell said he graduated from Allen's law school in 1894.[68] In 1896 E. Woodberry Brinkins and E. B. Burroughs graduated from the law school.[69] Brinkins was admitted to the South Carolina bar in 1897 and was subsequently admitted to the Georgia bar and practiced in Waycross. Later he moved to Thompkins, Georgia, where he farmed and practiced law.[70] Burroughs took the written South Carolina bar examination in December 1895, but he was one of three test takers not admitted the next day by the supreme court. He was examined again on May 21, 1896, and he and one of the two white applicants who had apparently failed the December exam were then admitted to the bar the next day.[71] Abraham L. Tucker was the only member of the law class of 1897. He was from Savannah, Georgia, and had applied for admission by a circuit court judge there as early as 1891 but was repeatedly denied even the opportunity to be examined.[72] He returned to Savannah after graduating from the law school; he finally gained admission and practiced law there until about 1920. He then moved to Philadelphia, where he practiced until at least 1930.[73] Thomas Hilton, who had graduated in 1891, was not admitted to the state bar until December 17, 1897. According to the Allen catalog, Hilton had died by 1910. There is no evidence he ever practiced law.

Green Jackson, L. M. Rice, and Edmund R. Anderson of the 1898 class were the law school's last graduates. Little is known about Rice and Anderson. Rice had died by 1910, and Anderson was a minister in Greenwood, South Carolina.[74] Green Jackson was the last Allen Law School graduate to be admitted to the South Carolina bar.[75]

The 1906 Report of the ABA Annual Meeting is the last one in which the Allen University Law School is listed. In 1906 Henry Wade Rogers, dean of the Yale University Law School, gave an "Address to the Association of American Law Schools," in which he had this to say about the Allen University Law School:

> South Carolina has two schools, both being established at Columbia, and each having a two years' course. The law school of South Carolina College exists for the white race and has 30 students. The law school of Allen University was established for the colored race. For the last few years it has had no students, but the President reports that there is a faculty which is ready to teach and that "they will probably have a student or two next term." This law school had graduated about forty men, but there seems to be no great demand for colored lawyers in South Carolina. The catalogue, however, states that the majority of those graduated "are meeting with a great degree of success in life." No admission requirements are prescribed, the catalogue simply announcing that "a knowledge of the Latin language is a great help in the study of law, and a course in liberal studies is recommended."[76]

Whites' reactions to black law schools and their graduates were predictable. The education reports of the secretary of the interior for 1892–93 provide some insight into the mind-set of even the most tolerant of American whites. While Secretary of the Interior John W. Noble was a Republican and Civil War army veteran, his views were condescending and racist.[77] One report refers to black people as descendants of "African savages" and declares that blacks were morally deficient as well as lacking in self-restraint. In what must have been a veiled reference to black lawyers, the report included the following statement:

> To a people thus lightly ballasted with independent social experience and racial prestige it is apt to seem that everything is a matter of language, and that the ability to talk effectively is an open sesame to every avenue of wealth, power, and consideration enjoyed by the dominant race, and that success in those avenues is obtained by the verbiage of sophistry rather than by patient foresight, and skillful energy. But by those who wish to secure what sanguinary battles and constitutional amendments can not secure, that is to say, the abolition of the slavery of ignorance, far different ideas are held.[78]

On the state level, there are no official reports about either Claflin or Allen.[79] However, attitudes toward the schools were evolving. In 1886 the legislature enacted a statute that allowed graduates of the "State Law School" to be admitted without taking the bar examination.[80] This statute could easily have been read to limit the "diploma privilege" to the graduates of the all-white University of South Carolina Law School, but according to reports filed with the secretary of the interior by the dean, Allen's law graduates were also granted the diploma privilege by the state supreme court.[81] However, in June 1888 the supreme court's records indicate that the diploma privilege had become restricted to graduates of the white law school. After 1890, these rolls clearly record that all Allen graduates were required to take the written bar examination, and by this same time, the school's report to the secretary of the interior no longer mentioned the diploma privilege.[82] The only "privilege" left was use of the library of the supreme court by Allen's law students.[83] The diploma privilege for graduates of the all-white University of South Carolina would endure until 1950, when the state was forced to open a separate state law school for black students. The diploma privilege had been condemned as early as 1901 by the American Bar Association, but the Deep South's racist practices would prevail over the attempt by the national bar leadership to elevate standards.[84]

After Saxon's departure, Allen University was not regularly reporting its law school statistics to the U.S. Department of Education or the American Bar Association. Joseph Morris did sporadically report some general information.[85] The university and law school had moments of triumph and challenge in this period. In 1891 the university's faculty suspended a number of students for insulting behavior.[86] In 1893 they built Arnett Hall at a cost of $25,000, but in 1895 its other building burned in a suspicious fire.[87] How much these stressors affected the operations of the law school is unknown. But, according to a former Allen faculty member, the Allen board of trustees voted to close the law school in 1899.[88] The school's catalog of 1908–10 reported the last graduates of the law school as the class of 1898. However, Allen continued to report that it had a law school. In the 1906 annual address of the president of the Association of American Law Schools, Allen University Law School was reported to have had no students for a few years, but the school had a faculty ready to teach any who enrolled. In fact, the president of Allen was quoted as saying that "they will probably have a student or two next term."[89] This same information was republished in June 1907.[90]

In sum, Allen had thirty law graduates between 1884 and 1898.[91] Twenty-one became members of the South Carolina bar, and at least five were admitted in other states, including two in Georgia.[92] Of those not admitted, four became teachers and preachers.[93] Some even became Allen faculty.[94] Various government reports, school catalogs, and one personal account provide some insight into black law schools such as Allen and suggest why the school ceased to produce lawyers. In the 1895 report on "Universities and Colleges for the Colored Race," the U.S. secretary of the interior reported to Congress that poverty and poor public schools in the South limited the number of black students who could attend college.[95] One Allen graduate, Edmund R. Anderson, related his difficulties as a student: he walked eleven miles each way to attend school and arrived with just fifteen dollars and his books.[96] By 1898, Anderson had earned both his bachelor's and law degrees from Allen. The 1895 report, which is based on 1891–92 information, asserts that the number of black lawyers was growing in the South. In fact, it singles out Allen University as one of the success stories in the South among the schools where the faculty was all black.[97] However, the fiscal state of the university may demonstrate Allen's lack of stability. The institution had buildings and grounds valued at only $20,000. Of the twenty-five black institutions reporting, Allen's physical plant had the lowest value. Clark University in Atlanta had property valued at $250,000. However, Allen was praised for keeping its tuition low, at $5.50 per month. Claflin University in Orangeburg cost $8.50 a month, and both schools required the students to work.[98]

In 1894 George Hoar wrote to the *Albany Law Journal* asserting that Howard was the only law school in the South open to black students.[99] Hoar was wrong in asserting Howard's uniqueness. As the secretary of the interior reported to Congress in 1895, there were in fact five law schools at colleges for black students.[100] In addition to Allen, the other southern black law schools included Walden, which operated from 1879 until 1917 in Nashville, Tennessee; Straight University in New Orleans, which was open from 1879 to 1886; and Shaw University School of Law in Raleigh, North Carolina, which produced fifty-four graduates between 1888 and 1914.[101] Wilberforce University in Ohio had a law school at the time of the interior secretary's report, but it had no students and was therefore not counted in the total.[102]

Of these out-of-state law schools, only Howard's and Shaw's graduates had any impact on South Carolina. Shaw University Law School attracted at least two South Carolinians. George Kilgore of Greenville graduated from the North Carolina law school in 1894. He was never admitted to the South Carolina bar but was practicing law in Virginia in 1900.[103] Charleston native John A. Gaillard attended Shaw; he graduated in 1897, returned to South Carolina, and was admitted to the bar in the same year. Raleigh native Mark A. Williams also graduated from Shaw that year and moved to South Carolina to be admitted in 1897.[104] Howard University Law School in Washington, D.C., produced more black lawyers than any other school during the Jim Crow era.[105] But few students from South Carolina attended Howard's law school. John F. Brown of Colleton and W. T. Andrews of Sumter graduated from Howard in 1884 and 1892, respectively. Both returned to the state. Talley R. Holmes, an Allen law graduate, was awarded an LLM by Howard in 1887. John F. Brown returned to South Carolina and was admitted by the supreme court in 1884.[106] The 1910 census says he was engaged in the general practice of law.[107]

~

As the nineteenth century came to a close, South Carolina still had twenty-nine black lawyers. Whipper, Lee, Wright, Straker, and the Claflin and Allen Law Schools had kept alive the vision of equal rights for the black community.

During the short period of time the two law schools operated, forty-two black lawyers were admitted to the bar in the state. By comparison, only twenty-four black lawyers were admitted from 1898 until 1950.

These black law schools in South Carolina represented a valiant effort to stanch the flood of Jim Crow injustice. They were part of the larger struggle that was compelled by the times, when the black community had to look inward and develop its own institutions. While these schools may have only served as a temporary beacon of hope for the black community, ultimately their legacy would bear the fruit of freedom. The role that the black legal profession played in the last twenty-five years of the nineteenth century was clearly one of hope, despite the failed promises of the U.S. Constitution.

Jonathan Jasper Wright.
Courtesy of the South Caroliniana Library, University of South Carolina, Columbia, S.C.

William J. Whipper.
Courtesy of the South Caroliniana Library, University of South Carolina, Columbia, S.C.

Francis L. Cardozo.
Courtesy of the South Caroliniana Library, University of South Carolina, Columbia, S.C.

Samuel J. Lee.
Courtesy of the South Caroliniana Library, University of South Carolina, Columbia, S.C.

Thomas E. Miller.
Courtesy of the South Caroliniana Library, University of South Carolina, Columbia, S.C.

Daniel J. Straker.
Courtesy of the Coleman Karesh Library, University of South Carolina School of Law.

Jacob Moorer.
Courtesy of the South Caroliniana Library, University of South Carolina, Columbia, S.C.

Nathaniel J. Frederick.
Courtesy of the ColumbiaSC63 Public History Collaborative.

In 1954, attorneys who practiced law in South Carolina were invited to attend the annual meeting of the NAACP held in Spartanburg, South Carolina, to discuss strategies and goals. Thurgood Marshall was the keynote speaker. This picture was taken of the attendees. Seated from left to right: William W. Bennett (Florence), Albert A. Kennedy (Columbia), Squire Morgan (Orangeburg), John Bolt Culbertson (Greenville), Thurgood Marshall (chief counsel of the NAACP), Robert Carter (deputy counsel of the NAACP), Donald J. Sampson (Greenville), John H. Wrighten (Charleston). Standing from left to right: William B. James (Sumter), Esau A. Parker (Sumter), John McCall (Cheraw), Lincoln C. Jenkins (Columbia), Edgar E. Thompson (Spartanburg), Harold Boulware (Columbia), Ernest J. Finney (Sumter), Frank Cain (Bennettsville), Cleveland Stevens (Loris), possibly Julius T. Williams (Savannah, Ga.), James M. Hinton Jr. (Augusta, Ga.), Vernoid R. Bunch (Georgetown), Willie T. Smith Jr. (Greenville), W. Newton Pough (Orangeburg), Matthew J. Perry Jr. (Spartanburg).

Courtesy of James P. Rogers.

Harold Boulware with Linda Brown, plaintiff in *Brown v. Board of Education*.
Courtesy of Cecil J. Williams.

Matthew J. Perry confers with Zack Townsend and Earl Coblyn.
Courtesy of Cecil J. Williams.

Ernest J. Finney.

Courtesy of the South Caroliniana Library, University of South Carolina, Columbia, S.C.

I. S. Leevy Johnson.

Courtesy of Johnson.

CHAPTER 7

Law Practice and Politics in the Gilded Age

The post-Reconstruction era was called the Gilded Age by Mark Twain to describe a time when there was a "thin but glittering layer of prosperity" that gilded the poverty and corruption permeating the nation.[1] In South Carolina the last quarter of the nineteenth century did not even offer a patina of prosperity for the black community. Instead, the white power structure engaged in an unrelenting assault on the civil, political, and economic rights of the black community.

Despite the dire conditions of the times, many black lawyers continued to practice, and new lawyers were attracted to the profession. In all areas, they faced challenges. Significantly, the continuing economic disadvantage of the black community meant that many were trapped by peonage, tenant farming, and forced labor in prison. Often their plight closely resembled slavery. But the chief challenge faced by the community was the determination of the white Democrats to deprive blacks of the right to vote. Without the vote, black citizens faced an increasingly hostile world. They could no longer expect to hold public office or benefit from any favorable policies from elected officials. Because of the whitewashing of the voter rolls, blacks faced antagonistic all-white juries in civil and criminal cases with devastating results. Consequently, the tasks for a black lawyer were daunting.

Law Practice

CHARLESTON BAR

With the loss of Macon Allen, George Lee, and Lewis Taylor, the Charleston bar was much reduced after Reconstruction. But the arrival of two prominent lawyers meant there would be black lawyers continuing to practice in the city. The most significant of these was Samuel J. Lee, the former Speaker of the House for the state of South Carolina. While law practice in Charleston did not bring Lee wealth, the volume of his practice was a sign of success in the courts.[2] In 1878, after the conclusion of Lee's testimony in the Cardozo trial and his own legal difficulties, he moved to Charleston and quickly began trying cases.[3] In June of that year, Lee won an acquittal for three black clients accused of murdering a white man in Charleston.[4] Between 1882 and 1892, Lee tried thirteen more murder trials in Charleston. Only two of his clients were found guilty of murder; four others were convicted of lesser crimes.[5] Six clients were found not guilty, and one had a mistrial and was not retried.[6] In Charleston County, Lee handled 196 separate criminal cases between 1882 and 1893.[7] In adjoining Berkeley County, Lee handled four murder cases; three of those clients were convicted of the reduced charge of manslaughter. Such a reduction meant at a minimum that the client was spared the death penalty. In just two years, Lee had forty-two cases on the criminal dockets in Berkeley County.[8] Lee also represented criminal defendants in federal court.[9]

In his study of the black bar, historian John R. Oldfield concluded that Lee had only a modest civil practice because he had just fifteen civil cases between 1878 and 1881 in Charleston County. However, in neighboring Berkeley County, Lee had more than 140 civil cases on the docket between 1883 and 1895.[10] Among Lee's civil cases in both Charleston and Berkeley Counties were at least thirty appeals from the trial justice courts, lower courts that handled cases with small monetary claims.[11] These appeals indicate that Lee had a substantial civil practice in these small claims courts as well as in the circuit court.

Lee was also effective in his appellate work. He argued 33 appeals in the South Carolina Supreme Court and won 10 out of 19 criminal appeals.[12] Most of these cases involved issues specific to his client, but two had broader impacts. One established the right of a criminal defendant to appeal from municipal courts, and another assured the right to a jury trial in city court criminal cases.[13] His record was not as stellar in his fourteen civil appeals.[14] He won only three of those. Overall, Lee had a winning percentage of nearly 40 percent before an all-white, all-Democrat appellate court.

Lee did not seek public office after Reconstruction and mostly kept a low profile politically. On one occasion, he joined a committee to assist some black men accused of lynching in Pickens County, South Carolina.[15] In 1888 he represented William Whipper in his ill-fated fight to retain his position as probate judge in Beaufort County. Lee was more successful in 1892 when he and Thomas Miller represented congressional candidate George Washington Murray in an appeal to the State Board of Canvassers. Murray was a black Republican, and E. W. Moise was his white Democratic opponent. In initial returns Murray lost to Moise by a count of 4,937 to 2,695. At the state board, Lee "spoke for one hour and forty-five minutes, and delivered his speech in a very impressive and dramatic manner."[16] The chief argument presented on Murray's behalf was that ballots had been disregarded by local officials on the spurious grounds that the ballots were on the wrong size paper. The supposedly defective ballots were no more than an eighth of an inch too wide. After the presentation by Lee and Miller, the all-white board awarded an additional 2,300 votes to Murray's total, giving him a victory by forty votes.[17]

Despite his skill, Lee did not become a wealthy man. A Charleston newspaper obituary said, "No doubt he would have been well-to-do if his clients had all been able to pay him."[18] However, he left a major legacy. At a time when the rights of black South Carolinians were under unrelenting assault, Lee proved that a black lawyer could succeed in the trial justice courts, before juries in murder cases, and in the state supreme court.

In addition to opening the Claflin College Law Department, Jonathan Jasper Wright had a small practice in Charleston. Two of his students, William F. Holmes and Robert L. Smith, represented clients with Wright.[19] In one case, Wright successfully defended two of his former students in a criminal libel case.[20] Wright handled a few criminal cases with some success, but his health was not good and he died in 1885.[21]

Some Charleston lawyers such as F. D. J. Lawrence, John M. Freeman, and Samuel Dickerson continued to practice after 1876. Lawrence tried a murder case in Charleston in 1877 and lost.[22] A Democrat, Lawrence was appointed as a trial justice in 1884 in Charleston and died in 1888.[23] John M. Freeman, admitted in 1875, had a limited practice. He never had more than four cases on the docket in Charleston in the 1880s. In 1888 he was recruited to assist the five black men accused of lynching a white man in Pickens County.[24] Freeman won his only case in the state supreme court.[25] He and R. C. Browne practiced law together from 1889 until 1895 but had only two civil cases in Berkeley County.[26] Freeman also represented Congressman Robert Smalls in an election dispute in 1886.[27] As an active Republican, Freeman benefited from federal government patronage jobs.[28] He died in 1892.[29]

Samuel Dickerson, admitted in 1870, was a former slave, a drummer in the Confederate army, and a trial justice during Reconstruction.[30] He had only one civil case in Charleston between 1878 and 1881, but seventeen criminal cases between 1882 and 1884. He served as a trial justice in the 1870s and after

Reconstruction probably had an extensive practice in those courts.[31] Although he died in 1885, his colorful oratory was recounted in the press even after 1900.[32]

Admitted in 1879, Joshua Williams Polite was the first black lawyer from Charleston admitted after Reconstruction. He practiced in Charleston and Berkeley Counties until his death in 1895.[33] Of four appeals to the state supreme court, he won two and lost two.[34] Polite was not active politically, but he was a witness in a congressional election contest in 1879.[35] Johnson C. Whittaker, born a slave, attended the University of South Carolina and then obtained an appointment to West Point. For three years, he survived a very hostile environment at the military academy. But in April 1880, he was found tied up and unconscious in his room, and in a bizarre turn of events he was accused of faking the attack. He was tried and convicted by a court-martial. In 1882 his conviction was reversed, but he was nonetheless dismissed from the academy.[36] He moved to Charleston to teach and was admitted to the bar in 1885, but then he moved to Sumter and practiced with John B. Edwards.[37] By 1900 Whittaker left practice and resumed teaching, which he continued until his death in 1931.[38] Edwards, an 1881 Allen Law School graduate, first practiced in Charleston then moved to Sumter, where he practiced for more than twenty-five years.[39] Edwards won two of four cases before the state supreme court, including his one criminal appeal.[40] In 1913 Edwards moved to Rhode Island and practiced there until 1936.[41]

Another law partner of Edwards in Charleston was Julius Linoble Mitchell, who graduated from Allen Law School in 1894.[42] Mitchell, a native of Moncks Corner, had attended the U.S. Military Academy and Hampton Institute in Virginia. Admitted in 1893, he practiced in the other Lowcountry counties of Berkeley and Georgetown. His most important case was representing John Brownfield, a Georgetown barber, in a murder case that was ultimately lost in the U.S. Supreme Court (see chapter 10). Mitchell had an active civil practice in Berkeley County between 1899 and 1907.[43] There are no Berkeley court records for criminal cases during this period. Between 1900 and 1901 in Georgetown County, he tried nine criminal cases.[44] After one trial, the press praised Mitchell for his advocacy.[45] After 1900, he had a busy civil practice in Berkeley County.[46] However, by 1904 Mitchell had moved to Rhode Island and was practicing there.[47] Mitchell and his former law partner, John B. Edwards, undertook a murder case with racial overtones, which resulted in one mistrial and two appeals to the Rhode Island Supreme Court.[48] Mitchell argued cases in the appellate courts of South Carolina, Rhode Island, Massachusetts, and New York with some degree of success.[49] He died in the 1920s in Brooklyn.[50]

Another Allen graduate, Eugene Hayne, was admitted in 1897 and tried to practice in Charleston. He and Alonzo Twine had cases together in Charleston and Berkeley Counties.[51] By 1910, Hayne had moved to and was practicing in New York City.[52]

BEAUFORT BAR

Unlike Charleston, the Beaufort County bar did not shrink with the end of Reconstruction; in fact, it grew. By some measures its lawyers made more contributions to the state than any other in this era. But like the Charleston lawyers, the Beaufort bar could not measure their success by monetary wealth. The leader of the Beaufort bar was William Whipper, who continued to have an active and successful trial court record. He handled both minor and high-profile cases. Newspaper accounts record Whipper as active in the police court of Beaufort and appearing in both civil and criminal cases in other courts.[53] In one month in 1877, Whipper lost the case of a client charged with keeping a house of prostitution but obtained an acquittal for twenty-four defendants in the murder trial dubbed "The Stafford's Cross Roads Case."[54] This case arose from a racial conflict between a white farmer and a group of blacks who lived on his place. Violence erupted and two whites and one black were killed. Two trials ensued: twenty-four blacks were charged with the murder of the two whites, and a white constable and another white man were charged with the black man's murder. When Whipper's clients were acquitted, the local press asserted that Whipper stacked the jury with blacks. But when the other jury composed of eleven whites and one black returned not guilty verdicts for the white defendants, the result was praised by the press.[55]

Whipper was not successful as an appellate lawyer—all of his thirteen appeals were unsuccessful. Two unpublished appeals were dismissed in 1897.[56] Of his published appeals between 1878 and 1901, six were civil cases and four criminal.[57]

When Whipper's wife Frances moved to Washington, D.C., in the 1880s, he moved there and tried practicing law so he could be with her and his children. He did not remain for long. The lure of politics and the possibility of a judgeship wooed him back to Beaufort.[58] Whipper finally achieved his judicial ambition when he was elected Beaufort County probate judge in 1882.

In 1887 Whipper represented Congressman Robert Smalls in an election contest, but the two men soon had a falling out.[59] Whipper as probate judge refused to release some minor children's money to Smalls, and the congressman became angry and had Whipper arrested for malfeasance in office.[60] Whipper's lawyers, Samuel J. Lee and Thomas H. Wheeler, got their client released, and he was ultimately exonerated.[61]

However, when Whipper sought reelection as probate judge on the Republican ticket in 1888, Smalls left the Republican Party and supported a "fusion" ticket for county offices that included a white Democrat candidate for the judgeship.[62] The fusion ticket won, and the Republicans cried foul. As related in chapter 4, Whipper refused to concede and was jailed for contempt of court. He appealed but after he lost in the state supreme court, he surrendered the office.

Despite his removal, Whipper remained active at the bar and in politics. His most noteworthy political activity was serving in the 1895 constitutional convention. However, his dramatic and eloquent speeches fell on deaf ears. Whipper's most important legal case was the politically charged murder trial of John Brownfield in Georgetown County in 1900 in which Whipper and Julius Mitchell challenged the exclusion of blacks from the jury (see chapter 10).

In the Beaufort bar, Whipper was joined by Thomas H. Wheeler, Thomas E. Miller, Samuel Bampfield, A. A. Bradley, L. S. Langley, A. H. Ezekiel, Dempsher Powell, John Mardenborough, Thomas J. Reynolds, A. S. Bascomb, William W. Still, Julius Washington, and Isaiah Reed.[63] This was the largest group of black lawyers in one county in the state's history. T. H. Wheeler, an active trial lawyer, also served as secretary to the county council, school commissioner, chair of the county Republican Party, and editor of the *Sea Island News*.[64] Wheeler was often counsel in congressional election contests; he represented Smalls in 1886.[65] But like Whipper, Wheeler became a critic of Smalls and even complained to President Benjamin Harrison of Smalls's treachery and fraud.[66] Wheeler represented Thomas Miller in congressional election contests for 1888 and 1890.[67] He succeeded in the 1888 contest by presenting evidence that voters had been denied the right to vote, that voters had been misled into depositing their ballots in the wrong box, and that ballot boxes had been stuffed.[68] His advocacy drew praise from the congressional committee as well as the black press.[69] In 1894 he and William J. Whipper represented George Washington Murray in his election contest at the State Board of Canvassers, and Wheeler made an elaborate presentation alleging fraud.[70] Failing there, Wheeler took the case to the Congressional Committee on Elections, but the Democratic majority committee rejected his claims.[71] In 1896 Wheeler left Beaufort and was employed in the census office in Washington, D.C.[72] He later practiced in Philadelphia, where he died in 1903.[73]

Thomas Miller had a law office in Grahamville in rural Beaufort County but practiced across the state.[74] He handled mostly civil, nonlitigation cases, and he had only two reported federal criminal cases.[75] His chief activity was politics, and he became the leading Republican in Beaufort County. Like Whipper and other black lawyers, Miller was an opponent of fusion and Robert Smalls.[76]

Miller served in the state house of representatives from 1874 until 1880. He then served one term in the state senate from 1880 to 1882, and he returned to the house in 1886. He also made multiple runs for Congress. As noted above, Miller was successful in challenging the results of the 1888 federal election and was seated by the U.S. House of Representatives in the fall of 1890. While in Congress he was a strong advocate for the Lodge Federal Elections Bill.[77] Known as the Lodge Force bill, the legislation would have required federal supervision of congressional elections and allowed the federal courts to monitor such elections. After the Republicans brokered a compromise on a tariff act and a silver bill, Lodge's bill was defeated. This compromise signaled the end of the Republican Party's efforts to protect the voting rights of African Americans in the South. Miller lost his bid for reelection in 1890 when many of his ballots were thrown out by state election officials because the paper was "tinged yellow."[78] Miller's attempt to prove to the Congressional Committee on Elections that his ballots and the Democrats ballots were the same size and color was thwarted when Samuel J. Bampfield, the Beaufort clerk of court and the son-in-law of Robert Smalls, refused to turn over the ballots.[79] Both Miller and Robert Smalls sought the Republican nomination for Congress in 1892, but George Washington Murray bested the two Beaufort County rivals for the nomination.[80] Miller was elected to the state house of representatives in 1894 and delegate to the state constitutional convention in 1895. Following that convention, Miller was appointed president of the newly created state college for African Americans in Orangeburg.

Samuel J. Bampfield attended Lincoln University in Pennsylvania, returned to South Carolina, read law with Judge P. L. Wiggin, and was admitted in 1875.[81] Bampfield was elected clerk of court in 1880 and joined the fusion ticket in 1888. He was appointed Beaufort postmaster in 1897.[82] He was also editor of the *New South* newspaper in Beaufort.[83] There is no evidence that he practiced law. He died in 1900.[84]

Some of Beaufort's lawyers had very limited law practices. Dempsher Powell, the adopted son of William Whipper, briefly practiced with his father.[85] Also practicing law with Whipper was Thomas J. Reynolds, who also read law with him.[86] He served in the state senate from 1884 to 1887 but had only one appellate case, which he lost, in 1892.[87] Reynolds was convicted by a jury in federal court in 1891 for overcharging a veteran's widow in a pension case.[88] He was also charged again in 1892 for a similar offense.[89] Reynolds died in 1896.[90]

John C. Mardenborough and L. S. Langley never practiced in Beaufort. Both worked for the federal government.[91] Augustus S. Bascomb graduated from Lincoln University in 1880 and was admitted to the bar in 1886. Instead of practicing law, Bascomb served as the elected school commissioner in Beaufort County and was an educator until his death in 1912.[92]

Three other Beaufort lawyers made further contributions. A. H. Ezekiel, admitted in 1877, was co-counsel with S. J. Lee and Thomas Wheeler in representing probate judge W. J. Whipper after his arrest.[93] Ezekiel had one appellate case, and in 1892 he represented the Republican Party in an election contest against the Beaufort fusionists.[94] Ezekiel had his own legal problems including an overturned conviction for forgery and a conviction for adultery and fornication with a white woman.[95] He died in 1926 in Savannah.[96] Isaiah R. Reed, admitted in 1893, was a delegate to the 1895 constitutional convention. Reed moved to Washington, D.C., about 1902, where he lived and worked for the government until 1940.[97] Julius Washington read law with Whipper and was admitted in 1887.[98] He served in the South Carolina House of Representatives from 1886 to 1889. He taught school, worked for the Customs Service, had a brief law practice in Beaufort with Thomas Miller, and then returned to government service.[99] After 1911, he opened a solo law practice in Beaufort and was joined by his son Charles in 1924. He died in 1938.[100]

Aiken County

After Reconstruction, Aiken County lost Samuel J. Lee and George Clyde but gained two new lawyers who tried cases and participated in public life. Edward J. Dickerson, admitted in 1885, and S. E. Smith, admitted in 1888, were active Republicans.[101] Dickerson had an active criminal law practice, winning his first trial in 1886.[102] He won two out of three jury trials in 1887.[103] He tried cases in almost every year between 1888 and 1904.[104] However, fourteen out of his sixteen cases resulted in guilty verdicts. Dickerson had only four civil cases from 1891 until 1907.[105] Dickerson also campaigned against lynching.[106] S. E. Smith had seven criminal cases between 1888 and 1898.[107] The press took note of his convention speeches, describing him in one account as "full of oratory and common sense."[108] He was appointed to a federal position in Charleston in 1900.[109] He resided in Charleston until at least 1919.[110]

Orangeburg and Richland

Orangeburg County had an active black bar during Reconstruction, but the firms from that era did not survive. Humbert and Fordham did not last a year, and there is no record of Taylor, Fordham and Lawrence after the newspaper's mention of its creation.[111] In the 1880s and 1890s, John Henry Fordham, who had been a member of two different Orangeburg firms, primarily worked for the federal government and in 1894 tried one criminal case in the county.[112] Richland County had had no black bar during Reconstruction other than the attempt by Robert Brown Elliott to form the Elliott, Straker, and Stewart law firm in 1876. When it dissolved, D. A. Straker emerged as the lawyer who would have the most impact and success in the two counties.[113]

Straker tried his hand at elective politics in Orangeburg but was unceremoniously removed from the state legislature in 1877. However, after moving to Columbia, Straker continued to make his opinions known. In 1881 he joined R. B. Elliott and Judge Samuel Lee in visiting James A. Garfield to urge federal intervention in the state.[114] Straker was a strong critic of disenfranchisement and asserted that the southern white "rape complex" was fabricated to destroy the views of sympathetic whites that blacks deserved the right to vote.[115] As a lawyer he tried to attack disenfranchisement, and in 1880 he represented former judge Samuel Lee in his congressional election contest.[116] In the first years after Reconstruction, the Republican Party did not run a statewide ticket, but in 1884 the party nominated Straker for lieutenant governor.[117]

Straker practiced in Orangeburg, Lexington, Kershaw, Fairfield, and Richland Counties.[118] With his training at Howard, his forceful manner, and his distinctive Barbadian accent, he stood out.[119] He was also willing to undertake challenging cases. In 1879 the legislature repealed the divorce statute, but Straker had filed a divorce petition for his client before the effective date of the repeal and argued that the repeal should not apply retroactively to his client. However, the supreme court ruled against his client.[120] His use of an insanity defense in the murder trial of James Coleman in Columbia demonstrated that he was an assertive and able trial lawyer.[121] But the murder was so gruesome that his efforts were to no avail. In a less sensational case, Straker was successful in compelling the trustees of an African Methodist Episcopal church in Columbia to accept a minister appointed by their bishop.[122] Straker's skill as a lawyer drew praise from Justice Samuel McGowan of the state supreme court, where Straker won two out of his five appeal cases.[123]

His recollections of law practice provide some insight into the difficulties black lawyers faced.[124] In an 1883 court hearing, a white witness testified he wanted to unload a six-shooter into Straker, but the trial judge refused to find the white witness in contempt.[125] During Reconstruction, black trial lawyers had often enjoyed success before majority black juries. In another trial Straker recounted that even though a majority of the jurors were black, the trial judge tried to have one of the five whites named as foreman. Much to the consternation of the judge, none of the whites could read or write, and a literate black juror had to be named. By the late 1880s, Straker noted that while some blacks were still being summoned for jury service, the prosecutor would strike all of them in favor of an all-white jury.[126] Despite the overwhelming black population of Richland and Orangeburg Counties, the whitewashing of juries made it even more difficult for a black lawyer to successfully represent his clients.[127] Consequently, Straker gave up on the South and moved to Detroit in 1887. The white-owned *Columbia Daily Register* offered this explanation for his departure: "The personal and property rights of his colored clients have been faithfully and in most cases successfully represented, their poverty as a class has left his labor in their behalf unremunerative and compels him to seek another field for the exercise of legal talents which will win renown and money under other conditions than those which interpose an insuperable barrier here."[128]

A similar economic reason was related in a biographical sketch of Straker published in 1912.[129] But other newspaper accounts reflect that something more than money may have been at the root of Straker's discontent with South Carolina. In early 1887 Straker engaged in a public dispute with a white judge. In an exchange of letters to the editor of the *Daily Register*, Straker and trial justice Charles Kinsler hurled accusations against each other. Straker accused the magistrate of unfairness, and the judge responded that Straker was a liar and a fool.[130] The dispute remained unresolved in the press, and in an interview Straker gave to a Detroit newspaper, he said he fled South Carolina shortly after this dispute "under twenty-four hours notice."[131]

Straker's law students at Allen University had even less success than their dean. Peter Flynn Oliver served two years as dean of the law school, but then he moved to Kansas to practice in 1888.[132] Within weeks of his arrival in Wichita, Oliver addressed a gathering of two thousand at the Young Men's Republican Club, praising Kansas for its progressive ideas as opposed to South Carolina's effort to deny the vote to blacks.[133] While Oliver found the politics of Kansas welcoming, his law practice was insubstantial.[134] By 1889 he and his wife had moved to El Reno in the Oklahoma Territory.[135] Oliver died at age thirty-four in 1895.[136]

Later Allen graduates had varying degrees of success. E. C. C. Washington and Benjamin E. Watson graduated in 1886. Both stayed in Columbia, but neither practiced law. Washington was active in civic affairs, including antilynching efforts.[137] Out of the Allen class of 1887, only Thomas A. Saxon and Andrew E. Hampton were admitted to the state bar. Hampton taught but never practiced law.[138] Saxon was appointed dean of Allen's law school in 1888. An active Republican, he served as a presidential elector for the Republican Party in 1888.[139] At a Republican Party meeting, Saxon asserted that some Democratic leaders were associated with the Ku Klux Klan.[140] His efforts to register black voters drew the ire of white Democrats, who complained to the governor about his activities.[141]

Walton Williams, Casper G. Garrett, and Butler W. Nance were admitted to the bar in 1890. There is no record of Williams's career. Garrett was reported to be "in the active practice of law," but he was also employed as an educator and edited a newspaper.[142] He served as an alternate delegate to the Republican National Convention in 1928.[143] Nance practiced and helped organize the NAACP in Columbia (see chapter 9).[144]

Other Counties

In the first two decades of the Jim Crow era, few black lawyers practiced in the more rural areas of the state. The most prominent and financially successful was Edward J. Sawyer of Bennettsville in Marlboro County. Admitted in 1885, Sawyer attended law school at the University of South Carolina and Allen University.[145] As the only black lawyer in Marlboro County—and in the northeastern part of the state—Sawyer maintained a law office, but he said, "The profession does not pay."[146] He published a newspaper, farmed, operated a general store, served as school superintendent and postmaster, founded a bank, and became a wealthy man.[147] By 1920 he owned more than 1,800 acres and businesses valued at more than $125,000.[148] An active Republican, he ran for Congress in 1892 and attended multiple national Republican conventions.[149] The only record of any legal advocacy work by Sawyer was his representation of a Republican congressional candidate in an election contest in 1895.[150]

In 1895 Governor Ben Tillman called for a convention to promulgate a new constitution that would deprive blacks of the vote. All voters had to reregister to cast a ballot for convention delegates. Sawyer protested in an editorial that black registrants have "the door closed in their faces and they were informed that although they would be expected to pay taxes right on, no further opportunity to register and vote would be allowed them."[151] In June 1895 the *Columbia State* ran an interview with Sawyer and quoted him as saying, "We could not support extreme Tillmanites when their leader has declared that it was his purpose to disenfranchise the negro, place exorbitant poll tax on him and abolish all free school funds."[152] Sawyer ran for convention delegate but failed in his bid.[153] Despite his political activities, Sawyer was praised by the white press for his conservative politics and his "industriousness."[154] As the ominous cloud of Jim Crow darkened the state, Sawyer still participated in party politics. In 1897 he was part of a delegation that met with Governor Ellerbe to urge law enforcement to prevent lynching.[155] He remained active until the late 1920s but died in 1929 after several years of declining health.[156] His obituary in a leading white newspaper had his name wrong but was very detailed about his life, including his attendance at the university's law school and his Republican Party activities. Noting his service as postmaster, the obituary claimed that "he was always courteous to the white people. He never had any trouble. He knew his place."[157]

Another University of South Carolina law student from the Reconstruction era was Paris Simkins of Edgefield. He was admitted to the bar in 1886; an active Republican, he served as postmaster, ran a store, and worked as a minister.[158] In 1888 he gave a speech in Oconee County on the topic of voting and accused the Democrats of passing registration and election laws designed to deprive black voters of their constitutional rights.[159] Simkins reportedly worked as a clerk writing briefs for Governor John B. Sheppard and did legal work for a benevolent society.[160]

Major McFarlan of Chesterfield County was admitted in 1884. There is little evidence that he practiced law. He served as postmaster, worked as a teacher, and ran for the state house of representatives in 1898.[161] He died in 1923.[162]

John F. Brown graduated from Howard University Law School in 1884, then he returned to Colleton County and was admitted to the bar. In 1888 he was a federal election supervisor, and his testimony aided in awarding a U.S. congressional seat to Thomas Miller.[163] Brown ran for the state senate in 1890 but lost.[164] The only evidence of his law practice consists of two civil appeals to the state supreme court, which he won.[165]

After his graduation from Allen Law School, Robert A. Stewart taught there and was offered the deanship but chose law practice instead.[166] Stewart moved to Clarendon County, where he supported his family from his income as postmaster.[167] Stewart said, "I desire to succeed as a lawyer if possible, but find it hard in these parts; prejudice is great." But he expressed some optimism when he said that "the condition of the people is favorable. In intelligence and morals they are improving."[168] In 1898 Stewart was still trying cases in Manning, and in 1900 he unsuccessfully ran for Congress.[169] By 1908 Stewart had taken a federal job in Orangeburg County, where his political activity drew a reprimand from the Civil Service Commission.[170] Stewart moved to Washington, D.C., where he was still living and working for the federal government in 1930.[171]

E. B. Burroughs was admitted to the bar in 1896, but he never practiced.[172] However, he was an active advocate for equal rights. He served as a minister at Wesley ME Church in Charleston, gave the commencement sermon at Claflin University, was appointed the superintendent for the Orangeburg School

District, and edited a newspaper.[173] Burroughs's protest against the disenfranchisement of black voters in advance of the 1895 constitutional convention drew the attention of the press, as did his other civil rights activities.[174] He ran as the Regular Republican Party nominee for state superintendent of education in 1896 but lost.[175] In 1897 he joined with E. J. Sawyer on a delegation urging the governor to condemn lynching. But the local press reported that Burroughs and the other ministers were going to teach "Their Race Not to Commit Usual Crimes. The Quickest Remedy."[176] After 1900, Burroughs remained active in the ministry and died in 1919.[177]

~

In 1888, after he had left the state, D. A. Straker reflected on South Carolina and the condition of its people of color. He correctly noted that the majority of the black citizens had been disenfranchised first "by blood and murder," and then by legislative schemes to restrict their vote. Straker decried the fact that blacks were being deprived of the right to sit on juries and questioned how Congress could be representative when so many legislators had been "elected" by fraud. On economic issues, Straker traced the history of the white "master" taking advantage of former slaves in labor contracts. He concluded that the great disparity in wealth in the South was the result of "poor wages, bad laws and race prejudice." Despite all that he had seen in South Carolina, Straker was optimistic that within twenty years the situation would be reversed. There is no doubt that Straker had identified the major problems that black lawyers and the black community faced. At the same time, his optimism seems emblematic of the hope and faith that his community held for the American legal system.[178]

While many lawyers such as Straker left, other lawyers stayed and had varying degrees of success in law practice, business, and other endeavors. None achieved wealth through law practice. Most were active in politics. While none succeeded in effecting real legal change, their political activities, their opposition to disenfranchisement, and their campaigns against lynching were at least heard. Their efforts ensured that the fight for equal rights was not over.

CHAPTER 8

A Last Stand

The Civil War brought freedom, and Reconstruction established civil rights for the state's black citizens, but the Jim Crow era saw a nearly complete reversal of those gains. In fact, blacks faced an organized attack by the Democratic Party on freedom and civil rights. The chief goal of white Democrats was to deprive blacks of the vote. Consequently, the chief political activity of the black bar in this era was struggling to preserve the right to vote.

The Ballot under Assault

While violence and intimidation had been the means of achieving white rule, perversion of the law was the chief tactic of whites in suppressing the black vote.[1] Although federal authorities prosecuted several cases of voter intimidation in the state, an order by the governor in 1884 impeded these prosecutions by requiring the state attorney general to defend anyone indicted for violating the federal election laws.[2] In furtherance of the effort, the legislature appropriated $10,000 to fund those defenses.[3] The state legislature also began enacting methods to circumvent federal authorities and hinder black voters. In 1877 the state legislature separated state and federal ballot boxes, which effectively prevented federal authorities from asserting any jurisdiction to protect black voters' ballots for state offices.[4] In 1882 new franchise provisions were enacted, justified by legislator Edward McCrady because of "the great and cruel injury done to the white race in the South by forcing upon us the ignorant negro vote."[5] Complete abrogation of the Fifteenth Amendment was the goal.[6] The 1882 registration law required all men to reregister by June 1882 or forever be barred from voting.[7] The only new voters to be allowed thereafter would be those who had turned twenty-one or who had moved into the state.[8] In addition, for the first time, payment of a poll tax was a prerequisite to the right to vote. The tax was an economic burden on most blacks, and to make matters worse, the legislature criminalized nonpayment of it.[9]

Every detail of voter registration was carefully planned to restrict black voting. For example, if a voter moved within a precinct, he had to reregister. This provision dramatically disenfranchised black farm laborers, who often moved with the crops and seasons.[10] The only way a person denied the right to register could contest the denial was by filing a written notice within five days and then appealing to the circuit court within ten days.[11] Precinct boundary lines were redrawn so that some black voters had to travel all day to vote.[12] Probably the most "effective" provision was the "Eight Box Law," which required voters to deposit a ballot for each office in a separate ballot box, and if a voter put his ballot in the wrong box, his vote did not count. The U.S. attorney for South Carolina estimated that this provision eliminated more than 80 percent of black ballots.[13]

Two other schemes developed during this period proved to have a long-lasting influence on black voting: the organization of all-white Democratic clubs and the creation of the white primary. In 1888 the legislature authorized the political parties to hold primary elections or conventions and to determine the rules under which they would be conducted and who was allowed to vote. This ultimately led to the all-white primary. Under this mechanism, white Democrats could keep blacks off the ballot in the primary elections, and only whites would be voting for the party's candidates.[14] The perversity of the white primary is almost unfathomable. The Democratic Party was not shy about which men were welcome to vote: "a white Democrat, or a negro who voted for General Hampton in 1876 and who has voted the Democratic ticket continuously since." Rule 2 of the Democratic Party further stipulated that "every negro applying for membership in a Democratic club, or offering to vote in a Democratic Primary election, must produce a written statement of ten reputable white men, who shall swear that they know of their own knowledge that the . . . voter, voted for General Hampton in 1876 and has voted the Democratic ticket continuously since."[15]

Despite these efforts, black voters persisted. They continued to run for local offices and to win elections in areas with a black majority. In response, the predominant white strategy became cheating: first, to prevent blacks from registering to vote, and second, not to count their votes. As mentioned previously, several federal prosecutions were instituted in egregious instances of such cheating, but the Department of Justice finally abandoned all of its enforcement efforts by the mid-1880s.[16] Left with few remedies, black voters tried to pursue their claims in state court, but virtually all of these cases proved futile. In *Ex parte Mackey* the South Carolina Supreme Court declined to overturn an election even though election officials refused to count the votes from majority black precincts; in *Ex parte Elliott* the court affirmed the election officials' refusal to count ballots for a black congressional candidate because of their color, their size, and their inclusion of the word "for" before the word "Congress."[17]

By the 1890s black citizens' right to vote faced extinction. In the 1870s there had been more than 91,000 registered black voters in the state; by 1888 this number had declined to under 14,000.[18] In the 1876 congressional campaigns, Republicans were able to elect three black congressmen out of five seats. In 1878 no blacks were returned to Congress from South Carolina. In 1880 Robert Smalls and white Republican Edward W. M. Mackey were sent to Congress, along with three white Democrats. In 1882 reapportionment, gerrymandering, and disfranchisement limited the Republicans to only one sure seat. Mackey defeated Smalls for that seat but died while in office, opening the seat for Smalls. From 1880 through 1897, the state had one lone black Republican congressman in all but two sessions of Congress.

Beginning in 1876, no black congressional candidates won their elections without postelection contests. Black lawyers played a pivotal role in these election disputes. When Congress investigated the 1876 South Carolina elections, sixteen black lawyers' names appeared in the committee's report as counsel, witnesses, or candidates.[19] In later years, black lawyers were critical to the election of three black congressmen: Robert Smalls, Thomas E. Miller, and George Washington Murray.

In 1880 Robert Smalls was only seated after he won a contest before Congress.[20] His lawyers included Thomas Wheeler, A. H. Ezekiel, Paris Simkins, and Laurence Cain. Such cases were heard by the Committee on Elections of the U.S. House of Representatives.[21] The decisions of the committee were then approved or disapproved by the full House. In Smalls's case in 1880, the committee overturned the white Democrat's victory, citing fraud, violence, intimidation, and illegal rejection of ballots by state election officials, and that decision was upheld by the full House.[22] In 1882 Smalls was defeated for the Republican nomination but won a special election in 1884. Smalls also won again in the regular election in the fall of 1884. In 1886, according to official state returns, Smalls was defeated by the white Democrat, William Elliott. Thomas Wheeler, John Freeman, and William Whipper represented Smalls in the contest, but they could not convince a congressional Democratic majority to overturn the election.

In the 1888 election, William Elliott was again declared the winner but this time over Thomas Miller, who had replaced Smalls as the Republican nominee. Miller contested his defeat and took the challenge to Congress. His lawyers, Thomas Wheeler and T. J. Reynolds, made multiple arguments that Miller be seated. First, they argued that the state's restrictive 1882 voter registration law conflicted with the more liberal provisions of the 1868 constitution of South Carolina.[23] Since the post–Civil War constitution was in part enacted to satisfy Congress's conditions on readmission of South Carolina into the Union, the constitution represented what was permissible in Congress's view of voter protection. This argument caused the congressional committee to call the state's 1882 registration law "an abridgement, subversion, and restraint" on the right to vote. Miller also argued that his ballots had been improperly excluded and that the boxes had been stuffed with Democratic ballots. The committee found the most egregious violation to be the use of the state's Eight Box Law. Evidence showed that white Democratic poll workers made every effort to confuse voters into placing their ballots in the wrong box. More than a thousand ballots for Miller had been excluded on that basis. Miller also presented evidence of wholesale ballot box stuffing. Again the committee found a violation and awarded 1,448 more votes to Miller. After the committee ruled for Miller, their decision was upheld by a House vote of 157 to 1.[24]

Miller ran for reelection in 1890 and faced the white Democrat Elliott and a white Republican, E. M. Brayton. (Miller's feud with Robert Smalls and the fusion faction caused the Republican split.) After the election, protests were filed with numerous county boards, who threw out Miller's ballots because of their yellow color, their size (1⁄16 inch too small), the print size and font, and the fact that they included the word "for" before Miller's name.[25] In the Beaufort returns, the board awarded the Democrat 644 votes, Brayton 32, and Miller 0. The official returns of the State Board of Canvassers for the entire district awarded Brayton 1,410 votes, Elliott 3,792, and Miller 3,315 votes. When it heard appeals by Elliott and Miller, the state board was evenly split.[26] Despite the fact that not a single vote had been awarded to Miller from his home county, the state supreme court ruled that the board should have issued a certificate of election to Elliott.[27] Miller then protested to Congress, but his challenge failed. The minority report of the Congressional Committee on Elections found that Miller proved he should have won by a majority of 3,233 votes, but the Democratic majority on the committee voted for the white Democrat.[28]

Black Republican George Washington Murray was elected to Congress in 1892 and 1894. In initial returns in 1892, Murray lost to the white Democrat, 4,937 to 2,695. Murray protested to the State Board of Canvassers represented by Samuel J. Lee and Thomas Miller. At the board hearing, Lee "spoke for one hour and forty-five minutes, and delivered his speech in a very impressive and dramatic manner."[29] Lee's chief argument was that ballots had been disregarded by local officials on the spurious grounds that they were an eighth of an inch too wide. After the presentation by Lee and Miller, the all-white board awarded an additional 2,300 votes to Murray's total, giving him a victory by forty votes.[30]

The board's decision on behalf of Murray was thought to have been the result of a split in the Democratic Party. The supporters of Benjamin R. Tillman on the board voted for Murray to defeat the conservative Democrat, E. W. Moise.[31] While the Democrats were split over national issues such as gold versus silver, Murray's biographer opined that the vote was more about humiliating the conservative Democrats and demonstrating the power of Ben Tillman than it was about silver.[32]

According to the county-certified returns and the state election board, Murray lost his 1894 congressional race.[33] Isaiah Reed, W. J. Whipper, Alfred Williams, and T. J. Reynolds appeared for him in Beaufort County.[34] Thomas Wheeler and William Whipper argued Murray's case before the state election commission.[35] Murray again relied on the grounds that his ballots had been illegally rejected.[36] This time the state board rejected his claims.[37] When Murray protested to Congress, the Congressional Committee on Elections found merit to his case and applied a logic that confirmed the obvious. The white minority had stolen the election from the black majority. In analyzing the returns from Charleston County, the committee noted that the county had eight thousand black voters and only six thousand whites, but Murray, the black candidate, was credited with only 397 votes while the white Democrat had 2,811.[38] In fact, Murray had carried four out of six counties in the district.[39] This time Wheeler and Whipper persuaded a majority of Congress to award the seat to Murray.

In another 1894 contest, congressional Republican candidate Thomas B. Johnston argued that 7,336 persons had been illegally barred from voting. W. F. Myers of Colleton County, J. H. Fordham of Orangeburg, J. C. Whittaker of Sumter, and Julius Mitchell of Moncks Corner represented Johnston in his congressional election contest.[40] The congressional committee decided there was no winner in the race between the white Republican Johnston and his white Democrat opponent J. William Stokes and declared the seat vacant.[41]

A New Constitution to Disfranchise Black Voters

The number of blacks elected to state offices declined steadily from 1878 to 1895. After the violent election of 1876 and the purge of the legislature in 1877, twenty-seven blacks still served in the state senate and house, but that number declined to twelve in 1878. It rose to fifteen in 1882 but dropped in every subsequent election until there were only two in 1894. A few blacks were elected to various town councils in the 1880s.[42] Georgetown and Beaufort County voters elected a number of blacks to county offices, including those of probate judge and school commissioner.[43] Beaufort also had both a black clerk of court and a black sheriff. In Georgetown blacks on the fusion ticket shared offices with whites until 1900. But in Beaufort, the battle between the Republicans and the fusionists nearly eliminated black officeholders. In 1892 Thomas Miller represented a slate of Beaufort black Republican candidates before the State Board of Canvassers; they were challenging the election of ten predominately white fusion ticket candidates. Initially the board agreed with Miller's arguments and held that the Republicans had won all local offices. But a few days later, the board reversed itself and ruled for the fusionists. In 1894, despite a challenge by the fusionists, Miller was elected to the state house of representatives, and other black Republicans won as well. This local battle continued in 1896, but thereafter, no blacks were elected to office in Beaufort until the 1970s. Likewise, until the 1970s the last blacks elected in Georgetown County were a state representative and a school commissioner in 1900.[44]

The only avenue for true black participation in politics was the Republican Party, and it was seriously divided. Historian John Marszalek observed that the two factions in the party differed not on issues but only in age. The Regulars were older and many had roots in Reconstruction, while the Reformers were younger and had become active in the politics of post-Reconstruction South Carolina.[45] Beyond these two factions, the fusion ticket battle in Beaufort infected the party statewide. Naturally, when two of the state's party leaders, Congressmen Smalls and Miller, were in different Beaufort camps, the Republican Party was seriously weakened not only in the county but also statewide. With both internal divisions and a reduced number of potential voters, the party was greatly diminished in its influence.

White Democrats were also divided. Their two camps were conservatives (supporters of Wade Hampton) and radicals (headed by Benjamin R. Tillman). The conservatives were generally identified with the planter class. While they favored white rule, they were less vehement in their opposition to civil rights of blacks. For example, the conservatives favored restrictive voter registration laws that emphasized property and educational requirements, but supposedly they did not object to an educated, prosperous black voter, and they supported major revisions to the registration laws in 1882. The radical Democrats, on the other hand, espoused the complete elimination of black voting. Ben Tillman feared that the conservatives could attract enough black voters to defeat him and his supporters' agenda. In 1890 Tillman ran for governor opposed by a conservative Democrat, Alexander C. Haskell, who bolted the Democratic Party and ran as an independent with the support of conservative Democrats and Republicans. With the black vote greatly diminished, Tillman was easily elected by a vote of 59,159 to 14,828.[46] One historian estimated that Haskell received about 5,000 black votes out of 14,000 registered blacks. To Ben Tillman, even those small numbers of black registered voters were more than could be tolerated. Looking for something more than fraud, intimidation, and mere legislation, Tillman called for a new constitution to protect "Anglo-Saxon Supremacy," and with that end in mind, he used the state of Mississippi as his model for action.[47] Mississippi's new constitution adopted in 1890 had virtually eliminated the black vote in that state. Consequently, Tillman worked tirelessly at getting a similar constitution adopted in South Carolina.[48] By December 1892 he finally had enough support in the legislature to authorize a referendum on whether to call a constitutional convention.[49]

However, Tillman's plan faced opposition from white "conservatives" and Republicans.[50] In fact, it was the combined opposition of the conservatives and the Republicans that Tillman used to support his assertion that if blacks were allowed to vote, they would always side with the conservatives. Black lawyers should have been the leaders in opposing Tillman and his proposed constitutional convention, but the divisions in the Republican Party led to inaction. Their only response was to meet. In September 1892 one Republican Party faction held its convention and condemned the state's election laws as depriving blacks of a republican form of government.[51] Nine black lawyers were delegates to this convention.[52] They even nominated black lawyer J. H. Fordham to run for attorney general on the party ticket. But they took no action to oppose the constitutional convention, and in the end they did not even run a ticket with Fordham or any other candidate for statewide office. In May 1893 this same group of black lawyers held a meeting in Columbia to protest lynching, but they ignored the approaching referendum.[53] While lynching was an important issue, clearly the more immediate matter was disenfranchisement.

The lack of action by the black legal community is confounding. Black lawyers had been contesting and litigating election cases for a number of years, but none litigated individual voter rights cases. Their failure to bring such cases was probably the result of their limited federal court experience, as well as internal struggles within the Republican Party. However, the reform faction of the party headed by Congressman George Washington Murray decided litigation was necessary. Backed by a secret alliance of conservative Democrats, Murray hired two white lawyers, Henry Obear and Charles A. Douglass, to bring lawsuits challenging the proposed referendum.

In order to vote in the referendum, the voter had to be registered under the restrictive 1882 registration law. This law allowed new voters to register only on the first Monday of each month only through July. If the potential voter failed to register accordingly, he could not cast a ballot in that year's fall election. The county boards of registration, who were appointed by the governor, vigorously prevented Republicans, especially black Republicans, from registering.[54] These discriminations ranged from requiring separate white and black lines for voters to outright denials of the right to register by others.[55]

The registration law required that those who had been eligible to vote in 1882 must have registered by June 30 in that year or be barred from voting in the referendum and all future elections. In anticipation of the coming referendum, Obear and Douglass filed legal challenges on behalf of three clients. Lawrence Mills, a black tailor, had first become eligible in 1890 but could not register because of long lines; he never gained admittance into the registration office. He was joined by two white plaintiffs: Joshua Lumsden had failed to register in 1882 because he was out of town when he turned twenty-one, and John J. Cormack had moved into the state in 1890 but did not register when he was eligible under the limited registration scheme, out of ignorance of the registration laws. All three cases were consolidated into applications to the state supreme court for an injunction that would prohibit the Richland County voter registrar from providing voter lists to the election managers and thus postpone the referendum.[56] The legal challenge did not fare well. The state's high court saw nothing wrong with refusing to register these new voters, and the application for an injunction was denied.[57]

Despite that failure, black citizens continued to try to register. One black voter in Orangeburg County managed to appeal his denial of a voter registration certificate to the local board of registration and obtained his certificate, but others were not so successful.[58] In Richland County, one black citizen failed in his appeal to the local board, while two others appealed unsuccessfully to the state supreme court.[59] If a black lawyer assisted in these cases, there is no record of it.

After the challenges in state court failed, the convention referendum was held and approved by a vote of 31,402 to 29,525, a margin of only 1,877 votes. There were outcries by conservative whites that Tillman had stolen the election, but the process for writing a new constitution continued.[60] The next step required the election of delegates to the convention. In a message to the legislature in November 1892, Governor Tillman criticized the 1882 registration law on the grounds that it disenfranchised "a large number of [white] citizens." In fact, he called the law unconstitutional.[61] Tillman's view of the law was clearly influenced by the close vote for the convention. The narrow margin indicated the need to increase the registration of white voters sympathetic to Tillman's views before the election of delegates. Of course, increasing voter registration for voters sympathetic to Tillman created the anomaly of increasing the opportunity for more blacks to register to vote. In December 1894 the legislature enacted a special statute for the election of convention delegates, which opened voter registration up to any male over twenty-one who had failed to register under the 1882 law. The grace period for registration was limited to ten days in March 1895, and the law also required the potential voter to produce a notarized affidavit that included the registrant's name, age, residence, all places of residence since becoming of age, and affidavits from two reputable citizens over the age of twenty-one attesting to the voter's eligibility.[62]

Clearly, the affidavit process was intended as a measure to exclude black voters. Naturally, it was assumed that blacks would have a hard time finding a notary and the two reputable citizens. But the scheme did not deter black citizens. In Manning, when the registrar's office opened on March 4, 1895, two hundred blacks sought registration and only one was allowed to register.[63] Similarly, in Marlboro County more than a hundred blacks waited in the cold and rain to register but were never admitted into the registrar's office.[64] Across the state, the black community was organized to take advantage of the ten-day grace period. But the white opposition had an ace up their sleeves. All notaries were appointed by the governor and could be removed by the governor. When black attorney W. T. Andrews of Sumter publicized the fact that he could notarize the affidavits necessary for registration, local whites complained, and the governor revoked Andrews's notary commission.[65] When challenged, John Gary Evans, who was Tillman's handpicked successor, simply asserted his gubernatorial right to revoke a commission, and later he said that he had taken the action because of a "request from respectable white citizens stating that [black notaries] had been soliciting business and making themselves particularly obnoxious to respectable white people."[66] Andrews was one of only three black notaries in Sumter. In Spartanburg a white Republican notary also had his commission revoked.[67] In Camden J. B. Middleton's commission was revoked again because his conduct was "heinous" and "abominable."[68] Middleton was simply notarizing affidavits for potential black voters. In Richland County two black notaries had their commissions revoked. In this case, former Allen Law School dean T. A. Saxon was accused of committing fraud when he wrote in the name of illiterate voters.[69] More than 250 applications for registration were rejected in

Richland County. In a letter to a Columbia newspaper, E. B. Burroughs accused the governor of engaging in "premeditated and unscrupulous methods" to keep 65,000 black voters from registering to vote in the delegate election.[70]

Efforts were launched to halt the election for convention delegates. Again, Congressman George Washington Murray led the effort.[71] He again hired Henry Obear and Charles Douglass, the same white lawyers who had challenged the referendum initially, and he stumped the state raising money from hundreds of blacks in order to fund the legal effort.[72] But Thomas Miller, one of the leading black lawyers in the state, sent an open letter to a Columbia newspaper objecting to Murray's litigation plan. In this letter, dated March 29, 1895, former congressman Miller asserted that the action filed by Murray's white lawyers was pursuing monetary damages and would not stop the election for delegates. Miller suggested that another legal action needed to be filed, and he offered the services of Samuel J. Lee, himself, and others to bring the suit. Failing that, Miller said he and other black lawyers could "register all eligible voters, or we will prevent a constitution being made."[73] This proposal to register voters was odd because the ten-day window under the registration law had already passed. Miller's opposition to the form of legal action was correct in that the first case filed, *Wiley v. Sinkler*, was for money damages. Murray responded that a new case was in the process of being prepared.[74] While Miller's criticism was partially valid, it was probably motivated more by his animosity toward Murray than by the merits of the case. In the 1894 congressional election, Murray had accused Miller of working on behalf of a white Democrat.[75] But Miller's letter also exhibits the failure of the black lawyers to take action as well as the divisions in the Republican Party. Miller and Samuel J. Lee were the leading black lawyers in the state, but neither one had the legal experience to fight a constitutional challenge in federal court nor the political viewpoints such that a congressman like Murray would trust them.

Mills v. Green was filed in federal court on April 13, 1895.[76] Again, the plaintiff was Lawrence P. Mills, the black tailor who had failed to reach the front of the line at the registration office. In an astounding decision dated May 8, 1895, federal judge Nathan Goff, a West Virginia Republican, declared the registration law unconstitutional and issued an injunction preventing the convening of the constitutional convention.[77] He described the state's registration laws as "unreasonable, burdensome, . . . harassing, . . . without reason, . . . vexatious, . . . cumbersome and peculiarly stringent."[78] Judge Goff noted that under the state's existing (1868) constitution, a potential voter had to be a twenty-one-year-old male, a one-year resident, and registered two months before an election to be eligible to vote. Thus, the 1882 registration law was clearly invalid under the state constitution. But the force of his opinion was that the Fourteenth and Fifteenth Amendments prohibited the race-based nature of the registration scheme.[79]

Mills's victory was short lived. On June 11, 1895, the U.S. Court of Appeals overturned Goff's decision. With Melville Fuller, chief justice of the U.S. Supreme Court, sitting as circuit justice, the court ruled that there was no proof of discrimination based on "race, color or previous condition of servitude." The constitutional convention had been held by the time the U.S. Supreme Court took up the matter of *Mills v. Green* in November 1895, so the high court dismissed the case.[80]

In July 1895 the Democratic Party held a primary to select its candidates for convention delegates. Few if any blacks voted in that primary, and white conservatives boycotted. In the August general election, some blacks were able to vote, and a number of blacks sought election as delegates. At least thirteen candidates were black lawyers: S. E. Smith in Aiken County; W. J. Whipper, T. E. Miller, and I. R. Reed in Beaufort County; J. L. Mitchell in Berkeley County; J. B. Edwards in Charleston County; W. F. Myers in Colleton County; W. F. Holmes in Florence County; Z. D. Greene in Georgetown County; E. J. Sawyer in Marlboro County; Butler Nance in Newberry County; J. W. Morris in Richland County; and W. T. Andrews in Sumter County.[81] Only Whipper, Reed, and Miller were elected. They were joined by nonlawyer black delegates Robert Smalls and James Wigg from Beaufort County, and Robert Anderson from Georgetown.

While the three black lawyers played an active role, they and the other black delegates had no influence on the body. However, the mere presence of the black delegates caused discomfort to the whites. Despite the fact that there were only six blacks out of 154 convention delegates, a rump session was called for whites only to iron out their differences.[82]

Racial animus infected the convention from the first day. In his opening address, temporary chairman Robert Aldrich demanded a repeal of the 1868 constitution because it had been drafted by "negroes" and was a "stain on the reputation of South Carolina."[83] Governor John Gary Evans, after being elected chairman of the convention, made clear that the goal was to draft a constitution that would ensure white supremacy. Evans called for "an educational qualification for right of suffrage if the supremacy of intelligence is to be preserved" (12). He explained that "we have experienced the cost and hardship of the rule of the ignorant" (12). In an amazingly forthright speech to the convention, Ben Tillman (now a U.S. senator) admitted that he and other whites had used "fraud and violence" and the election laws to deprive blacks from voting, but asserted that the constitution must go farther and "take from them every ballot" (463–64). To achieve that end, the convention adopted the so-called Mississippi Plan, which incorporated two of the legislative schemes already enacted in South Carolina, prolonged residency and payment of the poll tax, and presented two new ideas: disqualification for commission of so-called black crimes and the discretionary literacy clause.[84]

Disqualification from voting for criminal convictions was not new, but the Mississippi Plan was tailored to disqualify only certain voters.[85] The specific disqualifying criminal convictions were for burglary, arson, obtaining goods under false pretenses, robbery, bribery, adultery, bigamy, wife beating, housebreaking, receiving stolen goods, breach of trust with fraudulent intent, fornication, sodomy, incest, assault with intent to ravish, miscegenation, larceny, or crimes against the election laws.[86] These were supposedly crimes blacks would be more likely to commit than whites. Not included in the list were murder, treason, or dueling, which had been disqualifiers under the 1868 constitution, despite the fact that in 1890 South Carolina had three times more murders than were committed in all of the New England states combined.[87] In addition, the vast majority of the state's murders were committed by whites. Modern-day civil rights lawyer Laughlin McDonald pointed out that "a man could kill his wife and still vote, but if he merely beat her, he was denied the franchise."[88] McDonald explained that the crazy quilt of a law could only be understood by the fact that the law was intended to exclude black voters.

The most significant contributions to the goal of excluding blacks were the literacy provisions of the Mississippi Plan. These were supposedly facially neutral. First, the literacy test only applied if an applicant had not paid taxes on $300 worth of property. This was a major impediment to black voting because of the poverty of the community. In South Carolina only 15 percent of blacks owned their homes, so very few would own property valued at $300.[89] For non–property owners the alternative route to registration was the literacy test. Under the new scheme, until January 1, 1898, a potential voter was required to understand and explain any section of the constitution read to them by the registrar, but the literate voter merely had to be able to read the section presented. After January 1, 1898, a registrant had to be able to read *and* write any section presented to them by the registrar.[90] While a majority of blacks in the state were illiterate, the real animus of the new law was the discretion it granted to the voter registrar.[91] This mechanism meant that each registrar determined whether the applicant could read or write. As long as the voter registrar was willing to "lie" about whether a black citizen had passed the literacy test, no black could register. This provision was strongly attacked by the white press because of the danger that many whites could be denied the right to vote at the whim of one's political opponent.[92] But the literacy test had proved effective in Mississippi and promised to succeed in its devilish purpose in South Carolina as well.[93]

Outside the convention, black lawyer W. T. Andrews prepared a resolution for an assemblage of black citizens in Sumter. His resolution condemned the understanding clause as a vile surrender to "despotic demagogues."[94] Within the convention, the black delegates were united in their opposition to the clause. W. J. Whipper delivered a two-and-a-half-hour speech to the body in what the white press described "as [a] powerful one and did credit to the coal black man who delivered it."[95] Whipper not only spoke against the proposals but also offered a compromise that would have delayed any literacy requirement for five years, giving more people a chance to learn to read and write. Despite the moderation of his proposal, it was defeated 130 to 6.[96]

But that was not the only time Whipper was heard. On another occasion, Whipper confronted the convention and the very words of Senator Tillman. He chastised Tillman for resorting to the use of racial epithets such as "nigger."[97] He said,

> I am not here as a suppliant, nor do I put myself and my race in the attitude of a beggar. I am here as a man and a representative not representing simply the negro, but representing the people. The fact that I am a negro has nothing to do with my status here. And just here I will digress to speak of the flippant way the term "nigger" has been used in this convention. I am a negro. There are six others here that are negroes. We are proud of it, and we hope to be able to do something in and out of this convention that the negroes will be proud of and white men compelled to recognize. But when men selected from the various counties as it is fair to suppose with a view to their intelligence and their good standing at their grave duties and responsibilities resting upon them, and so flippantly use the word "nigger" spelled with two g's, it is hurtful, and I feel it keenly. It stings sharper than a serpent's tooth when it comes from the venerable gentleman from Edgefield, Mr. C. D. [Ben] Tillman.

Whipper defended the constitutional convention of 1868, saying, "I am proud of the work done in that convention. The way it has stood the test shows that there was nothing dangerous in it."[98] In contrast, Whipper pointed out that the 1895 convention was called to deprive citizens of the right to vote.

But the convention not only enacted new provisions to disenfranchise blacks; it also eliminated from the constitution's declaration of rights the provision that the right "to vote shall not be denied or abridged on account of race, color, or previous condition of servitude." This was nothing more than an attempt to do by silence what they could not do explicitly, which was deny the right to vote to all black citizens. On the convention floor, Thomas Miller attacked the provisions as a blow to universal suffrage and pointed out that the provision was nothing more than an attack on the U.S. Constitution and a folly like secession.[99]

I. R. Reed was also active in the convention. He appealed to the delegates to remember that the country had been founded on the principle of equality of all men.[100] Reed proposed that the new constitution include an antilynching provision.[101] His proposal would have authorized the governor to remove any county sheriff from whom a prisoner was seized and lynched. He further wanted the militia called out to prevent lynchings. His measure was referred to a committee and died.

The new constitution also provided that the legislature "shall provide by law for the regulation of party primary elections."[102] This was not new but would serve as one of the most effective tools of the white Democrats to prevent blacks from voting. The purpose was clear: the Democratic Party was clearly the white party. By allowing it to decide who could vote in its primary, only whites could vote in the election that mattered.[103]

Like much of the law of the Jim Crow era, the 1895 constitution was a hypocritical document. Article I, Section 9 declared that "the right of suffrage . . . shall be protected," but this section of the document's "Declaration of Rights" was simply a lie. Article II, titled "The Right of Suffrage," was as long as the entire "Declaration of Rights" article of the constitution and in minute detail devised a scheme to reduce if not eliminate the black vote.[104] When the convention adjourned, the new constitution became effective; unlike the 1868 document, it was not submitted to the voters for approval.[105]

Postconstitution: The Continuing Battle

With the 1895 constitution now in place, black lawyers would need a new resolve. Some congressional races had been challenged all the way to Congress and the black candidates had prevailed, both because it was clear that whites had stolen the elections and because the voter registration statutes were found to be invalid under the 1868 constitution.[106] However, the 1895 constitution created new dilemmas for black voters, candidates, and lawyers. Because of the new constitution's Machiavellian procedure of granting full discretion to local registrars, very few blacks would be allowed to register, much less vote, and consequently, there would be no need to commit fraud on election day. By virtue of the 1895 constitution, there was no conflict between the state constitution and the state's registration laws. Thus, congressional committees could no longer award a congressional seat to a black Republican on the basis that the state's registration laws were unconstitutional.[107]

The general elections in the fall of 1896 offered the first major opportunity to test the new constitution. Would the Republicans give up? Would fusion hold in the Lowcountry? Could the Democrats eliminate black voting? Would the new constitution be as egregious as predicted? Would black lawyers come to the fore to challenge it? The new constitution seemed to energize the Republicans, and for the first time since Reconstruction, the party fielded a slate of candidates for all statewide offices. Unfortunately, they split and ran a "Reorganized Republicans" ticket and a "Regulars" ticket. The only black lawyer on either ticket was Allen law graduate E. B. Burroughs, who ran for superintendent of education on the "Reorganized" ticket.[108] William Whipper and S. E. Smith joined George Washington Murray in supporting the Reorganized ticket, but Thomas Miller and Robert Smalls supported the Regulars and led the delegation to the national party convention.[109] The Regulars' nominee for governor received 2,780 votes; the Reorganized faction's gubernatorial candidate received 4,432 votes; and the Democrat won with 59,424 votes.[110] Neither Republican faction nominated a statewide ticket in 1898.

On the local level, there were few contested races in 1896. In Georgetown, fusion still held. George Herriott was reelected school commissioner, and Robert B. Anderson won one of the county's two seats in the state legislature with the other seat reserved for a white. Fusion was so strong that Anderson and his white counterpart had the exact same number of votes. Fusion would prevail in Georgetown in 1898 and 1900. Herriott was reelected in both elections, and Anderson was replaced by another black, John Bolts. Again, the white counterpart received the exact same number of votes as Bolts in 1898 and 1900. But in 1902 Bolts lost, receiving only 135 votes while his white opponent received more than a thousand. Herriott lost by an even larger margin, 1,067 to 98. In 1904 the only Republican candidate in Georgetown was for coroner, and he lost 702 to 131. In 1906 no Republican sought office in Georgetown.[111] In 1910 in Georgetown, whites were outnumbered 6,110 to 16,158.[112]

In Beaufort fusion was no more, but the Republicans did not give up. In 1896 a full Republican ticket ran with Julius I. Washington for clerk of court and William J. Whipper for a state house seat; however, no Republican candidate won. In 1898 the Beaufort Republican slate had fewer candidates but included Whipper running for the house and Washington running for superintendent of education. When they lost, they hired J. I. Washington to contest the election, but their challenge was unsuccessful. In 1900 the Republicans ran candidates for the four house seats, for county supervisor, and for the education post. Legislative candidate Julius I. Washington and his three fellow Republicans all received 267 votes, while the Democrats received 568, 569, 569, and 571 votes each. In Beaufort in 1902, the Republicans ran a slate for three legislative candidates and for three county offices, but all of the candidates were defeated by nearly identical margins. In 1904 the Beaufort Republicans ran a full slate in the county with William Whipper for the senate heading the ticket. He lost 597 to 262. The three house candidates and the four county office aspirants were defeated by similar margins. In 1906 the Republicans tried again with candidates for three county offices; they all lost.[113] In 1910 the county was 87 percent black.[114]

Congressional races continued to attract Republican candidates, even with the new constitution in effect. In 1896 the Republicans ran one black candidate and six white candidates for the state's seven congressional seats. All of these candidates lost and then contested the results.[115] Only B. P. Chatfield and George Washington Murray had lawyers. Chatfield was represented by E. J. Dickerson and S. E. Smith.[116] George Washington Murray, the lone black candidate and the only incumbent, was represented before the state board by William Whipper, J. I. Washington, John B. Edwards, and Thaddeus K. Sasportas.[117] All of the losing candidates contested the validity of South Carolina's 1895 constitution on the theory that the new literacy requirements violated the federal Reconstruction statutes of 1868; the federal law prohibited the state from restricting the franchise except as to age, sex, and conviction for a felony. In addition, Murray's lawyers argued that the county election boards fraudulently denied the vote to eligible black voters and allowed unregistered whites to vote. Murray lost at the state board, which certified returns that were not dramatically different from those that had been overturned in 1894. According to the state board, Murray had lost Charleston County by nearly two thousand votes and had won Beaufort County by three votes.[118] After Murray lost before the state board, he appealed to Congress and emphasized the challenge to the state constitution in his protest filed with Congress.[119]

The challenge to the congressional committee based on the 1868 Reconstruction statute was remarkably prescient in light of the fact that federal legislation in the form of the 1965 Voting Rights Act would effectively void the state constitution's literacy clause. However, while ahead of its time, the argument was not entirely new. It was a variant of an argument employed by Thomas Miller in the contest over the 1888 election as well as that used by Judge Nathan Goff in *Mills v. Green*. The argument had special weight because without the 1868 constitution, the state would not have been readmitted to the Union. The argument was so persuasive that even the chief justice of the South Carolina Supreme Court dissented in an 1895 appeal by a white litigant because he believed the state's registration laws were in conflict with the 1868 state constitution.[120]

Now the South Carolina Republican challengers used the old argument to attack the validity of the 1895 constitution. In a similar challenge to a local election in Mississippi, that state's supreme court held in 1892 that the federal statute could not control the election laws of a state.[121] In 1896 the supremacy argument was again rejected in three congressional challenge cases brought by candidates from Mississippi.[122] It fared no better with the seven Republican congressional candidates from South Carolina, all of whose challenges failed in 1896.[123] Nevertheless, black candidates continued to run. In 1898, according to state election officials, Murray lost 3,030 to 1,529 and was overwhelmed in Charleston County 1,612 to 240.[124] Murray only carried one county in the district. His attorneys J. I. Washington and W. F. Myers appealed again to the state board. Myers, along with Jacob Moorer, another black attorney, also filed a challenge to the 1895 constitution on behalf of Seventh Congressional District candidate J. H. Weston.[125] The certified returns, which had Weston losing 4,433 to 505, demonstrate just how effective the effort had been to eliminate the black vote. For example, Weston's Democratic opponent was recorded as receiving 1,456 votes to Weston's 81 votes in the majority black county of Orangeburg.[126] Moorer also represented Alexander Dantzler in contesting the 1900 election of the Seventh Congressional District, asserting that the 1895 constitution was in conflict with the U.S. Constitution.[127] In Orangeburg County Dantzler was recorded as only receiving 153 out of 2,764 votes cast.[128] The state board was not persuaded in these cases, and despite the clear deprivation of the right to vote, Congress did not overturn the results.

Nevertheless, candidates and their lawyers continued their election challenges well into the twentieth century.[129] In 1902 J. L. Mitchell made the argument on behalf of Aaron Prioleau, a black Republican candidate.[130] The official congressional election results in 1902 were dismal. In the overwhelmingly black First Congressional District, Prioleau lost 3,749 to 175. Redistricting had moved Beaufort County to the second district, where the Republican candidate received 213 out of 663 votes cast in Beaufort. He had received two votes in Aiken, one in Saluda, and none in Hampton and Edgefield.[131]

Black lawyers William Whipper, Jacob Moorer, John B. Edwards, E. J. Dickerson, Edward F. Smith, T. St. Mark Sasportas, Julius Washington, and Julius Mitchell all filed challenges. These lawyers did not rely exclusively on the state constitution argument. They sometimes asserted fraud and in other cases made challenges on very technical grounds—like those whites had used against them before 1895. For example, John B. Edwards, Julius I. Washington, and Julius Mitchell contested the color, the size, and the print of the ballots on behalf of William Beckett in the First Congressional District in 1900.[132]

Julius L. Mitchell appeared before the Committee on Privileges and Elections of the Fifty-Eighth Congress on behalf of Aaron Prioleau. According to state election officials, Prioleau was defeated in the 1902 election by his white Democratic opponent by a vote of 3,749 to 175. Mitchell asserted that there were 28,000 black voters in the district. According to newspaper reports, he proved that 3,811 Republican voters were denied the right to vote on Election Day by Democratic poll managers.[133] Despite the evidence, Mitchell's client did not prevail.

In 1904 Edward F. Smith of Mount Pleasant represented Prioleau and confronted another tactic used by the whites to suppress the black vote. Smith appeared before the state board asserting that predominately black precincts had been closed for the election of 1904, thus preventing many blacks from voting.[134] In the 1904 Seventh Congressional District election contest, the Washington law firm of Dudley and Michener made the constitutional argument on behalf of the Republican candidate, but again it was to no avail.[135]

Also in 1904, Jacob Moorer represented the black Republican candidate in a protest in the Second Congressional District contest.[136] In a 1906 contest Moorer represented the Republican in the Seventh Congressional District contending improper counting and tabulation of votes.[137] In 1908 Moorer protested on behalf of R. H. Richardson in the Seventh Congressional District for unlawful rejection of votes.[138]

Jacob Moorer attacked the 1895 constitution in congressional challenge cases in both state court cases and in the U.S. Supreme Court. He never succeeded in overturning the state constitution, but he managed to provoke some startling responses. For example, in one case the attorney for the state of South Carolina argued that because secession from the Union was illegal and invalid, South Carolina had never in fact left the Union.[139] The closest Moorer came to a victory was a moral victory. Alexander Dantzler ran for Congress in 1902, and after he lost, Moorer filed a challenge. The congressional committee hearing the case agreed that the constitutional argument had validity but reasoned that Congress would have to deny seats to white congressmen all across the South if they granted Dantzler relief. Not willing to do so, the committee suggested the U.S. Supreme Court needed to consider the issue.[140] Awaiting an opportunity to take the issue before the Supreme Court, Moorer continued to contest congressional election results on behalf of black candidates through at least 1910.[141]

Aaron Prioleau of Orangeburg was still running for Congress in 1914, and he used the constitutional argument in his challenge to that election. The congressional committee declared that "the House has repeatedly decided against contestant [Prioleau] as to the contention he makes with regard to the constitution and election laws of South Carolina."[142] In 1920 T. St. Mark Sasportas, a black lawyer, and L. A. Hawkins, a black real estate agent, ran for congressional seats. After losing, they protested the election results to the State Board of Canvassers. They lost, but the state board's records contain no information on the basis of their challenges.[143] However, according to a newspaper account, Hawkins argued that certain persons were not allowed to register, which might indicate the challenge to the 1895 constitution was still being used as late as 1920.[144] There is no record of any appeal by either Sasportas or Hawkins to Congress. While some black candidates continued to run for both Congress and lesser offices over the next thirty years, the appeal to the U.S. Congress based on the Reconstruction statute was last heard in Prioleau's case.[145]

After nearly thirty years of challenges to the election laws, the 1895 constitution, and various elections, the scorecard for the challenges was not very good. Judge Nathan Goff had momentarily halted the state's election system, but his decision was soon overturned. The campaign to stop the new constitution had generated a lot of attention and some eloquent arguments against disenfranchisement. A few election challenges resulted in black Republicans winning. But by the early 1900s, South Carolina was firmly under the control of white supremacists, and the black majority had been subjugated to a point that no black held public office in the state. Consequently, black lawyers had little to show for their efforts.

CHAPTER 9

From the Great Migration to the Great Depression

After the new constitution was finalized on December 3, 1895, the white supremacists were firmly in control, and the future for the state's black citizens was even more ominous. The new constitution defined who was black. Even though it mandated separate schools for black and white children, the legislature felt it necessary to further codify racial divisions and exclusions.[1] The constitution declared interracial marriages "unlawful and void," and the legislature criminalized such unions.[2] In 1898 segregated seating on trains was mandated by statute.[3] In 1904 the General Assembly applied such restrictions to steamboats and ferries.[4] In 1906 segregated train depot dining facilities were required by the legislature, and in 1912 separate waiting rooms were mandated.[5] Streetcars were segregated by city ordinances, and the Charleston city council required seating at the back of the car for blacks. Historian I. A. Newby pointed out that such ordinances exempted black maids and nurses when they were attending whites because the purpose of the laws was not so much physical separation as it was "white supremacy."[6] The cotton mills were required by law to segregate their workforces in separate workrooms and to provide separate entrances. In fact, the cotton mills were in many respects the most segregated place in any community. The statute even specified that the stairwells of the factories could not be occupied or used by both races at the same time. Under no circumstances could black and white millworkers use the "same lavatories, toilets, drinking water buckets, pails, cups, dippers or glasses."[7] If segregation was mandated in the workplace, the white supremacists viewed recreation as a sphere that required just as much separation. When the circus came to town, its tents had to have separate entrances.[8] In larger counties, completely separate public parks had to be established.[9] Poolrooms had to be segregated and could only be operated by a member of the same race as the patrons.[10] In its mania to segregate every aspect of life, the legislature also segregated the chain gangs and the reformatory.[11]

Segregation in voting was imposed, too. Before the promulgation of the new constitution, the legislature and the Democratic Party had effectively segregated voting through the white primary.[12] Despite their successes, the white supremacists never seemed satisfied. Almost every legislative session passed a measure to tighten the electoral process.[13] Furthermore, despite all the legal provisions that disenfranchised blacks, physical intimidation and violence were still employed. In 1898, when Republican poll watchers tried to document how many blacks had been denied the right to vote in Greenwood County, a confrontation resulted in the death of one white Democrat and the injury of one white Republican. The white Democrats were enraged and the "Phoenix riot" ensued. For several days, a mob of whites searched for the Republicans and killed at least seven blacks.[14] The black community in the area was terrorized for months afterward.

Earlier in 1898, one of the most infamous incidents in the Jim Crow era happened in Lake City. A black man, Frazier B. Baker, had been appointed postmaster in the small town. Soon after, a white mob set fire to Baker's home. Frazier died in the fire, and his wife and three children were fired on as they fled. As the mother tried to carry their twelve-month-old daughter to safety, the infant was shot and killed. State authorities did nothing. The U.S. government arrested and charged eleven white men. After a weeklong trial in federal court, the jury could not reach a verdict and the murderers went free.[15] As one of the prosecutors commented, "human life [was] cheaper in South Carolina than four cent cotton."[16]

Unfortunately, that statement was all too true. Racial clashes and near riots occurred in Georgetown, Sumter, Columbia, Norway, Carlisle, Newberry, and Beaufort. In 1919 white U.S. Navy sailors went on a rampage in Charleston, killing three black men and wounding twenty-five.[17] Historian Leon Litwack described the era as "the most violent and repressive period in the history of race relations in the United States."[18] The most common form of racial violence was lynching, which became an almost commonplace horror in the state.[19] One of the most conservative of South Carolina's historians recorded a hundred lynchings between 1895 and 1930.[20]

The cumulative impact of the myriad aspects of the white supremacist state was devastating. The Great Migration is dated by historians as beginning in 1910. Blacks had been leaving South Carolina since 1877, but after 1895 the migration accelerated; in fact, it was so substantial that white farmers feared they would not have enough cheap labor. Some claimed that labor agents recruiting workers to move west were the cause, and in 1898 the state tried to restrict these "migrant agents."[21] Labor agents were simply a symptom, not the problem, and migration continued to increase. South Carolina saw an outmigration of more than 175,000 blacks between 1900 and 1910.[22]

Black lawyers were still practicing, but many were those who had been admitted before 1895. In 1868 William Whipper had become one of the first three black lawyers in the state's history. Whipper continued to practice and stay active in politics until his death in 1907. The 1900 murder trial of John Brownfield in Georgetown County was in many ways the most significant trial and appeal he ever undertook. (This case is discussed in depth in the next chapter.) The case arose when a white constable tried to arrest Brownfield for failure to pay his poll tax. Brownfield resisted, and the constable was killed. At the murder trial, Whipper and his co-counsel Julius Mitchell challenged the exclusion of blacks from the jury. Unfortunately, the all-white jury convicted their client. Brownfield's death sentence was affirmed by both the South Carolina Supreme Court and the U.S. Supreme Court.[23]

Despite the result in *Brownfield*, Whipper's reputation as a lawyer was never in doubt. In early May 1900 one of his clients, George Thomas, was arrested for raping a white woman in Hardeeville in Beaufort County.[24] Despite sharp words between Whipper and the governor of South Carolina over Thomas's confinement, the state's leading newspaper complimented the black lawyer on his "tactful and considerate" cross-examination of the white woman victim. The article described Whipper's effort thusly: "His cross-examination of Mrs. Doubleby, while it brought out all the facts possible for his client, was tactful and unobjectionable. The defense put up no testimony. Whipper, who is noted for his eloquence[,] started his address to the jury by stating that he would as soon think of turning a Bengal tiger or a Numidian lion upon a community as a man guilty of the crime of which Thomas stood accused. He rested his defense on the fact that Thomas had not been fully identified."[25] If Whipper had obtained a not guilty verdict, the press probably would not have been so complimentary. The same newspaper the next year described William Whipper as the "Eloquent Negro Lawyer" in his wife's obituary, and Frances Rollin Whipper was described as "remarkably intelligent, of estimable character, and a fine writer."[26]

However, William Whipper's portrayal by the press was inconsistent. In 1902 he was criticized for supposedly counseling and aiding a client to resist arrest. The newspaper account, titled "Whipper Counsels Lawbreaking," claimed that Whipper was arrested with the approval of the black community.[27] There is no other record of the arrest, and the actual sentiment of the community toward Whipper is probably better illustrated by the fact that he was the Republican Party nominee for state senate from the county in 1904. The last case that Whipper tried was the murder trial of Robert Mack in 1906, but the result was not the desired end for the seventy-year-old lawyer's long career. His client was found guilty; however, the jury did recommend mercy, which meant his client was spared the death penalty.[28] Mack's appeal was undertaken by a white lawyer who asserted that Whipper's ill health and feeble physical condition before and during the trial had prevented him from properly representing his client. The state supreme court was not sympathetic to the argument, saying, "Jealous as the courts should always be that the rights of the ignorant and lowly should not be lost through ignorance and incapacity, the alleged sickness of the defendant's counsel is not a sufficient reason for suspending this appeal. [Whipper] is recognized as a man of capacity and experience and he went to trial without asking for a continuance or even mentioning his indisposition to the circuit court."[29] The court issued its order on July 16, 1907, and William James Whipper died July 29, 1907.[30] Despite Whipper's long career, no notice of his death has been found in any newspaper.

After 1895 the only other black lawyer in Beaufort was Julius Washington, who did not open his law office until 1911.[31] While it was reported that he built up a "good practice," Washington had only one appellate case. However, it was a complicated and financially significant case in which Washington persuaded the trial judge and ultimately the state's highest court to award $20,071 to an Odd Fellows lodge from the receiver of an insolvent bank.[32] Julius died in January 1938. His son, Charles E. Washington, had joined him in practice in 1924, creating the first multigenerational black law firm in the state.[33] Charles, who had graduated from Howard University School of Law, would practice in Beaufort until his death in 1967.[34] His legal work as well as his community activities and advocacy for equal treatment of blacks attracted the attention of the black press.[35] In one instance, he wrote to the editor complaining that the white school board in Beaufort was taking money from the black schools and spending it on white schools.[36]

William Fabriel Myers had been admitted in 1875. After Reconstruction, he was a federal government employee but remained active in Colleton County politics.[37] In 1897 he was co-counsel in an election contest representing a Republican candidate before Congress.[38] While he and his co-counsel did not succeed in having the candidate seated, the House of Representatives voted to declare the seat vacant, denying the Democrat a seat.[39] In 1903 Myers was convicted in federal court of receiving an illegal fee in a pension claim case and fined five dollars, but the conviction did not hinder him from practicing law or from remaining active in politics.[40] He addressed the Negro Business League convention in 1910 and read the Emancipation Proclamation at a Lincoln Memorial Association meeting in Columbia in 1913.[41] Myers was living in Columbia at the time of his death in 1917.[42] Another Colleton County lawyer, John F. Brown, who was admitted in 1884, practiced in Colleton County after 1895 until at least 1913.[43]

Another Reconstruction-era lawyer who continued practicing into the new century was Thomas J. Miller. The former congressman, state senator, state representative, and constitutional convention delegate remained an active lawyer and leader into the 1920s. In 1896 Miller was appointed president of the newly created college in Orangeburg for black students, the Colored Normal, Industrial, Agricultural, and Mechanical College of South Carolina.[44] The school grew under Miller's leadership. He also practiced law during his tenure as president. In correspondence from 1910, he reported he was associated with a white lawyer in a "$10,000 case."[45] In another letter, Miller complained that he had not had the time to properly prepare for the four cases he had to argue in court in January 1911.[46] These included two cases in Beaufort, one in Hampton County, and an oral argument in the state supreme court. The appeal was a civil matter that was decided in his client's favor in March 1911.[47]

The most significant legal matter undertaken by Miller was the Pink Franklin case. (A full discussion of this case follows in chapter 10.) After the U.S. Supreme Court affirmed Franklin's conviction and death sentence, Miller was contacted by the new civil rights organization, the NAACP, to explore a means to save Franklin's life. Miller said he thought the governor could be persuaded to pardon Franklin. With the NAACP's support, Miller worked tirelessly for weeks and ultimately convinced the governor to commute Franklin's death sentence.

Cole Blease was the governor-elect during the time Miller was working to save Franklin's life. In the gubernatorial election, Miller had publicly opposed Blease, a notorious racist on a par with Ben Tillman. After Miller's public efforts to save Franklin, Blease forced him to resign as president of the college in June 1911.[48] Miller moved to Charleston to practice law and handled both civil and criminal cases. He took three appeals to the state supreme court and handled one case with an estate of more than $200,000.[49] Miller was also active with the NAACP in Charleston. In 1919 he led an effort to convince the state legislature to reserve all teaching positions in the black schools in Charleston for black teachers and to forbid whites from teaching in these schools. Miller's committee collected signatures from five thousand black families. When Miller presented the petition, he was permitted to make a formal presentation to a legislative committee, and his efforts resulted in a positive response by the legislature.[50] Miller moved to Philadelphia in 1923 but returned to Charleston in 1934 and died there on April 8, 1938.[51]

After 1895, Edward J. Dickerson of Aiken continued to handle criminal and civil cases in the state courts.[52] In addition to his state court practice, he represented a Republican congressional candidate in an election contest.[53] In that case, he was opposed by former governor John C. Sheppard.[54] An active Republican, Dickerson was a delegate to the 1900 Republican National Convention.[55] In his obituary in 1903, Dickerson was identified as the lone black lawyer in Aiken and the surrounding area.[56]

One of the few lawyers who stayed in Charleston was Robert C. Browne. He had practiced with John Freeman in Charleston and Berkeley Counties before 1892 and was associated with Samuel J. Lee in Berkeley County in the 1890s, but he had no cases on the civil or criminal docket in Berkeley County after 1895. He was listed in the city directory as an "Attorney at Law" in 1902. Browne died in the city in 1915.[57]

Thaddeus St. Mark Sasportas was admitted in 1895, having read law with Samuel J. Lee. Sasportas started law practice in Charleston with John B. Edwards.[58] He moved to Georgetown in 1901 and had an active practice there until 1914.[59] Between 1901 and 1908, he had thirteen criminal trials and thirteen civil cases on the docket in Georgetown.[60] He returned to Charleston in 1915 and practiced there for more than twenty years.[61] During his career he took eleven appeals to the state supreme court and won two.[62] Sasportas was active in the Republican Party and ran for Congress in 1920.[63] During the Depression, he was the only black lawyer still practicing in Charleston.[64] He died October 12, 1937.[65]

As the nineteenth century came to an end, Charleston saw a brief upsurge in its black bar. Edward R. Culler was admitted in 1896 and practiced with Julius Mitchell and Eugene Hayne. However, he soon moved to Philadelphia and became a schoolteacher.[66] Eugene Hayne, admitted in 1897, was practicing in New York City by 1903.[67] Two other new Charleston lawyers, John A. Gaillard and Mark A. Williams, were admitted in 1897. Both attended law school in North Carolina. Williams, a native of North Carolina, returned there and was teaching in Raleigh in 1900.[68] Gaillard practiced law in Charleston until at least 1910. He had one appeal to the South Carolina Supreme Court.[69] Admitted in 1899, Alonzo E. Twine practiced in Charleston and Berkeley Counties with Eugene Hayne, Robert C. Browne, and Jacob Moorer and had three cases in the state supreme court.[70] Twine was a convert to the Baha'i faith, and because of his conversion, his former Methodist pastor had him committed to the state mental hospital, where he died at the age of thirty-six in 1914.[71] Edward F. Smith from Mount Pleasant in Charleston County was admitted in 1901. He had one criminal case in the state's highest court, which he lost, and he had a few civil cases on the docket in Berkeley County in 1920 and 1921.[72] Also admitted in 1901, Daniel B. Summers practiced in Charleston and Berkeley Counties. He had civil cases on the docket in Berkeley from 1912 to 1919 and handled a Charleston County case where his client was sentenced to death for killing a chain gang guard.[73] Summers was nearly lynched when he traveled to Florida to defend a client accused of killing a white man.[74] In one of his last cases, Summers along with Jacob Moorer represented Clinton Glover in Dorchester County. He was convicted of attempted assault of a white woman and sentenced to death. They appealed on several grounds, including the fact that the prosecutor commented on Glover's failure to testify, but the state supreme court found no error.[75] Summers died on March 30, 1915.[76]

Butler Nance, who had been admitted to the bar in 1890, taught in Fairfield County and then moved to Columbia in 1897 to work for the post office.[77] In Columbia Nance became active in civic affairs and led the effort to form the Capital Civic League, the city's first civil rights advocacy group. Within less than a year, the league was invited to join the NAACP, becoming an official chapter two years later in 1917.[78] As chapter president, Nance assisted the black community of Charleston in petitioning the state legislature to mandate the school board to hire black public schoolteachers for black children.[79] Nance used his legal education in his civil rights work and kept the national NAACP informed of the efforts of South Carolina blacks to assert their civil rights across the state. Two ministers were assaulted while trying to register to vote, and the national office became very interested in taking action. In the end, little could be done because, as Nance reported, the men would not give affidavits for fear of reprisal.[80] Led by fellow Allen graduate Green Jackson, Nance and the NAACP registered several hundred black voters in 1919, and Nance proudly reported to the national organization that black men were being called for jury duty.[81] In the fall of 1920 Nance sued the county voter registrar on behalf of thirty-two women who were denied the right to register to vote.[82] Nance's letterhead indicated that he was available to appear in "all Courts" and that his practice was limited to wills, real estate, and similar civil matters.[83] He had three appeals in the state supreme court.[84] He died February 19, 1923.[85]

William Trent Andrews of Sumter graduated from Fisk University in Tennessee and Howard University School of Law.[86] Admitted to the bar in 1894, Andrews was a prominent businessman and entrepreneur. His letterhead listed his commercial activities as law, real estate, and loans.[87] He operated a Sumter newspaper, served as a teacher and school principal, partnered with E. J. Sawyer in a real estate company, operated an icehouse and a mercantile store, and owned sixty houses and thirteen commercial buildings and stores.[88] He appears to have had a limited law practice; the only time his name appeared in a court decision was in connection to property he owned.[89]

Andrews was outspoken and active in both politics and civic life. In 1895 his notary commission was revoked by the governor because Andrews was helping register black voters.[90] Later that year Andrews helped organize a mass meeting in Sumter to protest the constitutional convention. He drafted a resolution adopted by the group that called the actions of the convention the work of "despotic demagogues."[91] Andrews was outspoken in editorials, in speeches to race conferences, and in a speech he was invited to give in Seattle, Washington on conditions in the South.[92] He was a Mason and a member of the Knights of Pythias, and he advocated for a reformatory for black youth.[93] As a Republican, he twice served as a delegate to the Republican National Convention.[94] He was on the executive committee of Booker T. Washington's National Negro Business League.[95] He chaired the arrangements committee when Booker T. Washington visited Sumter in 1909.[96] In 1911 not only was he was one of fifty black lawyers who formed the National Negro Bar Association, but he was also elected its treasurer.[97] Andrews wrote to the NAACP in 1914 concerning the lynching of Rosa Carson in Elloree, South Carolina.[98] In 1916 he helped the NAACP protest the lynching of Anthony Crawford in Abbeville, South Carolina. Crawford was a relatively wealthy black man who was lynched because he had the temerity to strike back when he was attacked by a white man. Roy Nash of the NAACP visited Abbeville to investigate and then asked Andrews to provide some legal research on lynching for him.[99] In a 1917 speech titled "The Causes of Negro Migration from the South," Andrews used the Crawford lynching to illustrate the horrors that were leading to the Great Migration.[100] Historian Lester C. Lamon has opined that Andrews was so perceptive in his speech that historians with the benefit of time, hindsight, and professional training have added little to the analysis of the causes of migration out of the South.[101] It is ironic that Andrews soon left South Carolina and moved to Baltimore, where he became the publisher and editor of the *Daily Herald* newspaper.[102]

S. S. Davis was the only black lawyer in Darlington County. Admitted in 1898, he practiced there and in Florence and Sumter Counties.[103] His law practice appears to have been limited to civil work. He brought two lawsuits against railroads in Sumter County in 1905 but lost both.[104] His only two appeals were a foreclosure case and a land partition action from Darlington County. He lost both of them in the state supreme court.[105]

Green Jackson was the last Allen Law School graduate to be admitted to the South Carolina bar. Jackson earned a living by practicing law, farming, teaching, and publishing a newspaper.[106] He was active in politics, church, innumerable civic organizations, and law practice.[107] Most importantly, he was very active with the NAACP in Columbia and registered hundreds of black voters in 1919.[108] Jackson still had a law office in 1929 but had retired by 1930.[109]

Marion J. Frederick graduated from Claflin University in 1900 and moved to Sumter in 1902 to teach in the Lincoln Graded School.[110] With whom he read law is not known. He gained admission to the bar on May 8, 1903.[111] A biographical sketch of Frederick published in 1919 reported that he had built up a "lucrative practice and is working out a large measure of success."[112] The first record of his practice is a 1907 case against a railroad.[113] Between 1906 and 1922, he had nineteen civil cases on the docket and handled numerous real estate transactions.[114] He also handled some minor criminal cases.[115] He had four appeals to the state supreme court, three civil and one criminal.[116] Frederick had co-counsel in two of his civil appeals, his brother Nathaniel in one and Jacob Moorer in both. Like W. T. Andrews, Frederick invested in real estate.[117] He and Andrews were both officers of a dry goods company, and both lawyers were on the committee that hosted Booker T. Washington in his visit to Sumter in 1909.[118] Frederick was active in a number of businesses, including a cotton gin cooperative and a bottling company.[119] His civic activities included the church, a farmer's association, World War patriotic organizations, the YMCA, the Sumter Colored Fair Association, the Urban League, and the Afro-American Improvement Association.[120] He was a Republican.[121] He and his wife moved to Cleveland, where he died in 1936.[122]

A Georgia native, John Adams was admitted in 1905.[123] He attended Lincoln University, Yale Divinity School, and Gammons Theological Seminary in Atlanta. Adams practiced primarily as a criminal defense lawyer in Columbia and Manning. In one case, Arthur Wright was tried for killing two men, and Adams was able to convince the jury to convict him only of manslaughter.[124] In a court-appointed case, the jury found his client not guilty.[125] When he and Jacob Moorer undertook the representation of Pink Franklin in 1907, Adams was a professor at Allen University. Franklin's was not the only case in which Adams and Moorer challenged all-white juries. In 1908 the two lawyers represented Henry Gloster on murder charges in Orangeburg. Their jury challenge failed, but they did manage to convince the jury to convict their client only of manslaughter.[126] Adams also tried a murder case in Fairfield County in 1908, and while it is unknown whether he challenged the jury composition, his client was saved from the death penalty by a recommendation of mercy from the jury.[127] After the Franklin case ended, Adams left the state and moved west. Adams told his son that he "was driven out of town by whites because of his unyielding advocacy for the rights of black people."[128] Adams practiced law in Washington and Colorado before settling in Omaha, Nebraska, in the early 1920s.[129] In Omaha he was a successful lawyer, a state senator, an active member of the NAACP, and a nationally prominent AME minister.[130]

Jacob Moorer, born during the Civil War, practiced law in Orangeburg from 1896 until his death in 1935.[131] He was a Voorhees College trustee, a Mason, a member of the Knights of Pythias, and an unsuccessful Republican candidate for the state house of representatives.[132] But he was a lawyer first and foremost. Moorer had a well-developed law practice and was an effective appellate advocate. He won five of twenty appeals he argued in the supreme court of South Carolina.[133] His earliest recorded case was in November 1898, when he appeared before the State Board of Canvassers on behalf of a black Republican candidate for Congress.[134] Over the next decade, he challenged numerous elections.[135] His innovative arguments, developed in those election cases, would serve as the primary basis for the appeal of Pink Franklin's conviction. His wife was a remarkable woman and also an advocate for civil rights. Lizelia Augusta Jenkins Moorer, a librarian at Claflin University in Orangeburg, taught African history and was a published poet.[136] Her volume *Prejudice Unveiled*, published in Boston in 1907, addressed prejudice, peonage, voting, juries, lynching, Jim Crow laws, and injustice in the courts.[137] Her poetry has been described by one modern commentator as "the best poems on racial issues written by any black woman until the middle of the [twentieth] century."[138]

Nathaniel J. Frederick was thirty-six years old when he was admitted to the bar in 1913.[139] He may have read law with his brother Marion in Sumter. Without question Frederick was one of the best-educated lawyers in the state. He held bachelor's degrees from Claflin College and the University of Wisconsin as well as master's degrees from Claflin and Benedict College in Columbia. Until 1915, his major source of income came from service as principal of Howard School in Columbia, one of the largest African American schools in the South.[140] While still principal of the school, Frederick opened a law office in 1914. He was an active Republican and served as a delegate to national conventions on multiple occasions.[141] He organized one of two black-controlled banks in the state and served as editor of two newspapers, the *Southern Indicator* and the *Palmetto Leader*.[142] His editorials advocated for civil rights and gave "voice to the anti-lynching crusade in South Carolina."[143] The *Palmetto Leader* kept its readership apprised of every important civil rights issue and case in the state and the nation.[144] The publisher of the newspaper, George H. Hampton, described his editor as "fearless."[145]

He had the opportunity to demonstrate his fearless and relentless advocacy in one of his first cases. In Bogus Sanders's trial in 1915, he and Jacob Moorer challenged the exclusion of blacks from their client's jury as well as the admitted racial prejudice of a potential juror.[146] That same year, Frederick was assaulted by a white constable. Frederick swore out a warrant against the officer, who was subsequently charged with assault and battery of a high and aggravated nature. Despite evidence that he had used a gun in the assault, the constable was only convicted of simple assault and fined.[147] Frederick had more success in defending a client accused of assaulting a police officer on a trolley car. John Caster had allegedly created a disturbance on the trolley, and the policeman, who was dressed in civilian clothes, attempted to arrest him. Caster, who was black, resisted and was shot by the white policeman. Frederick was able to convince the court that Caster had a right to defend himself, and the trial judge directed a verdict of not guilty.[148]

Frederick also handled many less dramatic civil cases. His clients included Dr. Matilda Evans, the first black woman medical doctor in South Carolina. From 1926 to 1930, he obtained nineteen judgments in civil cases in Richland County.[149] By the end of his career Frederick had appeared before the South Carolina Supreme Court thirty-three times, more than any other black lawyer.[150] All but four of these cases were civil matters. Of these cases, he won nine out of twenty-nine cases.[151]

His criminal appeal success rate exceeded that of his civil appeals. Although he handled only four criminal appeals, he won three of them and lost the fourth in an *en banc* decision.[152] In *State v. Sanders*, Frederick and Jacob Moorer succeeded in overturning their client's murder conviction and death sentence.[153] (*Sanders* is discussed in detail in chapter 10.) Two other criminal cases drew national attention. In the *Lowman* appeal, he represented a brother, a sister, and their cousin who had been convicted of murdering the Aiken County sheriff.[154] At their trial, the defendants had been represented by locally appointed white lawyers. The young men had been sentenced to death, and the young woman had received a life sentence. In a trial marked by threats of mob violence, the judge had charged the jury not to blame the white lawyers for their defense of the Lowmans. This charge in part led to the reversal that Frederick obtained for his clients. A unanimous court ordered a new trial. At the retrial, Frederick was assisted by a white lawyer, and they obtained a directed verdict of acquittal for Demond Lowman. The expectation was that a similar result would be had the next day for Bertha Lowman and her cousin, Clarence. Unfortunately, Demond

Lowman was immediately rearrested, and that evening of October 8, 1926, all three Lowmans were dragged from the county jailed and lynched.[155] Despite local and national editorial campaigns and three grand jury investigations, no one was ever brought to trial.[156]

In late 1926 Frederick began to reorganize the NAACP chapter in Columbia, which had grown dormant after the death of Butler Nance.[157] The local branch and the national organization provided assistance to Frederick with important cases such as the Ben Bess case. Unlike the Lowman case, the Bess case had a positive ending. Ben Bess had been convicted of the sexual assault of a white woman and had served thirteen years of a thirty-year sentence, but in 1928 the alleged victim recanted her testimony.[158] Using the recantation, Frederick obtained a commutation of Bess's sentence and a full pardon from Governor John G. Richards on May 4, 1928. After threats of prosecution for perjury, the alleged victim recanted her recantation, whereupon the governor attempted to withdraw his pardon and had Bess arrested.[159] Frederick immediately filed a habeas corpus petition. Frederick recruited A. L. King, a white lawyer, to assist him at the hearing because of the necessity of cross-examining the white woman. Circuit judge W. H. Townsend was assigned the case, and he appointed Richland County's master in equity to make a factual investigation to determine if Bess's pardon had been obtained by fraud. The master found no fraud, but Judge Townsend disagreed and refused to order the release of Bess. Frederick and King appealed to the South Carolina Supreme Court, challenging the right of the governor to revoke a pardon. The supreme court sat *en banc* with all the circuit court judges of the state and ruled 10 to 8 that the governor could not revoke his pardon.[160] Frederick had already made plans for Bess to leave the state to avoid any possibility of another Lowman tragedy, and when the decision was announced, Bess immediately boarded a train and departed the state.[161]

Frederick's lone loss in a criminal appeal was the case of *State v. Floyd*.[162] Clarence Floyd was charged with the rape of a white woman in Lexington County, a serious event in an ultraconservative, overwhelmingly white county. Because of the fears that a mob would storm the county jail, the sheriff called in law enforcement officers from outside the county to keep the peace.[163] When the trial began, four local white lawyers were appointed to represent Floyd.

The story of John D. Sutton and the alleged rape victim, Mary Cannon, was rife with suspicious circumstances. Cannon was separated from her husband, and Sutton had a wife and child at home. Sutton said he was giving Cannon a ride home, but they were on an isolated dirt road miles from her home. Sutton explained that as a salesman and collector for a furniture store, he worked at night, and that while he was giving Miss Cannon a ride he had to call on a customer. Cannon testified in a secret session of court that she lived in Columbia, in an adjacent county, and that on the evening in question she left home with Sutton because he was giving her a ride to see her father and then to a drugstore. If they had done what Cannon claimed, the pair would have driven about two miles to her father's workplace on Main Street and then seven blocks north on Main Street to a drugstore. But instead, they drove west from Columbia across the Congaree River to Brookland Village in Lexington County. Sutton testified that after seeing the customer, he stopped to light a cigarette when Floyd walked up and pulled a gun on him. Initially, Sutton claimed that he was robbed and then tied up while Floyd raped Cannon.[164] At the trial, Sutton changed his story and testified that Floyd simply held a gun on him during the rape. Moreover, after the incident, Sutton had reported that they were robbed but made no mention of the alleged rape. Sutton and Cannon reported the rape only after Floyd was arrested two days later. Floyd's court-appointed lawyers tried to cast suspicion on the relationship of Sutton and Cannon but never asked any questions about the improbability of driving into Lexington County when all Cannon needed was to go to Main Street in Columbia to see her father and then go to the drugstore.

In Floyd's defense, the lawyers called Floyd and four alibi witnesses. Floyd testified that he had worked for Sutton stealing cars and that Sutton "had it in for him" because Floyd had stolen money from him. Floyd claimed he spent the night in question at a boardinghouse with a woman who verified his story. Other witnesses testified they saw Floyd the next morning in the boardinghouse. The final witness was H. C. Oswald, the sheriff of Lexington County, who contradicted Sutton and said he definitely told him that Floyd had tied his hands behind his back.[165] After two hours of deliberation, the jury returned a verdict of guilty, and the judge imposed a sentence of death.[166]

Following the verdict, Floyd's court-appointed lawyers made no motions for a directed verdict or a new trial, nor did they appeal.[167] Despite the failure of these white lawyers to preserve Floyd's appellate rights, Nathaniel J. Frederick filed an appeal attacking the veracity of the white "victims" and asserted that the state had failed to carry its burden on disproving the defendant's alibi.

Although the appeal was filed in September 1933, the case was not heard until June 13, 1934, and the opinion was not issued until November 27, 1934.[168] The appeal was heard by an *en banc* panel that included the five justices of the supreme court and twelve circuit court judges. The only circuit court judge not to sit on the panel was the trial judge. Although Frederick had had an *en banc* court in the Ben Bess case, it was unusual for the state supreme court to convene such a court.[169] The state constitution allowed the court wide latitude in calling for such a hearing. All that was required was for two justices to request such a panel.[170] Unfortunately, there is no record of which justices requested the large panel, and no record of their reasons.

Frederick lost the *Floyd* case thirteen to four with two circuit judges and two supreme court justices dissenting.[171] The four dissenters may very well have thought that Floyd was innocent, but their opinions nevertheless reflected the white racism of the time overlaid with a layer of male chauvinism. Justice Milledge L. Bonham's opinion, which was joined by acting justice W. C. Cothran and two circuit court judges (C. J. Ramage and Philip H. Stoll), condemned Sutton: "I am not willing to believe that any white man, however weak and cowardly he may be, would have acted as the male prosecuting witness in this case swore he did." Bonham hinted that Cannon and Sutton had a motive to lie, but he did not directly call them liars. In contrast, Justice Cothran bluntly stated that Sutton and Cannon were lying, but he also believed that Floyd lied. Soon Floyd's date of execution was set, and no further appeals followed.[172] The twenty-year-old Floyd, still proclaiming his innocence, was executed in the state's electric chair on Sunday, January 4, 1935.[173]

In 1936 another of Frederick's clients was sentenced to death. Irvin Brown was convicted of murdering a white insurance salesman. The two men had argued over a twenty-cent refund on an insurance policy. Despite testimony that the salesman had attacked Brown, the jury convicted Frederick's client in fifteen minutes.[174] While his appeal was pending before the state supreme court, Brown died of pneumonia.[175]

Frederick never had a precedent-setting civil rights case, but for three decades as a lawyer and editor he advocated for civil rights, in particular the right to vote.[176] Frederick was one of the founders of the Columbia NAACP chapter and remained active with the civil rights organization throughout his career.[177] In April 1932 Frederick brought the first suit in the state's history challenging the white primary. Initially, his clients had been allowed to register, but the Board of Commissioners of Elections notified the men that they had to show that they had voted the Democratic tickets continuously since 1876 or their names would be stricken from the rolls because they were "of the negro race."[178] Frederick sought an injunction, but his motion was denied by state circuit court judge W. H. Townsend, and the primary proceeded the next day, with Frederick's clients not being permitted to vote. Frederick then sought relief in the federal court, but Judge J. Lyles Glenn refused to issue an injunction, declaring the case moot.[179] In a June letter, James Marshall, the NAACP's attorney in *Nixon v. Herndon*, suggested that Frederick bring a civil suit for damages.

Frederick demurred, noting that the whole issue would soon be moot as the state Democratic Party was seeking to have the legislature repeal all laws related to the primary.

In June 1932 Frederick was appointed to the National Legal Committee of the NAACP.[180] Also invited at the same time were such prominent men as Charles Houston, Louis Redding, and Jesse Heslip.[181] Heslip was president of the National Bar Association; Redding was a Harvard graduate and the first black lawyer in Delaware; Houston was dean of Howard Law School.[182] Writing in 1935, Charles Houston said Frederick was one of only three black lawyers in the South willing to do civil rights work. In 1935 National Bar Association secretary Thurgood Marshall announced that Frederick was appointed deputy regional director of the association.[183]

During his time, Frederick was the most active and successful African American lawyer in the state. Despite his successes, however, he died nearly destitute in September 1938.[184] His obituary in the *New York Amsterdam News* quoted him as stating, "God has made men that could whip me, but he has never made a man that I am afraid of."[185] Without Frederick, the state's capital city no longer had a black lawyer.

Between 1919 and 1924, a small group of lawyers educated at northern law schools were admitted to the state bar. Three were Howard graduates: Charles E. Washington (discussed above), Shadrack Morgan, and Herbert McGirt. William A. Dart and A. Chester Platt were graduates of Boston University. Dart and McGirt had very brief careers in the state. William Dart, a graduate of Boston University School of Law, was admitted in 1919. He was also admitted in Massachusetts in 1919 and New Jersey in 1920.[186] Under the tutelage of T. St. Mark Sasportas, Dart tried one case in Charleston, which he won but which was reversed on appeal.[187] He left Charleston and for a time was an assistant attorney general in New Jersey.[188] Herbert F. McGirt graduated from Howard University Law School and was admitted to the bar in 1922.[189] One newspaper described McGirt as "an ex-service man. . . . He is a very polite young colored man and has a number of friends, both white and colored, who wish him well in his profession."[190] McGirt was one of the Kershaw County delegates to the Republican State Convention in 1922.[191] There is no record of McGirt practicing law. He was arrested and convicted of arson in 1925, but his conviction was overturned by the state supreme court.[192] It appears he died in 1927.[193]

Like Dart, Arthur Chester Platt graduated from Boston University Law School.[194] Unlike Dart, Platt practiced in South Carolina for close to two decades. Admitted in 1922, Platt was the first African American lawyer in upstate

South Carolina.[195] He won two out of his four cases in the South Carolina Supreme Court.[196] Platt was reported to retain white co-counsel when he tried a case, but the two appeals he lost were ones with white co-counsel.[197] Despite the hard times of the Depression, he had some success in practice as counsel to Piedmont Building and Loan Association, and he owned his office and a home valued at $6,000.[198]

Platt also worked with the NAACP in the Upstate. In 1926 he contacted the NAACP on behalf of Jim Davis, who was accused of killing a white policeman. After Davis was tried and convicted of murder, the NAACP provided funds to help with his appeal and the subsequent retrial. Platt apparently made the effort to obtain the funds solely out of hope that Davis's life could be saved, since a white lawyer was representing Davis.[199] In 1927 Platt urged the NAACP to support the nomination of South Carolina's governor, Thomas G. McLeod, to the Federal Trade Commission.[200] Platt's support had been sought to show black support for the governor even though he had failed to act to prevent a lynching in the Lowman case. In a letter to Walter White of the NAACP, a New York lawyer described Platt as having been "hoodwinked."[201] The NAACP opposed McLeod's appointment, which did not succeed. In 1939, when a local hospital laid off its black nurses to create positions for white nurses, the Spartanburg Negro Civic League protested, and Platt was credited with saving the jobs of all the black nurses.[202] Platt died sometime before 1951; when Matthew J. Perry came to Spartanburg to practice, Annie Belle Platt, A. C.'s widow, gave the new lawyer her late husband's law books.[203]

The most prominent of the out-of-state law school graduates was Howard graduate Shadrack Morgan. Admitted in 1919, he was the grandson of a Reconstruction-era legislator.[204] Morgan practiced in Orangeburg and was often associated with Jacob Moorer and N. J. Frederick on cases. Between 1926 and 1939, he had eight civil cases on the circuit court dockets, three criminal cases, and two appeals to the state supreme court.[205] After the death of Nathaniel J. Frederick, Morgan served as the local counsel for the NAACP and was often consulted on South Carolina cases.[206] In 1939 Thurgood Marshall consulted Morgan about Charles B. Bailey's application to attend the University of South Carolina School of Law. In 1945 Thurgood Marshall recruited Morgan to serve as co-counsel in a teacher pay equalization case.[207] *Thompson v. Gibbes* did in fact result in equalized pay for black teachers.[208] Morgan died in 1962.[209]

The last lawyer admitted in the 1920s was not a law school graduate. Allen University professor Esau Allen Parker may have read law with Nathaniel J. Frederick and was admitted in 1924.[210] Parker started a newspaper in Sumter, the *People's Informer*, and according to civil rights activist Modjeska Simkins, he handled cases for black and white clients and was an early proponent of the NAACP.[211] His law practice was limited, and his only involvement in any appellate work was a case in which he served as executor of an estate.[212] Parker became ill in 1941 and retired. But he was coaxed out of retirement to serve as local counsel for the NAACP in *Wrighten v. Board of Trustees of the University of South Carolina*, which sought to desegregate USC's law school.[213] Parker had one other appeal, a foreclosure action against a church.[214] He died in 1963.

Beginning in 1899, the bar admissions of black lawyers began to decline. Only one black lawyer was admitted per year in 1899, 1900, 1901, 1903, and 1905. None were admitted in 1902 or 1904. No one was admitted again until 1913, followed by a drought until 1919, when two lawyers were admitted. Then two lawyers were admitted in 1922 and 1924. After 1924 no one was admitted until 1940.

The decline in the bar is consistent with the diminishing African American population in the state and in most of the South. For example, from 1900 until 1940 the white population of the state grew 94 percent, from 557,000 to 1,084,000; however, the black population grew by only 4 percent, from 782,000 to 814,000. In contrast, from 1890 to 1900 the state's black population had grown by 14 percent. But by the 1920s there was negative growth. Historian Walter Edgar described the 1920s in South Carolina as the "Draining Years."[215] Numerous factors accelerated the population decrease in the 1920s. Despite their service in World War I, returning veterans saw little hope and promise. Continued lynchings and race riots threw a pall over the hope of a more just and safe society.[216] The Nineteenth Amendment gave the vote to women, but voter registration efforts on behalf of black women were defeated just as they were for black men. The Ku Klux Klan returned to the state. The white community was as antagonistic as ever. Walter Edgar quotes Congressman James F. Byrnes as reflecting the attitude of the white community when he said, "The war has in no way changed the attitude of the white man toward the social and political equality of the negro." Moreover, although the Roaring Twenties were a time of substantial economic growth across the nation, South Carolina was suffering from the boll weevil, which devastated the cotton crop beginning in 1921. Cotton did not recover during the entire decade, and wages for cotton pickers had declined by half in 1930. The textile industry was expanding in the state, but it was an industry that offered few if any jobs to blacks. Educational opportunities were almost nonexistent. In the first five years of the 1920s, not a single black was awarded a high school diploma by the state.[217]

The cumulative effect of all of these factors led to the migration of thousands of blacks out of South Carolina, including 25 percent of the state's black lawyers. Of the thirty-eight lawyers discussed in this chapter, ten left the state and the region. Two others returned to Georgia and North Carolina, their home states. Of the ten who moved north and west, seven first tried practicing law in South Carolina but then migrated to better opportunities outside the South. Clearly, Jim Crow and poverty came together with a vengeance, and by 1930 there were no more than a handful of black lawyers still practicing in the state.

However, those who remained were some of the ablest and strongest advocates for civil rights. Jacob Moorer tried and appealed such cases as Pink Franklin's, one of the most important cases in the state's civil rights history. For fifteen years, Moorer would be the leading advocate for civil rights in the state. Two lawyers admitted in the 1890s, Butler Nance and Green Jackson, helped start the first NAACP chapter in state. In 1913 Nathaniel J. Frederick was admitted. Frederick tried some of the most important cases and for a time was identified as the only black lawyer in the state who would undertake a civil rights case. He had more positive impact for the rights of the black community than any other lawyer admitted in the first quarter of the twentieth century.

So while the era began under the shadow of the Jim Crow constitution and ended with the smallest number of black lawyers since 1868, a foundation for the future had been laid. Moorer and Frederick won few cases, but they offered hope to the community and demonstrated that the battle for equal rights was not over.

CHAPTER 10

All-White Juries and the Continuing Struggle for Voting Rights

The impact of the all-white jury on black defendants and the hypocrisy of the white-dominated judiciary of the state were on full display when trial judge Hayne P. Rice sentenced James "Bogus" Sanders to death in 1915. Judge Rice said, "Bogus, my advice to you is to prepare for death and make peace with your God. You have been given full opportunity to clear yourself; you have been given a fair trial, just as fair as if you had been the most prominent white man in the State, and I think you were justly convicted. You are sentenced to be electrocuted within the walls of the State penitentiary on Friday, July 16, between the hours of 10 a.m. and 2 p.m.; and may God have mercy on your soul."[1] Fortunately for Sanders, he was represented by Jacob Moorer and Nathaniel J. Frederick. While they failed to persuade Judge Rice that blacks had been intentionally excluded from Sanders's jury, they would successfully appeal his case and eventually save him from the electric chair.

Judge Rice's claim of equal justice for black defendants was a delusion that infected the justice system for decades. After the 1895 constitution was enacted, and the many congressional election challenges proved futile, the state's black lawyers had few avenues to advocate for civil rights. But in 1900 a remarkable black lawyer in Texas won a major victory in the U.S. Supreme Court in *Seth Carter v. Texas*. Wilford H. Smith appealed Carter's murder conviction on the basis that blacks had been intentionally excluded from the grand jury. Smith had tried to present evidence of the discrimination to the trial judge, and the Texas trial judge refused to hear it. The U.S. Supreme Court reversed the conviction and found that "it clearly appears by the record that the defendant . . . asked leave of the court to introduce witnesses . . . and that the court refused to hear any evidence upon the subject, and overruled the motion, without investigating whether the allegation was true or false."[2] Broadly read, the opinion promised that the exclusion of blacks from a jury, solely because of their race or color, denied the defendant the equal protection of the laws in violation of the Fourteenth Amendment.

Brownfield v. South Carolina

The promise of *Carter* was soon tested in South Carolina. John Brownfield was a black barber in Georgetown.[3] On the morning of Saturday, September 30, 1900, Brownfield was in his shop shaving a white customer when deputy sheriff J. C. Scurry walked in and announced that he had come to collect Brownfield's unpaid poll taxes. Brownfield refused to pay, and when Scurry tried to arrest him, Brownfield told the deputy that he could not be arrested for such an offense without a warrant. Scurry threw his gun in Brownfield's face and attempted to take Brownfield's razor from his hand. Brownfield resisted, and in the ensuing struggle the deputy was killed by his own gun.[4] Brownfield ran but was soon caught. The next day, when word spread across the county that whites had threatened to lynch him, a thousand blacks, including women laborers from nearby plantations brandishing rice hooks and hoes, encircled the jail yelling, "Save John." Whites were so intimidated by the show of black resistance that frantic calls were made to the governor to send in the militia armed with a Gatling gun. The demonstrations lasted two days, but by the time the militia marched into town, the crowd had dispersed. The white newspapers touted the impact of the militia with headlines such as "Prompt Dispatch of Troops Prevented Bad Results."[5] But in fact the troops had had no impact. It was the local integrated police force of six men aided by local black leaders who quelled what became known as the Georgetown Riot.[6] The demonstrators peacefully assembled, marched, and then went home when they were assured that Brownfield would not be lynched. The white community responded by holding a counterdemonstration under militia guard, and the white authorities arrested more than twenty black people, including ten women, for inciting the "riot."[7] One leader was sentenced to a year in the state penitentiary.[8] No one was attacked or injured in any way by the "riot." The only injury occurred when the editor of the white Georgetown newspaper was accidentally shot by a white militiaman.[9]

William J. Whipper and J. L. Mitchell, Brownfield's Attorneys

On November 16, 1900, John Brownfield was tried. His lawyer was Julius L. Mitchell, one of the community's leading "colored" men, whose courtroom advocacy had been praised by the local press.[10] But Brownfield also needed a more experienced trial lawyer, and William J. Whipper was brought in as co-counsel. The Radical Republican Whipper would not be welcomed by the white community in Georgetown.

The two lawyers began their defense of Brownfield by moving to dismiss the indictment because the grand and petit juries were all white.[11] Not only was Brownfield's jury all white, it was composed of prominent merchants, including one of the organizers of the "white parade."[12] Although it was obvious that the jurors were all white, circuit judge Ernest Gary quickly denied the challenge. Gary, the nephew of a founder of the Red Shirts, was not exactly a fair-minded jurist.[13] In another trial, he had demonstrated his bias when he charged the jury that it was appropriate to question the honesty of a witness simply because he was a Republican.[14] Opposing Whipper and Mitchell were solicitor John S. Wilson of Kingstree, Senator Legrand G. Walker of Georgetown, and J. A. Kelly, Walker's law partner.[15] Wilson had been a Red Shirt during the campaign to overthrow Reconstruction in 1876. He later recollected that he considered the *Brownfield* case the most important of his career because of the opportunity to defend the state's jury laws against the charge that such laws discriminated against blacks.[16] Walker was a member of the Georgetown Rifle Guards, which had been used to intimidate the black demonstrators.[17]

Six witnesses testified for the prosecution, including two doctors, and another six witnesses were called to rebut Brownfield's defense. The local press described these white witnesses as "competent and reliable gentlemen."[18] Brownfield testified in his own defense. His lawyers called four other witnesses to support his self-defense story.[19] White magistrate J. Jenkins Hucks testified for Brownfield that no warrant for Brownfield's arrest had been issued, thereby supporting Brownfield's defense that the deputy had no legal right to arrest him. The local press called Brownfield's black witnesses "Coons" and liars.[20]

After the evidence was concluded, all five lawyers argued to the jury.[21] In one of the more bizarre moments, one prosecutor made the perverted argument that the death penalty was the only "protection against lynch law."[22] The case went to the jury on Friday, November 16, at 6:00 p.m. The jury deliberated for ninety minutes and returned a guilty verdict. Judge Gary sentenced Brownfield to be hanged.[23]

Whipper and Mitchell appealed to the state supreme court citing the exclusion of blacks from the jury.[24] In an interview, Brownfield said, "I am a victim of Caucasian prejudice. I ought not to be hanged," citing the exclusion of blacks from his jury.[25] On the Sunday after the sentencing, Mitchell addressed a gathering at the black Methodist church in Georgetown to help raise money for the appeal. The white newspaper headlined its story "SENSATIONAL SPEECH—of

J. L. Mitchell, the Colored Lawyer—Says Brownfield Did Not Have a Fair trial and Will Not Hang." The newspaper said that "this kind of harangue" has surprised people coming from one of the "best colored citizens" and concluded that Brownfield had had one of the "most impartial trials that ever went before a jury." The newspaper warned that in any other place Brownfield would have been lynched and that the "white citizens of Georgetown maintained law and order, and the mandates of the law must and will be obeyed."[26]

John Brownfield's appeal was heard by the state supreme court in the April term of 1901. The appeal was based on the fact that the defense had filed a pretrial motion to quash the indictment because blacks were excluded from the grand jury. Despite an offer to present evidence, the trial judge denied the motion without hearing any testimony. Brownfield's lawyers had then orally challenged the racial makeup of the petit jury, which was also denied. Judge Gary wrote that he denied the motions because there were no facts to support the claim of racial discrimination, and because the petit jurors were unknown to him personally, he would not assume they were all white. Judge Gary's claim that he was unacquainted with the jurors is not credible. Georgetown historian and lawyer Tom Rubillo described Judge Gary's denial of the challenge to the all-white jury as "sophistry of the highest order."[27] The trial judge was not blind, so how could he not know whether the petit jurors were all white when he supervised their selection at the trial?

Justice Eugene B. Gary, the brother of the trial judge, wrote the unanimous opinion for the supreme court. In considering Brownfield's jury challenge, Justice Gary said, "The only question raised . . . is, whether his honor the presiding judge erred, in refusing to quash the indictment, simply because no member of the race, to which the defendant belongs, was on the grand jury that found the bill of indictment."[28] The court found no basis for granting the challenge to the jury because the constitution, statutes, and laws of South Carolina did not discriminate on the basis of race. No mention was made of the all-white petit jury.

Brownfield's appeal to the U.S. Supreme Court was again on the grounds that the trial court erred in failing to receive the testimony offered to prove the intentional exclusion of blacks from the grand jury and that there had been discrimination in the selection of the petit jury.[29] This argument was based on Wilford H. Smith's successful appeal in *Carter v. Texas*. In delivering the Supreme Court's decision, Justice Oliver Wendell Holmes said Brownfield failed to show that "all negroes were excluded from the Grand Jury by which he was indicted."[30] Holmes ignored the fact that the trial judge disingenuously said because he "was not personally acquainted with the jurors selected, I could not assume the facts to be as alleged."[31] Justice Holmes's opinion closely paralleled the state's brief. He accepted Judge Gary's statement as being dispositive as to whether Brownfield's counsel had attempted to offer proof.[32]

Had Whipper and Mitchell committed a terrible legal mistake? Their motion and affidavit were a verbatim repetition of the words used in the affidavit that the court considered in *Carter v. Texas*. The only difference was that in *Carter*, the Texas state trial judge put on the record his denial of the offer to present evidence. Despite the acceptance of trial judge Gary's statement that he was only ruling on the motion, the reality is that the denial of the motion was a refusal to hear evidence. The handwritten record of the trial from the journal of the clerk of court of Georgetown County says that the judge overruled the written motion, and then denied an oral motion.[33]

John Brownfield rebelled against confinement. In early spring of 1901, he dug a hole through the brick wall of the jail and was free for about an hour. That summer, after the South Carolina Supreme Court ruled against him, Brownfield attempted to commit suicide, but the jailers summoned help and saved his life.[34] In late 1902 Brownfield wrote a plaintive letter to the governor complaining of the conditions in jail.[35] There is no record of any reply. In early April 1903, after the U.S. Supreme Court's ruling, Brownfield took an overdose of Paris green (an insecticide), but again he survived.[36]

During the spring of 1903, Mitchell and others began organizing a public petition campaign to save Brownfield's life.[37] If such a petition was ever sent to Governor McSweeney, it cannot be found in his official papers.[38]

On June 17, 1903, with Judge Ernest Gary again presiding, the Court of General Sessions was called into session to set the date for Brownfield's execution. When asked by the court why the death sentence should not be carried out, Brownfield "said he knew the court could show him no mercy," but he requested a meeting with the mayor of Georgetown, a juror, and two other prominent Georgetown businessmen.[39] Judge Gary allowed the meeting, but the brother of the victim was summoned and his loud protest aborted the meeting. Brownfield was again brought before Judge Gary and asked why the sentence should not be carried out. Brownfield requested time to get up a petition.[40] Judge Gary pronounced the case "hopeless" and set the execution for Friday, June 26, 1903.[41] On June 23, 1903, as the gallows were being constructed in the jail yard, Brownfield finally succeeded in killing himself, apparently by another dose of poison.[42] The local white press complained in a headline that the law had been "Cheated Out of Its Just Deserts and All the Negroes Well Pleased with the Results." In a letter published by the paper, a writer identified as "Justice" asserted that the black community had "murdered" Brownfield by supplying him with the poison and called for a criminal investigation.[43] The

waving a red flag in the face of the all-white jury.[61] In addition to the jury, the lawyers faced mobs and a hostile press.[62]

Despite the tense atmosphere, Adams and Moorer challenged the racial composition of the jury and the constitutionality of the criminal peonage statute.[63] They also contested the validity of the state's constitutional provisions restricting who could vote and, consequently, who could serve on juries. Moorer used his argument from the election cases that the 1868 Reconstruction statute readmitting the state's congressional delegation prohibited the state from restricting the franchise. The 1895 South Carolina Constitution had done just that in its measures designed to disenfranchise blacks. A well-respected member of the judiciary, Judge J. C. Klugh was actually a cut above most of the state's judges, having graduated from both college and law school.[64] Nonetheless, he was not receptive to their arguments, and he denied their motions.[65]

The prosecutor was solicitor P. T. Hildebrand of Orangeburg, who had been admitted to the bar in 1888.[66] He was assisted by three other experienced Orangeburg lawyers, W. L. Glaze, D. O. Herbert, and Robert Lide.[67] These three had probably been retained by Valentine's family to assist in the prosecution, a common South Carolina practice.

The trial began on Monday, September 9.[68] Fearing trouble, Sheriff Dukes summoned constables from across the county to reinforce his deputies, and the governor closed the state-run liquor store (known as the state dispensary). These measures kept the community sober and under control, and violence was avoided.[69]

At the trial, the state called two physicians, W. S. Jennings and A. S. Hydrick. The state's other witnesses were W. M. Carter, Magistrate Valentine, Sol Spires, Tony Jerry, J. H. Easterling, Walter Hutto, and Fisher Keckley. The two physicians testified as to the deceased's wounds. One said Valentine was never conscious, and the other said Valentine gained consciousness only briefly to say he had been shot. However, both Easterling and Hutto testified of conversations with Valentine. Both said he knew he was going to die, which permitted the admission of his "dying declarations." They claimed Valentine said that he never fired a shot, and that Franklin shot him as soon as he opened the door.[70]

In his defense, Pink Franklin testified that he heard nothing until Valentine "busted" into the bedroom shouting for him to put his hands up, but before he could comply, Valentine shot him in the shoulder, and in an ensuing struggle he shot Valentine. Franklin's version was more consistent with the physical and medical evidence than the deathbed story. Valentine's gunshot wound was surrounded by gunpowder residue, which meant that he had been shot at close range, rather than just as he entered the bedroom. Moreover, both Franklins had been shot. How and why would Franklin have shot himself in the shoulder and his wife as well?

Legally, the case presented problems for the state. If Valentine had not identified himself or announced that he had a warrant, the arrest would have been illegal.[71] Moreover, if Franklin was threatened with death or serious bodily injury, he also had a right to use deadly force.[72] Since the peonage statute had been declared unconstitutional, Franklin had a right to resist arrest. Despite having a witness, W. M. Carter, who had accompanied Valentine that night, the state presented no testimony that Valentine ever identified himself or announced he had a warrant. The state tried to show that Franklin knew the constable was coming to arrest him. Tony Jerry was called to testify that Franklin told him the night before the shooting that "no one could arrest him." Franklin's lawyers challenged the voluntariness and truthfulness of Jerry's testimony with his admission that he had been seized, beaten, and jailed by the mob that had pursued Franklin.[73] In fact, three years later, Jerry recanted his story, stating that his testimony had been coerced.[74]

After the testimony, Adams and Moorer moved the court for a directed verdict of acquittal on the jury issue, the invalidity of the warrant, self-defense, and on the fact that no evidence had been presented as to the guilt of Patsy Franklin. Judge Klugh refused to direct a verdict even for Mrs. Franklin. Even though one juror did ask for a clarification on the question of legality of the attempted arrest, the jury ultimately found Pink Franklin guilty. They did, however, acquit his wife. The judge sentenced Pink Franklin to be hanged.[75]

An appeal to the state supreme court followed. The chief justice of the court was Young John Pope; the associate justices were Eugene B. Gary, Ira B. Jones, and Charles A. Woods. Pope was a Confederate veteran who had represented Ku Klux Klansmen in the 1870 federal prosecutions. Before becoming chief justice, he had been elected attorney general on the same ticket with Pitchfork Ben Tillman. Justice Eugene B. Gary had read law under his uncle, General Matthew W. Gary, founder of the Red Shirts.[76] Justice Ira Jones had been the lawyer for Governor Tillman and a leader in the 1895 constitutional convention. The newest member of the court, Charles A. Woods, was the only justice not politically identified with Tillman.[77] He had authored the opinion in *Ex parte Hollman*, issued just four months before the *Franklin* decision, which had declared the criminal peonage statute unconstitutional.[78] But the decision in *Hollman* was not even mentioned by the court in the *Franklin* case.

When the court issued its decision on March 17, 1908, an Orangeburg newspaper headlined its story, "Slayer of Valentine Must Die."[79] Chief Justice Pope wrote the opinion for the court. He ignored the conflict between the 1895 constitution and the 1868 Reconstruction statute. Regarding the challenge to the jury laws, the court found no merit because the state constitution and state statutes did not mention race. The opinion was similarly dismissive of the other appellate grounds. Notwithstanding prior decisions to the contrary, the court found no merit to Franklin's claim that he had a right to defend himself and his family.[80]

In the U.S. Supreme Court

Franklin's appeal to the nation's highest court attracted the attention of southern congressmen who were concerned that the case was a threat to the region's peonage system as well as civil rights groups who wanted to challenge this modern version of slavery.[81] One of those civil rights groups was the Constitution League, which later merged into the NAACP.[82] The league hired former U.S. attorney general Charles J. Bonaparte to write a brief on Franklin's behalf.[83] Bonaparte, the great-nephew of the French emperor, wanted complete control of the case, but Moorer and Adams refused to step aside, and Bonaparte refused to appear in the Supreme Court with the two black lawyers.

The Supreme Court decisions in *Carter v. Texas* and *Brownfield v. S.C.* molded how Franklin's lawyers approached their case. In order to prevail under *Carter* and avoid the mistake of *Brownfield*, Moorer and Adams needed to have produced testimony that blacks had been intentionally excluded from the jury. Perhaps Moorer and Adams recognized that they had no witnesses who could testify as to the intent of white officials. Consequently, the two lawyers must have believed their argument about the conflict between the 1868 Reconstruction statute and the state's constitution would not involve any factual or intent questions and would appeal to the high court on strictly legal grounds. If successful, the argument would have established a precedent on the jury question, and on the franchise question as well. However, the Supreme Court treated Franklin like other black defendants who claimed discrimination in jury selection. The court said that even if it could be held that the federal statute and the 1895 state constitution were in conflict, there was no evidence of actual discrimination against blacks in the selection of the jurors. In other words, without an admission by a state official that blacks were not permitted to sit on juries because of their race, the high court would not intervene.[84]

The defense based on the peonage statute had also seemed promising. After all, the federal district court in South Carolina and the state supreme court had both ruled the statute unconstitutional. Defending oneself against an unconstitutional warrant had a commonsense appeal, but the U.S. Supreme Court rejected it, holding that even if the statute were void as unconstitutional, it was a jury question as to whether Pink Franklin had a right to resist.[85]

Despite the defeat in Washington, Moorer and Adams did not give up. They filed a motion for a new trial based on the affidavit of Tony Jerry in which he retracted his trial testimony.[86] While this strategy did buy some time, it was not successful. Judge Klugh, the original trial judge, had expressed reservations about Franklin's guilt; however, he was ill, and another judge was assigned to hear the motion and to resentence Franklin.[87] This new judge denied Franklin a new trial and resentenced him to hang on December 23, 1910. On top of that, the need to find the right course of action quickly became even more urgent. On September 13, virulent racist Cole Blease won the Democratic runoff primary for governor.[88] With there being no Republican opposition, Blease would become governor, an event that would foreclose any possibility of clemency. The two lawyers again appealed to the state supreme court.[89]

In June 1910 Franklin's lawyers had begun a clemency petition to Governor Martin Ansel; however, they apparently never presented it to him.[90] Nonetheless, it was a good idea. Boston lawyer and NAACP supporter Albert E. Pillsbury wrote the civil rights group's executive secretary, Frances Blascoer, suggesting that a new clemency petition for Franklin be drafted. And so began the NAACP's first legal case.

The NAACP's chief South Carolina contact was Thomas Miller, who advised that Adams and Moorer be replaced by white South Carolina lawyers and that the appeal be dismissed.[91] Miller's attitude toward Adams and Moorer was derived in part from white lawyer Claude Sawyer, who told Miller he would not help as long as the two black lawyers were associated with the case. Miller also claimed that Moorer and Adams were demanding to be paid $1,000, the same fee Bonaparte had been paid.

Eventually Miller admitted that he had been misinformed about the monetary demand, but the NAACP was determined to remove Moorer and Adams.[92] Charles Bonaparte clearly influenced NAACP board members with his assertion that Moorer and Adams were incompetent. He also supported Miller's view that the NAACP must hire a "white, South Carolina lawyer."[93] Blascoer sent Miller fifty dollars, a petition, and instructions to hire Claude Sawyer. Sawyer in turn recruited Charleston lawyer Ben Hagood, a former U.S. attorney.

The national organization's resources were soon in motion. President William Howard Taft wrote two letters to the governor about the case.[94] Booker T. Washington exhorted his supporters to help, and W. E. B. DuBois tried to convince Moorer and Adams to withdraw.[95] Sympathetic newspaper articles and editorials appeared across the country.

Blascoer traveled to South Carolina to meet with Moorer and Adams and convince Pink Franklin to fire his lawyers and drop his appeal.[96] Although Blascoer described Moorer and Adams as "impossible," they did withdraw, and Franklin gave her a power of attorney. In addition to persuading Adams and Moorer to withdraw, she conferred with Miller, Sawyer, Hagood, and Ambrose Gonzales, a Columbia newspaper editor. Gonzales called the governor, and his newspaper ran sympathetic stories.[97] Blascoer's whirlwind visit culminated with a visit to the governor.

After Blascoer returned to New York, Miller, Sawyer, and Hagood met with Governor Ansel, and Miller presented him with a petition containing 975 signatures from black citizens. A commutation by Ansel was critical because his term expired January 17, 1911, and the newly elected governor, Cole Blease, would be inaugurated. Blease was infamous for his demagoguery and his endorsement of lynching as "necessary and good."[98]

Despite a counterpetition to the governor with more than five hundred signatures of whites, the mood was turning in Franklin's favor. The trial juror who had raised questions about the legality of the attempted arrest called for commutation and persuaded a Charleston newspaper to do the same.[99] Even the trial judge and the state's attorney general recommended commutation.[100] On January 5, 1911, Governor Ansel commuted Franklin's sentence to life. Over the next several years, Pink Franklin continued to seek the NAACP's help.[101] Ambrose Gonzales and NAACP board member Oswald Villard also continued to work on his behalf. Then in January 1919, Governor Richard Manning paroled Pink Franklin. Despite inquiries from the NAACP, he seemed to disappear. In reality, however, he took a new name and moved with his family about twenty miles away from Willow Township.[102] After a life of sharecropping, he died in 1949.[103]

The Bogus Sanders Case

The next major challenge to the criminal justice system in the state came in June 1915 in Columbia, the state capital. This time Jacob Moorer was joined by Nathaniel J. Frederick as defense counsel. James and Adlee Sanders, husband and wife, were charged with the murder of a white man. The case was prosecuted by solicitor Wade Hampton Cobb, whose trial co-counsel was former governor Cole Blease. A favorite of white mill workers, Blease had just completed his term as governor in January.

On May 25, 1915, James Sanders fired four shots at a group of white mill workers who had harassed his wife and threated him with a knife. Charlie

Ellers died of his wounds and E. J. Crouch was superficially wounded.[104] After a coroner's inquest, James and Adlee Sanders were indicted for murder.

Fifteen days after the shooting, the trial began. The courtroom was "filled to its capacity," and circuit judge H. F. Rice initially barred reporters. Moorer and Frederick began by challenging the selection of both the grand jury and the venire called to serve on the petit jury. They asserted that blacks were discriminated against in the jury selection process and had subpoenaed both the clerk of court and two jury commission members. The three white officials all denied any discrimination and asserted that jurors were chosen on "merit and morality."[105] The *State* reported that the chairman of the commission testified that of the 5,000–6,000 voters in the county, 1,500 were black, and that there were no marks on the voter rolls to allow racial identification. However, Moorer and Frederick produced the registration rolls and asked the chairman what the "c" and "cols" markings meant. He had to admit that the marks did in fact designate race. When the defense lawyers tried to introduce the books into evidence, the trial judge refused their request.[106] Then the judge denied their motion challenging the grand jury and the petit jury venire. But when jury selection finally began, Judge Rice and the defense had the following exchange with a potential juror:

COURT: Have you formed or expressed any opinion as to the guilt or innocence of these people?

BAILEY: I have not.

COURT: Are you conscious of any bias in your mind for or against them?

BAILEY: It is not exactly bias, your honor, but I feel a resentment in this particular case which might prejudice me in rendering a verdict.

~

COURT: Mr. Bailey, do you think your feeling would have any effect upon any verdict you might render after you hear the evidence and the law.

BAILEY: I believe I could render a verdict based on the law and the evidence. But, as I stated, I feel a prejudice in this particular case.

~

Cross Examination by (Frederick?)

ATTORNEY: How did you get that feeling that you spoke of a while ago?

BAILEY: I am listening to it.

ATTORNEY: And from what you listen to, that creates a feeling in you?

BAILEY: Yes; and a natural resentment for one of your race pleading to a jury that I am on.

Despite the obvious racial prejudice of Mr. Bailey, Judge Rice found him competent for service and refused to excuse him, forcing Sanders's lawyers to use a preemptory strike to keep Bailey off the jury. Thirty-four white men were called for jury service. The defense struck twenty venire men, and the state and the court struck one each. Of course the seated jury was all white. Once the trial began, the state called fourteen witnesses, and the defense called seven, including Adlee and James Sanders. The newspaper accounts are quite brief.

The case was a swearing contest. The white mill workers testified that they had been shot without provocation. The Sanderses both testified that the mill workers had been drinking, and that the white men had grabbed Mrs. Sanders and made insulting and suggestive remarks. Mr. Sanders admitted he came to his wife's rescue, but he said that the men attacked him with a knife.

After two days of testimony, Mr. Cobb began closing arguments for the state. He spoke nearly an hour, then Jacob Moorer argued for an hour. Nathaniel J. Frederick also argued for nearly an hour, and court adjourned. When court resumed the next day, Frederick spoke for another hour and fifteen minutes. Former governor Blease concluded the closing arguments for the state, speaking for an hour. Finally, Judge Rice charged the jury for fifty-five minutes. The judge's notes questioned the morals of Mrs. Sanders and ended with this statement: "We want law enforced but not by negroes with pistols in their pockets shooting down white men."[107] The jury was out for about an hour and a half and found James Sanders guilty of murder without mercy, which meant the death sentence would be imposed. Despite the judge's animosity toward Adlee Sanders, the jury failed to convict her. Following the verdict, the atmosphere was tense. Slowly the packed courtroom emptied, and then Sanders was surrounded by ten officers and taken to a waiting police car "which hurried him to the penitentiary."[108]

Moorer and Frederick moved for a new trial citing the improper selection of the grand jury, the failure to allow the defense to offer the registration books to prove discrimination in the jury selection, an improper charge on malice, and after-discovered evidence. Judge Rice denied the motion and added, "I wish to say that I think the jury was right in convicting Sanders." Moorer was quoted that he would "appeal to the supreme court and, if the judgment of the circuit court was affirmed, would doubtless carry the case to the supreme court of the United States."[109]

Following the losses in the *Brownfield* and *Franklin* cases, the *Sanders* case looked like a good one to take to the Supreme Court. Unlike the other cases, Sanders's lawyers had actually presented or tried to present evidence of discrimination in jury selection. The two lawyers argued to the state supreme court that the grand jury and petit jury were "unlawfully constituted, in that . . . discrimination was made against the Negro race because of race and color."[110]

The South Carolina Supreme Court ruled against Sanders and cited the U.S. Supreme Court's decision in *State v. Franklin* as its authority. Despite the fact that the trial judge had refused to allow Sanders's attorneys to introduce the county voter registration lists, which clearly identified black voters, the appellate court held that the refusal was not error.[111] The court also found that Sanders's lawyers had not offered any evidence to support their claims, despite the fact that the two black lawyers had moved to quash the grand jury's indictment and had called witnesses in support of their claim of discrimination. Two of those witnesses were the members of the jury commission who had admitted they chose grand jurors based on "merit and morality" or nothing more than their arbitrary choices.[112] Since the officials admitted there were many black voters, and if Moorer and Frederick had been allowed to introduce the registration records, they could have conclusively proved that the chairman of the election commission was lying and was in fact using marks to identify black voters and exclude them from jury service. Certainly the two lawyers had tried to establish a record that would allow them to avoid the "lack of evidence" issue that had been so problematic in the *Franklin* and *Brownfield* cases. The evidence of the use of "merit and morality," the use of racial identifiers on the rolls, and the fact that one in four voters was black might have even come close to establishing a challenge equivalent to the 1880 *Neal v. Delaware* case.[113]

The two lawyers also had another ground for an appeal, which was the failure of the trial judge to excuse the juror who had a bias and "a natural resentment for one of your race pleading to a jury I am on."[114] The state supreme court seized on this argument and reversed Sanders's conviction, ruling that the trial judge erred in failing to excuse the juror. With a new trial ordered and their client's life saved for the moment, Moorer and Frederick could not take the jury discrimination argument to the U.S. Supreme Court. It is easy to assume the South Carolina court recognized that the record in this case was different than in *Brownfield* and *Franklin*, and that reversing the conviction would prevent the case from going to the nation's highest court.

At the retrial, Moorer and Frederick again tried to attack the selection of the grand jury and the petit jury and again called witnesses to try to prove discrimination against black voters.[115] After a long trial and lengthy jury deliberations, Sanders was again convicted, but this time the jury recommended mercy, and he was sentenced to life. Although Moorer and Adams apparently considered it, the verdict was not appealed.[116] Sanders's life had been saved, and a third trial might have subjected him to the death penalty again. In 1921, five years later,

Sanders was paroled by the governor for good behavior, based on the recommendation of the parole board, which had received requests for parole from the trial judge and nine out of the twelve jurors.[117]

Voting Rights

After the losses in *Brownfield*, *Franklin*, and *Sanders*, the outlook for civil rights was bleak. Since the number of black lawyers was declining in the state, the activities of the remaining few were critical in advancing civil rights and laying a foundation for the next generation. The jury cases had failed to overturn the Jim Crow era's all-white juries in the state, but the battle for voting was not abandoned by the black bar. The association of Jacob Moorer and Nathaniel J. Frederick in the *Sanders* case was beneficial in two ways. The trials and appeal helped prepare the inexperienced Frederick for numerous battles ahead. Moreover, their collaboration helped lead to the formation of an important civil rights organization. In June 1915 Moorer and Frederick helped create the Capital City Civic League.[118] The Civic League became the cornerstone for the presence of a national civil rights organization in the state. The national office of the NAACP had played a significant role in the Pink Franklin case, but the organization of the league meant there would be a continuing local presence in the state.

The league's chief goal was to serve as the black community's advocate of voting rights, and Moorer and Frederick were soon joined in the battle against Jim Crow voter registration laws by two other black lawyers, Butler Nance and Green Jackson. In 1915 Nance reported to W. E. B. DuBois that the league had registered eight hundred black voters in Richland County.[119] Two years later, the Civic League became the first NAACP chapter in the state.[120] Green Jackson worked tirelessly for the newly formed NAACP chapter on voter registration.[121] The league also tried to assist across the state. In 1919 a black preacher successfully registered to vote in Greenwood County, but when other black citizens tried to register, local whites reacted with violence. Nance sought the assistance of the NAACP's national office.[122] In turn, the NAACP asked Nance to investigate. But with meager financial resources, his investigation had little impact, and no legal action was taken.[123]

After the approval of the Nineteenth Amendment granting women the right to vote, a group of black women tried to register in Columbia. Although many were college graduates, their registration attempts were rejected. The state constitution required only that the potential voter be able to read and write any section of the state or federal constitution, but the registrars required them to explain legal terms such as "mandamus" and "civil code." Other women, some of whom were certified public schoolteachers, were denied because the registrar claimed that they mispronounced words.[124] Butler Nance filed the first NAACP suit in the state's history on behalf of thirty-two women.[125] The action was technically an appeal to the county court after the county board of registration refused to register the women. Nance pointed out that many of the women were graduates of "the State College at Orangeburg" and had the signature of the state's governor on their diplomas.[126] The case was dismissed by the county court judge for want of jurisdiction, and the dismissal was then appealed to the Court of Common Pleas.[127] There is no record of the case after this appeal was filed; it was probably dismissed because the election had been held before the court was in session.

In the mid-1920s Nathaniel J. Frederick, publisher of the *Palmetto Leader* newspaper, became the chief lawyer for the NAACP in Columbia. He filed an action against local officials for refusing to register black voters who qualified as property owners.[128] Frederick actually obtained a court order requiring the registrar to issue certificates to the black property owners, but the registrar ignored the order.

Through Frederick's work with the NAACP, the white primary was also starting to receive attention.[129] Writing in a 1926 editorial, Frederick addressed the absurdity of the white primary. He pointed out that a black voter could vote in the Democratic primary only if he met two conditions. First, the potential voter would have to have voted for Wade Hampton for governor in 1876, and second, he would need ten white men who would attest to that fact. Under this Democratic Party rule the potential black voter and his ten male witnesses would have to be at least seventy-one years old in 1926.[130] Furthermore, since no black woman could have voted in 1876, no black woman could ever qualify to vote in the Democratic Party primary. But Frederick did not pursue a challenge to the white primary. As the lone NAACP lawyer in the state, he was probably overwhelmed with requests for help and had few economic resources to pay for litigation. Also in 1926, Frederick was the lawyer for the Lowmans in their retrial. When they were lynched, Frederick was certainly distracted.[131] The local NAACP chapter in Columbia was in the process of being revived, and Frederick must have hoped some other lawyer would rise to the occasion.[132] In fact, the national office of the NAACP tried to obtain copies of the South Carolina Democratic Party primary rules through a white lawyer in Spartanburg, but no action followed.[133]

But the battle over the white primary was not over. After the same system was thrown out in Texas, that state's legislature established a different voter registration scheme that simply allowed the political parties to establish whatever rules they wished on the qualification of voters. In 1932 the NAACP sued Texas, and the U.S. Supreme Court ruled for the second time that the Texas primary was unconstitutional.[134] While the Texas case was pending, Frederick filed suit challenging the white primary in South Carolina. But he lost in both state and federal court, and since the Democratic primary had already been held that year, the federal district court judge ruled Frederick's case moot.[135] In response to the new Texas case, the South Carolina Democratic Party called on the state legislature to repeal all laws relating to the party primary. This forced Frederick to forestall another suit since he saw little value in filing a case against a yet-to-be-determined scheme.[136]

In July 1932 Nathaniel J. Frederick became one of the first three black lawyers appointed to the National Legal Committee of the NAACP.[137] But his activities on behalf of the NAACP gradually began to diminish. He was one of only seven black lawyers left in the state, and the only one willing to take civil rights cases.[138] Facing the Great Depression, Frederick struggled to earn a living. At his death, he was nearly destitute.[139] According to the obituary in the *Palmetto Leader*, Frederick's last editorial appeared on May 7, 1938, when he attacked the Democratic Party's exclusion of black voters. By 1939 there were only four black lawyers left in the state, none of whom practiced in Columbia, Greenville, or Charleston, the largest cities.[140] No lawyer remained in the state who was willing to challenge the denial of the vote to the black citizens of South Carolina.

~

The cases discussed in this chapter were not landmark civil rights cases. All three fell short in their attack on the all-white jury. The voter registration and primary challenges were simply aborted as failures. But all three cases are historic in the story of civil rights and the legal profession in South Carolina. In *Brownfield*, black lawyers stood in a South Carolina courtroom for the first time and directly challenged the Jim Crow legal system. Again in *Franklin* and *Sanders*, black lawyers challenged the legal system that was derived from the 1895 constitution. The all-white jury survived the attack in the *Franklin* case. The NAACP did not succeed in making the case a test of peonage, and Adams and Moorer failed to overturn the 1895 constitution. But Franklin's life was saved, demonstrating that legal efforts could achieve some meaningful results. The actions of blacks and whites from the South and across the nation showed the power of a biracial, multiclass coalition. In *Sanders*, Moorer again tried to challenge the all-white jury, and with the aid of Nathaniel J. Frederick, he mounted the most serious challenge yet. Although Jim Crow justice survived, a client avoided the death penalty, and a firm foundation had been laid for future civil rights efforts.

These particular lawyers' lives tell the story of the black legal profession in the first three decades of the new century. *Brownfield* was the last major case of William Whipper's career. South Carolina's first black lawyer would die in 1907, but his legacy would live on. Julius Mitchell and John Adams left the state. Both had remarkable careers in their adopted states, but without question the loss of young, strong advocates for civil rights would be felt in South Carolina for more than a quarter century. Jacob Moorer would use his experience in the *Franklin* case to help James Sanders. Moorer continued to practice after the *Sanders* case but did not handle a major case again. He died in 1935. Nathaniel J. Frederick emerged from the *Sanders* case with a partial victory and an experience that helped mold him into the state's leading civil rights lawyer.

The jury cases had failed to overturn the Jim Crow era's all-white juries. Of course, in *Franklin* and *Sanders*, the client's life was saved. In *Sanders*, Moorer and Frederick did lay the groundwork for a test case to the U.S. Supreme Court, but saving their client's life took precedence. It is conceivable that the evidence produced in *Sanders* might have persuaded the high court to overturn a conviction because of racial discrimination in jury selection, but its record between 1900 and 1935 suggests otherwise. In 1904 the court overturned the conviction of an Alabama defendant on the grounds that he had not been allowed to present evidence of jury discrimination.[141] Otherwise, the court continued to ignore the systematic exclusion of blacks from juries in the South and continued to require evidence that was nearly impossible to produce.[142] It was not until 1935 in one of the infamous *Scottsboro* cases that another conviction was overturned because of race discrimination in jury selection. In *Norris v. State of Alabama*, the U.S. Supreme Court was persuaded that blacks had been systematically excluded from the jury based on the testimony of multiple witnesses, the presence of qualified blacks on the voter rolls, the fact that nonblacks had been called for jury service for more than thirty years, and the forgery of jury lists by white officials.[143]

CHAPTER 11

The 1940s and the Civil Rights Era

The Great Depression drained South Carolina of both financial and human resources. Coupled with decades of Jim Crow, the impact on the black community was devastating. In "looking at the life and lot of South Carolina Negroes in the early 1930's," one historian said he got "the impression of a people trapped in a morass."[1] Many blacks simply gave up and left the state. Between 1920 and 1940 the black population declined from 865,000 to 814,000, making South Carolina no longer majority black. This decline also affected the legal profession. Not a single black lawyer was admitted to the bar from 1925 through 1939.

However, the black community did not give up the struggle for civil rights.[2] By the late 1930s the NAACP had not only survived, but for the first time, it was organized in the Upstate, in rural counties, and on the state level.[3] Local NAACP leaders such as Levi Byrd, a Cheraw plumber, were helping revitalize the organization.[4] Charles Houston, litigation director, made repeated visits in the late 1930s, speaking on behalf of the civil rights organization's campaign to challenge inequality in education. In 1938 two Charleston high school graduates petitioned the local school board to provide a means for blacks to obtain a college education. In 1939 another Charleston high school graduate asked the board to pay his tuition at South Carolina State because the city's college (Charleston College) was only for whites.[5]

These actions had been inspired by the NAACP's efforts outside South Carolina. In 1936 the NAACP's suit on behalf of Donald G. Murray had desegregated the University of Maryland School of Law.[6] The following year the NAACP filed a similar lawsuit against the University of Missouri for its failure to admit Lloyd L. Gaines to its law school. The state court refused to admit Gaines, but on appeal the U.S. Supreme Court ruled that Missouri had denied

Gaines a privilege enjoyed by white residents and that he should be admitted to the law school. The court indicated, however, that if Missouri provided a separate legal education for black residents, Gaines would have no complaint. State officials promptly established a law school at Lincoln University. Charles Houston was preparing to appeal that decision when his client disappeared and the appeal had to be abandoned.[7] The Lincoln University Law School did open in September 1939 with thirty students.

South Carolina's white leadership was well aware of the threat to segregation posed by the *Murray* and *Gaines* cases. In fact, H. C. Byrd, the acting president of the University of Maryland, informed Leonard T. Baker, the president of the University of South Carolina, that the *Murray* decision would affect every state law school in the South.[8] Soon after, University of South Carolina law dean J. Nelson Frierson also informed President Baker that the issue of equal facilities for black law students demanded attention.[9]

Two years later, in April 1938, Charles B. Bailey, a black resident of Columbia and a 1932 graduate of Morehouse College, applied to the all-white University of South Carolina School of Law.[10] Bailey informed Charles Houston of his application and that his primary objective was to gain financial assistance from the state so that he could attend an out-of-state law program.[11] Houston encouraged Bailey, explaining that his goal matched the short-term strategy of the NAACP, which was to compel southern states to financially support black students who wanted to attend out-of-state graduate and professional programs. Houston emphasized, however, that the NAACP's "ultimate goal is to reestablish the right of Negro citizens to attend the State university just the same as they did during the Reconstruction days."[12]

Bailey wrote to the law school dean, the president of the university, and the school's board of trustees seeking admission or financial aid.[13] Finally, Solomon Blatt, a member of the university's board of trustees as well as speaker of the South Carolina House of Representatives, informed Bailey that his application would be considered. Six months later and after another letter from Bailey, Blatt once again indicated that the application was "receiving consideration."[14] Blatt already had publicly proclaimed that "the white people of South Carolina need not have any fear as to what the outcome of this application is going to be. The board of trustees will do everything in their power to maintain the University of South Carolina for white students only."[15]

When the *Gaines* decision was handed down three months later, Blatt introduced legislation in the statehouse to establish a law school at State College in Orangeburg. "We know of no other way to meet this," the speaker declared, "than to establish a chair of law at the state Colored college."[16] The measure to create the black law school passed in the house, but with arguments that the state could not afford a new law school, the senate proposed that the law school at the University of South Carolina admit any applicant "regardless of race, color, creed, or sex" with the proviso that any application to the law school would require a certificate signed by two members of the General Assembly testifying to the applicant's "good moral character." The house refused to accept the senate proposal, and the separate law school died.[17]

In the meantime, Bailey's application remained in limbo. In 1940 Bailey wrote to Thurgood Marshall seeking help. Marshall reassured him that indeed "we have by no means abandoned your case," but he explained that the NAACP was swamped with other civil rights litigation. With no legal help forthcoming, Bailey took a job with the U.S. Post Office in Columbia and gave up his efforts to be admitted to University of South Carolina School of Law, where his grandfather, Paris Simkins, had graduated in 1876.[18]

Other citizens of the state were also growing frustrated and started taking action. After a long hiatus, black candidates were running for both local office and for Congress.[19] Shadrack Morgan ran for the state legislature in Orangeburg County, becoming the first black lawyer to seek office since before 1900.

In 1942, at the behest of the NAACP, the U.S. Justice Department prosecuted South Carolina white election officials for violating the rights of a black citizen trying to register to vote.[20] This was the first federal effort to enforce voting rights in the state in more than sixty years. Much like earlier nineteenth-century efforts, the prosecution of the Cherokee County election officials failed, and the woman who instigated the charges was fired from her job with the public schools.[21] While such reprisals would continue, the community did not relent. In Charleston schoolteachers organized to demand equal pay.[22] Whites were confronted "with forceful, sustained, and militant civil rights agitation."[23] Their reaction was often violent. In November 1942 an elderly black man who had advocated for black voting rights was severely beaten by whites in Greenville.[24] The need for local civil rights lawyers remained urgent.

New Lawyers

With the death of Nathaniel J. Frederick in 1938, the black bar was at its lowest point numerically since 1868. However, in 1940 and 1941, four new lawyers were admitted. Harold Boulware was admitted in 1940, followed by Harold A. Stevens, Cassandra Maxwell, and Walter Frederick Robinson in 1941. Boulware, Maxwell, and Robinson were all graduates of Howard University Law

School. Stevens, a Boston College Law School graduate, never practiced in South Carolina.[25]

Walter Robinson was secretary of the Columbia chapter of the NAACP in 1947 and 1948.[26] He practiced in Columbia into the 1950s and served on the NAACP state conference's Legal Redress Committee with Harold Boulware and W. B. James of Sumter.[27] He also served as co-counsel in a lawsuit seeking to desegregate the University of South Carolina School of Law.

Cassandra Maxwell of Orangeburg was the first woman of her race admitted to the state's bar.[28] Maxwell provided some assistance to Boulware and the NAACP, but she would not take a public role for fear of its impact on her family's grocery business, which had a substantial white clientele.[29] She practiced law for a short time and then joined the faculty of South Carolina State School of Law. After leaving that institution in 1951, she practiced in Georgia and Pennsylvania.[30] She died in Philadelphia in 1974.[31]

Boulware would become an able successor to N. J. Frederick and the state's chief civil rights lawyer in the 1940s and early 1950s. He opened an office in Columbia in 1940. One of his early cases was *Grant v. Richardson*, a habeas corpus action on behalf of two clients, Alchrist Grant and Cyrus Pinckney, who had been sentenced to death for assault with intent to rape. At trial, the defendants had been abandoned by their retained lawyer, and the defense was provided by two lawyers appointed at the last minute. An appeal in state court challenged the conviction on the grounds that the appointed lawyers had not been allowed sufficient time to prepare and that blacks were excluded from the jury. The state supreme court rejected these claims.[32] In a last-minute effort to save the men's lives, Boulware filed a federal habeas action, but it too was rejected, and Grant and Pinckney were executed.[33]

In 1943 Boulware filed his first civil rights case, a challenge to the pay disparity for teachers in Charleston. Unfortunately, his client, Melissa Smith, was terminated because of her lawsuit and her case mooted. As historian R. Scott Baker observed, Boulware and other NAACP leaders were "determined to bring the issue to court" and found a new plaintiff, Viola Duvall. She was a science teacher at Burke High School in Charleston making only twelve dollars a week, while white teachers were making twice as much.[34] The case was heard by U.S. district court judge Waties Waring of Charleston. In a ruling that surprised white South Carolina, in February 1944 Judge Waring ruled for Boulware's client, which resulted in her pay increasing to $100 a month.[35] Boulware had obtained his first major civil rights victory.[36]

Following the success in *Duvall*, the NAACP wanted Boulware to file a challenge to the white primary, but he was drafted into the U.S. Army in April

1944.[37] With Boulware gone, the NAACP recruited Shadrack Morgan to serve as Thurgood Marshall's local counsel.[38] In 1944 the U.S. Supreme Court in *Smith v. Allwright* held that Texas's attempt to classify the white primary as a private activity did not comport with the Fourteenth Amendment.[39] Despite the *Smith v. Allwright* decision, Governor Olin D. Johnson of South Carolina called the legislature into special session to privatize the state's Democratic Party primary by repealing all state primary election laws.[40] Illustrating the underlying racist intent of the extraordinary session, Governor Johnson said, "History has taught us that we must keep our white Democratic primaries pure and unadulterated so that we might protect the welfare and homes of all the people of our State."[41] The legislature then eliminated all references to the party primaries from the state's statutes.

Naturally, when Boulware returned from the war, a ready-made test case was waiting. When George Elmore tried to vote in the Richland County Democratic primary in 1946, the party officials turned him away. Boulware filed *Elmore v. Rice* challenging the actions of the Democratic Party. Thurgood Marshall was lead counsel on the case with Robert Carter. The NAACP lawyers won a declaration from Judge Waring that the white primary was unconstitutional. In an extraordinary ruling, Judge Waring said, "It is time for South Carolina to rejoin the Union. It is time to fall in step with the other states and to adopt the American way of conducting elections."[42] That decision was affirmed by the U.S. Court of Appeals, and the state's petition to the U.S. Supreme Court was denied.[43] However, the still-defiant white Democrats promulgated rules that vested control of the party primaries in clubs that blacks could not join and allowed black voters only if they would take "an oath that [they] believed in social and educational separation of the races."[44] Again Harold Boulware filed suit. In issuing a temporary injunction, Judge Waring described the conduct of the state Democratic convention as the result of "a flagrant disregard of basic rights [which] must have sprung from either gross ignorance or a conscious determination to evade the issue and to refuse to obey the law of the land."[45] In the fall of 1948 Judge Waring issued a permanent injunction against the new scheme and declared it unconstitutional. The judge observed:

> To say that these rules conform or even pretend to conform to the law as laid down in the case of *Elmore v. Rice* is an absurdity. Under the rules adopted by the State Party a Negro could never become a member, could never attend any meeting, could never have any vote in the election of the officials in charge of the party affairs, could never have a vote or even a voice in the adoption of rules, platforms or any

> part whatsoever in the government of the party. In other words, he was granted the privilege of voting at a primary election under certain conditions and upon certain qualifications, not applicable to white voters or voters of any other race under rules, terms and conditions in the adoption of which he had no part. We cannot escape the inevitable conclusion that this in no way complied with and was in contravention of the law of the land as enunciated by our courts in prior decisions and distinctly laid down in the Elmore case.[46]

The state again appealed and lost in the U.S. Court of Appeals for the Fourth Circuit.[47] The white primary was finally dead.

The New Law School

In January 1947 Boulware filed another major civil rights case. *John Wrighten v. University of South Carolina* was a long time in the making.[48] When Charles Bailey was attempting to gain admission to the University of South Carolina School of Law in 1938, Harold Boulware was completing his last year of law school at Howard University. His senior moot court project was designed to prepare Boulware to argue for the creation of a law school for African Americans under the doctrine of "separate but equal" as established by the U.S. Supreme Court in *Plessy v. Ferguson*.[49] Black veterans returning from World War II were eager to take advantage of the GI Bill. In 1946 veteran John Wrighten, a twenty-four-year-old black student at South Carolina State College, applied for admission to the University of South Carolina Law School and was rejected because of his race.[50] Wrighten then sought the support of the NAACP. Thurgood Marshall and Robert Carter, with Harold R. Boulware, E. A. Parker, and W. F. Robinson as local counsel, filed a suit on Wrighten's behalf.[51] The case challenged the state's denial of admission to Wrighten as violating the equal protection clause for the Fourteenth Amendment, but the lawyers hedged their bets and employed some of Boulware's moot court arguments from 1938 by pointing out that there was "no other law school supported by state funds which plaintiff and other Negroes similarly situated can conveniently attend."[52]

John Wrighten's suit was heard by U.S. district court judge J. Waties Waring on June 5 and 6, 1947. The state called USC School of Law dean Samuel L. Prince as an expert witness on legal education to support the position that "an equal law school" could be established at South Carolina State College. Law student Matthew Perry, who witnessed the trial, remembered that Thurgood Marshall embarrassed Prince by producing a stack of articles on legal education and getting Prince to admit that he had read none of the articles and had never even attended law school.[53]

Also testifying was Miller F. Whittaker, the president of South Carolina State College. Whittaker was obligated to support the contention of political leaders that a legitimate law school could quickly be created at South Carolina State. Whittaker complained privately: "They are putting me in the middle between the plaintiff and the defendants in this Law School business."[54] Whittaker must have been doubly torn with his role. He was the son of Johnson C. Whittaker, who had been forced out of West Point more than seventy years earlier because of his race.

In response to Thurgood Marshall's inquiry, President Whittaker readily conceded that no legal education was available in South Carolina for its black citizens. He further testified that no funds for a law school at South Carolina State had been allocated in 1945–46 or 1946–47, and that the college had hired no law professors and had no law library. Marshall then drove to the heart of the NAACP's case and asked Whittaker if, in view of "the fact that you don't have a faculty yet, nor a dean, nor a librarian, do you, in your own mind, believe you can set up a law school by September that would be the full and complete equal of the law school at the University of South Carolina?" Whittaker replied: "No, I don't think so."[55]

Despite the poor quality of the state's case, Judge Waring did not order Wrighten's admission to USC's law school. Citing the *Gaines* case, Waring decided to give the Orangeburg school and the state until September to establish such facilities. But Waring cautioned that if a law school was not established for black South Carolinians that was substantially equal to USC's, then either Wrighten would be admitted to the university's law school, or South Carolina's all-white school would be abolished.[56]

Within two weeks of the decision, Whittaker hired Benner C. Turner, a law professor at the all-black North Carolina College of Law in Durham, as dean. A Georgia native, Turner was a graduate of Phillip Andover Academy, Harvard College, and Harvard University School of Law. State College Board of Trustees vice chairman C. F. Brooks said of Turner, "We want nothing less than a man of ability, character, and with a correct understanding of the American way of life especially here in South Carolina."[57]

Whittaker and Turner then hired two additional law professors, one of whom was Cassandra Maxwell, and purchased hundreds of books for the law library. One classroom, some bookshelves, and student desks were made available in the college library. That building, Wilkinson Hall, also housed offices of the president and the business manager, as well as the college bookstore.

Located across the street in a women's dormitory were office spaces for the law school dean and faculty. The first class consisted of eight men and one woman.[58]

Marshall and the NAACP appealed Waring's decision to the federal court of appeals. The board of trustees and administrators of the University of South Carolina were obligated under Waring's order to admit Wrighten to the university's law school if the law school in Orangeburg was not established or if it was deemed to be unequal to the university's law school. It was obvious to Marshall that the hastily established law school in Orangeburg was not equal "in every respect" to the law school at the university.[59] But Wrighten informed him that local NAACP leaders told him to enroll in the new law school. Marshall reacted with fury and demanded that Wrighten provide him with their names, saying, "If ever I hear of any NAACP official speaking in favor of segregation . . . I will personally file charges against that member or officer." Marshall reminded Wrighten, "I had advised you not to go to the Jim Crow law school."[60] Shortly thereafter, Wrighten expressed the desire to quit the case. An exasperated Marshall finally gave up on Wrighten and directed Columbia attorney Harold Boulware in a "*confidential*" letter to "withdraw, without prejudice, the last motion we filed for further relief in this case and to leave it as it is."[61]

John Wrighten entered the South Carolina State Law School in 1949 and graduated in 1952. It was clear that, whether segregated or not, South Carolina needed a law school that would educate black lawyers. As of 1947, South Carolina had admitted only fifteen blacks lawyers in the twentieth century.[62] Another five were admitted by 1950, two of whom were S.C. State graduates. This number also included Benner C. Turner, the first law school dean of S.C. State, who was admitted on motion of Dean Samuel Prince of USC School of Law.

Other Civil Rights Cases

While the *Wrighten* case proceeded, a group of parents in Clarendon County had grown tired of the poor conditions in their children's schools. In particular, they wanted the same transportation provided to their children as was given to white students. In the summer of 1947, the state NAACP requested that Boulware represent the parents, and Boulware petitioned the school board to provide "school bus transportation" for the children of Levi Pearson.[63] After no response from the school board, he filed suit on March 16, 1948, in federal court. It was the first case in the state's history to challenge segregated schools. Clarendon County was one of the most oppressive of South Carolina's rural counties. While African Americans constituted 70 percent of the county's population, they earned less than $1,000 a year and owned less than 15 percent of the land. The local school board annually expended $179 for each white child and only $43 for each black child.[64]

In the lawsuit Boulware asserted that Pearson's children were suffering irreparable damage and asked the court to enjoin the school board from providing free bus service to white students while denying it to blacks. Boulware's co-counsel was Thurgood Marshall, the NAACP's lead counsel. Unfortunately, Levi Pearson had sued the wrong school district. His farm was located right on the school district line, and while he paid property taxes to one school district, his children attended another. Without the legal standing, Pearson's suit had to be dismissed.

Pearson suffered serious economic reprisals by the white community. However, he and the other parents did not give up. In March 1949 they met with Thurgood Marshall, Harold Boulware, and other NAACP officials to pursue a new course of action. At this meeting Thurgood Marshall informed the Clarendon County parents that the NAACP did not wish to pursue only a school transportation case; rather, Marshall urged that the lawsuit should challenge all areas of inequality in the schools. In addition, at least twenty families were needed to sue jointly if the NAACP were to be involved. The Rev. Joseph Delane, chief leader of the Clarendon County group, feared that it would be very hard to convince twenty families to jeopardize their wherewithal and possibly their lives for such a lawsuit.[65] But the parents came through.

Having a lawsuit with multiple plaintiffs meant that an individual's standing could not force dismissal of the case, and with multiple parties, intimidation would not likely scare away all of the plaintiffs. Despite the numbers, the parents suffered. Harry Briggs lost his job at a local gas station, and his wife lost her job as a maid at the Summerton Motel. Likewise, other named plaintiffs lost their jobs and were denied credit at the feed store or access to bank financing for their farms and businesses.[66]

Before the lawsuit could be filed there was much work to be done both locally and nationally. Boulware prepared a petition to the school board contrasting the conditions of white and black schools in Clarendon County. On February 20, 1950, the school district attorney flatly denied any inequality in the schools. The school's attorney claimed that Scott's Branch had a library with 1,678 books, including 56 encyclopedias, 21 progressive reference sets, 3 dictionaries, and other books. A woman who had been a student in the ninth grade the year the report was written noted that her homeroom had doubled as the school's library, and she remembered only three dictionaries. She said that the "count must have included all student textbooks in the school, the entire supply of outdated magazines that had not yet been confiscated for use as toilet paper, and photographs of encyclopedias and 'progressive reference sets' (whatever they are)."[67]

While the larger case was prepared by the national NAACP lawyers, Harold Boulware was called on to assist in grievances the parents had against the principal of the Scott's Branch High School. One observer noted that Harold Boulware became the "master of the Clarendon County Courthouse. It was the first time that a black lawyer had stood in those halls in more than a generation."[68] Boulware's successful efforts led to the removal of the principal.

On May 16, 1950, the new lawsuit captioned *Briggs v. Elliott* was filed, seeking sweeping relief. The complaint cited inequality not only in transportation but also in buildings, teachers, teacher pay, and materials. The case was heard initially by Judge Waties Waring. While Marshall had wanted to directly challenge the state's segregation constitution, he had taken the more cautious approach of challenging the equality of the separate schools under *Plessy v. Ferguson*. The conditions were so inadequate that such a claim would have been easy to prove. For example, Scott's Branch High School served six hundred students but provided them only with two outhouses and schoolyard water spigots.[69]

As the case progressed, NAACP lawyers discovered that Judge Waring wanted nothing to do with a separate but equal suit and suggested that a direct challenge be made to segregation in the schools.[70] The judge's comments compelled the NAACP lawyers to withdraw their case and draft a new complaint which would directly challenge separate but equal. The new petitions now had twenty-nine families as plaintiffs. Filed in December 1950, the case challenged the constitutionality of South Carolina's segregation clause and as such required a three-judge court. Judge Waring was joined by U.S. District Judge George Bell Timmerman, a staunch segregationist, and U.S. Circuit Judge John Parker of West Virginia.[71]

The trial in Charleston was dramatic. It included the testimony of Kenneth Clarke, the social psychologist from the City College of New York who had developed the famous black and white doll test that he conducted in Clarendon County. Clarendon County school board lawyer Robert McCormick Figg surprised Marshall by conceding that the Clarendon County schools were deplorable and unequal but stated that the board needed a reasonable period of time to right the wrong. On June 23, 1951, the three-judge court issued its opinion accepting the concession that the black schools were inferior but also agreeing that the board needed more time to improve the schools. In responding to the NAACP's position about the inherent inequality of the segregated system, the court simply relied on *Plessy v. Ferguson* and found "segregation of the races in public school so long as equality of rights is preserved, is a matter of legislative policy for the several states with which the federal courts are powerless to interfere." Judge Waring dissented from the majority opinion, writing that the federal court should "face, without evasion or equivocation the question as to whether segregation in education is legal in [light] of the 14th amendment of the Constitution." Waring ended his dissent by asserting that "the system of segregation education adopted in practice by the state of South Carolina must go and must go now."[72]

The South Carolina case was soon appealed to the U.S. Supreme Court, where it was ultimately joined with *Brown v. Board of Education of Topeka, Kansas*, becoming the landmark case that ended segregated schools in the United States. Although Harold Boulware had a secondary role in the appeal, he had played a pivotal role as counsel in the most important civil rights case in American history.

In addition to civil rights cases, Boulware undertook important individual cases for clients. In 1947 Willie Earle became the last man lynched in the state's history, but the jury in the subsequent trial of twenty-eight white men failed to convict them. Boulware was then approached by Earle's family, and he won a lawsuit on their behalf under a state law that made counties liable to the families of lynching victims.[73]

In 1949 Boulware was retained to represent a young man charged with rape in Greenwood County. This case, *State v. Willie Tolbert*, would prove to be one of the most difficult of Boulware's career. Tolbert had been charged with intent to rape, which was a capital offense. In the South black men convicted of even attempted rape of a white woman were routinely sentenced to death. White rapists seldom faced such a sentence.[74] Moreover, the alleged victim was the local prosecutor's daughter. On September 12, 1949, when Boulware traveled to Greenwood for the trial, he was followed and kidnapped by a group of white men. The men took the lawyer into the woods and assaulted him. Boulware said they "tapped" him a few times and then threatened him with worse "if that Damn Nigger gets off."[75] The next day, Boulware was again physically attacked on the courthouse steps. Despite the presence of some of his assailants in the courtroom, Boulware challenged the racial composition of the grand jury and the petit jury venire. In what the press noted as the first action of its kind in the state, the trial judge granted his motions.[76] A new grand jury was hastily called with its first ever black member, but it quickly reindicted Tolbert that afternoon, and the trial began the next day with an all-white jury, the court having excused the only black called for the venire.[77] The state's evidence consisted of the young white woman and her boyfriend, who both identified

Tolbert and testified that Tolbert raped her. After the close of the state's case, Boulware announced that his client refused to testify and rested his case. After deliberating only ten minutes, the jury convicted Tolbert, and he was sentenced to death.[78] After the trial, Boulware had to have highway patrolmen escort him home to Columbia.[79]

Tolbert was executed on October 28, 1949. Two different articles were published detailing Tolbert's claim that the victim had consented to sexual intercourse with him. On October 1, black newspaperman John McCray published a detailed version of the story. In addition, a white reporter interviewed Tolbert just before his execution and also related Tolbert's claim. The stories outraged the father of the victim, and criminal libel charges were filed against both reporters. Ultimately, the case against the white reporter was dropped, but McCray, facing a sure conviction and a prison sentence, took Thurgood Marshall's advice and pled guilty.[80] He was fined and placed on probation.[81]

McCray claimed that he based his version of Willie Tolbert's story on notes provided to him by Harold Boulware.[82] After Boulware had died, McCray explained that Boulware had called him to say that he had been visited by investigators and denied being the source of McCray's story. Boulware had apologized to McCray, who remembered thirty-seven years later that Boulware was upset and "still shaken" by the Tolbert trial and the investigation. In an interview in 1986, McCray said that after the Tolbert case, Boulware withdrew from school desegregation cases and was reluctant to take on new NAACP cases.[83]

While Boulware may have been unsettled by the trial as well as McCray's problems, he remained active in the *Briggs* case through the 1954 and 1955 U.S. Supreme Court decisions.[84] In 1954 he was still the NAACP lawyer in the state.[85] In 1957 he was involved in a case suing the Elloree schools for terminating teachers who were members of the NAACP.[86] Boulware was counsel in four major criminal appeals to the state supreme court between 1952 and 1960.[87] Boulware also had an active civil practice at the trial level in Columbia.[88] He ran for office at least twice in the 1960s.[89] He became a municipal judge in 1968 and was appointed by Governor John C. West as a Richland County family court judge in 1974.[90] He retired from that judgeship in 1982 and passed away just a few months later in February 1983.[91]

Other Lawyers

Three other lawyers were admitted in the 1940s. William B. James, admitted in 1947, had attended Robert Terrell Law School in Washington, D.C. He practiced law in Sumter from 1947 to 1954. After he ran for Sumter City Council in 1954 and lost, he moved to Washington to work for the Federal Trade Commission.[92] In 1971 he returned to Sumter and was active in community affairs. He died in 1989.[93]

From the mid-1930s Charleston had no black lawyers until 1948, when Richard C. Fields was admitted.[94] A native of Charleston, Fields attended West Virginia State College and Howard University School of Law. He studied for the bar exam in Harold Boulware's office in Columbia and was admitted in 1948. Fields was never active as a civil rights lawyer but quickly earned the respect of the white bar in Charleston. He often served as co-counsel on cases with white lawyers and was successful doing personal injury work for plaintiffs. He credits Gedney Howe, the solicitor in Charleston, with mentoring him. Another white lawyer who was of assistance to Fields was J. D. E. Meyer, uncle of U.S. senator Fritz Hollings. When Fields needed to search a title in Orangeburg, Col. Meyer called ahead to the clerk of court on his behalf. When Fields arrived he was greeted graciously by the clerk and given the grand tour of the clerk's office with tips on searching titles in the county records. However, when Fields needed the restroom, the clerk of court called the courthouse janitor, who was black, to take him to the janitor's water closet in the basement. Twenty-five years later, when Fields returned to that same courthouse as a sitting circuit court judge, things had changed.[95] Fields was made municipal court judge in Charleston in 1969, becoming the first black judge in the state since the nineteenth century. Fields was elected a family court judge by the South Carolina General Assembly in 1975, and in 1980 the state legislature elected him a circuit judge.[96] He retired from the bench in 1992 and resumed law practice.

Lincoln C. Jenkins of Columbia was admitted in 1949. After graduating from Howard University School of Law, Jenkins, the son of a prominent minister, returned to Columbia and opened a law office on Washington Street next door to Harold Boulware's. Jenkins co-counseled with Boulware in two criminal cases in the early 1950s.[97] Probably because of Boulware's withdrawal from some NAACP work, Jenkins was asked to take on cases, and for a time he was considered the chief counsel for the civil rights organization.[98] In 1955 he served as local co-counsel for Jack Greenberg of the national office when the Sumter branch was sued for libel.[99] Likewise in 1956, when Thurgood Marshall sued the Elloree school district for terminating teachers who were members of the NAACP, Jenkins was local counsel instead of Boulware.[100] By 1958 he was representing the plaintiffs in the Clarendon County school desegregation case.[101] By 1959, however, Jenkins and the leaders of the state NAACP had persuaded Matthew J. Perry to become its chief counsel.[102] Jenkins then invited Perry to join him in practice in Columbia. They remained law partners until Perry went on the bench.

Jenkins continued to play a significant role in civil rights cases. In 1961 he and Perry argued a case in the state supreme court contesting the constitutionality of the conviction of students arrested at a sit-in in Columbia.[103] When the Greenville airport was ordered to desegregate its waiting rooms, Jenkins was the lawyer for the plaintiff.[104] In 1962, while Perry was working on Henri Monteith's case against the University of South Carolina, Jenkins was handling the case that resulted in ending segregation of the state parks of South Carolina.[105] The state parks case was another sad example of South Carolina's response to civil rights. A month after the decision, all of the state parks were closed.[106] That response was not new. In 1956, when a suit was brought to desegregate Edisto Beach State Park, the state admitted in court that segregated state facilities were unconstitutional but the legislature simply closed the park.[107] In 1964 the state parks were reopened with restricted use of swimming and camping facilities, and in 1966 all of the parks, including Edisto, were fully reopened.[108]

Jenkins served on the Richland County School District One Board of Trustees and was a municipal judge in Columbia. His son Lincoln Jenkins III was also a lawyer and a city judge in Columbia. The elder Jenkins died May 14, 1986.[109]

The lawyers admitted in the 1940s were the vanguard of the modern civil rights movement. Because of their efforts the state was forced to change. While a lawyer such as Richard Fields did not play a role in the civil rights movement, the very fact that he practiced law successfully in Charleston meant that the city became a different place. Cassandra Maxwell played a minor role in the civil rights struggle, but becoming the first woman of her race admitted to the South Carolina bar was a significant event in and of itself. W. F. Robinson and William B. James had only supporting roles in the civil rights struggle; nonetheless, their presence made a difference. Lincoln Jenkins was overshadowed by his law partner, Matthew Perry, but without question, Lincoln Jenkins's contribution to civil rights in the state has been underappreciated. Of course, the role that Harold Boulware played in the civil rights struggle was critical to the advancement achieved by the black community in the state. There is no question that Harold Boulware was South Carolina's first true civil rights lawyer.

CHAPTER 12

The Modern Civil Rights Era

With the successes of the NAACP's South Carolina cases, the civil rights revolution was well under way by the early 1950s. But the state remained a bastion of segregation. More blacks were able to vote, but no black was elected to public office in the 1950s or 1960s. Also, because of white resistance, the dual secondary and elementary school systems would not be eliminated until 1970.

The South Carolina State Law School

Paradoxically, the creation of the "separate but equal" law school at South Carolina State College would serve as one of the most important NAACP victories, since the graduates of the law school would launch a series of legal assaults on segregation in the state. The new law school had been created to prevent the desegregation of the University of South Carolina's School of Law. Historian William Hine has pointed out that the state legislature never adequately funded the new law school, and in fact, the meager monies provided for legal education deprived the undergraduate program at South Carolina State of critically needed funds. The college's enrollments surged following World War II as veterans applied in record numbers. The college desperately needed both faculty and facilities. Many students were housed in surplus army barracks. During the life of the law school from 1947 until 1966, the college annually rejected hundreds of undergraduate students because of inadequate space.[1]

In 1947 the college's president, Miller F. Whittaker, complained to the legislature that the pending budget bill for construction on college campuses seriously shortchanged his institution. The legislature had proposed allocations ranging from $600,000 to $3.1 million for the state's white colleges and only

$350,000 to South Carolina State. In total, only 4.6 percent of state monies for higher education were allocated to the state's only black public college. Although the state's black population was 39 percent, legislators ignored Whittaker's complaint and passed the bill with no changes.[2]

The first building erected on the campus following World War II was Moss Hall, the law school. Completed in 1949 at a cost of $200,000, it was named after Adam H. Moss, a local white attorney who served on the college's board of trustees.[3] While the funds for the law school deprived the undergraduate program of needed sustenance, it was never sufficient to earn full accreditation by the American Bar Association. South Carolina State had the lowest-paid law faculty of all forty-five state-supported law schools in the nation.[4]

The underpaid faculty, however, were well qualified and dedicated. Benner C. Turner, the first dean, was a graduate of Harvard Law School and had been a law professor at North Carolina Central University. He served as dean from 1947 to 1950 and then was president of State College for seventeen years. Leo Kerford graduated from the University of Kansas Law School and taught for the law school's entire nineteen-year existence. Harvard graduate Paul A. Simmons was on the faculty for three years in the early 1950s and later became a federal district judge in Pittsburgh. LeMarquis DeJarmon, a graduate of Western Reserve Law School in Cleveland, taught at State from 1948 to 1955. University of Iowa law graduate Blinzy Gore was on the faculty for sixteen years; Howard law graduate Charles Washington Jr. taught at the school for fourteen years. Earl Coblyn, a graduate of Suffolk Law School, served on the faculty from 1961 to 1966. Fordham Law School graduate Samuel C. Scott was on the faculty only one year. Cassandra Maxwell, a Howard law graduate, was on the faculty three years. The second dean, Peter H. Whittaker, the nephew of Miller F. Whittaker, succumbed to heart failure in 1954. Theodis R. Gay, a graduate of Wayne University Law School, served as dean from 1955 to 1961, and Leo Kerford was the last dean, serving from 1961 to 1966.[5]

Publicly, the school's law professors were not active in the civil rights movement.[6] In the aftermath of *Briggs v. Elliott*, the General Assembly enacted a statute prohibiting membership in the NAACP by local, county, and state employees. Any public involvement in civil rights by faculty would have meant termination.[7] In fact, public schoolteachers in Elloree in Orangeburg County were terminated because of their NAACP membership.[8] The law school sponsored seminars for attorneys, but civil rights was not among the topics.[9] However, by the 1960s, as the civil rights struggle accelerated, Earl W. Coblyn, who was hired in 1961, actively supported a black candidate in a legislative campaign. In addition, Charles Washington Jr. provided private counsel and advice to Matthew Perry and organized a mooting of one of Perry's major civil rights cases.[10]

On the other hand, while some of State's graduates moved away, thirty of the fifty-one graduates were admitted to the South Carolina bar, and most of them engaged in significant civil rights litigation.[11] Major cases were handled by Albert A. Kennedy, W. Newton Pough, Frank E. Cain, John Wrighten, Ernest A. Finney, Willie T. Smith Jr., William Bennett, Russell Brown, Ruben L. Gray, Zack E. Townsend, George A. Payton, and Matthew Perry.[12] Other State graduates assisted in trial work and in advising civil rights groups. For example, Cleveland Stevens handled many trials for student demonstrators in Orangeburg. Alphonso Pendergrass assisted Charles Washington Jr. in civil rights cases in Beaufort County.[13] Franklin DeWitt, Daniel E. Martin, George Allen Anderson, and John E. McCall represented the NAACP in various counties.[14] These lawyers represented thousands of civil rights demonstrators in city courts, magistrate's courts, state circuit court, the state supreme court, the federal district courts, the federal appellate courts, and the U.S. Supreme Court.

"Chief Counsel"

Without a doubt, the lawyer who had the greatest impact on civil rights in the state's history was Matthew J. Perry. He represented thousands of clients in civil rights cases and co-counseled with other State Law School graduates in many of these cases.[15] His fellow lawyers considered him their leader and affectionately called him "chief counsel."[16]

Perry was born in Columbia, South Carolina, in 1921. His father, a tailor, contracted tuberculosis because of exposure to mustard gas in World War I. This illness necessitated the family's moving to Alabama because the only Veterans Administration hospital that accepted African Americans was in Tuskegee, Alabama. When the senior Perry died in 1932, Mrs. Jenny Liles Perry moved her family back to Columbia to live with her father, William Liles, a railroad brakeman who could provide a modest but stable home for his daughter and grandchildren. Mrs. Perry had attended Benedict College and worked as a domestic worker, a seamstress, and a clerk to help support her three children. After high school Matthew Perry, a good student, attended South Carolina State College.[17] The Japanese attack on Pearl Harbor occurred during Perry's sophomore year, and by January 1943 he was in the army. He served in England, France, and Germany before returning home in 1946 as a sergeant.[18] Perry had often thought about becoming a lawyer, but his World War II experiences cemented the decision. A pivotal moment occurred on a cold night in Alabama while his troop train stopped. Hungry and tired, he sought a meal at the train station café, only to be directed to a window to buy his sandwich and eat it outside in the cold. Peering into the windows of the café, Perry saw Italian prisoners of war being served inside the station. In fact, the young white waitresses even appeared to be flirting with them. To Perry, there was no greater indignity than for a prisoner of war to be treated better than an American soldier in uniform. After the war, he finished his undergraduate education at State and then entered the second class at the new law school.

While he was a law student, Perry established a close relationship with Harold Boulware and was often invited to accompany him to court. Boulware's tutelage coincided with the inspiration that Perry was receiving from the NAACP's civil rights litigation victories. Unlike Boulware, Perry's formal legal education was not oriented toward civil rights. The law school at South Carolina State was not training lawyers to be "social engineers" as had the Howard School of Law. In fact, despite the ever-increasing numbers of federal civil rights cases, Perry recalled no formal discussion of them in his classes.[19]

The law school's first two graduates, Albert A. Kennedy and Julius T. Williams Jr., were admitted to the state bar in 1950 by the diploma privilege without having to take the bar exam, like the white graduates of USC's law school. But after that first class, the privilege was abruptly ended. David Robinson, the lead attorney for the state in John Wrighten's case, led the South Carolina Bar Association's effort to persuade the General Assembly to revoke the privilege. The legislator who introduced the bill was blunt in explaining that requiring law school graduates to pass the bar exam would "bar Negroes and some undesirable whites" from practicing law.[20] In 1951 Perry was the only member of his class to pass the bar exam on the first try.

After law school, Perry moved to Spartanburg, where he was the city's first black lawyer since the 1930s. He opened a small office equipped with a typewriter and a few law books given to him by the widow of A. C. Platt, the last black lawyer who had practiced in the city. His wife, Hallie Perry, taught high school to help support them, but soon Matthew Perry was earning a living in the courtroom. He was assertive, inventive, and always professional. In the local municipal court, Perry's black clients were treated more severely than white defendants, and Perry was on more than one occasion faced with the necessity of appealing the city judge's decision. The appellate rules required written notice to be served to the judge within twenty-four hours of his decision. The next time the judge ruled without allowing Perry to present any argument, Perry immediately filed a notice of appeal. The white judge responded, "How could you know the grounds for your appeal so fast?" Perry responded, "Your honor, you always do this to my clients."[21] Not only were Perry's clients treated more fairly thereafter, but his victory attracted more clients. His income was bolstered by the state's Prohibition laws, which created a large underground business of selling liquor. Unlike most criminal defendants, these bootleggers were financially able to afford a lawyer, and a good criminal defense lawyer such as Matthew Perry often got them off.[22]

After a few years in practice, Perry was invited to Washington, D.C., to watch the mooting of *Brown v. Board of Education* at Howard University School of Law on the night before the oral arguments in the U.S. Supreme Court. The next day Perry was also able to observe the historic arguments in the court itself.

His success as a trial lawyer attracted the attention of the NAACP. In June 1954, some seventeen months before Rosa Parks started the bus boycott in Montgomery, Alabama, Sara Mae Flemming had taken a seat in the front of a bus in Columbia, South Carolina, where she was immediately ordered by the white driver to move to the back. When she attempted to exit the bus by the front door, she was physically barred by the driver. Humiliated and angry, Flemming found a sympathetic white lawyer, Philip Wittenberg, to sue the bus company and the state. State law required the bus driver to enforce segregated seating on the bus, and the utility company defended on that basis. The case was assigned to pro-segregation district court judge George Bell Timmerman, who twice dismissed her suit. Both his decisions were reversed by the Fourth Circuit Court of Appeals and sent back for trial. Because of death threats and a cross burning, Wittenberg withdrew, and the NAACP needed a new lawyer to try the case. Lincoln Jenkins recruited Matthew Perry, and three years after her saga began, Perry managed to get her case to the jury. As could have been expected, the all-white, all-male jury ruled against her in just thirty minutes. After this case, however, the bus no longer had segregated seating, and Matthew J. Perry had become the NAACP's lawyer.[23]

In 1960 Perry became chairman of the NAACP's state legal committee. He was soon representing hundreds if not thousands of clients. In Orangeburg alone, State students, teachers, parents, and community activists generated hundreds of cases. This level of community activity compelled Perry to organize a team of black lawyers. Just in 1960, this team represented over a thousand South Carolina State students who were arrested for demonstrating.

Perry and his local lawyers were careful to make a good trial record so that the cases could be appealed by the NAACP lawyers in New York. Although Jack Greenburg argued *Edwards v. South Carolina* in the U.S. Supreme Court, it was Perry who had represented the 189 students charged with breach of the peace in the Columbia municipal court trials.[24] The students had been arrested for marching on the state capitol grounds "protesting the antiquated and unjust pattern of segregation" in the state.[25] They were permitted to walk around the statehouse once but they could not stop, walk around a second time, or sing while on the statehouse grounds, and they had to disperse within fifteen minutes. By contrast, white students from the University of South Carolina had been allowed to hold boisterous political rallies on the statehouse grounds.[26] Perry proved that his clients had obeyed all orders except to disperse and end their demonstration. Instead of leaving, his clients remained to listen to a religious speech and sing religious and patriotic songs. Perry argued they had committed no unlawful acts, but the state countered that the students had caused traffic congestion and public inconvenience, and they had attracted "potential troublemakers" to the scene.[27] In fact, even the troublemakers caused no disturbance. In an opinion full of footnotes quoting the trial testimony, the U.S. Supreme Court reversed the convictions, holding 8–1 that the students' First Amendment rights had been violated.[28]

In 1962 Perry tried a demonstration case in Greenville on behalf of ten students arrested for sitting in at a lunch counter. This case resulted in his first appeal to the Supreme Court, which he argued and won, *Peterson v. City of Greenville*.[29] Perry won seven appeals in the U.S. Supreme Court, which overturned more than seven thousand demonstrators' convictions.[30]

A decade after *Brown v. Board of Education* and *Briggs v. Elliott*, no public primary or secondary school in South Carolina had been desegregated. Working with local counsel and the NAACP lawyers from New York, Perry attacked segregated education. In 1962 he sued Clemson College for Harvey Gantt, who had been denied admission because of his race. Gantt prevailed and in January 1963 became the school's first black student. In that same year, Perry brought suit against the University of South Carolina on behalf of Henri Monteith and again won. Ms. Monteith, along with James Anderson and James Solomon, became USC's first black students since 1877. However, no secondary or elementary school had been desegregated. In 1955 the parents of Minerva Brown petitioned for their daughter to be admitted to all-white Charleston High School. The case dragged on for six years, Minerva graduated, and the case appeared mooted. Her father, J. Arthur Brown, president of the state conference of the NAACP, approached Perry for guidance, and Perry amended the complaint to substitute the youngest Brown daughter, Millicent. The case was soon heard and won.[31] For the first time in state history, a public secondary school was desegregated when Millicent Brown, the named plaintiff, and ten other black students enrolled at all-white schools in Charleston in September 1963. Similar suits had to be brought across the state. In 1964 Perry was able to desegregate the schools in Sumter, Orangeburg, and Clarendon Counties.[32]

These cases resulted in so-called freedom of choice plans. Such plans did little to desegregate schools because no whites chose to attend black schools, and any black student who attended a white school suffered harassment, threats, and intimidation. In 1966 Perry filed six cases challenging freedom of choice plans. The lead case was, sadly enough, against a school district in Clarendon County, where *Briggs v. Elliott* arose, and where schools were still segregated more than a decade later. U.S. district court judge Robert Martin found that the district's freedom of choice plan was nothing more than a means to "maintain separation of the races" and enjoined the school board from continuing to operate a biracial school system.[33] In 1968 the U.S. Supreme Court held that freedom of choice plans were unconstitutional, and in 1969 the court ordered that desegregated school systems be achieved "at once," thus ending dual school systems.[34] Perry again was counsel when in 1970 the Fourth Circuit Court of Appeals ordered the immediate implementation of the Supreme Court's mandate to end segregated schools.[35] After the court ruled that busing was appropriate to achieve desegregation, Perry became lead counsel in the primary busing case in South Carolina.[36] More than twenty years had passed since the school desegregation fight had begun in South Carolina. Perry biographer Robert J. Moore noted that "by 1971 a unitary system was in place; 93 percent of black pupils in South Carolina attended schools with white children."[37]

Not all of Perry's cases were on behalf of civil rights demonstrators or students. Because of the racial disparities in the criminal justice system, the national NAACP and later the NAACP Legal Defense Fund launched a campaign against the death penalty.[38] As chairman of the NAACP's legal committee, Perry effectuated that policy in South Carolina. His first case was the appeal of Quincy Bullock, an illiterate dishwasher who had been convicted and sentenced to die for murdering Carolyn Barfield, a white woman described by the press as a "pretty, 25 year old Lake View mother."[39] The story was that on August 3, 1958, Barfield and a male companion, Jeremy Horne, were parked in a cemetery when someone fired into their car and caused them to flee.[40] Jeremy Horne said he was shot in the shoulder while running, and he lost Carolyn Barfield along the way.[41] Barfield's body was discovered the next day.[42] Quincy Bullock, who had served time for attempted criminal assault and lived in the area, was arrested.[43] His arrest attracted a mob, forcing the police to move Bullock from jail to jail.[44] Initially Bullock claimed he had been in North Carolina on the night of the murder, but after relentless questioning, he confessed, "If you say I done it, I done it."[45] Then three days later, Bullock signed two written confessions prepared by the police. At his trial, Bullock recanted his confessions, claiming he signed because he was beaten by the law enforcement officers.[46] His two court-appointed white lawyers could not prevent the confession being admitted. While Bullock was not charged with rape, highly prejudicial evidence was introduced that the victim had been raped. Before the trial Jeremy Horne, the companion of the deceased, had implicated Bullock, but at the time of the trial Horne was hospitalized and was never cross-examined in court. Two state's witnesses were in conflict about Bullock's gun. One claimed that the bullet found in Horne's shoulder was from the gun, but the other expert testified that it could not be determined if the bullet came from the gun.[47]

Bullock testified in his own defense, asserting he was innocent and that he had been beaten into confessing. Bullock's wife corroborated her husband's claim that he was beaten. Bullock was convicted by the all-white Dillon County jury and sentenced to death.[48] Perry, Lincoln Jenkins, and Donald Sampson were asked to handle the appeal to the South Carolina Supreme Court.[49] They argued that Bullock's confession was obtained "under duress" and that the prejudicial evidence of a rape should not have been admitted.[50] The state supreme court affirmed Bullock's conviction.[51] Perry then appealed to the U.S. Supreme Court chiefly on the grounds that Bullock's confession was not voluntary. He asserted that there had been sustained questioning at multiple jails "punctuated by beatings while a sheet was placed over his head."[52] The U.S. Supreme Court granted oral arguments in the case but ultimately denied relief.[53] Quincy Bullock was electrocuted on April 28, 1961, maintaining his innocence with his last words.[54] Bullock's case was the only U.S. Supreme Court appeal Matthew Perry ever lost, and Bullock was his only client to be executed.[55]

A chief target of the NAACP campaign was the use of the death penalty in rape cases.[56] According to Jack Greenberg of the NAACP Legal Defense Fund, when the campaign began, "almost 90 percent of the 455 defendants executed for rape since the 1930's were blacks convicted of raping white women."[57] Perry had one of the first cases in the state to challenge the death sentence in a rape case. On Tuesday, November 28, 1961, two young white women reported they had been raped in a motel in Kingstree. Suspected immediately was a nineteen-year-old convicted rapist, David White, who had just escaped from a prison farm. The two women said a black man entered their room, held a butcher knife on them, and assaulted them.[58] White's fingerprints were found in the motel room, and the alleged victims picked out White from photographs as their rapist.[59]

White turned himself in, and he was taken to the state penitentiary for "safekeeping."[60] Charged with rape, he had two local court-appointed lawyers.[61] Both of White's accusers testified at trial. One woman positively identified White as the rapist, but the other failed to identify him. The sheriff testified that White admitted to being in the hotel room and taking money, but he denied hurting the girls. The all-white, all-male jury convicted White of rape, and the judge sentenced him to death.[62]

White appealed and was granted a stay of execution.[63] Subsequently, Matthew Perry and Lincoln Jenkins were appointed as White's counsel.[64] They appealed to the South Carolina Supreme Court, and the court reversed White's conviction because the trial judge had refused to charge the jury that White's decision not to testify could not be used against him.[65]

At the new trial, Perry's extensive questioning of each potential juror caused the press to complain of the delays, but the trial proceeded as before.[66] The most dramatic moment of the trial came when Perry objected to the solicitor's closing argument: "If a snake would bite you or one of your children would you let him go and bite again? . . . How would you like to see [the defendant] coming into your bedroom or your daughter's bedroom, with this butcher knife? What if it was your sister's bedroom? What if the defendant was coming in your mother's bedroom window with that butcher knife?"[67] Even though the argument was clearly an appeal to passion and prejudice, the trial judge allowed it. Again White was convicted of rape and sentenced to death.[68] Perry appealed, and this time the Supreme Court reversed the conviction because the prosecutor's arguments prejudiced the right of the defendant to a fair trial.[69] At the time, Matthew Perry was representing seven of the twelve men on death row and was described by the press as "probably the most widely-known fighter to end the death penalty."[70] White was never executed.[71]

In 1963 Perry undertook the representation of Lewis Bostick, whose case was similar to such cases as *Brownfield*, *Franklin*, and *Sanders*. Like John Brownfield and Pink Franklin, Bostick was charged with killing a law enforcement officer. In Bostick's case it was for murder of the sheriff of Jasper County, C. W. Floyd. Bostick, a seventeen-year-old, signed a statement in which he admitted that he set up a roadblock to stop cars and rob the drivers. Bostick claimed that when Sheriff Floyd arrived at the roadblock, Floyd shot at him first, and he returned fire.[72]

Lewis Bostick, represented by local white attorneys and tried by an all-white jury, tried to plead guilty to avoid the death sentence, but the state refused to accept the plea.[73] He was convicted and sentenced to death.[74] In his appeal to the South Carolina Supreme Court, Bostick's attorneys argued only that the state had failed to prove the location of the murder. Otherwise, Bostick's attorneys told the state supreme court that their client received a fair trial.[75] The court found "no prejudicial error" in the trial, and Bostick's appeal was denied.[76]

Matthew Perry and Charles Washington Jr. took on the case and obtained a stay of execution.[77] They then filed in state circuit court a *habeas corpus* petition for Bostick.[78] They argued that blacks "were systematically excluded from the grand and petit juries in Jasper County."[79] In 1960 the county was 62 percent black. At the state court hearing before Judge John Grimball, Perry called various county officials who all denied any discrimination in jury selection, but Perry established that in 1954 a state court judge had found that Jasper County engaged in discriminatory jury selection practices.[80] Perry then proved that the county had ignored the order and not changed its method of choosing jurors. They used county registration records that designated voters by race. The clerk of court asserted that the names were blindly drawn, but he also admitted that "I know as soon as I see their names whether they are white or colored."[81] Perry then asked who was excluded and the clerk claimed that only those over age sixty-five, disabled, or in ill health were presumptively excluded, but he conceded that they struck voters who could not read and write. Despite the fact that there were 974 white males registered to vote and 256 black males, only one black voter had been drawn for the grand jury that indicted Bostick, and while two had been on the petit jury venire, none served on his jury. In fact, only one black had ever been drawn for either the grand or the petit jury service. When asked to explain how it was possible that only one black had ever been selected for grand jury service, the clerk replied that he did not know. Despite this evidence, the jury discrimination argument was rejected by Judge John Grimball.[82] The case again went to the state supreme court, which also rejected the appeal and affirmed the circuit judge ruling.[83]

Perry then sought review by the U.S. Supreme Court.[84] Earlier that term, the court decided *Whitus v. State of Georgia*, which found a Georgia scheme similar to Jasper County's to be discriminatory. In *Whitus* juror names were drawn from records that identified taxpayers by race, then potential jurors were selected by jury commissioners based on their personal knowledge of the qualifications of the juror.[85] On March 27, 1967, the U.S. Supreme Court reversed Bostick's conviction because of "discrimination in jury selection."[86]

Soon after the high court decision, the solicitor announced that he planned to try Bostick again.[87] Six years after the original trial, Bostick was again convicted of murder, but the jury recommended mercy, and Bostick received a mandatory life sentence. His jury in this second trial included seven black men and five white men.[88]

In April 1969 Perry was again representing college students, this time from

Voorhees College in Denmark, South Carolina. The students had occupied a college administration building demanding the creation of a black studies program. Unfortunately, they were armed and had proudly displayed rifles and bandoliers to the press.[89] The arrested students were charged with riot.[90] Although represented by Matthew Perry, Lincoln Jenkins, and Fred Henderson Moore, the students were convicted.[91] Moore and Matthew Perry then appealed on behalf of two students, but the convictions were affirmed.[92]

Perry's cases changed every facet of life in the state. One of his clients, Gloria Rackley, illustrates the wide-ranging impact of Perry's work. Her children were able to attend desegregated schools as a result of a suit filed by Perry.[93] Ms. Rackley was fired from her job as a schoolteacher because of her civil rights activities, and Perry sued on her behalf, resulting in her reinstatement with back benefits.[94] In 1965 Perry successfully sued the Orangeburg Regional Hospital on behalf of Ms. Rackley, challenging their segregation practices.[95] For other clients, he brought suits that desegregated public libraries, state parks, municipal golf courses, movie theaters, restaurants, bus stations, and airports.[96] Perry participated in at least two dozen school desegregation cases. He saved the lives of numerous men sentenced to death. He dismantled at-large elections, which led to the election of a substantial number of blacks to seats in the state legislature. In 1972 Perry was lead counsel in a lawsuit that caused the reapportionment of the South Carolina House of Representatives into single-member districts. Consequently, the number of African Americans in the state legislature increased from three to thirteen, the largest number it had been since Reconstruction.[97] The attack on at-large elections also led to the election of large numbers of blacks to county councils across the state.[98] Biographer Robert Moore believed that Perry's success in the reapportionment cases torpedoed his chances of being elected to a state court judgeship, because too many of the legislators were angered by them.[99] They would also prove to be the last major civil rights cases Perry would bring.

In addition to his civil rights work, Perry served in many other capacities. Despite his representation of the Voorhees College student protestors, he served as chairman of the college's board of trustees.[100] Perry was on the national board of the NAACP; in 1968 he was their interim general counsel and was even mentioned as a candidate to be chairman of the board.[101] He was offered a position as a professor at the University of South Carolina School of Law in 1972, but he declined and instead accepted a part-time lecturer position.[102] He was elected to the Democratic National Committee in 1973.[103]

In 1974 Perry was the unsuccessful Democratic nominee for Congress.[104] In 1975, in his first ever meeting with Senator Strom Thurmond, Perry was offered a presidential appointment to the U.S. Military Court of Appeals. After consultation with friends and family, he accepted. On February 18, 1976, U.S. Supreme Court justice Thurgood Marshall administered to him the oath of office, making Perry the first black from the Deep South appointed to a federal judgeship. In 1979 Matthew J. Perry Jr. was appointed to the U.S. District Court for South Carolina by President Jimmy Carter, becoming the state's first black federal judge.

Judge Perry retired in 1995 but continued to hear cases in senior status. In 2004 the new U.S. Courthouse in Columbia was named in his honor. On Friday, July 29, 2011, less than a week before his ninetieth birthday, Perry worked a full day and died that evening at home. His funeral was attended by nearly two thousand mourners. He was eulogized by such luminaries as former U.S. senator Fritz Hollings and South Carolina chief justice Jean Toal. In his *New York Times* obituary, Harvard law professor Randall Kennedy praised Perry for helping "create federal law that enlarged our liberty."[105] Retired federal public defender Langdon D. Long, who appeared before Perry many times, described Perry as the "quintessential judge. He was determined to be sure every single individual who came before him understood his or her rights under the Constitution. He could be tough with lawyers but he treated each defendant with dignity and respect. If all judges were as keen of intellect and sincere in compassion as Matthew Perry our judicial system would be much fairer."[106] With more than ninety reported civil rights cases litigated from South Carolina by Perry, his record is without equal in the history of the South Carolina bar.[107] The "separate but equal" South Carolina State Law School managed to produce the most important civil rights lawyer in the state's history.

From Waiter to Chief Justice

In some ways, Ernest A. Finney's contributions to civil rights in South Carolina were as important as those of Matthew J. Perry. Finney graduated from S.C. State School of Law in 1954 and was admitted to the bar that same year. Finney's mother had died when he was ten days old in 1931, and he was raised by his father, who worked for the War Department in Washington, D.C. As a youngster, Finney saw the African American bar of D.C. in action and was inspired to pursue a legal career. In 1946 his father became dean of Claflin College in Orangeburg. The young high school student was warned by his Washington friends "you won't last thirty days" in the South, but he thrived in Orangeburg. He attended Claflin College, where he graduated in 1952, and then enrolled in the South Carolina State Law School. During law school, he married Frances Davenport, and on graduation they moved to Conway, South Carolina. To support themselves, they both taught. Ernest Finney also started a part-time law practice above the office of dentist Peter Kelly. However, one of his first interactions with the bar was not in court. The state bar association held its annual convention at the Ocean Forest Hotel in Myrtle Beach and instead of being an attendee, Finney was employed as a waiter.[108]

As the civil rights movement accelerated, Ernest Finney chose to move to Sumter, a town that offered greater opportunities for involvement in civil rights. Although Finney and his wife both held other jobs, Finney also opened a law office. One of his first clients was Irene Sampson Williams, a teacher who lost her job because of her civil rights activities. Finney sued the school district on her behalf, and Williams was awarded back benefits.[109]

Representation of civil rights protestors presented many different challenges. In 1961 Finney was called to Rock Hill to represent a group of Friendship Junior College students who had been arrested for the state's first sit-in. Finney found that the "Friendship Nine" did not want a lawyer, because they were determined to serve their sentences and not be bailed out. The "Jail No Bail" tactic reenergized the Rock Hill movement and produced even more clients for Finney. Demonstrations continued for months, and the arrests led to convictions and appeals.[110] Ultimately Finney was able to get many of their convictions reversed by the U.S. Supreme Court.[111]

In Sumter, demonstrations, sit-ins, and picketing led to numerous arrests. In a single day, students were arrested at the S. H. Kress lunch counter, others at Lawson Pharmacy, another client at Mitchell's Drugstore, nine students at Rowe's Drugstore, and twenty-eight more at the Sumter Cut Rate Drugstore. Despite the pressures and constant work, Finney had a remarkable record in these cases, winning three appeals in the state supreme court.[112] With mass arrests, the bail quickly added up. On one occasion, fifty-eight individuals were arrested and charged with parading without a permit, breach of peace, destruction of county property, and malicious mischief, resulting in Finney's having to raise $29,000 for bail. While he was seeking funds, forty-four more individuals were arrested for marching at a drive-in restaurant.[113]

In addition to the Sumter cases, Finney served as counsel for the Congress of Racial Equality, which required him to travel to Washington, D.C., with James Farmer (CORE's national director) and Carl Rachlin (general counsel) to meet with John Doar, the assistant attorney general in charge of the Civil Rights Division. The meeting was in response to a request made by President John Kennedy to investigate the treatment of sit-in demonstrators in Rock Hill and

Sumter. While he was in Washington, more arrests were made in those towns, as well as in Columbia.[114]

In 1965 Finney filed a suit to desegregate the public schools in Dorchester County.[115] He served as co-counsel in school desegregation cases in Sumter, Dorchester, Greenville, Darlington, and Clarendon Counties.[116] He also sued to desegregate the Carnegie Public Library in Sumter.[117] He co-counseled a number of cases with Matthew Perry, including a successful attack on the segregated state parks, and the two were able to enjoin the state board of education from providing private school scholarships to white students so they did not have to attend desegregated schools.[118]

Throughout the 1960s, Finney continued to develop his law practice and advocate for civil rights. By 1964 Finney had developed such a reputation that he received a significant number of write-in ballots for Congress.[119] In 1966 Finney ran for the legislature and lost.[120] In 1968 he was a delegate to the National Democratic Convention and again unsuccessfully ran for the state legislature. Following the assassination of Martin Luther King Jr., President Lyndon Johnson named Finney chairman of the South Carolina Advisory Commission to the U.S. Civil Rights Commission.[121] He was also named to the State Elections Commission in 1968.[122] In 1972 he was elected to the South Carolina House of Representatives, defeating a white incumbent.[123]

Finney served on the house judiciary committee, one of the most powerful in the body, for four years.[124] In 1976 the General Assembly elected him circuit court judge, and when he was sworn in, he became the first African American circuit judge in state history.[125] In 1985 Finney was elected to the South Carolina Supreme Court, becoming only the second African American to ever serve on the court and the first since Reconstruction. His opponent for the seat in 1985 was his close friend Jean Toal. Toal withdrew from the race, thus clearing the way for Finney's selection. (Toal would subsequently be elected to the court in 1986.) On May 11, 1994, Finney was elected chief justice of the South Carolina Supreme Court. He considered the court's decision in *Abbeville County School District v. South Carolina* his most significant judicial contribution.[126] The suit on behalf of numerous poor rural districts challenged the method used to allocate funds for public schools. In the decision, authored by Finney, the court held that the state constitution's education clause required that each child be provided with adequate and safe facilities in which to learn, read, and speak the English language, and gain knowledge of mathematics, physical science, economic, social and political systems, history, governmental processes, and academic and vocational skills.

He retired from the court in March 2000 and practiced law for a short time as counsel to his son Jerry's law firm. He served a year as interim president of South Carolina State University. Thereafter, Judge Finney retired again and now resides with his wife Frances Davenport Finney in Columbia, South Carolina.[127]

Other State Graduates

Albert A. "Blue" Kennedy graduated from S.C. State Law School in 1950 and practiced in Columbia with Harold Boulware.[128] He had a limited career.[129] For a time, Kennedy was active in civil rights and on one case successfully challenged Fairfield County's exclusion of blacks from its grand jury.[130] Kennedy was suspended indefinitely by the South Carolina bar in 1970 for negligent failure to perform legal services.[131]

W. Newton Pough graduated from S.C. State Law School in 1952 and was admitted to the bar that year. He began law practice in Orangeburg in 1956 and practiced there for fifty years. As a law student, he assisted in doing research on the Clarendon County desegregation case, and as a lawyer, he was active in civil rights litigation with Matthew Perry and Zach Townsend. Pough filed one major civil rights case even before Perry became an active civil rights lawyer, when he and John H. Wrighten challenged the segregation of Edisto Beach State Park in 1955. This case illustrates the level of harm the state would inflict on all of its citizens to preserve segregation. The popular beachfront park was closed by the state to moot the suit and remained closed for ten years.[132]

Pough, Matthew Perry, and Zack Townsend were co-counsel in a series of trials and appeals for Edward Richburg, who was charged with the murder of a white deputy sheriff. Richburg's trial began in January 1966, in front of a Orangeburg "biracial jury."[133] Richburg and the deputy had both shot each other, and the evidence was quite conflicting at the trial. Richburg took the stand to claim self-defense in the shooting. When the case was handed to the jury, it deliberated most of the day and was unable to reach a verdict, resulting in a mistrial.[134]

At his second trial, the state struck all but one black juror, and Richburg was found guilty of murder and sentenced to death.[135] In the appeal that followed, his lawyers attacked Richburg's conviction on the grounds that women and blacks had been excluded from the jury, but the state supreme court reversed on more technical grounds and avoided the question of jury discrimination.[136] Venue for the third trial was moved to Columbia so the jury pool would not know the details of his prior trials.[137] In his third trial, Richburg was convicted of manslaughter by a jury of nine whites and three blacks.[138] He was sentenced to eighteen years in prison and served five years.[139]

Like many of his colleagues, Pough was active in the community. He worked with the NAACP, Boy Scouts, and the Democratic Party, serving as a national delegate in 1972. When Pough died in 2006, he was eulogized at his funeral by Judge Matthew Perry.[140]

In 1953 the five African Americans admitted to the South Carolina bar were graduates of South Carolina State. William W. Bennett of Lane, a World War II veteran, practiced in Florence. He was co-counsel on numerous civil rights cases with Lincoln Jenkins and Matthew Perry.[141] In 1955 Bennett and Elliot Turnage represented a group of parents who attempted to desegregate the school system in Florence, South Carolina.[142] In 1960 Bennett represented forty-eight high school students charged with parading without a permit.[143] He also served on the NAACP team of lawyers who represented college student demonstrators in Orangeburg in 1960.[144] From April 1954 until 1969, Bennett had an active civil law practice.[145] He ran for the Florence County council and school board but did not win either office.[146] He became a trustee at Allen University and was director of the Florence County antipoverty agency when he died in an automobile accident in 1969.[147]

Also admitted in 1953, Frank E. Cain Jr. of Bennettsville was a 1951 State College law graduate. His most significant civil rights case was *State v. Hamm*. Gene Hamm was described by state supreme court justice Thomas Bussey as "a locally well known, young, black, bearded, civil or human rights activist."[148] Charged with possession of illegal drugs, Hamm asserted that marijuana was planted on him by law enforcement officers. Cain was joined on this case by Mordecai C. Johnson as well as Jack Greenberg of the NAACP Legal Defense Fund. They were unsuccessful in their defense of Hamm, but on appeal, two state supreme court justices dissented on the grounds that the trial judge refused to inquire as to racial prejudice by potential jurors. Hamm's conviction was appealed by the NAACP Legal Defense Fund to the U.S. Supreme Court, which overturned the conviction because of the failure of the trial judge to question the venire of potential racial prejudice.[149] While Cain and Johnson's advocacy for Hamm ultimately resulted in a favorable decision by the high court, Hamm was convicted of additional charges, including assault with a deadly weapon and distribution of heroin, and was sentenced to fifteen years.[150] Cain practiced law for sixty years and still maintained an office in 2014.[151]

Vernoid Bunch, a veteran, graduated from law school in 1952 and was admitted to the bar in 1953. Bunch was co-counsel with Harold Boulware in *State v. Waitus*, a murder case tried in Bunch's hometown of Georgetown.

Waitus's conviction and death sentence were affirmed on appeal. Bunch also lost his only other appellate case.[152] In addition to his legal work, he taught at Howard High School in Georgetown.[153] Bunch died in 2002.[154]

John H. Wrighten had been the plaintiff in the lawsuit that resulted in the creation of South Carolina State Law School. Graduating from the law school in 1952, he was admitted in 1953. He practiced in Charleston and was active in civil rights activities. He and J. Arthur Brown, president of the Charleston NAACP, plotted a legal strategy to attack segregation in the city. Wrighten served as local counsel when a group of high school students sat in at lunch counters.[155] Matthew Perry and Lincoln Jenkins were summoned to help Wrighten in the trials.[156] On appeal, Wrighten and Perry were able to convince the state supreme court to overturn the resisting arrest convictions, but the trespassing guilty verdicts were affirmed. However, all the convictions were summarily reversed by the U.S. Supreme Court in 1964.[157] Wrighten worked with W. Newton Pough in the attempt to desegregate Edisto Beach State Park.[158] Wrighten was also co-counsel with Matthew Perry and Ernest Finney in *State v. White*, the rape case in which the verdict and death penalty were overturned because of prejudicial arguments by the prosecutor.[159] Wrighten handled criminal and civil matters in both state and federal court.[160] His legal career came to an end in 1971 when the South Carolina Supreme Court disbarred him for irregularities with client funds.[161]

In 1953 John E. McCall of Cheraw graduated from S.C. State Law School and was admitted to the bar that year. A veteran, McCall had attended South Carolina State College before enlisting in 1944. In the 1950s he was legal adviser to the Cheraw NAACP branch and vice president of the Southeastern Lawyers Association, as well as being active in community affairs.[162] His only reported case was the successful appeal of a rape conviction with his co-counsel Frank Cain.[163]

Ernest Finney's class of 1954 included Herman G. Boyd of Columbia, Cleveland Stevens of Loris, Edgar Thompson of Spartanburg, and Willie T. Smith of Columbia. Boyd had been a high school principal before going to law school. Although he had a law office in Columbia, he practiced very little and died in 1971.[164] Stevens had a general practice in Conway. He led a Horry County voter registration campaign in 1963.[165] He was on the NAACP's team of lawyers who represented student demonstrators in Orangeburg.[166] In 1971 he helped defend John Wrighten in disbarment proceedings.[167] He also served as the public defender in Horry County, undertaking some notorious cases.[168] A disability forced him to retire from practice in 1989.[169] Edgar Thompson practiced in Rock Hill and Spartanburg, taught in elementary school, and then became a chemist with Firestone.[170] Willie Smith, a veteran of World War II and the Korean War, settled in Greenville to practice law, where he served as local counsel for the NAACP. In 1957 Smith and Donald Sampson succeeded in convincing a federal jury to award punitive damages to their client for an illegal search of his home. However, it was only a moral victory because the federal district judge set aside the jury's verdict and ruled that an illegal search did not violate the federal Civil Rights Act.[171] In February 1959, when Richard Henry, a civilian employee of the air force, was forcibly removed from the Greenville airport, Smith and Lincoln Jenkins represented him.[172] In July 1960 Smith and Donald Sampson sued the Greenville County library for refusing to serve black students. The federal judge refused relief, and the board of trustees voted to close all of the library's branches. But within a week the board reversed its decision and reopened to all patrons regardless of race.[173] Smith represented students arrested for sitting in at lunch counters in Greenville and Rock Hill.[174] *Peterson v. Greenville* began when fourteen high school students were arrested at a lunch counter in a Kress dime store.[175] Their convictions were overturned by the U.S. Supreme Court in 1963.[176] Smith also served as co-counsel with Matthew Perry and Constance Baker Motley in representing Harvey Gantt against Clemson.[177] In 1967 Smith became a legal services attorney and was executive director of Legal Services of Greenville from 1970 to 1977. In 1978 he was elected a family court judge by the General Assembly. Smith died in 2002.

Between 1955 and 1958, no State graduates remained in South Carolina to practice.[178] This trend was broken in 1959 by Russell Brown of Ravenel; he passed the bar and practiced in Charleston for more than thirty years. Brown also was elected president of the Charleston NAACP.[179] Among his clients were civil rights demonstrators in the town of Saint George, students arrested for sit-ins in Charleston, and Charleston hospital worker strike-marchers.[180] He and Fred Henderson Moore represented Louis Moorer, who was convicted of rape and sentenced to death. On appeal, after the conviction and death sentence were affirmed, Brown and Moore filed an unsuccessful habeas corpus action on the grounds that blacks had been systematically excluded from the jury.[181] Brown continued to practice in Charleston until 2003, when he resigned from the bar following a public reprimand by the state supreme court.[182]

Between 1960 and 1962, the only S.C. State graduate who was admitted to the state bar, Ned Felder, never practiced in the state. However, Ruben Lee Gray, a 1963 graduate of the law school, was admitted that year and would continue the tradition of being a civil rights lawyer. A native of rural Georgetown County, Gray walked five miles to the Deep Creek School and had to ride a bus thirty miles or more to attend Howard High School in Georgetown.

After graduating from high school, Gray worked for a year and then enrolled in South Carolina State College's six-year program that would lead to a law degree. When he graduated in 1963, Gray was offered a job by Ernest Finney. He immediately began representing student demonstrators. In one case, his seventy-five student clients continued their protest in the jail, destroying all the dishes and throwing the food. The county threatened to send the students to the state prison. Gray intervened with the white authorities and managed to calm both his clients and the sheriff. Gray's legal career was soon interrupted by the draft and two years of military service. When he returned in 1965, the civil rights era was far from over.[183] The atmosphere in Sumter was tense with few if any sympathetic whites. A more typical response was the drugstore owner who used a cattle prod on black women students when they tried to sit in.

Gray practiced with Finney until Finney was elected to the circuit bench in 1976. Gray continued on his own until 1992, when he was elected a family court judge. Over the years, he mentored a number of young lawyers including Chip Finney, Ernest's son. He served seven years on the Sumter County Council. After ten years as a family court judge, Judge Gray retired and resumed law practice with an office on South Washington Street in Sumter. In 2013 he was still practicing.[184]

Also graduating from the law school in 1963 was Zack Townsend. A graduate of Benedict College in Columbia, Townsend was in the army in Germany when Emmett Till was lynched in Mississippi. This horrendous murder motivated Townsend to attend law school. He returned to South Carolina, graduated from S.C. State Law School, and was admitted to the bar in 1963.

Townsend became a civil rights lawyer more quickly than any lawyer before him. On the day after he was admitted to the bar in August 1963, Matthew Perry telephoned and informed Townsend that he had three hundred clients in the Orangeburg jail. Their trial was less than a week away. Townsend admitted that he was terrified but jokingly says he managed to make a decent appellate record by citing every amendment to the U.S. Constitution. Townsend had hundreds of trials over the next eighteen months.[185] Professor Earl Coblyn, one of Townsend's law professors, suggested that they form a law firm and practice together, which they did for three years.

Townsend worked with Matthew Perry on numerous civil rights cases, including all of the Gloria Rackley cases that had so transformed Orangeburg and the state. Townsend was also co-counsel in *State v. Richburg* (discussed above). Townsend remembered that even after their client was sentenced to death, Matthew Perry confidently predicted that Richburg would not be executed. It seemed an improvident boast to Townsend. But after three trials, not only had their client emerged with only a conviction of manslaughter, he was released after five years. In 2013 Townsend still maintained a law office but considered himself retired. His daughter Ariel Townsend Rosamond is a lawyer and continues the Townsend law firm in Orangeburg.[186]

In 1964 graduate Ernest Simmons was admitted to the bar but never practiced. Franklin DeWitt of Conway graduated in 1964 and practiced in Conway. In 1976 DeWitt and Matthew Perry represented Archie Allen in his death penalty case. They lost their appeal before the South Carolina Supreme Court, but Allen's life was spared by the U.S. Supreme Court's decision in *Furman v. Georgia*.[187] After the legislature enacted a new death penalty statute to comply with *Furman*, the state attempted to retroactively apply the death penalty. DeWitt, Perry, and Robert Hallman were successful in preventing the state from imposing death in these cases.[188] DeWitt practiced in Conway until his death in 2008.[189]

George A. Payton, a 1965 S.C. State Law School graduate, initially practiced with Richard Fields in Charleston. In 1969 Payton, with Fred Henderson Moore, Russell Brown, and Anthony Amsterdam, served as counsel for Ralph David Abernathy, Hosea Williams, and Andrew Young when they were arrested for holding a prayer vigil in the middle of a street in Charleston. As leaders of the Southern Christian Leadership Conference (SCLC) they were in Charleston to support a strike by hospital workers. One night they tried to lead a group of 250 supporters to a park for a prayer vigil. The march had proceeded about two blocks when the Charleston police chief ordered Abernathy to stop because they did not have a parade permit. The SCLC leaders had received permits in Charleston for previous assemblies, but the Charleston city code expressly prohibited parades after 8:00 p.m.[190] Abernathy asked the chief whether the group could split up and walk the remaining distance to the park in small groups or singly in order to avoid the prohibition of the ordinance. Conroy told Abernathy that neither he nor any member of his group could continue to the park for the prayer vigil. Abernathy knelt in the street and began praying. The chief ordered him to stop. Abernathy refused and admonished him not to interrupt the prayer. Abernathy and the three other leaders were arrested and charged with riot, and at a preliminary hearing, the judge set a $50,000 bond.[191] A federal court challenge to the arrests failed.[192] Eventually, Abernathy was released, and the strike was settled.[193] Payton was also counsel in the unsuccessful challenge to the expulsion of student protesters from Voorhees College.[194] Payton had an active law practice, including handling criminal appeals to the South Carolina Supreme Court.[195] George Payton was murdered in his law office in Charleston on March 18, 1975, and the crime was never solved.[196]

The class of 1965 had six other graduates, but of those only three were admitted to the state bar. As a student George Allen Anderson was active in the Orangeburg protests and was identified as a leader when nearly a thousand students were arrested over four days in October 1963.[197] After graduating from law school, Anderson accepted a job with the Aiken Community Action Agency and in 1967 became its executive director.[198] He has also practiced law and was co-counsel with Matthew Perry on two cases.[199] He still had a law office in 2013.[200] Ernest Deveaux graduated from S.C. State Law School in 1965 and practiced briefly in Charleston. He ran for the legislature in 1972 as a Republican.[201] He died in 2008.[202] George Marion Crawford of Orangeburg, who graduated in 1965, had suffered a spinal cord injury while in college and was paralyzed. Nevertheless, he practiced law in his hometown until his death in 2006.[203]

Daniel E. Martin graduated from S.C. State Law School in 1966 and was admitted that same year. A graduate of Allen University, Martin practiced in Charleston and for a time served as an assistant solicitor in the Ninth Judicial Circuit. At one point, he was in practice with Fred Henderson Moore.[204] In 1991 Martin and Armand Derfner represented probate judge Bernard Fielding in an election contest and were successful in the state supreme court in protecting Fielding's election.[205] Martin served in the state legislature from 1984 until 1992. In 1992 he was elected by the General Assembly to the circuit court bench. He retired from the bench in 2001 and was still practicing in 2014.[206]

~

South Carolina State School of Law, that inferior law school that Thurgood Marshall once dismissed as a "Jim-Crow dump in South Carolina," produced superior lawyers whose impact went far beyond the fifty men and one woman who earned their law degrees there.[207]

Following World War II, across the South the black legal profession began to grow (see table 3). This growth was clearly affected by the "separate but equal" law schools such as S.C. State. Other state-supported all-black law schools were established at North Carolina Central University (1939), Texas Southern University (1947), Southern University in Louisiana (1947), and Florida A&M (1949).[208] A comparison of the black bars in six southern states—Arkansas, Alabama, Florida, Louisiana, Mississippi, and South Carolina—illustrates that such schools were a major catalyst for growth of the profession. Their black bars grew from 1950 to 1970 as follows: Alabama from 10 to 20; Arkansas from 9 to 12; Florida from 15 to 64; Louisiana from 6 to 26; Mississippi from 5 to 11; and South Carolina from 12 to 60. In this period only Arkansas and Louisi-

TABLE 3. Number of Black Lawyers in Old Confederate States, 1950–1970

	1950	*1960*	*1970*
Alabama	10	13	20
Arkansas	9	19	12
Florida	15	25	64
Georgia	17	12	60
Louisiana	6	30	26
Mississippi	5	4	11
North Carolina	29	58	118
South Carolina	12	36	60
Tennessee	18	28	46
Texas	26	50	91
Virginia	55	59	58

Note: This chart is partially based on the U.S. Census. However, other sources provided more accurate information in a number of cases.

For Arkansas, see Judith Kilpatrick, "(EXTRA)Ordinary Men: African American Lawyers and Civil Rights in Arkansas before 1950," *Arkansas Law Review 53* (2000): 299, and "Wiley Branton and the Voting Rights Struggle," *Arkansas Little Rock Law Rev 26* (2004): 642.

For Mississippi, the census appears correct for 1950 and wrong for 1960, where no blacks are reported. According to a newspaper article, there were four black lawyers in Mississippi in 1964. Obituary of R. Jess Brown, *New York Times*, January 3, 1990. For more information on Mississippi, see http://digilib.usm.edu/cdm/ref/collection/coh/id/8308 (accessed November 18, 2014).

Alabama's census numbers are also incorrect. Only a total of nineteen black lawyers had been admitted by 1964. See http://blog.al.com/spotnews/2013/05/before_the_civil_rights_moveme.html (accessed November 18, 2014). Fred D. Gray said there were eight lawyers in Alabama when he passed the bar in 1954. See Fred D. Gray, *Bus Ride to Justice* (Montgomery: Black Belt, 1995).

Louisiana's census figure for 1960 is also incorrect. Southern University graduated twenty-eight men who were admitted to the Louisiana bar between 1950 and 1960. See http://www.sulc.edu/Departments/Alumni/Recognitions.html (last visited November 24, 2014). Also, Loyola University Law School in New Orleans admitted black law students in the early 1950s. See http://law.loyno.edu/100-years (accessed November 24, 2014). The Louisiana number for 1960 would therefore exceed thirty.

My own research convinces me that the South Carolina number for 1950 is accurate, the 1960 number is quite erroneous, and the 1970 number is probably right.

ana had public white university law schools that admitted blacks.[209] The states with the "separate but equal" law schools had much stronger growth in their black bars. Alabama's bar grew about 2.5 times and Arkansas's remained stable, but Florida's bar quadrupled, Louisiana's bar quadrupled, and South Carolina's black bar grew 500 percent. "Separate but equal" law schools also contributed to a more robust black bar in North Carolina and Texas. North Carolina's black bar grew from 29 to 118, and Texas's grew from 26 to 91. Clearly the presence of a public black law school supported a healthy growth in the African American bars in the South.

That growth was felt in every corner of the state of South Carolina. At least twenty-seven State graduates stayed and practiced law in South Carolina. For the first time, black lawyers were located in every major city and were able to provide a range of legal services for the community. They became community leaders and eventually served in public office and in the judiciary. Some of them rose to the highest levels of the judiciary.

In November 1965 the South Carolina State College Board of Trustees voted to close the law school. The 1966 state budget authorized the transfer of the 21,000-volume law library to the University of South Carolina School of Law. Meanwhile, the University of South Carolina began to accept black students.[210] Though the S.C. State Law School was short lived, its impact is almost immeasurable. Clearly, the greatest contribution of its graduates was in their advocacy for civil rights. They transformed the state from a rigidly segregated society to a far more open and inclusive place. The law school had been created to reinforce the walls of segregation. Instead, its graduates succeeded in demolishing them.

CHAPTER 13

A New Generation

Not all of the lawyers admitted in the 1950s and 1960s were graduates of S.C. State Law School. For various reasons, some attended law school out of state, and two read law. Nonetheless, these lawyers chose to practice law in South Carolina. These lawyers would contribute significantly to the struggle for civil rights in the state.

The 1950s and Graduates of Other Law Schools

Of the thirty men admitted to the bar in the 1950s, ten were graduates of other schools. Four of those were S.C. State Law School faculty, and only one of those, Charles E. Washington Jr., actually ever practiced law in the state.[1] The other six were Donald Sampson, James M. Hinton Jr., Elliott Turnage, Bernard Fielding, Ira Claiborne, and Aaron Harvey. Sampson, Turnage, and Fielding were active participants in civil rights cases.

Donald J. Sampson, a graduate of Temple University Law School, was admitted in 1951. He was Greenville County's first black lawyer and co-counsel in a number of significant civil rights cases including *School District of Greenville County v. Whittenberg*, *Gantt v. Clemson*, *City of Rock Hill v. Hamm*, and *State v. Edwards*.[2] As lead counsel in a civil rights action aimed at desegregating Greenville's public skating rinks, he saw his case mooted when the city closed the rinks.[3] As previously mentioned, in *Mackie v. Chandler*, Sampson and Willie T. Smith obtained a $100 jury verdict for an illegal search of their client's home.[4] Sampson and Smith also were appointed to defend Charles E. Brooks, charged with raping two white women. The evidence against Brooks was clear, and the chance of an acquittal was weak. Brooks was convicted and sentenced to death, which was upheld on appeal. However, Sampson and Smith had one significant achievement in this case. Recognizing that the death penalty for rape was imposed only on black men convicted of assaulting white women, the two lawyers were able to convince trial judge G. Badger Baker to *voir dire* the potential jurors about racial prejudice. Badger agreed to ask the question "Would you have any prejudice against a defendant because of his Color?"[5]

Sampson also shared the misfortune with Matthew Perry and Lincoln Jenkins of representing Quincy Bullock in the failed appeal of his death sentence for the murder of Carolyn Barfield in Dillon County.[6] Sampson and Perry were more successful in *State v. Gist*, obtaining a reversal of their young client's sixty-six month sentence for making profane telephone calls.[7] In 1962 his client, Noigra C. Yarn, was twice convicted in municipal court for violating Greenville's "white block" ordinance, which prohibited blacks from living in certain areas. In an appeal to the state circuit court, judge Frank Eppes declared the ordinance unconstitutional.[8] One historian described Sampson's legal work as forcing white Greenville "to bow" to the inevitability of desegregation.[9] Sampson passed away on May 26, 2001.[10]

South Carolina native Elliott D. Turnage graduated from Harvard Law School in 1927.[11] During the 1930s he practiced in Oklahoma, appearing before the Oklahoma Supreme Court and in the federal courts.[12] From 1935 until 1954, he lived in Pennsylvania and North Carolina, where he worked at various jobs ranging from menial to white collar, and his activities with a summer camp that conducted an "interracial school" in Harrisburg, Pennsylvania, drew the attention of the House Un-American Activities Committee.[13] He returned to South Carolina and was admitted to the bar in 1954. He practiced with William Bennett in Darlington. Their caseload was mostly civil, and Turnage handled thirteen appeals before the state supreme court.[14] He also had an active civil rights practice. When Clarence Mitchell of the Washington, D.C., NAACP was arrested in Florence for entering the local railroad station by the front door, Turnage, Bennett, and Lincoln Jenkins were successful in having the charges dismissed.[15] In the summer of 1960, Darlington enacted an ordinance requiring a permit before anyone could "parade" on the streets. After the passage of the ordinance, four young men walked a few blocks to a school carrying signs that read "Old Jim Crow has got to go," "Desegregation is Democracy," and "We want equality and Justice for all." They were arrested and charged with parading without a permit. Despite Turnage's efforts, they were convicted and sentenced to thirty days or a fifty-five-dollar fine. Turnage and Matthew Perry were unable to overturn their convictions on appeal.[16] Another case handled by Turnage arose from the boycott by S.C. State students of Orangeburg businesses that were members of the White Citizens' Council.[17] One of the targets was Coble Dairy. When fifty students at Mayo High School in Darlington attempted to support the boycott by refusing to drink Coble Dairy milk, they were summarily expelled by their principal. Turnage filed an action for an injunction in federal court trying to overturn the suspensions, but the request was refused.[18] Turnage then tried the state courts in an attempt to oust the principal but did not succeed.[19] In addition to his civil rights law practice, Turnage was active in politics; he served as a delegate to the Republican National Convention in 1956 and also served as executive secretary of the Palmetto State Voters Association. Turnage died in 1962.[20]

Bernard R. Fielding graduated from Hampton University and Boston University School of Law. A Charleston native, Fielding returned home to operate his family's funeral home and was admitted to the bar in 1957. He was an active civil rights lawyer, serving as counsel for the NAACP in Charleston.[21] In 1968 he filed a suit to challenge the full-slate law, which required voters in at-large legislative races to vote for a candidate for each seat. If the voter cast a ballot for less than a full slate, her ballot was void.[22] The case was unsuccessful, but in 1972 Fielding was co-counsel in the landmark victory of *Stevenson v. West*, which compelled the state to redistrict its house of representatives into single-member districts.[23] Fielding also served as co-counsel with Matthew Perry representing black high school students such as Harvey Gantt, arrested for sitting in at a lunch counter in Charleston.[24] In the late 1970s and the 1980s Fielding was associate probate judge in Charleston County, and in 1991 he was elected probate judge in a contested election that required the state supreme court to declare him the winner.[25] He served one term. In 2014 Fielding was still practicing law and operating his family's business.

Three out-of-state graduates admitted in the 1950s never handled civil rights cases, and two never even practiced in the state. Ira W. Claiborne, a graduate of Lincoln University Law School in Saint Louis, was admitted in 1952, but the Charleston native practiced in the city only for a short time. He moved to Los Angeles, where he died in 1976.[26] James M. Hinton Jr. graduated from American University Law School and was admitted in 1954 but moved to Augusta, Georgia.[27] Admitted in 1957, Aaron Harvey took a correspondence law course from LaSalle Extension University in Chicago and read law with Richard Fields in Charleston. In 1970 he became the first black magistrate in Charleston since the 1870s.[28] He was magistrate for more than a decade and was deceased by 1990.[29] In December 1956 Suzanna Blackwell of Hodges, South Carolina, became the second black woman admitted to the state's bar.[30] She had attended night law school in Washington, D.C., in the early 1920s.[31] There is no record of her practicing law in South Carolina.

The 1960s and the Demise of South Carolina State

As the civil rights revolution intensified in the 1960s, S.C. State Law School continued to produce graduates, but between 1960 and 1966, only eleven of twenty-three law graduates were admitted to the bar. In some years, no graduates were admitted. In November 1965 the college's board of trustees voted to close the law school. Historian William Hine believes the school closed because of poor funding.[32] Financial constraints meant that the school would never be accredited, nor would its faculty be adequately paid. College president Turner expressed the concern that the quality of students was declining. Certainly the school's enrollment and bar passage rates were not good. The school's last class had three students in 1966, and Daniel E. Martin and Damon Thomas became the last two state graduates admitted to the bar.

The University of South Carolina School of Law had been desegregated in 1964 with the admission of Paul Cash. In September 1965 Jasper Cureton transferred from State to USC, and Johnny Lake transferred in September 1966. Lake and Cureton would graduate in June 1967, becoming USC's first black graduates since Reconstruction. In 1965 I. S. Leevy Johnson was admitted to USC's law school as a freshman and would be the school's first black graduate to attend the school for three years.

Between 1960 and 1968, twenty-three blacks were admitted to the state's bar. For the first time since the creation of the law school at State, a majority of the new black lawyers had graduated from another law school. Four were graduates of the Howard University School of Law. Two graduated from Florida A&M. Two more came from Suffolk Law School in Boston and from North Carolina Central. One read law, and three were graduates of USC School of Law.

The 1960 Howard School of Law graduating class produced four South Carolina lawyers.[33] Two, Mordecai C. Johnson and Fred Henderson Moore, would be prominent civil rights attorneys. A Florence native, Mordecai Johnson graduated from State in 1951. After service in the army, he attended Howard Law School and also earned an LLM from George Washington University. For four years he worked for the U.S. Department of Health, Education and Welfare and the U.S. Commission on Civil Rights.[34] When Johnson returned to South Carolina, he became active in the civil rights movement and served as co-counsel in three NAACP school desegregation cases.[35] In 1970 he and Frank Cain represented Gene Hamm, the young civil rights worker who claimed drugs had been planted on him. As noted earlier, despite their efforts, Hamm was convicted of additional charges, including assault with a deadly weapon and distribution of heroin, and was sentenced to fifteen years.[36]

In 1980 Johnson was lead counsel in an NAACP suit seeking to require single-member districts in the South Carolina Senate.[37] That suit was filed on the eve of elections and was rejected by the federal court.[38] Despite the failure to enjoin that election, Johnson's efforts were not in vain. The senate enacted single-member districts in 1983.[39] In addition to his civil rights litigation, Johnson was a leader in local, state, and regional civic and political affairs. He served on the South Carolina Council on Human Relations and on the board of directors of one of the South's most prestigious organizations, the Southern Regional Council.[40] In 1970 and 1972 he ran unsuccessfully for Florence City Council and the South Carolina House of Representatives on the United Citizens Party ticket.[41] In 1977 Johnson and another candidate were the first blacks elected to the Florence City Council since 1895.[42] He served from 1977 to 1981 and in 1990 was elected municipal court judge of Florence.[43] Johnson died in 1994.[44]

Fred Henderson Moore, a native of Charleston, attended State as an undergraduate, where he was president of the student body and active in the local civil rights movement.[45] Moore's activities nearly derailed his career before he could even graduate from college. Following the *Brown v. Board of Education* decision, the White Citizens' Council was organized in Mississippi and soon spread to South Carolina, where it was supported by major businesses in Orangeburg. The black community began boycotting these businesses in the spring of 1957. In support of the community, Moore marshaled fellow State students to observe the boycott. The campaign was so successful that the white community pressured the college's president and the all-white board of trustees to demand that Moore call it off. When Moore refused just two weeks shy of graduation, he was expelled. Moore was forced to attend other schools to obtain his undergraduate degree. With the help of Harold Boulware and others, Moore enrolled at the Howard University School of Law. He graduated in 1960 and passed the South Carolina bar that same year.

Moore returned to Charleston and was befriended by the city's black bar. In particular, John Wrighten, Russell Brown, and Mack Davis took him under their wing but not before engaging in some mild hazing. They knew that Moore wanted to be a civil rights lawyer, so they told him they had a discrimination case for him. When Moore sat down with his new client, he discovered that the client's black dog had been attacked by a white dog. Despite his disappointment, Moore investigated the attack and discovered that the white dog's owner had homeowner's insurance. Consequently, Moore had the last laugh on his fellow lawyers when he was able to convince the lawyer for the insurance company to pay $1,200 to the owner of the injured black dog.[46]

Moore soon was engaged in more serious work and became one of the city's most active civil rights lawyers. When J. Arthur Brown, president of the Charleston NAACP, wanted the Charleston municipal golf course desegregated, John Wrighten refused to be involved, thinking there were more important matters than a golf course. Brown turned to Matthew Perry, who in turn recruited Moore as local counsel. They soon tried the case, and in July 1961 a federal judge ordered the course to be desegregated.[47] Moore was also asked to assist Perry and Constance Baker Motley with Harvey Gantt's lawsuit to desegregate Clemson College. Moore also served as third chair in Millicent Brown's lawsuit to desegregate Charleston's public schools. Moore later related that he discovered just how brilliant Motley was. She was to cross-examine an anthropologist who testified that segregation was justified because of the supposed intellectual inferiority of blacks. As the expert's testimony dragged on, Moore observed Motley either reading a newspaper or writing letters but never taking notes about the testimony. However, on cross Motley quickly eviscerated the professor when she asked him about the U.S. Army's IQ tests of recruits during World War II, which had shown the clear superiority of northern blacks to southern whites. The Charleston school board's entire defense collapsed, and U.S. district court judge J. Robert Martin issued an order desegregating the city's schools.

In 1968 Moore represented Cleveland L. Sellers Jr., who was prosecuted for inciting a riot in which three State students were killed. Moore and many observers believe Sellers was prosecuted because he was a "black militant." Sellers, a native of Bamberg County, was one of the leaders of the Student Nonviolent Coordinating Committee (SNCC) in Mississippi and other southern states. In 1967 Sellers returned to South Carolina and began organizing college students in Orangeburg.[48] On February 8, 1968, State college students faced off against heavily armed police on the campus. Three students were killed by state police, and Sellers and numerous others were wounded. Fred Henderson Moore and Howard Moore of Atlanta represented Sellers. Fred Moore believes he was the only South Carolina lawyer who would undertake Sellers's defense, because Sellers espoused "black power."[49] The evidence against Sellers was that on the evening of the shooting he was seen moving about and talking to groups of students. Supposedly these students had then become boisterous, demanding, and threatening. Sellers was convicted, and his conviction was affirmed by the state supreme court.[50] Sellers remains the only person tried and convicted for any crime related to what became known as the Orangeburg Massacre.[51]

In 1969 the Medical University of South Carolina hospital workers in Charleston tried to organize a union. Unionization of state employees was illegal in South Carolina, and when the medical school refused to negotiate, more than a thousand employees struck. Tensions mounted and numerous marches and demonstrations followed. Major civil rights figures and union leaders such as Coretta Scott King and Walter Reuther came to Charleston to support the workers. One march alone attracted more than demonstrators. When Ralph David Abernathy and other leaders of the SCLC marched one evening and then kneeled to pray in the street, they were arrested. Fred Moore was their lawyer.[52]

During the hospital workers' strike, student protests at Voorhees College also erupted. As mentioned earlier, on April 28, 1969, more than two dozen students took over the Voorhees College administration building. The next day, the *State* newspaper in Columbia carried a front-page story headlined "Armed Students Occupy Building at Voorhees," accompanied by three photographs of students brandishing weapons in the windows of the occupied building.[53] The students vacated the building, but thirty-six were arrested and charged with riot.[54] When the students went on trial in July 1970, former student activist Moore represented them, along with Matthew Perry and Lincoln Jenkins. The students were convicted and received sentences ranging from 18 to 24 months.[55] Moore and Perry represented two students on appeal, but their convictions were affirmed.[56]

There was more trouble to come at Voorhees. In February 1970 the college terminated five popular faculty members, and a student boycott closed the school.[57] In response, the school expelled 165 of its 700 students and requested that the governor send in the National Guard and state police to seal the campus "against students and faculty."[58] Moore, George Payton, and Mordecai Johnson filed suit for the students in *Counts v. Voorhees College* challenging their expulsion, but the case was dismissed.[59]

In 1973 Moore and Ray McClain sued the state's board of bar examiners on behalf of four black law school graduates who had failed the bar exam.[60] They alleged that the exam unfairly discriminated against black applicants.[61] Having lost in the federal district court, they appealed to the Fourth Circuit Court of Appeals. That court ruled that two of the applicants had been treated "arbitrarily and capriciously" in the grading of their exams and ordered their admission.[62] However, the bar examiners requested a rehearing, and the appellate court sitting *en banc* reversed the ruling and denied all relief.[63]

Moore was counsel in a number of voting rights cases including *Stevenson v. West*, which forced the election of the South Carolina House of Representatives in single-member districts.[64] In 1980 Moore and Mordecai Johnson brought suit to challenge single-member districts in the South Carolina Senate, but it was unsuccessful.[65] Throughout his career Moore had a very active practice that included a number of serious criminal and civil cases.[66]

Moore's legal career was not without difficulties. Beginning in 1972, he was disciplined multiple times by the state supreme court.[67] Moore has asserted that the first disciplinary action was in retribution for his civil rights work.[68] A public reprimand by the court in 1980 certainly seems excessive. The panel that investigated the case described Moore's actions as mere negligence and recommended the complaint be dismissed, but the bar's executive committee recommended a private reprimand, and the state supreme court imposed a public sanction. In 1984 Moore was suspended by the court for irregularities in his trust account, but he was reinstated five years later.[69] Following more difficulties, in 2000 the Supreme Court disbarred Moore.[70] Moore sincerely believes that he was treated unfairly because of his civil rights work. In 2014 Moore was a Reformed Methodist minister but continued efforts to regain his law license.[71]

Benjamin L. Cook Jr., admitted in 1961, graduated from South Carolina State with a degree in electronic engineering. He then read law and was mentored by John Wrighten.[72] In 1963 Cook ran for city council in Charleston, thus becoming the first black candidate for such a seat in the twentieth century.[73] Cook practiced law with Fred Henderson Moore; they handled civil cases as well as criminal trial work, including one death penalty case.[74] Moore and Cook integrated the South Carolina bar convention in 1962.[75] Moore described Cook as brilliant and a superb cross-examiner. Cook was also active in the civil rights movement serving as co-counsel with Matthew Perry and other lawyers in the suit to desegregate Greenville schools in 1966.[76] He had a law office in Charleston until his death in 1975.[77]

Hemphill Pride II was admitted to the bar in 1963. His parents were Dr. Hemphill Pride, a dentist, and Maud Pendergrass Pride, a successful businesswoman and schoolteacher. While a college student his interest in the law was sparked when he attended court hearings where the state of Georgia tried to force the NAACP to disclose its membership rolls. After graduating from Johnson C. Smith College in Charlotte, Pride enrolled at South Carolina State Law School. In his second year, he was arrested for participating in civil rights demonstrations; the president of the college did not approve and "requested" that Pride take a leave of absence. After working in Washington, D.C., Pride graduated from Florida A&M Law School in 1963 and was invited by Lincoln Jenkins and Matthew Perry to join their firm. His association with the two senior civil rights lawyers meant that Pride participated in such major cases such as *Newman v. Piggie Park Enterprises*, a landmark public accommodations case.[78] Pride often went to court with Perry and Jenkins and was delighted on one occasion when they asked him to give the closing argument. Pride admits that he was naïvely convinced he could persuade the all-white Orangeburg County jurors to find his black college student clients not guilty. Of course, Perry and Jenkins tried such cases to make a record so that they could win on appeal and simply saw the closing arguments as good practice for Pride. He failed to convince the white jurors, but the experience was of benefit to Pride and his subsequent clients.

By 1970 Pride was a trial lawyer who attracted both clients and press. He often challenged the systematic exclusion of blacks from juries.[79] In one highly publicized case, he represented a black state police officer charged with robbing drug dealers and convinced a jury that his client was not guilty.[80] In 1973 Pride formed an alliance with Tom Turnipseed, a former aide to George Wallace. They challenged the state law that allowed a utility company to raise consumers' electric rates under bond without a hearing. The case was lost in the district court and U.S. Supreme Court, but it started a series of consumer cases challenging rate increases.[81]

In October 1977 Pride was indicted in federal court for misusing federal money.[82] Pride had built an apartment complex financed through the Department of Housing and Urban Development (HUD). He fell behind in his mortgage payments, and HUD foreclosed. Because Pride had not paid all of the rent he had collected to HUD, he was charged with misappropriation. Pride believed that he was prosecuted because he had been an aggressive African American criminal defense lawyer.[83] His indictment caused a group of community leaders to assert that it was a case of harassment and injustice.[84] After a ten-day trial, Pride was convicted.[85] In 1981, while he was serving a three-year prison sentence, the South Carolina Supreme Court suspended him from the practice of law. The court, however, refused to disbar him.[86] After Pride's release, he petitioned for readmission to the bar, repassed the bar exam, and was readmitted. He has been practicing law in Columbia ever since.

Another lawyer who had troubles with the bar was Dorothy Sampson. A Sumter county native, Sampson was the third black woman admitted to the state's bar. The sister of Donald Sampson, she attended law school at North Carolina Central University, where her other brother, Daniel G. Sampson, was a professor. She graduated in 1963 and returned to Sumter, where she became active in civil rights. She ran for the legislature in 1968.[87] During the campaign she transported black citizens to the voter registration office. While she waited for them, a deputy sheriff ordered her to move. She refused and was arrested and subsequently convicted of resisting arrest.[88] In 1969, after a confrontation with a white bank teller, she was convicted of disorderly conduct. Then in 1971 she was charged in a bar disciplinary proceeding of taking a fee in excess of that allowed by a probate court order and "improperly" intervening between a fellow attorney and his client.[89] According to Hemphill Pride, one of her lawyers, since nothing in the alleged misconduct was based on dishonesty, a reprimand was expected. But the state's highest court indefinitely suspended her, citing her arrest and conviction in the voter registration incident and her disorderly conduct conviction following a confrontation with a white bank teller. Pride believes that Sampson was suspended because she was an aggressive black woman who had been active in the civil rights movement.[90]

Thomas D. Broadwater attended South Carolina State College, Kentucky State College, Suffolk University, and Florida A&M School of Law, and he was admitted to South Carolina's bar in 1966. In 1970, with Modjeska Simkins and John Roy Harper, Broadwater helped organize the United Citizens Party and ran as its candidate for governor. He was elected as a Democrat to the South Carolina House of Representatives in 1980 and 1982.[91] Broadwater had a substantial civil law practice, including some civil rights work. He filed one case against the City of Columbia police for racial discrimination.[92] He was also co-counsel with Leonard Boudin of the National Lawyers' Guild on behalf of U.S. Army soldiers protesting the Vietnam War.[93] Broadwater's representation of the "Fort Jackson Eight" was unsuccessful because the court ruled that soldiers gave up their First Amendment rights while in uniform on the base. Broadwater has expressed pride in his defense of the soldiers but felt it hurt him personally and professionally.[94] He practiced law for more than thirty years before suffering a stroke.[95] He recovered but did not resume an active practice.

James L. Felder, a native of Sumter, South Carolina, graduated from Clark College in Atlanta. He served two years in the U.S. Army's honor guard ceremonial unit and was a pallbearer for President John F. Kennedy. He graduated from the Howard University Law School in 1967 and was admitted to the South Carolina bar in 1968. In 1970 Felder, along with I. S. Leevy Johnson and Herbert Fielding, was elected to the South Carolina House of Representatives. They were the first African Americans elected to the legislature since 1900. Felder practiced law in Columbia until he was disbarred in 1975 for misappropriation of client funds.[96]

Johnny Lake and Jasper Cureton began their legal education at State but transferred to the University of South Carolina when the Orangeburg school closed. Both graduated in 1967, becoming USC's first black graduates since Reconstruction. Both passed the bar that year, but their lives took very different paths. Lake had a troubled career and was nearly destitute when he was disbarred in 1977.[97]

Jasper Cureton has had a distinguished career. Born in Oconee County and raised on a farm, Cureton graduated from South Carolina State College in 1960, planning to attend veterinary school. However, finances forced him to take a job with the welfare department in New York City. In 1961 he was called to active duty as an army lieutenant; his interest in the law was piqued when he represented soldiers in military discipline cases. After two years in the army, he returned to his welfare department job and began applying to law schools. He enrolled at South Carolina State Law School, only to learn in his first semester that the school was closing. He consulted with Matthew Perry and Paul Cash, the first black student law student at modern-day USC, and scheduled an appointment with Dean Robert Figg. Figg advised him to complete his first year at South Carolina State and then transfer. When he arrived the next fall, Cureton felt ostracized for several months until fellow student Martha Garrison sat down next to him in class. Soon he was befriended by others, including Jean Toal. He had an uncomfortable moment in class when Prof. Harry Lightsey used a derogatory racial term. Lightsey was embarrassed, quickly apologized, and soon befriended Cureton. He visited Cureton and his wife when their six-month-old baby died and took up a collection to help with medical expenses.[98]

When Cureton graduated he was hired by local Legal Aid director Edward A. "X" Harter. Harter once assigned Cureton to represent a client in magistrate's courts in rural Richland County. When Cureton requested a jury trial, the magistrate reluctantly summoned a jury of only four men. When deliberations began, the jurors requested a private meeting with the judge. Cureton objected, but the judge met with them nonetheless, and the jury came back with a conviction. Cureton then appealed. The magistrate was livid that the young black lawyer had appealed and complained to Harter. Harter supported Cureton, and Cureton was able to obtain a reversal of the conviction. After a year at legal services, Cureton went into practice with Tom Broadwater and handled hundreds of closings for low-income housing loans. He also handled domestic cases and a few criminal cases, most notably that of a conscientious objector who was charged criminally for failing to submit to induction. Despite the animosity of the federal judge, Cureton's client was found not guilty by the jury.[99]

In 1976 Cureton was elected master in equity for Richland County. As master in equity, Cureton made many rulings, one of which was reversed by circuit court judge Ernest Finney. He and Judge Finney were good friends, but it was a historic event to have a black judge reverse another black judge. In 1981 he was elected to the family court bench, and in 1983 to the South Carolina Court of Appeals, thus becoming only the second African American appellate court judge in South Carolina history. Cureton's most significant decision on the Court of Appeals was in challenging the exclusion of blacks from a civil jury. His decision was overturned by the South Carolina Supreme Court; however, Justice Finney wrote a dissent that agreed with Cureton.[100] Ultimately, Cureton's decision that the exclusion of blacks from juries without a nondiscriminatory basis was illegal was vindicated by the U.S. Supreme Court.[101] Cureton retired from the court in 2010 but continues to hear cases.[102]

Isaac Samuel Leevy Johnson was raised in Columbia, South Carolina, where he graduated from the segregated C. A. Johnson High School. He then obtained a degree in mortuary science from the University of Minnesota. Johnson was mentored by his grandfather I. S. Leevy, who was a prominent community leader and funeral home owner. After college, Johnson worked in his grandfather's funeral home "washing cars, embalming bodies, and digging graves." While working for his grandfather Johnson obtained a business degree from Benedict College, and he was promoted to the front office, where he was put to work "washing cars, embalming bodies, and digging graves."[103] In 1968 Johnson obtained a law degree from the University of South Carolina. He hoped the degree would enhance his business skills and help him run Leevy Funeral Home. Unfortunately, Mr. Leevy died, and there was no place for Johnson in the funeral home. Instead, Johnson was forced into law practice. His office was above Harold Boulware's and a block away from the firm of Jenkins, Perry, and Pride. Johnson never felt he had a solo practice because Boulware and Jenkins mentored him. Even the secretary at Jenkins, Perry, and Pride did secretarial work for him. By this time, the era of civil rights litigation was nearly over. However, the African American lawyer retained his traditional role in criminal defense, and Johnson honed his skills and developed his reputation handling minor criminal cases in the crowded municipal court, where his quick wit, eloquence, and hard work often gained acquittals for his clients.

Johnson was proudest of what he called big victories for small clients. His representation of Eva Mae Middleton was one of those cases. She was charged with murder for shooting her sleeping husband. In opening remarks to the jury, Johnson related that for many years the victim came home drunk every Friday after work and beat his wife. Johnson did not deny his client had shot her husband but stated that he would prove she was a victim of the "Battered Wife Syndrome."[104] During the trial, Johnson used his client's humble demeanor and small size to contrast her with the six-foot-seven police detective who was the chief witness against her. The five-foot-six Johnson played up the large size of the detective to demonstrate how intimidating the detective had been in interrogating his client.

The local press called the trial "a tale of marital brutality, terror, depression—and love."[105] The two adult Middleton children testified they heard the shots that killed their father, then saw their dazed mother come out with a gun in her hand, saying, "Oh my God! The man made me kill him!" The defense called more than fourteen witnesses, including a medical school professor who was an expert witness on the battered wife syndrome. Mrs. Middleton took the stand on her own behalf, and Johnson had her tell a harrowing tale of repeated beatings, including one that induced a miscarriage. Mrs. Middleton testified that on the day of his death, her husband was drunk, angry, and threatening to kill her. After dinner, he knocked her to the floor, and as she crawled away, he picked her up and threw her into the bedroom. He then went to bed uttering another threat before falling asleep. His wife shot him three times. The final witness was the medical school professor who tested Mrs. Middleton and testified that she fit the profile of a battered woman suffering from the syndrome. In closing arguments, I. S. Leevy Johnson effectively used the syndrome to criticize the failure of the courts and the police to recognize the defense. The jury returned with a verdict of not guilty.

Johnson's law firm, Johnson, Toal, and Battiste, has been one of Columbia's more successful small law firms. His law partners, William T. Toal and Luther Battiste, are well-known and accomplished trial lawyers. Battiste, a native of Orangeburg, was a longtime member of the Columbia City Council. Toal, a native of Columbia, was Johnson's law school classmate and the two have remained friends ever since. Toal had been a professor at the University of South Carolina Law School before joining the firm. In 1995 Johnson was able to once again become active in the family's funeral home business when he became the owner of Leevy's funeral home.

In 1970 Johnson was elected to the South Carolina House of Representatives. He was not reelected in 1972 but returned to the legislature in 1974, serving three more terms. As a legislator, Johnson worked at removing the Confederate flag from the statehouse, creating single-member house and senate districts, and protecting voting rights.[106] He also filed an unsuccessful legal challenge to Columbia's at-large city council election.[107] After the suit, the city modified its council election process to include four single-member district seats and two at-large seats.[108] Johnson has remained active in the Democratic Party and was an early supporter of Barack Obama.[109] He has also held community service leadership positions outside the political arena. He has been active in the National Bar Association, the American Bar Association, American College of

Trial Lawyers, the South Carolina Association for Justice, the Fourth Circuit Judicial Conference, and the American Board of Trial Advocates. In 1985 Johnson was elected the first African American president of the South Carolina Bar Association. Before 1968 the bar association had no black members.[110]

While the South Carolina State Law School laid the foundation for the modern African American bar in the state, men such as Elliot Turnage, Donald Sampson, Mordecai Johnson, and Fred Henderson Moore, graduates of other law schools, also made significant contributions to the civil rights struggle in the state. Jasper Cureton helped desegregate the University of South Carolina School of Law and became the first black to serve on an appellate court since Reconstruction. Hemphill Pride became a leading criminal defense lawyer. Bernard Fielding and Mordecai Johnson were active in civil rights litigation, community affairs, and politics, and both became judges. I. S. Leevy Johnson was elected to the legislature, formed a successful leading law firm, and became president of the state bar association.

With the closing of South Carolina State's law school and the admission of blacks to the University of South Carolina School of Law, a significant shift in the state and the legal profession was at hand. The civil rights revolution had forced the state to change. Consequently, more and more doors were opening. As the 1960s closed, it was clear that black lawyers would be leaders in the profession, the legislature, and the judiciary.

CONCLUSION

In 1968 the *Charleston News and Courier* ran a story headlined "Negro Lawyers Note Tremendous Improvement."[1] The reporter had interviewed a group of black lawyers about their experience practicing law. He did not mention that he was writing on the hundredth anniversary of the admission to the bar of the first black lawyers in the state's history, probably because he was not aware of it. The modern-day lawyers described the near impossibility of practicing before the 1950s. The only pre–World War II lawyer mentioned in the article was T. St. Mark Sasportas, described as a "lone and legendary figure" with a very limited practice. In fact, it was his death in the "early 1930's" that seemed significant, because there was no black lawyer in the city after his death until Richard Fields returned in 1949.

These lawyers lamented that Charleston had produced "a good number" of black lawyers in the past but that they never returned to the city to practice. Now, however, the situation had changed. At the time of the article, there were more than thirty black lawyers in the state, more than a third of whom were in Charleston. They disagreed to some degree about their acceptance in the bar. John Wrighten said that the courts and other lawyers were "most receptive to any needs or problems I may have." George Payton was as upbeat as Wrighten, stating, "I don't believe anything really hinders my practice." While acknowledging tremendous improvements in race relations, Bernard Fielding said, "When I walk into a courtroom, I can't dismiss the possibility that there will be some degree of discrimination directed against my Negro client." Fred Henderson Moore said, "Negro lawyers are treated better and are more acceptable now," but he also thought that progressive lawyers who were active in civil rights were treated unfavorably in the courts. All complained of residual prejudice within the black community against the black lawyer. Moore said the feeling was gradually disappearing as black lawyers achieved success and won cases, but he felt that the myth of white superiority still endured.[2]

This view was not new. In the *History of the American Negro*, published in 1919, the plight of the black lawyer was often mentioned. Apparently, many black lawyers complained that the community did not support them. Editor A. B. Caldwell summarized that frustration by explaining, "The colored preacher has no competition in the white minister. The same is true of the colored teacher in the South. With the negro lawyer it is different. For legal advice and direction, his people . . . are accustomed to going to the white attorney."[3] While there may have been some truth in that statement, the plight of the black lawyer must not be attributed to a lack of community support. Jim Crow and economic factors were most certainly the chief villains in the difficulties the lawyers faced. It is not easy to judge how many black clients went to white lawyers. However, the reality was that the black community suffered severe economic stress in every era discussed in this book and struggled simply to feed their families, much less afford any legal representation.

The 1968 article offered another interesting but limited perspective on the black lawyer in South Carolina. Apparently, neither the reporter nor the lawyers knew the whole history of the black legal profession in Charleston and the state. They had heard of Sasportas, but Charleston's other leading black lawyers were not mentioned. William Whipper, Charleston's first black lawyer, had opened a law office with Robert Brown Elliott in 1868. In 1869 they were joined by Macon B. Allen, who had become America's first black lawyer in Maine in 1844. Where was mention of Charleston's George Lee, one of the country's first black judges, or Reconstruction-era congressman Robert DeLarge, also a member of the Charleston bar? Numerous other black lawyers hailed from the city. Lewis Taylor read law with Macon B. Allen and had a substantial trial practice in Charleston in the 1870s and 1880s. Even as Jim Crow began to diminish the opportunities for black lawyers, Jonathan Jasper Wright practiced in the city and established the Claflin Law School there. Samuel J. Lee moved to the city in the late 1870s and handled hundreds of cases in Charleston's courts. In fact, it was under Lee's tutelage that T. St. Mark Sasportas read law and became a member of the bar in 1895.

These modern-day lawyers' knowledge of their profession's history is understandable. The role of blacks in the state during Reconstruction had been distorted and downplayed by historians. Almost a fourth of the lawyers admitted by the state supreme court during Reconstruction were black.[4] The role the black lawyer had played in politics, the legislative branches, and the courts during the prior century was entirely missed by the *News and Courier* article. In 1868 African American lawyers helped write South Carolina's first democratic constitution. They advocated for civil rights in the state legislature, in Congress, in the courts, and on the bench. They defended the civil rights of the newly freed slaves during Reconstruction. Even the fall of Reconstruction did not daunt them. Jonathan Jasper Wright and D. A. Straker founded law schools. Samuel J. Lee and William Whipper mentored numerous lawyers. As a result, the legal profession remained an option for young blacks even in the 1880s and 1890s. Many of the early lawyers had remained active in politics. They were elected to office, and two served as judges in this era. These lawyers contested stolen elections and challenged the disenfranchisement of black voters. William Whipper and Thomas Miller fought the Jim Crow constitution of 1895. Others confronted the exclusion of blacks from juries, and on two occasions in the first decade of the twentieth century, black lawyers from South Carolina took jury discrimination cases to the U.S. Supreme Court.

However, by the end of the nineteenth century the black bar was under enormous stress. The Great Migration affected the black bar just as it affected the community as a whole. According to the U.S. census, only North Carolina had an increase in its black bar between 1900 and 1940 (14 to 27; see table 2 in the introduction). All other southern states had a net decline. In that same period, South Carolina had the most precipitous decline, going from 29 lawyers to 5. Yet despite the 1895 constitution and other constraints, there was no immediate exodus of lawyers from the state. In fact, among lawyers the reaction was subdued, and for a short time new lawyers continued to gain admission to the bar. In the five years before the Jim Crow constitution, nine black lawyers were admitted to the bar. In contrast, from 1896 to 1901 thirteen new lawyers were admitted. Allen University's law school continued to educate new lawyers, but its last graduate was in 1898.

It is true that by the early twentieth century, the number of African American lawyers in the state had declined, and opportunities for new lawyers were diminished. But even then, black lawyers continued to oppose injustices in the courts and in the electoral process. Beginning in 1915 and continuing in the 1920s and 1930s, Nathaniel J. Frederick and others organized the NAACP and helped maintain it through the Great Depression. The modern civil rights era began in 1940 as Harold Boulware and others teamed with the NAACP to begin a relentless series of civil rights lawsuits, the most monumental of which arose from South Carolina and was initially filed by Boulware under the guidance of Thurgood Marshall. Following the victories in *Briggs v. Elliott* and *Brown v. Board of Education*, other lawyers such as Lincoln Jenkins began to file civil rights cases. Soon Jenkins recruited Matthew Perry to become chief counsel for the NAACP in the state.

The successes of Matthew Perry, Ernest Finney, and other lawyers who graduated from South Carolina State's law school are a testament to its crucial importance in the advancement of civil rights in South Carolina. While the Charleston lawyers in 1968 may not have known all of the rich heritage of the black legal profession, they recognized that the closure of State's law school was a significant loss. Wrighten, the plaintiff in the lawsuit resulting in the school's establishment, saw the closing as a tragedy. Danny Martin, one of the school's last graduates, lamented the loss of the individualized attention that the students at the Orangeburg law school had received because of the small class sizes. And despite Fred Moore's troubled history with S.C. State, even he did not welcome the loss. But thanks to the work of these lawyers and their clients, the system that had demanded "separate but equal" was irrevocably breaking apart.

When Zack Townsend first started to practice in 1963, there were essentially no blacks on any juries, and the courthouse still had separate restrooms and water fountains. He remembered clearly the first time he argued before a black juror. By the 1970s and 1980s, Townsend noted that he no longer appeared before all-white juries and even had black judges presiding over his trials. He knew the world had changed the day he observed a trial presided over by a black judge in which the white defendant was prosecuted by a black assistant solicitor and convicted by an all-black jury. As the 1960s came to a close, Richard Fields and Harold Boulware had become judges. In 1970 I. S. Leevy Johnson and James Felder were elected to the legislature. After that, black lawyers would continuously occupy seats in the state legislature. Blacks were elected judges on the family court, the circuit court, the court of appeals, and the state supreme court and were appointed to the federal bench.

With South Carolina State School of Law closed, the University of South Carolina School of Law began admitting black students. In the early 1970s the formerly all-white law school had some serious problems with its black student retention rate.[5] But over time the school changed, minority student enrollment grew, and more and more black law students graduated. In 1976 the law school hired its first full-time black faculty member, James E. Bowers. Bowers stayed only one year, but in 1978 the school hired Kenneth W. Gaines, who is still teaching at the school. O'Neal Smalls was hired in 1989 and retired in 2006. Burnele Powell became dean of the law school in 2003 and retired from the faculty in 2014. Danielle Holley Walker joined the faculty in 2005 and served as associate dean from 2011 until 2014, when she departed to become dean of Howard Law School. Today, the school's faculty and student body are more diverse than ever. Averaging almost 15 percent minorities in its classes, the formerly all-white bastion of legal education has produced hundreds of black lawyers for the state.

In the 2010 census the state's black population was 28 percent. In 2015 the state supreme court and the court of appeals each had a black member. Out of 46 circuit court judges, 5 were black, and 8 out of 57 family court judges were black.[6] In 2010 only 4.6 percent of the lawyers in the United States were black, but 8.7 percent or 855 out of South Carolina's 9,800 lawyers were black.[7]

Between 1868 and 1968, the South Carolina bar admitted 165 black men and

3 black women. Many of these lawyers advocated for civil rights throughout their careers. Others had more limited roles in the struggle. Some did not even practice in South Carolina. But it is remarkable that these 170 individuals chose to enter the legal profession in the Deep South in this era. The curse of slavery, the shadow of the confederacy, and the legacy of Jim Crow remained ever present. Despite all the obstacles they faced, these lawyers were all for equal rights.

APPENDIX A

African American Lawyers in South Carolina, 1868–1968

Name	*Education*	*Date of Admission*	*Hometown*
1. Jonathan J. Wright	read Pa	Sept. 1868SC	Beaufort
2. William J. Whipper	read Mich.	Sept. 1868SC	Beaufort
3. Robert B. Elliott		Sept. 1868SC	Aiken
4. Macon B. Allen	read Maine	Nov. 1869CC[1] Dec. 1875SC	Charleston
5. George Lee	J. J. Wright	June 1870CC[2]	Charleston
6. John Patterson Green	Ohio Union	Sept. 20, 1870CC[3]	Bennettsville
7. Edwin T. Belcher	Howard	Nov. 1871SC	Augusta, Ga.
8. Eugene R. B. Belcher	Howard	Nov. 1871SC	Augusta, Ga.
9. John F. Quarles	Howard	Nov. 1871SC[4]	Augusta, Ga.
10. Theophilus J. Minton	USC/Elliott/ Whipper	Mar. 6, 1872SC[5]	Columbia
11. Robert DeLarge	Elliott/Whipper	Mar. 6, 1872SC	Charleston
12. W. H. Jones Jr.	Elliott/Whipper	Mar. 6, 1872SC	Georgetown
13. Stephen A. Swails	Elliott/Whipper	Mar. 6, 1872SC	Kingstree
14. Samuel J. Lee	Elliott/Whipper	Mar. 6, 1872SC	Hamburg
15. Henry J. Maxwell	Elliott/Whipper	Mar. 6, 1872SC	Bennettsville
16. John L. Humbert	T. H. Cooke[6]	May 1872CC[7]	Orangeburg
17. T. K. Sasportas	Cooke	May 1872CC[8]	Orangeburg
18. Lewis J. Taylor Jr.	M. B. Allen	June 11, 1872CC[9]	Charleston
19. Richard H. Gleaves*		Unknown CC?	Beaufort
20. James A. Bowley	M. B. Allen	Nov. 16, 1872CC[10]	Charleston/ Georgetown
21. A. W. Watson	W. J. Whipper	Nov. 8, 1872CC[11]	Charleston/ Aiken
22. A. A. Bradley*	read Maine	1873CC?[12]	Beaufort
23. George C. Clyde	S. J. Lee	Nov. 1873SC	Aiken
24. Benjamin Byas	Whipper	June 6, 1874CC[13]	Charleston
25. Walter R. Jones	USC	Nov. 1874SC	Columbia
26. John Hammond Fordham	*	1874CC[14]	Orangeburg
27. William Hannibal Thomas		Jan. 1875, Nov. 1876SC	Newberry
28. Samuel Dickerson	C. W. Buttz	Nov. 10, 1875CC[15]	Charleston
29. Joseph H. Boston	USC	July 1875CC[16]	Newberry
30. F. D. J. Lawrence	Buttz	1875CC, April[17] 1882SC	Charleston
31. Daniel A. Straker	Howard	July 1875SC	Charleston
32. William F. Myers		Dec. 1875SC	Colleton
33. T. McCants Stewart	USC	Dec. 1875SC	Sumter
34. Thomas E. Miller	USC	Dec. 1875SC	Lawtonville
35. William A. Hayne		Dec. 1875SC	Marion
36. John M. Freeman Jr.		Dec. 1875SC	Charleston
37. Samuel J. Bampfield	P. L. Wiggin	Dec. 1875SC	Beaufort
38. Joseph H. Stuart	USC	Dec. 1875SC	Camden
39. Francis L. Cardozo	USC	July 1876SC	Columbia

Name	*Education*	*Date of Admission*	*Hometown*
40. Thomas H. Wheeler	Howard	Oct. 16, 1873CC,[18] April 1876SC	Beaufort
41. John Charles Mardenborough	Seymour[19]	March 24, 1876CC[20]	Edgefield
42. Styles L. Hutchins	USC	Nov. 1876SC	Columbia
43. Joseph W. Morris	USC	Nov. 1876SC	Columbia
44. Richard T. Greener	USC	Dec. 1876SC	Columbia
45. Laurence Cain	USC	1876CC*[21]	Edgefield
46. Samuel J. Picksley		1876CC*[22]	Hamburg
47. L. S. Langley	Whipper	Feb. 1877CC[23]	Beaufort
48. A. H. Ezekiel	Whipper	Feb. 1877CC	Beaufort
49. Dempsher W. Powell	Whipper	Feb. 1877CC	Beaufort
RECONSTRUCTION ENDS (all subsequent admitted by the supreme court unless indicated)[24]			
50. Henry B. Johnson	USC	Nov. 1877	Charleston
51. Joshua Williams Polite		May 1879	Charleston
52. William J. Bowen	Lee	Dec. 1881	Charleston
53. Robert Lloyd Smith	Claflin	1882	Charleston
54. George O. Marshall	Claflin	1883	Charleston
55. William F. Holmes	Claflin	Dec. 1883	Charleston
56. Talley R. Holmes	Allen	May 1884[25]	Columbia
57. John B. Edwards	Allen	May 1884	Columbia
58. Peter Flynn Oliver	Allen	May 1884	Columbia
59. Robert A. Stewart	Allen	May 1884	Columbia
60. Major D. McFarlan		Dec. 1884	Cheraw
61. John F. Brown	Howard	1884	Colleton
62. E. C. C. Washington	Allen	May 1885	Columbia
63. Benjamin E. Watson	Allen	May 1885	Columbia
64. E. J. Sawyer	Allen	May 1885	Bennettsville
65. J. C. Whittaker		May 1885	Charleston
66. Edward J. Dickerson	Allen	Dec. 1885	Aiken
67. Thomas J. Reynolds		Dec. 1885	Beaufort
68. Robert C. Browne	Lee	May 1886	Charleston
69. Paris Simkins	USC	Nov. 1886	Edgefield
70. A. S. Bascomb		Dec. 1886	Beaufort
71. Andrew E. Hampton	Allen	May 1887[26]	Columbia
72. Thomas A. Saxon	Allen	May 1887	Laurens
73. Wm. W. Still		May 1887	Beaufort
74. Julius I. Washington	Whipper[27]	Dec. 1887	Beaufort
75. Seymour E. Smith		1888	Aiken
76. Casper G. Garrett	Allen	May 1890	Laurens
77. Butler W. Nance	Allen	May 1890	Newberry
78. Zachariah D. Greene	Allen	Dec. 1890[28]	Georgetown
79. Walton W. Williams	Allen	Dec. 1890	Columbia
80. Dock J. Jordan	Allen	May 1892	Columbia
81. Isaiah R. Reed		1893	Beaufort
82. Julius L. Mitchell	Allen	1893	Moncks Corner
83. W. T. Andrews		Dec. 1894	Sumter
84. T. St. Mark Sasportas	Lee	May 1895	Charleston
1895 CONSTITUTION			
85. E. B. Burroughs		May 21, 1896	Cheraw
86. Edward R. Culler		Dec. 18, 1896	Charleston

Name	Education	Date of Admission	Hometown
87. Jacob Moorer		Dec. 18, 1896	Orangeburg
88. E. Woodbury Brinkins	Allen	May 1897	Columbia
89. Eugene R. Hayne	Allen	May 1897	Charleston
90. John A. Gaillard	Shaw	May 1897[29]	Charleston
91. Mark A. Williams	Shaw	May 1897[30]	Charleston
92. Thomas T. Hilton	Allen	Dec. 1897	Marion
93. Green Jackson	Allen	May 1898	Columbia
94. S. S. Davis		1898	Darlington
95. Alonzo E. Twine		May 1899	Charleston
96. Edward F. Smith		Dec. 1900	Mount Pleasant
97. Daniel B. Summers		1901	Charleston
98. Marion J. Frederick		1903	Orangeburg, Sumter
99. T. T. Henry		1903CC*	Columbia
100. John Adams		1905	Columbia
101. Nathaniel J. Frederick	Read	1913	Columbia
102. Shadrack Morgan	Howard	1919	Orangeburg
103. William A. Dart	Boston University	1919	Charleston
104. Booker T. Smith		1920CC*	Spartanburg
105. Herbert F. McGirt	Howard	1922	Camden
106. Arthur Chester Platt	Boston University	1922	Spartanburg
107. Esau Allen Parker		1924	Columbia, Sumter
108. Charles English Washington	Howard	1924	Beaufort
109. Harold R. Boulware	Howard	1940	Columbia
110. Harold A. Stevens	Boston College	1941	Columbia
111. Cassandra Maxwell	Howard f**	1941	Orangeburg
112. W. F. Robinson	Howard	1941	Columbia
113. William B. James	Robt Terrell	1947	Sumter
114. Benner C. Turner	Harvard f	1948	Orangeburg
115. Richard Fields	Howard	1948	Charleston
116. Lincoln C. Jenkins Jr.	Howard	1949	Columbia
117. Albert A. Kennedy	SCSt	1950	Columbia
118. Julius Thomas Williams Jr.	SCSt	1950	Orangeburg
ALL BY WRITTEN EXAMINATION			
119. Matthew J. Perry	SCSt	1951	Columbia
120. Donald James Sampson	Temple	1951	Sumter
121. W. Newton Pough	SCSt	1952	Orangeburg
122. Charles E. Washington Jr.	Howard	1952	Beaufort
123. Ira W. Claiborne	Lincoln	1952	Charleston
124. William W. Bennett	SCSt	1953	Lane
125. Frank E. Cain	SCSt	1953	Bennettsville
126. Vernoid R. Bunch	SCSt	1953	Georgetown
127. Leo J. Kerford	Kansas f	1953	Orangeburg
128. John H. Wrighten	SCSt	1953	Charleston
129. John E. McCall	SCSt	1953	Cheraw
130. Ernest A. Finney Jr.	SCSt	1954	Orangeburg
131. Cleveland Stevens	SCSt	1954	Loris
132. Willie T. Smith Jr.	SCSt	1954	Columbia
133. Herman G. Boyd	SCSt	1954	Columbia
134. Elliott D. Turnage	Harvard	1954	Darlington

Name	*Education*	*Date of Admission*	*Hometown*
135. James M. Hinton, Jr.	American	1954	Columbia
136. Edgar E. Thompson	SCSt	1954	Spartanburg
137. LeMarquis DeJarmon	Wes Res f	1955	Orangeburg
138. Blinzy L. Gore	Iowa f	1955	Orangeburg
139. John J. Rodgers	SCSt	1955	Walhalla
140. Suzanna Blackwell		1956	Hodges
141. Mack Evans Davis	SCSt	1957	Varnville
142. Aaron Harvey	read law & Lasalle correspondence[31]	1957	Charleston
143. Paul Rainey Webber III	SCSt	1958	Orangeburg
144. Bernard R. Fielding	Boston University	1958	Charleston
145. Alphonso Walter Pendergrass	SCSt	1959	St. Stephens
146. Russell Brown	SCSt	1959	Ravenel
147. Mordecai C. Johnson	Howard	1960	Florence
148. Fred Henderson Moore	Howard	1960	Charleston
149. Arthur J. Howard Clement III	Howard	1960	Charleston
150. Leroy Nesbitt	Howard	1960	Charleston
151. Ned Edward Felder	SCSt	1961	Charleston
152. Benjamin L. Cook Jr.	read law[32]	1961	Charleston
153. Hemphill P. Pride II	Fla. A&M	1963	Columbia
154. Ruben Lee Gray	SCSt	1963	Hemingway
155. Zack E. Townsend	SCSt	1963	Orangeburg
156. Earl Coblyn	Suffolk f	1963	Orangeburg
157. Dorothy V. Sampson	North Carolina CU	1964	Sumter
158. Ernest Simmons Jr.	SCSt	1964	Columbia
159. Franklin R. DeWitt	SCSt	1964	Conway
160. Thomas D. Broadwater Jr.	Fla. A&M	1966	Columbia
161. George A. Payton	SCSt	1966	Charleston
162. George Allen Anderson	SCSt	1966	Aiken
163. Danny E. Martin	SCSt	1966	Charleston
164. Damon George Thomas	SCSt	1966	Charleston
165. Johnny Lake Jr.	USC	1967	Greenwood
166. Jasper Marshall Cureton	USC	1967	Columbia
167. Ernest G. Deveaux	SCSt	1967	Charleston
168. George Marion Crawford	SCSt	1967	Orangeburg
169. James L. Felder	Howard	1968	Columbia
170. Isaac Samuel Leevy Johnson	USC	1968	Columbia

* There is no official record of these men being admitted to the bar. They have been included because of secondary sources indicating that they were lawyers. Some of them practiced in the state's courts, but no proof of their admission to the bar has been found. Some may never have been admitted but have been included for the sake of completeness.

** An f indicates that person was a member of the faculty at South Carolina State.

1. Admitted by Judge L. C. Carpenter. See "Court in Charleston," *Orangeburg News*, November 6, 1869.

2. "Crumbs," *Charleston Daily News*, June 23, 1870; "Deaths," *Columbia Daily Phoenix*, February 20, 1873.

3. By Judge J. M. Rutland on September 20, 1870. See John P. Green, *Fact Stranger than Fiction: Seventy-five Years of a Busy Life with Reminiscences of Many Great and Good Men and Women* (Cleveland: Riehl, 1920), 136. See also Marlboro County Court of Common Pleas Journal, September 20, 1870, South Carolina Department of Archives and History, Columbia, South Carolina (SCDAH).

4. Quarles was admitted to practice in Augusta, Georgia, in January 1873, which may have made him the first black admitted to practice in a Georgia court. See "Our South Atlantic Neighbors: Georgia," *Charleston Daily News*, January 9, 1873.

5. Minton, DeLarge, Jones, Swails, Lee, and Maxwell were all admitted by the supreme court after an examination by a committee made up of D. H. Chamberlain, William Whipper, and H. C. Worthington.

"Supreme Court," *Columbia Daily Phoenix*, March 7, 1872. Oddly, Worthington was not a member of the South Carolina bar.

6. Cooke was the Republican solicitor in Orangeburg County. *Charleston Daily News*, March 22, 1872.

7. By Judge Robert F. Graham, on motion of T. H. Cooke. "Local," *Orangeburg News*, May 18, 1872; Criminal Journal, Orangeburg County Court of General Sessions, May 9, 1872, 405.

8. By Judge Robert F. Graham. "Local," *Orangeburg News*, May 18, 1872.

9. By Judge Graham. Charleston County Court of Common Pleas, June 11, 1872, SCDAH.

10. By Judge Graham. Charleston County Court of Common Pleas, November 16, 1872, SCDAH.

11. By Judge Graham. Charleston County Court of Common Pleas Civil Journal, November 8, 1872, SCDAH.

12. E. Merton Coulter, *Negro Legislators in Georgia during the Reconstruction Era* (Athens: Georgia Historical Society, 1968), 112, 118.

13. Admitted by Judge Graham. Court of Common Pleas, Charleston County, Civil Journals, June 6, 1874, 40.

14. On April 4, 1874 the *Orangeburg Times* noted the formation of the law firm of Humbert and Fordham. It is assumed that Fordham was admitted by a circuit judge.

15. Admitted by Judge J. P. Reed on December 3, 1875. Court of Common Pleas, Civil Journals, Charleston County. C. W. Buttz was a white Republican. See Hyman Rubin III, *South Carolina Scalawags* (Columbia: University of South Carolina Press, 2006).

16. Admitted by Judge Montgomery Moses on July 20, 1875. Thomas H. Pope, *History of Newberry County, South Carolina*, vol. 2 (Columbia: University of South Carolina Press, 1992), 64.

17. Admitted by Judge Reed on February 5, 1875. Court of Common Pleas, Charleston County, Civil Journals, 267.

18. *Beaufort Republican*, October 16, 1873. Whipper moved Wheeler's admission on the basis that Wheeler was a member of the bar in the District of Columbia.

19. R. W. Seymour was a white Republican. See *Columbia Daily Phoenix*, October 17, 1874.

20. By Judge R. B. Carpenter, Edgefield County Court of Common Pleas, Minute Session Journal 1868–1879, SCDAH.

21. Cain was counsel for Robert Smalls in a contested federal election case. See Tillman v. Smalls at 255 (45th Cong., 1st Sess., March 1877).

22. Picksley is identified as a lawyer twice in the state treasurer's monthly reports. See "Treasurer's Monthly Statement," (Columbia) *Daily Union Herald*, July 3, 1876. He is also mentioned in "The Sable Citizens," (Columbia) *Daily Phoenix*, April 18, 1875.

23. On Langley, Ezekiel, and Powell, see "Court of General Sessions," *Beaufort Tribune and Port Royal Commercial*, February 8, 1877.

24. In 1878 the legislature amended the statute relating to admission to the bar and provided that no license to practice could be issued by any court other than the supreme court. Act 442 (March 12, 1878).

25. All of the lawyers sworn in 1884 were orally examined in open court and then admitted. See "Young Lawyers," *(Sumter) Watchman and Southron*, June 3, 1884.

26. On December 22, 1886, the legislature granted the diploma privilege to law school graduates. Act 272, "An Act to Amend Section 2160 Relating to Attorneys," Acts and Joint Resolutions of the General Assembly of the State of South Carolina Regular Session 1886 (Columbia: Charles Calvo, 1887), 521.

27. "Death of Attorney J. I. Washington," *Beaufort Gazette*, January 17, 1938.

28. Greene passed a written bar examination and was admitted on December 18, 1890. "New Legal Timber," *(Sumter) Watchman and Southron*, December 24, 1890.

29. Gaillard had previously been admitted in North Carolina. See *"The State Supreme Court," (Columbia) State*, May 13, 1897.

30. Williams had previously been admitted in North Carolina. See *ibid.*

31. Judge Richard Fields mentored Harvey. Effective March 1, 1958, the supreme court amended its rules requiring that applicants for admission to the bar be graduates of an ABA-approved law school. Under this new rule, if an applicant had begun study in a law office prior to January 1, 1957, they could petition the court for a waiver of the graduation requirement. Rule 5 of the Rules of Examination and Admission of Persons to Practice Law in South Carolina, Rules of the Supreme Court of South Carolina, Code of Laws of South Carolina 1952 (Cum. Supp. 1960).

32. Zack Townsend and Judge Richard Fields confirm that Cook read law. Judge Fields thought Cook was bright enough to have done it on his own but opined that he may have read law in John Wrighten's office. Presumably Rule 5 was waived for Cook.

APPENDIX B

Alphabetical List

Name	Year of Admission	Hometown
John Adams	1905	Columbia
Macon B. Allen	1869	Charleston
George Allen Anderson	1966	Aiken
W. T. Andrews	1894	Sumter
Samuel J. Bampfield	1875	Beaufort
A. S. Bascomb	1886	Beaufort
Edwin T. Belcher	1871	Augusta, Ga.
Eugene R. B. Belcher	1871	Augusta, Ga.
William W. Bennett	1953	Lane
Suzanne Blackwell	1956	Hodges
Joseph H. Boston	1875	Newberry
Harold R. Boulware	1940	Columbia
William J. Bowen	1881	Charleston
James A. Bowley	1872	Charleston
Herman G. Boyd	1881	Charleston
A. A. Bradley	1873	Beaufort
E. Woodbury Brinkins	1897	Columbia
Thomas D. Broadwater Jr.	1966	Columbia
John F. Brown	1884	Colleton
Russell Brown	1959	Ravenel
Robert C. Browne	1886	Charleston
Vernoid R. Bunch	1953	Georgetown
E. B. Burroughs	1896	Cheraw
Benjamin Byas	1874	Charleston
Frank E. Cain	1953	Bennettsville
Laurence Cain	1876	Edgefield
Francis L. Cardozo	1876	Columbia
Ira W. Claiborne	1952	Charleston
Arthur J. Howard Clement III	1960	Charleston
George C. Clyde	1873	Aiken
Earl Coblyn	1963	Orangeburg
Benjamin L. Cook Jr.	1961	Charleston
George Marion Crawford	1967	Orangeburg
Edward R. Culler	1896	Charleston
Jasper Marshall Cureton	1967	Columbia
William A. Dart	1919	Charleston
Mack Evans Davis	1957	Varnville
S. S. Davis	1898	Darlington
LeMarquis DeJarmon	1955	Orangeburg
Robert DeLarge	1872	Charleston
Ernest G. Deveaux	1967	Charleston
Franklin R. DeWitt	1964	Conway
Edward J. Dickerson	1885	Aiken
Samuel Dickerson	1875	Charleston

Name	*Year of Admission*	*Hometown*
John B. Edwards	1884	Columbia
Robert B. Elliott	1868	Aiken
A. H. Ezekiel	1877	Beaufort
James L. Felder	1968	Columbia
Ned Edward Felder	1961	Charleston
Bernard R. Fielding	1958	Charleston
Richard Fields	1948	Charleston
Ernest A. Finney Jr.	1954	Orangeburg
John Hammond Fordham	1874	Orangeburg
Marion J. Frederick	1903	Orangeburg
Nathaniel J. Frederick	1913	Columbia
John M. Freeman Jr.	1875	Charleston
John A. Gaillard	1897	Charleston
Casper G. Garrett	1890	Laurens
Richard H. Gleaves	1870s	Beaufort
Blinzy L. Gore	1955	Orangeburg
Ruben Lee Gray	1963	Hemingway
John Patterson Green	1870	Bennettsville
Zachariah D. Greene	1890	Georgetown
Richard T. Greener	1876	Columbia
Andrew E. Hampton	1887	Columbia
Aaron Harvey	1957	Charleston
Eugene R. Hayne	1897	Charleston
William A. Hayne	1875	Marion
T. T. Henry	1903?	Columbia
Thomas T. Hilton	1897	Marion
James Miles Hinton Jr.	1954	Columbia
Talley R. Holmes	1884	Columbia
William F. Holmes	1883	Charleston
John L. Humbert	1872	Orangeburg
Styles L. Hutchins	1876	Columbia
Green Jackson	1898	Columbia
William B. James	1947	Sumter
Lincoln C. Jenkins Jr.	1949	Columbia
Henry B. Johnson	1877	Charleston
Isaac Samuel Leevy Johnson	1968	Columbia
Mordecai C. Johnson	1960	Florence
W. H. Jones Jr.	1872	Georgetown
Walter R. Jones	1874	Columbia
Dock J. Jordan	1892	Columbia
Albert A. Kennedy	1950	Columbia
Leo J. Kerford	1954	Orangeburg
Johnny Lake Jr.	1967	Greenwood
L. S. Langley	1877	Beaufort
F. D. J. Lawrence	1882	Charleston
George Lee	1870	Charleston
Samuel J. Lee	1872	Aiken
John Charles Mardenborough	1876	Edgefield

Name	Year of Admission	Hometown
George O. Marshall	1883	Charleston
Danny E. Martin	1966	Charleston
Cassandra Maxwell	1941	Orangeburg
Henry J. Maxwell	1872	Bennettsville
John E. McCall	1953	Cheraw
Major D. McFarlan	1884	Cheraw
Herbert F. McGirt	1922	Camden
Thomas E. Miller	1875	Lawtonville
Theophilus J. Minton	1872	Columbia
Julius L. Mitchell	1893	Moncks Corner
Fred Henderson Moore	1960	Charleston
Jacob Moorer	1896	Orangeburg
Shadrack Morgan	1919	Orangeburg
Joseph W. Morris	1876	Columbia
William F. Myers	1875	Colleton
Butler W. Nance	1890	Newberry
Leroy Nesbitt	1960	Charleston
Peter Flynn Oliver	1884	Columbia
Esau Allen Parker	1924	Columbia
George A. Payton	1966	Charleston
Alphonso Walter Pendergrass	1959	Saint Stephens
Matthew J. Perry	1951	Columbia
Samuel J. Picksley	1875?	Hamburg
Arthur Chester Platt	1922	Spartanburg
Joshua Williams Polite	1879	Charleston
W. Newton Pough	1952	Orangeburg
Dempsher W. Powell	1877	Beaufort
Hemphill P. Pride II	1963	Columbia
John F. Quarles	1871	Augusta, Ga.
Isaiah R. Reed	1893	Beaufort
Thomas J. Reynolds	1885	Beaufort
W. F. Robinson	1941	Columbia
John J. Rodgers	1955	Walhalla
Donald James Sampson	1951	Sumter
Dorothy V. Sampson	1964	Sumter
T. K. Sasportas	1872	Orangeburg
T. St. Mark Sasportas	1895	Charleston
E. J. Sawyer	1885	Bennettsville
Thomas A. Saxon	1887	Laurens
Paris Simkins	1886	Edgefield
Ernest Simmons Jr.	1964	Columbia
Booker T. Smith	1920?	Spartanburg
Edward F. Smith	1900	Mt. Pleasant
Robert Lloyd Smith	1882	Charleston
S. E. Smith	1888	Aiken
Willie T. Smith Jr.	1954	Columbia
Cleveland Stevens	1954	Loris
Harold A. Stevens	1941	Columbia
Robert A. Stewart	1884	Columbia

Name	*Year of Admission*	*Hometown*
T. McCants Stewart	1875	Sumter
Wm. W. Still	1887	Beaufort
Daniel A. Straker	1875	Charleston
Joseph H. Stuart	1875	Camden
Daniel B. Summers	1901	Charleston
Stephen A. Swails	1872	Kingstree
Lewis J. Taylor Jr.	1872	Charleston
Damon George Thomas	1966	Charleston
William Hannibal Thomas	1875	Newberry
Edgar E. Thompson	1954	Spartanburg
Zack E. Townsend	1963	Orangeburg
Elliott D. Turnage	1954	Darlington
Benner C. Turner	1948	Orangeburg
Alonzo E. Twine	1899	Charleston
Charles English Washington	1924	Beaufort
Charles E. Washington Jr.	1952	Beaufort
E. C. C. Washington	1885	Columbia
Julius I. Washington	1887	Beaufort
A. W. Watson	1872	Charleston
Benjamin E. Watson	1885	Columbia
Paul Rainey Webber III	1958	Orangeburg
Thomas H. Wheeler	1873	Beaufort
William J. Whipper	1868	Beaufort
J. C. Whittaker	1885	Charleston
Julius Thomas Williams Jr.	1950	Orangeburg
Mark A. Williams	1897	Charleston
Walton W. Williams	1890	Columbia
Jonathan J. Wright	1868	Beaufort
John H. Wrighten	1953	Charleston

APPENDIX C

Read Law

Determining who mentored a lawyer is quite difficult in some cases. I have footnoted the source for a number of the mentors. However, those with a question mark (?) are based on an educated guess. Under the date for admission, those admitted only in the circuit court are noted with "cc."

	W/Whom/Where	*Year of admission*	*Hometown*
1. Jonathan J. Wright	In Pa.[1]	1868	Beaufort
2. William J. Whipper	In Ohio	1868	Beaufort
3. Macon B. Allen	In Maine[2]	1869	Charleston
4. George Lee	J. J. Wright[3]	1870	Charleston
5. John L. Humbert	T. H. Cooke[4]	1872cc	Orangeburg
6. T. K. Sasportas	Cooke[5]	1872cc[6]	Orangeburg
7. Lewis J. Taylor Jr.	M. B. Allen[7]	1872cc[8]	Charleston
8. James A. Bowley	M. B. Allen[9]	1872cc[10]	Charleston/ Georgetown
9. A. W. Watson	W. J. Whipper[11]	1872cc[12]	Charleston/Aiken
10. Theophilus J. Minton	R. B. Elliott[13]	1872[14]	Columbia
11. Robert DeLarge	Elliott?[15]	1872	Charleston
12. W. H. Jones Jr.	Elliott?	1872	Georgetown
13. Stephen A. Swails	Elliott?	1872	Kingstree
14. Samuel J. Lee	Elliott?	1872	Hamburg
15. Henry J. Maxwell	Elliott?	1872	Bennettsville
16. A. A. Bradley	read in Maine[16]	1873cc[17]	Beaufort
17. George C. Clyde	S. J. Lee[18]	1873	Aiken
18. Benjamin Byas	C. W. Buttz[19]	1874cc[20]	Charleston
19. Samuel Dickerson	Buttz[21]	1875cc[22]	Charleston
20. Samuel J. Bampfield	P. L. Wiggin[23]	1875	Beaufort
21. F. D. J. Lawrence	Buttz[24]	1875cc,[25] 1882	Charleston
22. John C. Mardenborough	Seymour[26]	1876cc[27]	Edgefield
23. L. S. Langley	Whipper[28]	1877cc	Beaufort
24. A. H. Ezekiel	Whipper[29]	1877cc	Beaufort
25. Dempsher W. Powell	Whipper[30]	1877cc	Beaufort
26. William J. Bowen	Lee[31]	1881	Charleston
27. Thomas J. Reynolds	Whipper[32]	1885	Beaufort
28. Robert C. Browne	Lee[33]	1886	Charleston
29. A. S. Bascomb	Whipper?[34]	1886	Beaufort
30. Wm. W. Still	Whipper?	1887	Beaufort
31. Isaiah R. Reed	Whipper?	1893	Beaufort
32. T. St. Mark Sasportas	Lee	1895	Charleston
33. Nathaniel J. Frederick	read[35]	1913	Columbia
34. Aaron Harvey	read law & Lasalle correspondence[36]	1957	Charleston
35. Benjamin L. Cook Jr.	read law[37]	1961	Charleston

	W/Whom/Where	Year of admission	Hometown
UNKNOWN WITH WHOM THEY READ LAW			
1. Robert B. Elliott		1868	Aiken
2. Richard H. Gleaves		CC?	Beaufort
3. John Hammond Fordham		1874CC[38]	Orangeburg
4. William Hannibal Thomas		1875/1876	Newberry
5. William F. Myers		1875	Colleton
6. William A. Hayne		1875	Marion
7. John M. Freeman Jr.		1875	Charleston
8. Samuel J. Picksley		Unknown CC[39]	Hamburg
9. Joshua Williams Polite		1879	Charleston
10. Major D. McFarlan		1884	Cheraw
11. J. C. Whittaker		1885	Charleston
12. S. E. Smith		1888	Aiken
13. Edward R. Culler		1896	Charleston
14. Jacob Moorer		1896	Orangeburg
15. S. S. Davis		1898	Darlington
16. Alonzo E. Twine		1899	Charleston
17. Edward F. Smith		1900	Mount Pleasant
18. Daniel B. Summers		1901	Charleston
19. Marion J. Frederick		1903	Orangeburg, Sumter
20. T. T. Henry		1903?CC[40]	Columbia
21. John Adams		1905	Columbia
22. Booker T. Smith		1920?CC[41]	Spartanburg
23. Esau Allen Parker		1924	Columbia, Sumter

1. Wright read law with the firm of Bentley, Fitch, and Bentley in Susquehanna County and then with Judge O. Collins in Wilkes-Barre. See Richard Gergel and Belinda Gergel, "To Vindicate the Cause of the Downtrodden," in James L. Underwood and William Lewis Burke, eds., *At Freedom's Door: African American Founding Fathers in Reconstruction South Carolina* (Columbia: University of South Carolina Press, 2005), 36.

2. He was tutored by a "liberal white lawyer" in Maine. J. Clay Smith Jr., *Emancipation: The Making of the Black Lawyer, 1844–1944* (Philadelphia: University of Pennsylvania Press, 1993), 112.

3. Obituary in the *Columbia Daily Union*, February 20, 1873.

4. He was admitted on the motion of T. H. Cooke. See Criminal Journal, Orangeburg County Court of General Sessions, May 9, 1872, 405. Cooke was solicitor in Orangeburg County. See "The County Solicitorship," *Charleston Daily News*, March 22, 1872.

5. Criminal Journal, Orangeburg County Court of General Sessions, May 9, 1872, 405.

6. By Judge Robert F. Graham. (N.t.), *Orangeburg News*, May 18, 1872. See Criminal Journal, Orangeburg County Court of Sessions May 9, 1872, 405.

7. Civil Journal, Charleston County Court of Common Pleas, June 4, 1872, South Carolina Department of Archives and History, Columbia, South Carolina (SCDAH).

8. By Judge Graham. Charleston County Court of Common Pleas, June 11, 1872, SCDAH.

9. Civil Journal, Charleston County Court of Common Pleas, November 15, 1872, SCDAH.

10. By Judge Graham. Charleston County Court of Common Pleas, November 16, 1872, SCDAH. Bowley read law with Macon B. Allen.

11. Civil Journal, Charleston County Court of Common Pleas, November 6, 1872, SCDAH.

12. By Judge Graham. Civil Journal, Charleston County Court of Common Pleas, November 8, 1872, SCDAH.

13. M. Harrison Wayman, "The Quaker City," *Colored American Magazine* 6 (1903): 288.

14. Minton would also graduate from USC School of Law.

15. Since Minton, DeLarge, Jones, Swails, Lee, and Maxwell were all admitted by the supreme court on the same day and examined by the same committee, it is possible that all six were mentored by R. B. Elliott. See "Supreme Court," *Columbia Daily Phoenix*, March 7, 1872.

16. Admitted in Maine and Massachusetts. See "Colored Lawyer Not Allowed to Practice in Georgia," *Charleston Daily News*, January 23, 1867. Also see Smith, *Emancipation*, 100.

17. Since Bradley's few court cases were in the criminal court of Charleston in 1873, it is possible he was admitted by one of the judges in that court. However, one source indicates that Bradley claimed to have been admitted by the circuit court in 1870. See E. Merton Coulter, *Negro Legislators in Georgia during the Reconstruction Era* (Athens: Georgia Historical Society, 1968), 112, 118.

18. Since he lived in Aiken, it is likely that Clyde would have read law with S. J. Lee. One historian opined that Clyde learned the law by serving a clerk of court. See John Oldfield, "The African American Bar in South Carolina, 1877–1915," in Underwood and Burke, *At Freedom's Door*, 117.

19. Civil Journal, Charleston County Court of Common Pleas, June 10, 1874, SCDAH.

20. Admitted by Judge Graham. Civil Journal, Charleston County Court of Common Pleas, June 10, 1874, 40, SCDAH.

21. Civil Journal, Charleston County Court of Common Pleas, November 10, 1875, SCDAH.

22. Admitted by Judge J. P. Reed, December 3, 1875. Civil Journal, Charleston County Court of Common Pleas, SCDAH. Buttz was a white Republican. See Hyman Rubin III, *South Carolina Scalawags* (Columbia: University of South Carolina Press, 2006), 119.

23. I. Garland Penn, *The Afro-American Press and Its Editors* (Springfield, Mass.: Wiley, 1891), 205.

24. Civil Journal, Charleston County Court of Common Pleas, November 10, 1875, SCDAH.

25. Admitted by Judge Reed, February 5, 1875. Civil Journal, Charleston County Court of Common Pleas, 267, SCDAH.

26. R. W. Seymour was a white Republican. See "Independent Republican Party," *Columbia Daily Phoenix*, October 17, 1874.

27. Admitted by Judge R. B. Carpenter, Edgefield County Court of Common Pleas, Minute Session Journal 1868–1879, SCDAH.

28. "Court of General Sessions," *Beaufort Tribune and Port Royal Commercial*, February 8, 1877.

29. Ibid.

30. Demps Whipper Powell, "A Providential Revelation, Relationship with the Whipper Family," Whipper Papers, Moorland-Spingarn Research Center, Howard University, Washington, D.C.

31. "Limbs of the Law," *(Charleston) News and Courier*, December 14, 1881. Also see Oldfield, "African American Bar in South Carolina," 117.

32. Alrutheus Ambush Taylor, *The Negro in South Carolina during the Reconstruction* (Washington, D.C.: Association for the Study of Negro Life and History, 1924), 295.

33. "Limbs of the Law," *(Charleston) News and Courier*, December 14, 1881. Also see Oldfield, "African American Bar in South Carolina," 117.

34. I assume Whipper was also the mentor for Bascomb, Still, and Reed. All were located in Beaufort and were political allies.

35. According to his obituary, he read law "under the direction of some of the best legal minds of the state bar." See *Palmetto Leader*, September 10, 1938.

36. Judge Richard Fields mentored Harvey. Effective March 1, 1958, the supreme court amended its rules requiring that applicants for admission to the bar have graduated from an ABA-approved law school. Under this new rule, if an applicant had begun to study law in a law office prior to January 1, 1957, they could petition the court for a waiver of the law school graduation requirement. Rule 5 of the Rules of Examination and Admission of Persons to Practice Law in South Carolina, Rules of the Supreme Court of South Carolina (1958). Code of Laws of South Carolina 1952 (Cum. Supp. 1960).

37. Zack Townsend and Judge Richard Fields confirm that Cook read law. Judge Fields thought Cook was bright enough to have done it on his own but opined that he may have read law in John Wrighten's office. Presumably Rule 5 was waived for Cook.

38. The *Orangeburg News* noted the formation of a new law firm (Humbert and Fordham) in the town, so it is assumed that Fordham had been admitted by circuit judge. "A New Law Firm," April 4, 1874.

39. Picksley is identified as a lawyer twice in the state treasurer's monthly reports. See "Treasurer's Monthly Statement," *Daily Union Herald*, July 3, 1876. He is also mentioned in the *Daily Phoenix*, April 18, 1875.

40. T. T. Henry is listed as an attorney in the Columbia City Directory (1904), 536, available at ancestry.com.

41. Booker T. Smith is listed in the 1920 and 1930 census and multiple times in the Spartanburg city directory as a lawyer. In 1937 a legal notice lists Smith as executor of an estate. See "Legal Notice," *(Spartanburg) Herald Journal*, September 19, 1937.

APPENDIX D

Law School Attended

Lawyer	*Law School*	*Date of Admission*	*Residence at Admission*
John Patterson Green	Ohio Union	Sept. 20, 1870CC	Bennettsville
Edwin T. Belcher	Howard U.	Nov. 1871SC	Augusta, Ga.
Eugene R. B. Belcher	Howard U.	Nov. 1871SC	Augusta, Ga.
John F. Quarles	Howard U.	Nov. 1871SC	Augusta, Ga.
Theophilus J. Minton	USC[1]	Mar. 6, 1872SC	Columbia
Walter R. Jones	USC	Nov. 1874SC	Columbia
Joseph H. Boston	USC*	July 1875CC	Newberry
Daniel A. Straker	Howard U.	July 1875SC	Charleston
T. McCants Stewart	USC	Dec. 1875SC	Sumter
Thomas E. Miller	USC*	Dec. 1875SC	Lawtonville
Joseph H. Stuart	USC	Dec. 1875SC	Camden
Francis L. Cardozo	USC	July 1876SC	Columbia
Thomas H. Wheeler	Howard U.	Oct. 16, 1873CC, April 1876SC	Beaufort
Styles L. Hutchins	USC	Nov. 1876SC	Columbia
Joseph W. Morris	USC	Nov. 1876SC	Columbia
Richard T. Greener	USC	Dec. 1876SC	Columbia
Laurence Cain	USC	1876CC	Edgefield
Henry B. Johnson	USC	Nov. 1877	Charleston
Robert Lloyd Smith	Claflin	1882	Charleston
George O. Marshall	Claflin	1883	Charleston
William F. Holmes	Claflin	Dec. 1883	Charleston
Talley R. Holmes	Allen U.	May 1884	Columbia
John B. Edwards	Allen U.	May 1884	Columbia
Peter Flynn Oliver	Allen U.	May 1884	Columbia
Robert A. Stewart	Allen U.	May 1884	Columbia
John F. Brown	Howard U.	1884	Colleton
E. C. C. Washington	Allen U.	May 1885	Columbia
Benjamin E. Watson	Allen U.	May 1885	Columbia
E. J. Sawyer	Allen U./ USC*	May 1885	Bennettsville
Edward J. Dickerson	Allen U.	Dec. 1885	Aiken
Paris Simkins	USC	Nov. 1886	Edgefield
Andrew E. Hampton	Allen U.	May 1887	Columbia
Thomas A. Saxon	Allen U.	May 1887	Laurens
Casper G. Garrett	Allen U.	May 1890	Laurens
Butler W. Nance	Allen U.	May 1890	Newberry
Zachariah D. Greene	Allen U.	Dec. 1890	Georgetown
Walton W. Williams	Allen U.	Dec. 1890	Columbia
Dock J. Jordan	Allen U.	May 1892	Columbia
Julius L. Mitchell	Allen U.	1893	Moncks Corner
W. T. Andrews	Howard U.	1894	Sumter
E. Woodbury Brinkins	Allen U.	May 1897	Columbia
Eugene R. Hayne	Allen U.	May 1897	Charleston
John A. Gaillard	Shaw U.	May 1897	Charleston

Lawyer	*Law School*	*Date of Admission*	*Residence at Admission*
Mark A. Williams	Shaw U.	May 1897	Charleston
Thomas T. Hilton	Allen U.	Dec. 1897	Marion
Green Jackson	Allen U.	May 1898	Columbia
Shadrack Morgan	Howard U.	1919	Orangeburg
William A. Dart	Boston U.	1919	Charleston
Herbert F. McGirt	Howard U.	1922	Camden
Arthur Chester Platt	Boston U.	1922	Spartanburg
Charles English Washington	Howard U.	1924	Beaufort
Harold R. Boulware	Howard U.	1940	Columbia
Harold A. Stevens	Boston C.	1941	Columbia
Cassandra Maxwell	Howard U.	1941	Orangeburg
W. F. Robinson	Howard U.	1941	Columbia
William B. James	Robt Terrell	1947	Sumter
Benner C. Turner	Harvard U.	1948	Orangeburg
Richard Fields	Howard U.	1948	Charleston
Lincoln C. Jenkins Jr.	Howard U.	1949	Columbia
Albert A. Kennedy	SCSt	1950	Columbia
Julius Thomas Williams Jr.	SCSt	1950	Orangeburg
Matthew J. Perry	SCSt	1951	Columbia
Donald James Sampson	Temple U.	1951	Sumter
W. Newton Pough	SCSt	1952	Orangeburg
Charles E. Washington Jr.	Howard U.	1952	Beaufort
Ira W. Claiborne	Lincoln U.	1952	Charleston
William W. Bennett	SCSt	1953	Lane
Frank E. Cain	SCSt	1953	Bennettsville
Vernoid R. Bunch	SCSt	1953	Georgetown
John H. Wrighten	SCSt	1953	Charleston
John E. McCall	SCSt	1953	Cheraw
Ernest A. Finney Jr.	SCSt	1954	Orangeburg
Cleveland Stevens	SCSt	1954	Loris
Willie T. Smith Jr.	SCSt	1954	Columbia
Herman G. Boyd	SCSt	1954	Columbia
Elliott D. Turnage	Harvard U.	1954	Darlington
Edgar E. Thompson	SCSt	1954	Spartanburg
LeMarquis DeJarmon	Western Reserve	1955	Orangeburg
Blinzy L. Gore	U. of Iowa	1955	Orangeburg
John J. Rodgers	SCSt	1955	Walhalla
Mack Evans Davis	SCSt	1957	Varnville
Paul Rainey Webber III	SCSt	1958	Orangeburg
Bernard R. Fielding	Boston U.	1958	Charleston
Alphonso Walter Pendergrass	SCSt	1959	St. Stephens
Russell Brown	SCSt	1959	Ravenel
Mordecai C. Johnson	Howard U.	1960	Florence
Fred Henderson Moore	Howard U.	1960	Charleston
Arthur J. Howard Clement III	Howard U.	1960	Charleston
Leroy Nesbitt	Howard U.	1960	Charleston
Ned Edward Felder	SCSt	1961	Charleston
Hemphill P. Pride II	Fla. A&M	1963	Columbia
Ruben Lee Gray	SCSt	1963	Hemingway
Zack E. Townsend	SCSt	1963	Orangeburg
Earl Coblyn	Suffolk U.	1963	Orangeburg
Dorothy V. Sampson	NCCU	1964	Sumter

Lawyer	*Law School*	*Date of Admission*	*Residence at Admission*
Ernest Simmons Jr.	SCSt	1964	Columbia
Franklin R. DeWitt	SCSt	1964	Conway
Thomas D. Broadwater Jr.	Fla. A&M	1966	Columbia
George A. Payton	SCSt	1966	Charleston
George Allen Anderson	SCSt	1966	Aiken
Danny E. Martin	SCSt	1966	Charleston
Damon George Thomas	SCSt	1966	Charleston
Johnny Lake Jr.	USC	1967	Greenwood
Jasper Marshall Cureton	USC	1967	Columbia
Ernest G. Deveaux	SCSt	1967	Charleston
George Marion Crawford	SCSt	1967	Orangeburg
James L. Felder	Howard U.	1968	Columbia
Isaac Samuel Leevy Johnson	USC	1968	Columbia

* Indicates *did not graduate*

1. Minton read law with R. B. Elliott and later graduated from law school.

Law School Graduates by Institution

	Year of Admission		*Year of Admission*
SOUTH CAROLINA STATE (30)			
Albert A. Kennedy	1950	Mack Evans Davis	1957
Julius Thomas Williams Jr.	1950	Paul Rainey Webber III	1958
Matthew J. Perry	1951	Alphonso Walter Pendergrass	1959
W. Newton Pough	1952	Russell Brown	1959
William W. Bennett	1953	Ned Edward Felder	1961
Frank E. Cain	1953	Ruben Lee Gray	1963
Vernoid R. Bunch	1953	Zack E. Townsend	1963
John H. Wrighten	1953	Ernest Simmons Jr.	1964
John E. McCall	1953	Franklin R. DeWitt	1964
Ernest A. Finney Jr.	1954	George A. Payton	1966
Cleveland Stevens	1954	George Allen Anderson	1966
Willie T. Smith Jr.	1954	Danny E. Martin	1966
Herman G. Boyd	1954	Damon George Thomas	1966
Edgar E. Thompson	1954	Ernest G. Deveaux	1967
John J. Rodgers	1955	George Marion Crawford	1967
ALLEN UNIVERSITY (20)			
Talley R. Holmes	1884	Casper G. Garrett	1890
John B. Edwards	1884	Butler W. Nance	1890
Peter Flynn Oliver	1884	Zachariah D. Greene	1890
Robert A. Stewart	1884	Walton W. Williams	1890
E. C. C. Washington	1885	Dock J. Jordan	1892
Benjamin E. Watson	1885	Julius L. Mitchell*	1893
E. J. Sawyer	1885	E. Woodbury Brinkins	1897
Edward J. Dickerson	1885	Eugene R. Hayne	1897
Andrew E. Hampton	1887	Thomas T. Hilton	1897
Thomas A. Saxon	1887	Green Jackson	1898
UNIVERSITY OF SOUTH CAROLINA (17)			
Theophilus J. Minton	1872	Richard T. Greener	1876
Walter R. Jones	1874	Laurence Cain	1876CC
Joseph H. Boston*	1875CC	Henry B. Johnson	1877
T. McCants Stewart	1875	E. J. Sawyer*	1885
Thomas E. Miller*	1875	Paris Simkins	1886
Joseph H. Stuart	1875	Johnny Lake Jr.	1967
Francis L. Cardozo	1876	Jasper Marshall Cureton	1967
Styles L. Hutchins	1876	Isaac Samuel Leevy Johnson	1968
Joseph W. Morris	1876		
CAPLIN UNIVERSITY (3)			
Robert Lloyd Smith	1882	William F. Holmes	1883
George O. Marshall	1883		
HOWARD UNIVERSITY (21)			
Edwin T. Belcher	1871	John F. Brown	1884
Eugene R. B. Belcher	1871	W. T. Andrews	1894
John F. Quarles	1871	Shadrack Morgan	1919
Daniel A. Straker	1875	Herbert F. McGirt	1922
Thomas H. Wheeler	1873/1876	Charles English Washington	1924

Law School Graduates by Institution (*continued*)

	Year of Admission		*Year of Admission*
Harold R. Boulware	1940	Mordecai C. Johnson	1960
Cassandra Maxwell	1941	Fred Henderson Moore	1960
W. F. Robinson	1941	Arthur J. Howard Clement III	1960
Richard Fields	1948	Leroy Nesbitt	1960
Lincoln C. Jenkins Jr.	1949	James L. Felder	1968
Charles E. Washington Jr.	1952		

BOSTON UNIVERSITY (3)

William A. Dart	1919	Bernard R. Fielding	1958
Arthur Chester Platt	1922		

OTHER UNIVERSITIES AND COLLEGES

	Law School	*Year of admission*
Harold A. Stevens	Boston C.	1941
Hemphill P. Pride II	Fla. A&M	1963
Thomas D. Broadwater Jr.	Fla. A&M	1966
Benner C. Turner	SCStf, Harvard U.	1948
Elliott D. Turnage	Harvard U.	1954
Blinzy L. Gore	SCStf, U. Of Iowa	1955
Ira W. Claiborne	Lincoln U. (Mo.)	1952
Leo Kerford	Kansas	1954
Dorothy V. Sampson	NCCU	1964
John Patterson	Green Ohio Union	1870CC
William B. James	Robert Terrell (D.C.)	1947
John A. Gaillard	Shaw U.	1897
Mark A. Williams	Shaw U.	1897
Earl Coblyn	Suffolk U.	1963
Donald James Sampson	Temple U.	1951
James Miles Hinton, Jr.	American	1954
LeMarquis DeJarmon	Western Reserve	1955

* Indicates *did not graduate*

African American Students of the Law School, 1873–1877

Joseph Boston
Lawrence Cain, Class of 1876
Francis L. Cardozo, Class of 1876
Richard T. Greener, Class of 1876
Styles Linton Hutchins, Class of 1876
Henry Barton Johnson, Class of 1875
Walter Raleigh Jones, Class of 1874
Thomas E. Miller
Theophilus J. Minton, Class of 1876
Paul J. Mishow
Joseph White Morris, Class of 1876
William F. Myers
Arthur O'Hear
Edward James Sawyer
Paris Simkins, Class of 1876
Charles H. Sperry
Thomas McCants Stewart, Class of 1875
Joseph Henry Stuart, Class of 1875
C. M. Wilder

White Students of the Law School, from the Reorganization of 1873 to 1877

Charles L. Anderson, Class of 1874
Charles J. Babbitt, Class of 1876
Thomas M. Canton, Class of 1876
Edgar Capless, Class of 1874
H. C. Corwin
Charles W. Cummings, Class of 1874
Erastus W. Everson
Gil Dixon Fox
Henry A. Fox, Class of 1875
Barnett B. Goins
William Jackson
James O. Ladd
George T. McIntyre
Niles Gardner Parker, Class of 1874
Mortimer A. Warren, Class of 1875
T. M. Wilkes
John Wingate

Racial Composition of the Graduating Classes of the Law School, 1868–1876

Year	*White*	*Black*	*Year*	*White*	*Black*
1868	2	0	1873	4	0
1869	0	0	1874	4	1
1870	5	0	1875	2	3
1871	3	0	1876	2	7
1872	6	0			

Allen Graduates

Name	*Year*	*Bar Admission**	*Law Practice*	*Residence*
John B Edwards	1885	May 1884	yes	Sumter
Talley R. Holmes	1885	May 1884		
Peter Flynn Oliver	1885	May 1884		
Robert Adger Stewart	1885	May 1884		Washington, D.C.
Edward James Sawyer	1886	May 1885	businessman	Bennettsville
E. C. C. Washington	1886	May 1885		
Benjamin E. Watson	1886	May 1885		
A. J. Jamison	1887	Little Rock		
Thomas A. Saxon	1887	May 1887	law faculty	Columbia
Andrew E. Hampton	1887	May 1887	yes?	Columbia
James L. Bumgardner	1890			Tampa
Butler Nance	1890	May 1890	yes?	Columbia
Caspar G. Garrett	1890	May 1890		
Zachariah D. Greene	1890	Dec. 1890	yes	Georgetown
Walton T. Williams	1890	Dec. 1890		
Charles Brown Jr.	1891			Horatio, S.C.
N. W. Edwards	1891			
Thomas T. Hilton	1891/1893	Dec. 1897		
James W. Goudlock Jr.	1892			Rock Hill
Eugene R. Hayne	1892?	May 1897		Charleston
Dock J. Jordan	1892	May 1892		
S. Simmons	1892			
Edmund R. Anderson	1896?			
E. Woodbury Brinkins	1897	May 1897		Columbia
Abraham L. Tucker	1897	Ga.?		Waycross, Ga.
Green Jackson	1898	May 1898		Columbia
L. M. Rice	1898			
E. R. Anderson	1898?			

* Admitted in South Carolina unless otherwise noted

APPENDIX E

White Lawyers and Black Lawyers in Southern States

	1890	1900	1910
Alabama	1298/13	1587/6	1470/12
Arkansas	1052/30	1345/27	1328/20
Florida	561/13	598/13	697/14
Georgia	1713/16	2352/33	2215/18
Louisiana	1040/30	1293/15	1217/13
Mississippi	872/26	999/24	1196/21
North Carolina	978/14	1238/25	1294/19
South Carolina	748/23	818/29	890/17
Tennessee	2029/35	2643/73	2053/43
Texas	/12	/28	/33
Virginia	1611/38	1972/53	1772/37
	1920	1930	1940
Alabama	1388/11	1583/4	1612/4
Arkansas	1307/26	1469/16	1518/8
Florida	1113/13	2570/10	2676/10
Georgia	2479/27	2750/14	2621/8
Louisiana	1181/8	1595/8	1856/6
Mississippi	1537/14	1225/6	1280/3
North Carolina	1537/27	2335/27	2388/27
South Carolina	960/14	1108/13	1137/5
Tennessee	1986/33	2431/26	2604/16
Texas	/31	20	/22
Virginia	1923/52	2334/57	3120/48
	1950	1960	1970
Alabama	1790/10	2308/18(13)	2306/20 (25)
Arkansas	1332/9	1268/19	1458/12?
Florida	3524/15	5780/25	8559/64
Georgia	2923/17	3199/12	4298/58
Louisiana	2249/6	3022/19(30)	3941/26?
Mississippi	1373/5	1403/0 (4)	1964/54(11?)
North Carolina	2283/29	2745/58	3547/118
South Carolina	1304/6(12)	1642/13(36)	1930/60
Tennessee	2649/18	3020/28	3575/46
Texas	8056/26	10338/50	1343/91
Virginia	4343/55	5545/59	8585/58

NOTES

INTRODUCTION

1. Irvin C. Mollison, "Negro Lawyers in Mississippi," *Journal of Negro History* 15 (1930): 38.

2. Charles H. Houston, "The Need for Negro Lawyers," *Journal of Negro Education* 4 (1935): 49; Carter G. Woodson, *The Negro Professional Man and His Community* (Washington, D.C.: Association for the Study of Negro Life and History, 1934); Fitzhugh Lee Styles, *Negroes and the Law in the Race's Battle for Liberty, Equality and Justice under the Constitution of the United States; with Causes Celebres* (Boston: Christopher, 1937).

3. Judith Kilpatrick, "(Extra)Ordinary Men: African American Lawyers and Civil Rights in Arkansas before 1950," *Arkansas Law Review* 53 (2000): 299.

4. John Oldfield, "The African American Bar in South Carolina, 1877–1915," in James L. Underwood and William Lewis Burke, eds., *At Freedom's Door: African American Founding Fathers in Reconstruction South Carolina* (Columbia: University of South Carolina Press, 2005), 116.

5. For example, see August Meier and Elliott Rudwick, "Attorneys Black and White: A Case Study of Race Relations within the NAACP," *Journal of American History* 62 (1976): 913; Kenneth W. Mack, "Social History of Everyday Practice: Sadie T. M. Alexander and the Incorporation of Black Women into the American Legal Profession, 1925–1960," *Cornell Law Review* 87 (2001–2002): 1405, and *Representing the Race: The Creation of the Civil Rights Lawyer* (Cambridge, Mass.: Harvard University Press, 2012); J. Clay Smith Jr., ed., *Rebels in Law: Voices in History of Black Women Lawyers* (Ann Arbor: University of Michigan Press, 1998).

6. J. Clay Smith Jr., *Emancipation: The Making of the Black Lawyer, 1844–1944* (Philadelphia: University of Pennsylvania Press, 1993).

7. South Carolina's bar percentage of blacks was 3.8 percent in 1880, nearly 3 percent in 1890, and 3.4 percent in 1900, which were the highest percentages of any Deep South state.

8. Eric Foner, *Reconstruction* (New York: Harper & Row, 1988), 1.

9. The simplest source on place of origin is Thomas Holt, *Black over White: Negro Political Leadership in South Carolina during Reconstruction* (Urbana: University of Illinois Press, 1977), Table 5, Summary of Biographical Data.

CHAPTER 1. The Coming of Freedom

1. John Belton O'Neall, *The Negro Law of South Carolina* (Columbia: John G. Bowman, 1848), chap. 1, sec. 1, at p. 5.

2. Ibid., chap. 2, sec. 36 (contract); sec. 37 (marry); sec. 44 (assemble); sec. 31 (own property); sec. 41 (literacy); sec. 39 (testify or take an oath); sec. 48 (clothing); sec. 51 (if

more than seven slaves travel without a white person accompanying them they could be seized and whipped with twenty lashes); sec. 53 (gun).

3. Ibid., chap. 1, sec. 48 (testify); sec. 50 (take an oath).

4. Ibid., chap. 1, sec. 37.

5. Ibid., chap. 1, sec. 57.

6. Ibid., chap. 3, secs. 14, 15, 16, 8, 9, 4.

7. *Kinloch v. Harvey*, 16 S.C. Law 508 at 514 (Harpers Law 1830).

8. Thomas D. Morris, *Southern Slavery and the Law*, 1619–1860 (Chapel Hill: University of North Carolina Press, 1996), 272–74; Walter Edgar, *South Carolina: A History* (Columbia: University of South Carolina Press, 1998), 329–30; John Hope Franklin, *From Slavery to Freedom* (New York: Knopf, 1967), 207–9; O'Neall, *Negro Law of South Carolina,* chap. 3, sec. 40.

9. Edgar, *South* Carolina, 329, 330–38.

10. "Provost Court," *Charleston Daily News*, July 21, 1866, 5.

11. "Civil Rights Bill," *Charleston Daily News*, August 14, 1866, 5.

12. See Wright to Maj. Gen. R. K. Scott, April 8, 1867, American Missionary Association Papers (hereafter cited as AMA Papers). Wright was advocating on Christopher's behalf to retain the boat that had been given to him by the navy. A reply written on April 24, 1867, from E. L. Duncan, assistant commissioner of the bureau, recognized Christopher's rights. E. L. Duncan to Wright, April 24, 1867, AMA Papers.

13. Willie Lee Rose, *Rehearsal for Reconstruction: The Port Royal Experiment* (Oxford: Oxford University Press, 1976), 15.

14. Kate Clifford Larson, *Bound for the Promised Land: Harriet Tubman, Portrait of an American Hero* (New York: Ballantine, 2004).

15. Joel Williamson, *After Slavery: The Negro in South Carolina during Reconstruction, 1861–1877* (Chapel Hill: University of North Carolina Press, 1965), 5.

16. Rose, *Rehearsal for Reconstruction*, 56–57.

17. Edgar, *South Carolina*, 383.

18. South Carolina, Constitutional Convention, *Journal of the Convention of the People of South Carolina held in Columbia, S.C., September 1865* (Columbia: J. A. Selby, 1865), 27–29.

19. Edgar, *South Carolina*, 383.

20. *Journal of the Convention of the People of South Carolina,* 59–65. See also Edgar, *South Carolina*, 383 and Williamson, *After Slavery*, 72.

21. Williamson, *After Slavery*, 73.

22. South Carolina Constitution of 1865, art. IV.

23. *Proceedings of the Colored People's Convention of the State of South Carolina* (Charleston: South Carolina Leader, 1865), 11, 51–53.

24. "Resolution of November 24, 1865, Colored People's Convention of the State of South Carolina, held in Zion Church, Charleston, November 1865," in Philip Sheldon Foner and George E. Walker, eds., *Proceedings of the Black State Conventions, 1840–1865* (Philadelphia: Temple University Press, 1979), 279.

25. *Proceedings of the Colored People's Convention*, 292, 294.

26. Ibid., 298.

27. Ibid., 300.

28. J. J. Wright Letter, September 23, 1865, Beaufort, South Carolina, AMA Papers.

29. J. J. Wright Reports, October and December 1865, AMA Papers.

30. J. J. Wright Report, January 1866; Jonathan J. Wright to M. E. Stribey, July 27, 1865, AMA Papers.

31. Jonathan J. Wright to S. Hunt, February 5, 1866, and September 23, 1865, AMA Papers.

32. Act nos. 4730, 4731, 4732, 4733, 1865 South Carolina Acts 271–304. These codes regulated African Americans in minute detail, including their "domestic relations" (Act no. 4730), their right to sell farm produce (4731), their right to own guns (4731), and their right to work (4733).

33. South Carolina Constitution of 1865, art. IX, §11; Williamson, *After Slavery*, 72–77.

34. Act nos. 4730, 4731, 1865 South Carolina Acts 271.

35. Ibid., Act no. 4730.

36. "Major General D. E. Sickles, HQ, Dept. of S.C., *General Orders, No. 1, January 1, 1866,*" *(Columbia) State*, January 23, 1866, 2; *see also* Act no. 4798, 1866 South Carolina Acts 393.

37. Act no. 4798, 1866 South Carolina Acts 393–94.

38. An Act to Provide for the More Efficient Government of the Rebel States, 14 Stat. 153 (1867).

39. Gen. E. R. S. Canby assumed command of the military district on September 5, 1867, and supervised voter registration and the elections. Max L. Heyman Jr., *Prudent Soldier: A Biography of Major General E. R. S. Canby, 1817–1873* (Glendale, Calif.: Arthur Clark, 1959), 305–32.

40. Richard Gergel and Belinda Gergel, "To Vindicate the Cause of the Downtrodden," in James L. Underwood and William Lewis Burke, eds., *At Freedom's Door: African American Founding Fathers in Reconstruction South Carolina* (Columbia: University of South Carolina Press, 2005), 39.

41. Suzanne Stone Johnson and Robert Allen Johnson, eds., *Bitter Freedom: William Stone's Record of Service in the Freedmen's Bureau* (Columbia: University of South Carolina Press, 2008), 4, 8, 12.

42. Message of the President to Congress and Accompanying Documents to the Two Houses of Congress (39th Congress 1866), 668. Also see Johnson and Johnson, *Bitter Freedom*, 53.

43. Wright to Freedmen's Bureau, February 5, 6, and 7, 1867, *Records of the Field Offices of the State of South Carolina, Bureau of Refugees, Freedmen, and Abandoned Lands, 1865–1872*, microfilm set #M1910, Reel 57—Beaufort District, Letters Received and Endorsements Sent, February–December 1867 and March–June 1868, National Archives and Records Administration, Washington, D.C.

44. Ibid.

45. Message of the President, 738, 64.

46. A. P. Aldrich to B. F. Perry, August 8, 1865, in B. F. Perry Papers, cited in Donald G. Nieman, *To Set the Law in Motion: The Freedmen's Bureau and the Legal Rights of Blacks, 1865–1868* (Millwood, N.Y.: KTO Press, 1979), 42n14.

47. Nieman, *To Set the Law in Motion*, 42.

48. Message of the President, 65, 66–67.

49. Ibid., 312–14, 305 (quotation); Heyman, *Prudent Soldier*, 311; "Judge Aldrich and Gen. Canby," *Charleston Mercury*, October 23, 1867.

50. Message of the President, 672, 669.

51. "Report of the Proceedings of the U.S. Provost Court," *Sumter News*, June 7, 1866, 3.

52. Johnson and Johnson, *Bitter Freedom*, 16, 43, 68, 15.

53. Nieman, *To Set the Law in Motion*, 10.

54. Thomas D. Morris, "Equality, 'Extraordinary Law,' and Criminal Justice: The South Carolina Experience, 1865–1866," *South Carolina Historical Magazine* 83 (1982): 15, 33.

55. After the suspension of the bureau courts, William Stone also held court as a Freedmen's Bureau agent. Stone noted that criminal matters were sent to the state courts and complained that little justice was to be had there. The provost courts were reestablished in March 1867 in response to the outrages by whites against black citizens. Johnson and Johnson, *Bitter Freedom*, 31–33.

56. Monthly Report of J. J. Wright, Agent to the Bureau, February to November 1867, *Records of the Field Offices of the State of South Carolina, Bureau of Refugees, Freedmen, and Abandoned Lands, 1865–1872*, microfilm set #M1910, Reel 57—Beaufort District, Letters Received and Endorsements Sent, February–December 1867 and March–June 1868, National Archives and Records Administration, Washington, D.C.

57. "A Planter's View," *(Beaufort) New South*, June 16, 1866.

58. Williamson, *After Slavery*, 174.

59. Nieman, *To Set the Law in Motion*, 54–55.

60. Laura Towne quoted in Dylan C. Penningroth, *The Claims of Kinfolk: African American Property and Community in the Nineteenth Century South* (Chapel Hill: University of North Carolina Press, 2003), 114.

61. Martin Abbott, *The Freedmen's Bureau in South Carolina, 1865–1872* (Chapel Hill: University of North Carolina Press, 1967), 62.

62. Nieman, *To Set the Law in Motion*, 59–60.

63. Harry Augustus Volz III, "The Administration of Justice by the Freedmen's Bureau in Kentucky, South Carolina and Virginia" (master's thesis, University of Virginia, 1975), 57.

64. Eric Foner, *Freedom's Lawmakers: A Directory of Black Officeholders during Reconstruction* (Baton Rouge: Louisiana State University Press, 1996), 226.

65. *Proceedings of the Constitutional Convention of South Carolina* (New York: Arno, 1868), 556–57.

66. See Stephen Smith, Frederick Camp, Lucious Barbour, and George White, *Record of Service of Connecticut Men in the Army and Navy of the United States during the War of the Rebellion* (Hartford, Conn.: Lockwood & Brainard, 1889), 890; Demps Whipper Powell, "A Providential Revelation, Relationship with the Whipper Family," Leigh Whipper Papers, Manuscript Department, Moorland-Spingarn Research Center, Howard University, Washington, D.C., 1–2.

67. Whipper to Scott, November 21, 1866, Records of Provost Marshal Field Organizations (Civil War) 1861–70, microfilm, Frame 099–0901, National Archives and Records Administration, Washington, D.C.

68. Gergel and Gergel, "Vindicate the Cause," 40.

69. See indictment in *U.S. v. William T. Bennett*, March 7, 1867, *Records of the Field Offices of the State of South Carolina, Bureau of Refugees, Freedmen, and Abandoned Lands, 1865–1872*, microfilm roll 15, National Archives and Records Administration, Washington, D.C.

70. See Stephen R. Wise and Lawrence Rowland, *Rebellion, Reconstruction, and Redemption, 1861–1893: History of Beaufort County, South Carolina*, Vol. 2 (Columbia: University of South Carolina Press, 2015), 458–59.

71. Thomas Holt, *Black over White: Negro Political Leadership in South Carolina during Reconstruction* (Urbana: University of Illinois Press, 1977), 74; Roll of Attorneys, South Carolina Supreme Court, 1869–1876 (on file with South Carolina Supreme Court, Columbia).

72. Foner, *Freedom's Lawmakers*, 16.

73. Abbott, *Freedmen's Bureau in South Carolina*, 62.

CHAPTER 2. Reconstruction and the Birth of a New Kind of Lawyer

1. An Act to Provide for the More Efficient Government of the Rebel States, 14 Stat. 153 (1867).

2. Alrutheus Ambush Taylor, *The Negro in South Carolina during Reconstruction* (1924; reprint, New York: AMS Press, 1971), 126–27.

3. Richard Zuczek, *State of Rebellion: Reconstruction in South Carolina* (Columbia: University of South Carolina Press, 1966), 41. Freedmen had voted first in Mitchellville, South Carolina, in March 1865 in electing town officers. See Thomas Holt, *Black over White: Negro Political Leadership in South Carolina during Reconstruction* (Urbana: University of Illinois Press, 1977), 11–12.

4. Zuczek, *State of Rebellion*, 41.

5. Carol Bleser, *The Promised Land: History of the South Carolina Land Commission, 1869–1890* (Columbia: University of South Carolina Press, 1969), xii.

6. James Lowell Underwood, "African American Founding Fathers," in James L. Underwood and William Lewis Burke, eds., *At Freedom's Door: African American Founding Fathers in Reconstruction South Carolina* (Columbia: University of South Carolina Press, 2005), 2.

7. Elliott claimed to have been trained by an English barrister, but his biographer is doubtful. See Peggy Lamson, *The Glorious Failure: Black Congressman Robert Brown Elliott and the Reconstruction in South Carolina* (New York: Norton, 1973), 24–25.

8. "Death of Judge George Lee," *Columbia Daily Union*, February 20, 1873, 3.

9. *Proceedings of the Constitutional Convention of South Carolina* (Charleston: Denny & Perry, 1868; reprint, New York: Arno Press, 1968), 9, 13–15, 20–24, 26, 27, 31, 32, 34, 35, 39, 41, 42. The proceedings will hereafter be cited parenthetically in the text.

10. Lamson, *Glorious Failure*, 50.

11. Cardozo proved to be quite foresighted on this issue. Later, he would serve as the state land commissioner and tried to purchase land for the freedmen. However, few blacks obtained sufficient lands to support themselves, and many were forced into sharecropping.

12. Article I, Section 20, 1868 Constitution.

13. The Declaration of Rights abolished debtor's prison and provided for the exemption of a homestead.

14. Act No. 16, 14 Statutes at Large of South Carolina 19 (September 9, 1868). The exemption was lowered to $500 by Act No. 273, Act and Joint Resolution of the S.C. General Assembly (March 1, 1870), and raised again to $1,000 in Revised Statutes of the State of South Carolina, Chp. XCVI, Sec. 1 (1873).

15. See Art. X, Sec 10, 1868 Constitution.

16. He lost the fight, but in the late twentieth century the South Carolina Supreme Court declared the religious test unconstitutional. See *Silverman v. Campbell*, 326 S.C. 208, 486 S.E.2d 1 (1996).

17. James Lowell Underwood, "African American Founding Fathers," in James L. Underwood and William Lewis Burke, eds., *At Freedom's Door: African American Founding Fathers in Reconstruction South Carolina* (Columbia: University of South Carolina Press, 2005), 7.

18. Carol Tone, *Pride of the Family: Four Generations of American Women of Color* (New York: Summit, 1991), 167.

19. Art. VIII, 1868 Constitution.

20. Underwood, "African American Founding Fathers," 25n208.

21. Holt, *Black over White*, 96–98.

22. Walter B. Edgar, ed., *The Biographical Directory of the South Carolina House of Representatives* (Columbia: University of South Carolina Press, 1974), vol. 1, 409–10; Louise Bailey, Mary L. Morgan, and Carolyn R. Taylor, eds., *The Biographical Directory of the South Carolina Senate, 1776–1985* (Columbia: University of South Carolina Press, 1986), vol. 3, 1894–95.

23. W. Lewis Burke, "Post-Reconstruction Justice: The Prosecution and Trial of Francis Lewis Cardozo," *South Carolina Law Review* 53 (Winter 2002): 361, 366–67.

24. An Act to Admit the States of North Carolina, South Carolina, Louisiana, Georgia, Alabama, and Florida, to Representation in Congress, 15 Stat. 73 (1868).

25. Presidential Proclamation No. 15, 15 Stat. 711–712 (December 25, 1868).

26. Zuczek, *State of Rebellion*, 53.

27. Slave patrols were both official and unofficial gangs of nonslaveholding whites who patrolled the rural areas to control slaves and apprehend runaways. Often because of their nonproprietary interest in the slaves, the patrols could be especially violent. See Leon Litwack, *Been in the Storm So Long* (New York: Knopf, 1979), 28.

28. Zuczek, *State of Rebellion*, 55–57.

29. Lamson, *Glorious Failure*, 74, citing "The Leaders of the People," *Charleston News*, September 12, 1868.

30. Holt, *Black over White*, 150.

31. Ibid., 4, 163.

32. Franklin Johnson, *The Development of State Legislation Concerning the Free Negro* (New York: Arbor Press, 1918; reprint, Whitefish, Mont.: Kessinger, 2008), 29.

33. The senators were Jonathan J. Wright of Beaufort (1868–70), Henry Maxwell of Marlboro (1868–77), Stephen A. Swails of Williamsburg (1868–77), Laurence Cain of Edgefield (1872–76), William H. Jones of Georgetown (1874–76), and William H. Myers of Colleton (1874–78). See Bailey, *Biographical Directory of the South Carolina Senate*, vol. 1. The representatives were Robert Brown Elliott of Barnwell (1868–70), William J. Whipper of Beaufort (1868–70), Robert DeLarge of Charleston (1868–70), George Lee of Charleston (1868–70), Samuel J. Lee of Edgefield and Aiken (1868–74), William H. Jones of Georgetown (1868–70), Joseph Boston of Newberry (1868–76), James A. Bowley of Georgetown (1869–74), Benjamin Byas of Orangeburg (1870–72), Paris Simkins of Edgefield (1872–76), John M. Freeman of Charleston (1874–76), Thomas E. Miller of Beaufort (1875–80), William Hannibal Thomas of Newberry (1876–77), and D. A. Straker of Orangeburg (1876–77). Thomas and Straker were elected in 1876 and served in the Mackey House but were refused their seats in the Wallace House because of "gross contempt and defiant attitude." See Edgar, *Biographical Directory of the South Carolina House of Representatives*, Vol. 1.

34. Lamson, *Glorious Failure*, 82–86, quotation on 84.

35. The First Enforcement Act, passed on May 31, 1870, barred state officials from discriminating against voters based on race, color, or previous condition of servitude in the application of local election laws; outlawed the use of "force, bribery, threats, and intimidation" to keep voters from going to the polls; and made it a misdemeanor to deprive a citizen of "employment or occupation" in order to control his vote. The most important provision prohibited disguised groups such as the Klan from traveling on "public highways, or upon the premises of another" with the intent of interfering with constitutional liberties. An Act to Enforce the Right of Citizens of the United States to Vote in the Several States of This Union, and for Other Purposes, 16 Stat. 140–46 (1870); see also Everette Swinney, "Enforcing the Fifteenth Amendment, 1870–1877," *Journal of Southern History* 28 (May 1962): 202–3. The Second Enforcement Act, passed on February 28, 1871, following the November 1870 election, extended federal control of the election process. An Act to Amend an Act Approved May 31, 1870, entitled "An Act to Enforce the Rights of Citizens of the United States to Vote in the Several States of This Union, and for Other Purposes," 16 Stat. 433–40 (1871); see also Swinney, "Enforcing the Fifteenth Amendment," 203. The Third Enforcement Act, popularly known as the Ku Klux Klan Act, made it a federal offense to conspire to prevent persons from holding public offices, serving on juries, enjoying equal protection of the laws, and voting, or to conspire to overthrow or "destroy by force the government of the United States." An Act to Enforce the Provisions of the Fourteenth Amendment to the Constitution of the United States, and for Other Purposes, 17 Stat. 13–15 (1871); see also Swinney, "Enforcing the Fifteenth Amendment," 203.

36. Lou Falkner Williams, *The Great South Carolina Ku Klux Klan Trials, 1871–1872* (Athens: University of Georgia Press, 1996), 113. Williams notes that Johnson was supposedly the highest paid lawyer in the country (54–55).

37. Ibid., 113. After Reconstruction, these convictions were even used to aid in reestablishing white rule. After whites regained power, the state prosecuted two prominent black Reconstruction leaders on spurious corruption charges. In exchange for a presidential pardon of some of these Klansmen, the two black leaders were pardoned by the South Carolina governor. See W. Lewis Burke, "Reconstruction Corruption and the Redeemers' Prosecution of Francis Lewis Cardozo," *American Nineteenth Century History* 2, no. 3 (September 2001): 67, 93–94, 98.

38. *Journal of the House of Representatives of the State of South Carolina Being the Regular Session of 1868* (Columbia: John W. Denny, 1868), 44–46.

39. Ibid., 45.

40. Ibid.

41. Ibid., 46.

42. Edgar, *Biographical Directory of the South Carolina House of Representatives*, 1:407.

43. *Journal of the House of Representatives, 1868*, 50–51.

44. Holt, *Black over White*, 96, 226–42.

45. Act No. 98 (approved February 13, 1869): "An Act to Enforce the Provisions of the Civil Rights Bill of the United States Congress" made it unlawful for licensed common carriers and businesses to discriminate based on race or color. It imposed a penalty of a $200 fine and/or six months' imprisonment. See "First Step Toward Social Equality," *Charleston News*, August 17, 1868.

46. Holt, *Black over White*, 143, quoting (*Charleston*) *Daily Courier*, August 17, 1868.

47. "Official," *Orangeburg News*, August 22, 1868.

48. "Joint Resolution Ratifying the Fifteenth Amendment to the Constitution of the United States." Joint Resolution No. 12, Acts and Joint Resolutions of the General Assembly of the State of South Carolina (approved March 16, 1869), 288.

49. "An Act to Alter and Amend the Criminal Law." Acts and Joint Resolutions of the General Assembly of the State of South Carolina, Act No. 91 (approved February 4, 1869), 175.

50. "An Act to Secure Equal Civil Rights, and to Provide for the Enjoyment of All Remedies in Law by All Persons, Regardless of Race or Color." Acts and Joint Resolutions of the General Assembly of the State of South Carolina, Act No. 233 (approved February 14, 1870), 337.

51. "An Act to Enforce the Provisions of the Civil Rights Bill of the United States Congress, and to Secure to the People the Benefits of a Republican Government in This State." Acts and Joint Resolutions of the General Assembly of the State of South Carolina, Act No. 279 (approved March 1, 1870), 386.

52. *Journal of the House of Representatives, 1868*, 152.

53. Williams, *Ku Klux Klan Trials*, 16.

54. *Journal of the House of Representatives, 1871–72* (Columbia: Republican Printing Co., 1872), 420.

55. Act No. 333 (approved February 26, 1873): "An Act to Provide for the Establishment and Support of a State Normal School"; Act No. 193 (approved December 18, 1869): "An Act to Incorporate the Claflin University."

56. See Acts and Joint Resolutions #161, An Act for the Relief of Widows and

Orphans of Persons Killed because of their Political Opinions (March 13, 1872); #165, An Act to Establish a School at the State Penitentiary (March 13, 1872); #330, An Act to Incorporate the Carolina Orphan Home in the Town of Spartanburg, S.C. (February 26, 1873); #333, An Act to Provide for the Establishment of a State Normal School (February 26, 1873); #338, An Act to Make an Appropriation to Pay Claims for Reporting Klansmen (July 28, 1871); #413, An Act to Provide for the Establishment of a House of Refuge and Industrial School in the Cities of Charleston and Columbia (November 25, 1873); #462, An Act to Establish Certain State Scholarships in the University of South Carolina (February 20, 1874); #550, An Act to Require the County Commissioners of Charleston County to Erect a Poor House in Said County ("open to all classes of indigent poor") (March 14, 1874); #598, An Act to Amend an Act Entitled "An Act for the Relief of Widows and Orphans of Persons Killed because of their Political Opinions" (amended to embrace Abbeville County) (March 17, 1874); #616, An Act to Punish Persons for Ill-Treating Children, Apprentices, Idiots, Servants and Helpless Persons (March 17, 1874); #655, An Act to Amend an Act Entitled "An Act for the Relief of Widows and Orphans of Persons Killed because of their Political Opinions" (January 28, 1875); #694, An Act to Declare and Protect the Rights of Women and Children under Policies of Life Insurance Taken Out for Their Benefit (March 5, 1875); #719, An Act to Amend Section 1, Chapter CXXXVI of Part IV of the Revised Statutes, Relative to Offenses against Civil Rights (March 11, 1875); #722, An Act to Amend Section 2 of "An Act to Regulate the Issuing of Checks to Laborers upon Plantations or Elsewhere" (March 11, 1875); #776, An Act to Amend an Act Entitled "An Act for the Relief of Widows and Orphans of Persons Killed because of their Political Opinions" (March 24, 1875); #124, An Act to Provide for the Education of Minor Children in the City of Columbia and County of Charleston (March 10, 1876).

57. *Report of the Commissioners on the Revision and Consolidation of the Statute Laws of the State* (Columbia, S.C.: Republican Printing Company, 1871). Pages iii through v have the three-page report of the commissioners, W. J. Whipper, Charles W. Montgomery, and D. T. Corbin, dated November 28, 1871. Whipper presented the commissioners' report to the house on November 23, 1869. *Journal of the House of Representatives of the State of South Carolina, Regular Session 1869–70 (November 23, 1869)* (Columbia: John W. Denny, 1870), 11. "State Legislature," *(Columbia) Daily Phoenix*, January 27, 1870, referred to "Corbin and Whipper's code" being read the third time (3).

58. "Good for Young Lawyers," *Orangeburg News*, February 5, 1870.

59. J. Clay Smith, "The Reconstruction of Jonathan Jasper Wright," in Underwood and Burke, *At Freedom's Door*, 72.

60. "The Supreme Three," *Orangeburg News*, February 19, 1870, quoting the *Edgefield Advertiser*.

61. Smith, "Reconstruction of Wright," 78, citing Walter Allen, *Governor Chamberlain's Administration in South Carolina* (New York: G. P. Putnam's Sons, 1888; reprint, New York: Negro Universities Press, 1969), 430.

62. The only mention appears to be in a legal scholar's work. See J. Clay Smith, *Emancipation: The Making of the Black Lawyer, 1844–1944* (Philadelphia: University of Pennsylvania Press, 1993), 215.

63. Journal of the House of Representatives (1871–72), 187–88, 465.

64. "Death of Judge Lee," *Charleston Daily News*, February 20, 1873.

65. "Death of Judge George Lee," *Columbia Daily Union*, February 20, 1873, 3; *Journal of the House of Representatives of the State of South Carolina, 1872–1873* (Columbia: Republican Printing, 1873), 551.

66. *Journal of the House of Representatives (1872–1873)*, 551.

67. 1875 S.C. Acts 824. On December 22, 1874, Allen protested the abolition of the court to Governor D. H. Chamberlain. Papers of Governor D. H. Chamberlain, 1874–1877, South Carolina Department of Archives and History, Columbia, South Carolina (hereafter cited as SCDAH).

68. "Annual Report of the Secretary of State to the General Assembly of South Carolina," *Reports and Resolutions of the General Assembly of the State of South Carolina at the Regular Session, 1876–77* (Columbia: Republican Printing, 1877), 230, 407.

69. *Journal of the Senate of the State of South Carolina Being in Regular Session of 1874–75* (Columbia: Republican Printing, 1875), 182.

70. See Court of General Sessions (Charleston County) Bar Dockets, Volume 2, Bar Docket 1873–1875, SCDAH.

71. See Court of Common Pleas of Charleston County, Calendars 1872–1874, SCDAH.

72. See the various city directories for Charleston from 1868 to 1876. D. T. Corbin was the U.S. attorney in 1868 and had a law practice with William Stone, and future U.S. attorney L. C. Northrup also practiced in Charleston. D. H. Chamberlain and Seabrook also had their primary law office in Charleston. Chamberlain was attorney general and later governor. Seabrook was the solicitor. Corbin and Stone represented the city and county of Charleston. D. H. Chamberlain represented the county treasurer. See Court of Common Pleas of Charleston County, Calendar No. 1, "Issues of fact to be tried by a Jury" (1872), SCDAH.

73. See *State v. Hayne*, 4 S.C. 403 (April Term 1873). The case was tried in the Charleston criminal court at the July term 1872. W. J. Whipper was the solicitor. See "The Inferior Court," *Charleston News*, May 10, 1872, for Whipper's initial appointment as interim solicitor.

74. Eric Foner, *Freedom's Lawmakers* (Baton Rouge: Louisiana State University Press, 1996), 123, 23, 189; Legal Notice at *Beaufort Republican and Sea Island Chronicle*, December 21, 1871; John David Smith, *Black Judas: William Hannibal Thomas and the American Negro* (Athens: University of Georgia Press, 2000), 100, 108; "The Death of Sam Dickerson," *(Charleston) News and Courier*, April 12, 1885, 8; "Annual Report of the Secretary of State," 230.

75. Holt, *Black over White*, 103–5.

76. Ibid., 110.

77. See Francis Butler Simkins and Robert Hillard Woody, *South Carolina during Reconstruction* (Chapel Hill: University of North Carolina Press, 1932), 477. Also see "Reed Elected Judge," *(Charleston) News and Courier*, December 12, 1874.

78. Journal of the House of Representatives of the State of South Carolina, Being in Regular Session, December 16, 1875 (Columbia: Republican Printing, 1875), 192–203.

79. Both quotations from Hyman Rubin III, *South Carolina Scalawags* (Columbia:

University of South Carolina Press, 2006), 102. Also see John S. Reynolds, *Reconstruction in South Carolina* (Columbia: State, 1905; reprint, New York: Negro Universities Press, 1969), 322–23.

80. See *Whipper v. Reed*, 9 S.C. 5 (1877) where the court upheld the governor's action by holding that the incumbent judge's term had not expired.

81. Rubin, *South Carolina Scalawags*, 102.

82. For example, his letter to the editor. "Strong Letter," *Beaufort Republican*, December 28, 1871.

83. Reynolds, *Reconstruction in South Carolina*, 227–29.

84. Journal of the House of Representatives, December 10, 1872, 86.

85. *Report of the Joint Investigating Committee on Public Frauds made to the General Assembly of South Carolina at the regular Session* 1877–78, 1242–45, 1270, 1277. A complete list of the endorsed checks is at 1366–93.

86. Eric Foner, *Reconstruction: American's Unfinished Revolution, 1863–1877* (New York: Harper & Row, 1988), 507.

87. Holt, *Black over White*, 187–93.

88. *Biographical Directory of the United States Congress, 1774–2005* (Washington, D.C.: Government Printing Office, 2005), 942, 1013.

89. Three other black lawyers served in Congress during Reconstruction. All three were elected later than Elliott and DeLarge. See Foner, *Freedom's Lawmakers*, 138 (John R. Lynch), 177 (James Rapier), and 222 (Josiah T. Wells).

90. Lamson, *Glorious Failure*, 75, 123.

91. Walter Edgar, ed., *South Carolina Encyclopedia*, 100 (Columbia: University of South Carolina Press, 2006).

92. Lamson, *Glorious Failure*, 122–23.

93. Ibid., 132, 146.

94. Ibid., 175 (first quotation), 181–82, second quotation on 181.

95. *The Civil Rights Cases*, 109 U.S. 3 (1883).

96. "Death of R. C. DeLarge," *(Aiken) Journal*, February 21, 1874, 1. "The death of this colored ex-member of Congress, who took a prominent part in the politics of this city and State after the close of the war, occurred yesterday morning, at his residence in Calhoun street. He had been in bad health for some time, and for three weeks prior to his disease was confined to his bed. Before the war he conducted the tailoring business. He figured as a member of the Reconstruction Convention, and was subsequently appointed a magistrate by Gov. Scott. He became a member of the General Assembly and then land commissioner, and ran for Congress against Sheriff Bowen, got the credentials and held a seat for a while in that body. A contest ensued, which resulted in his being ousted—neither he nor his opponent being seated by the committee which investigated the election. After sojourning in Columbia for some time, he was appointed a trial justice, an office he held until his death, and the duties of which he performed in connection with an occasional appearance in the Criminal Court as an attorney."

97. Congressional Globe, 42nd Congress, First Session (Washington, D.C.: Government Printing Office, 1872), 230–31.

98. See generally Stephen Hahn, *A Nation under Our Feet* (Cambridge: Belknap Press of Harvard University Press, 2003).

99. John Belton O'Neall, *The Negro Law of South Carolina* (Columbia: John G. Bowman, 1848), chap. 2, sec. 41.

100. Foner, *Reconstruction,* 283–85.

101. Lewis Henry Reece, "South Carolina's Route to Disenfranchisement, 1867–1895" (PhD diss., Bowling Green State University, 2001), 14, 17.

102. Suzanne Stone Johnson and Robert Allen Johnson, eds., *Bitter Freedom: William Stone's Record of Service in the Freedmen's Bureau* (Columbia: University of South Carolina Press, 2008), 54.

103. Holt, *Black over White*, 114.

104. On activities of the various Union League chapters, see Holt, *Black over White*, 29–31; Foner, *Reconstruction,* 284.

105. See the following articles from *Beaufort Republican and Sea Island Chronicle*: "References," May 21, 1870; "Emancipation," December 21, 1871; "Political Speaking," May 23, 1872; "Local Politics," August 1, 1872; "State Convention," August 29, 1872; "A Card. Whipper vs. Smalls," September 12, 1872; "Elliott on the Pattersonians," January 16, 1873; "Annual Meeting of School District," July 3, 1873. See also "Council Meeting," *Port Royal Commercial and Beaufort County Republican,* December 11, 1873; "Dinner at Gillisonville," *Port Royal Commercial and Beaufort County Republican*, April 16, 1874; "Brunson," *Port Royal Standard and Commercial*, October 5, 1876; "A Large Republican Meeting," *Port Royal Standard and Commercial*, October 19, 1876.

106. See Burke, "The Radical Law School," in Underwood and Burke, *At Freedom's Door*, 94–104.

107. "Meeting at Sellers Store," *Orangeburg News,* May 18, 1872; "Grand Mass Meeting," *Orangeburg News,* August 16, 1873.

108. "Minutes of the Mass Meeting," *Orangeburg News*, September 9, 1871.

109. "Excursion to Orangeburg," *(Orangeburg) Free Citizen*, July 24, 1875.

110. "Orange Peelings," *Orangeburg News,* June 24, 1871 (lecture); "The Annual Examination," *Orangeburg News,* June 10, 1871 (graduation).

111. Burke, "Radical Law School," 94.

112. For example, see "Woman's Suffrage Movement," *(Charleston) Daily Republican*, January 20, 1871.

113. "Fourth in the City," (*Charleston) News and Courier*, July 6, 1874.

114. "Town and Country News, Fourth of July," *Aiken Tribune*, July 11, 1874. "A telegram was read from R. B. Elliott, who had been selected as orator of the day, announcing his detention, and inability to reach Aiken until four o'clock in the afternoon, when the meeting was adjourned until that hour, the crowd, which consisted of seven or eight hundred people, resorting to tables where a generous barbecue had been spread for their entertainment. At five o'clock the meeting re-assembled, and General Elliott, having arrived on the Charleston train, was introduced, and for an hour kept the audience engrossed by a speech replete with pertinent advice, and characterized by that impassioned oratory which always distinguishes his eloquent addresses."

115. John P. Green, *Fact Stranger than Fiction: Seventy-five Years of a Busy Life with*

Reminiscences of Many Great and Good Men and Women (Cleveland: Riehl, 1920), 142, 143.

116. Smith, *Black Judas*, 101, 102, 106.

CHAPTER 3. The Education of the New Lawyers

1. "Supreme Court," *(Columbia) Daily Phoenix*, September 24, 1868; "By Telegram," *Charleston Daily News*, September 24, 1868. Some sources indicate that Whipper had been admitted in Michigan and Ohio. See Eric Foner, *Freedom's Lawmakers* (Baton Rouge: Louisiana State University Press, 1996), 226. If Whipper had been admitted in another jurisdiction, he could have been admitted on motion.

2. "By Telegram," *Charleston Daily News*, September 24, 1868; "Admitted to Practice," *Anderson Intelligencer*, September 30, 1868.

3. "By Telegram," *Charleston Daily News*, September 24, 1868.

4. See appendix A.

5. "By Telegram," *Charleston Daily News*, September 24, 1868.

6. J. Clay Smith, *Emancipation: The Making of the Black Lawyer, 1844–1944* (Philadelphia: University of Pennsylvania Press, 1993), 113.

7. "Court in Charleston," *Orangeburg News*, November 6, 1869. Under Act. No. 46, after two years of practice, anyone admitted in the circuit court could be admitted in the supreme court.

8. "Court Proceedings," *Beaufort Republican and Sea Island Gazette*, October 16, 1873.

9. Act 48, Statutes at Large of South Carolina (1868) Section 1.

10. See, for example, *Columbia Register*, December 12, 1876. T. McCants Stewart was appointed to a three-member panel.

11. Charleston County Court of Common Pleas Journals, SCDAH. James A. Bowley was admitted by Judge R. F. Graham on November 16, 1872, after being examined by Chas. W. Buttz, John G. Mackey, and Macon B. Allen. Allen certified that Bowley had read law under him for two years. L. J. Taylor was admitted by Judge R. F. Graham on June 11, 1872, after being examined by D. T. Corbin, J. G. Mackey, and Macon B. Allen, and on motion of Whipper, Elliott, and Allen. A. W. Watson was admitted on November 8, 1872, on motion of Whipper, Elliott, Allen, and Taylor, and after passing an examination given by E. B. Seabrook, J. G. Mackey, and L. J. Taylor.

12. *South Carolina in 1876, Testimony as to the Denial of the Elective Franchise in South Carolina at the Elections of 1875 and 1876*, 44th Congress, 2d Session, Senate Misc. Doc. No. 48, Vol. 2 (Washington, D.C.: Government Printing Office, 1877), Testimony of John Martinborough [*sic*], Columbia, South Carolina, January 10, 1877, 623. The three Democrats were W. D. Ramey, J. R. Abney, and A. J. Norris. See Edgefield County Court of Common Pleas Minutes, March 24, 1876, Sessions Journal 1868–1879, SCDAH.

13. John P. Green, *Fact Stranger than Fiction: Seventy-five Years of a Busy Life with Reminiscences of Many Great and Good Men and Women* (Cleveland: Riehl, 1920), 137–38.

14. "Death of Sam Dickerson," *(Charleston) News and Courier*, April 12, 1885, 8.

15. "Three Members of the Bar," *Orangeburg News*, May 18, 1872.

16. "Local Items," *Beaufort Tribune*, June 14, 1877.

17. Anton-Hermann Chroust, *The Rise of the Legal Profession in America* (Norman: University of Oklahoma Press, 1968), 2:175.

18. Richard Gergel and Belinda Gergel, "To Vindicate the Cause of the Downtrodden," in James L. Underwood and W. Lewis Burke, eds., *At Freedom's Door: African American Founding Fathers in Reconstruction South Carolina* (Columbia: University of South Carolina Press, 2005), 37.

19. Foner, *Freedom's Lawmakers*, 226.

20. "From the State Capital," *Charleston Daily News*, September 25, 1868. According to the article, Elliott told the court that he had attended the Massachusetts School of Law and had read law for nine months. "Robert B. Elliott," in William J. Simmons, ed., *Men of Mark: Eminent, Progressive and Rising* (Cleveland: G. M. Rewell, 1887), 466–67; *Charleston Daily News*, September 24, 1868; John Wesley Cromwell, *The Negro in American History* (Washington, D.C.: American Negro Academy, 1914), 179.

21. "Macon Bolling Allen—A Milestone for Maine," *Maine Bar Journal* 15 (October 2000): 735. There is no record of a Sergeant Fitzherbert with whom he claimed to have read law. Nor is there any record of a Massachusetts Law School.

22. "Trouble among the Negroes," *Charleston Daily News*, January 23, 1867. Also see Smith, *Emancipation*, 100.

23. Smith, *Emancipation*, 410.

24. "Death of Judge George Lee," *Columbia Daily Union*, February 20, 1873, 3.

25. M. Harrison Wayman, "The Quaker City," *Colored American Magazine* 6, no. 4 (1903): 288.

26. Court of Common Pleas, Charleston County Journal (November 15, 1872), SCDAH.

27. Court of Common Pleas, Charleston County Journal (June 4, 1872), SCDAH.

28. Court of Common Pleas, Charleston County Journal (November 6, 1872), SCDAH.

29. Demps Whipper Powell, "A Providential Revelation, Relationship with the Whipper Family," Whipper Papers, Moorland-Spingarn Research Center, Howard University, Washington, D.C.

30. Holt, *Black over White*, 54.

31. See *Papers in the Tillman v. Smalls, Fifth District of South Carolina*, 45th Congress, 1st Sess., House Misc. Doc. 11 (Washington, D.C.: Government Printing Office, 1877).

32. Roll of Attorneys, South Carolina Supreme Court, November 10, 1875.

33. See Hyman Rubin III, *South Carolina Scalawags* (Columbia: University of South Carolina Press 2006), Appendix A, 119–22.

34. Civil Journal, Charleston County Court of Common Pleas, June 10, 1874, SCDAH. E. B. Seabrook was active with the Independent Republican Party. See "Independent Republican Party," *(Columbia) Daily Phoenix*, October 24, 1874. Henry W. Schroder was on the Union ticket in 1865. "Union Ticket," *Charleston Daily News*, August 22, 1865. He was identified as a member of the Radical Ring by the press in 1869. "Radical City Ring," *Charleston Daily News*, May 17, 1869.

35. See letter of John G. Mackey to the editor printed in "The Solicitorship," *Charles-*

ton Daily News, August 30, 1872, in which Mackey claims to be a "respectable Republican." He was running as a candidate for solicitor of the First Judicial Circuit against C. W. Buttz. Mackey claimed that Buttz was the candidate of the "court clique." See also Holt, *Black over White*, 155.

36. T. Y. Simons and Charles H. Simonton were on the committee. See George C. Rogers Jr., *Generations of Lawyers: A History of the South Carolina Bar* (Columbia: South Carolina Bar Foundation, 1992) for multiple references to Simonton. As to Simons, see the *Charleston City Directory* (1867), 148, available at ancestry.com.

37. Roll of Attorneys, November 10, 1875; *Biographical Directory of the United States Congress, 1774–2005* (Washington, D.C.: Government Printing Office, 2005), 942.

38. Robert Brown Elliott may have mentored T. J. Minton, Robert DeLarge, Samuel J. Lee, Henry Maxwell, and W. H. Jones. Elliott moved their admission to the bar. See "Supreme Court," *(Columbia) Daily Phoenix*, March 7, 1872, 2. Samuel Dickerson of Charleston was mentored by C. W. Buttz. George C. Clyde of Aiken was probably mentored by S. J. Lee. There is no known mentor for Richard H. Gleaves of Beaufort, John H. Fordham of Orangeburg, William A. Hayne of Marion, John M. Freeman of Charleston, and Samuel J. Bampfield of Beaufort.

39. Green, *Fact Stranger than Fiction*, 117–18.

40. *Recent Election in South Carolina*, 44th Congress, 2d Session, House of Representatives (Ordered to be printed January 12, 1877) (Washington, D.C.: Government Printing Office, 1877), 213.

41. Chroust, *Rise of the Legal Profession*, 2:75.

42. *South Carolina Bar Association Transactions of the Thirty-First Annual Meeting*, February 7th and 8th, 1924, Columbia, South Carolina (Columbia: McCaw, 1924), 68.

43. Rogers, *Generations of Lawyers*, 14–15.

44. Kermit L. Hall, *The Magic Mirror: Law in American History* (New York: Oxford University Press, 1989), 210.

45. Smith, *Emancipation*, 33.

46. Smith, *Emancipation*, 218; Edmund L. Drago, *Black Politicians and Reconstruction in Georgia* (Baton Rouge: Louisiana State University Press, 1982), 59–61.

47. Smith, *Emancipation*, 195, 218. See United States Census, 1880, 1900, 1910, and 1920, Population, Ga., Richmond County, available at ancestry.com.

48. Green, *Fact Stranger than Fiction*, 138.

49. "The Fall of the University," *(Charleston) News and Courier*, October 13, 1873.

50. "The State University," *Edgefield Advertiser*, October 16, 1873.

51. Quoted in "Deferred Editorials," *Edgefield Advertiser*, October 23, 1873.

52. "The Opportunity of the White South," *Columbia Daily Union*, February 9, 1875, 1, quoting the *(Charleston) News and Courier*.

53. Edwin L. Green, *A History of the University of South* Carolina (Columbia: State, 1916), 90; "South Carolina University—Facts for the Thinking," *Columbia Daily Union Herald*, February 11, 1875, 2; *Register of South Carolina College*, 1874–75, South Caroliniana Library, University of South Carolina (hereafter cited as SCL). The university had 231 students in 1875. See David Duncan Wallace, *South Carolina: A Short History* (Chapel Hill: University of North Carolina Press, 1951), 590. Edwin L. Green, in his *His-*

tory of the University of South Carolina, refused to list any enrollments for the "Radical" period. According to Green's enrollment figures for the non-Reconstruction eras, the university's enrollment did not exceed 231 until 1886 (437–38).

54. "The University," *Columbia Daily Union Herald*, February 10, 1875, 2.

55. Green, *History of the University of South Carolina*, 413, quoting John S. Reynolds, *Reconstruction in South Carolina* (Columbia: State, 1905).

56. "Colored Students in the South Carolina University," *Abbeville Medium*, October 15, 1873.

57. Ibid.

58. Daniel Walker Hollis, "College to University," in *University of South Carolina*, vol. 2 (Columbia: University of South Carolina Press, 1956), 72.

59. U.S. Senate, *Miscellaneous Documents of the Senate of the United States for the 2nd Session of the Forty-Fourth Congress: South Carolina in 1876 Testimony as to the Denial of the Elective Franchise in South Carolina at the Elections of 1875 and 1876*, vol. 1 (Washington, D.C.: Government Printing Office, 1877), 238 (hereafter cited as *South Carolina in 1876*).

60. Professor Fisk Brewer's written statement dated 1876, Papers of Fisk Brewer, SCL.

61. By comparison, in the first eight years of the post-Reconstruction era, 1883 to 1891, the law school had fifty-three graduates. See Roll of Students, 1805–1905—South Carolina College (University of South Carolina Archives, Columbia, hereafter cited as USC Archives).

62. Racial identification of students is based on university records, census records, city directories, and secondary sources.

63. "When Negroes Attended the State University," *(Columbia) State*, May 8, 1911, 9.

64. Those admitted to the bar were Thomas E. Miller, William F. Myers, Joseph Boston, and Edward J. Sawyer. Arthur O'Hear, C. M. Wilder, Charles H. Sperry, and Paul J. Mishow were the other four students. O'Hear was from a prominent Charleston family and had attended Avery Institute and Oberlin College. He died of tuberculosis on August 3, 1876. See Willard B. Gatewood, "Alonzo Clifton McClennan: Black Midshipman from South Carolina, 1873–1874," *South Carolina Historical Magazine* 89 (1988): 24, 30n18; Edmund L. Drago, *Initiative Paternalism and Race Relations: Charleston's Avery Normal Institute* (Athens: University of Georgia Press, 1990), 54. Wilder was a delegate to the constitutional convention in 1868, served one term in the legislature, and was Columbia's postmaster for many years. See Michael E. Thompson, "Blacks, Carpetbaggers, and Scalawags: A Study of the Membership of the South Carolina Legislature, 1868–1870" (PhD diss., Washington State University, 1975), 194; *Columbia City Directory* (1885), 105. Boston, who was a freeborn educator, represented Newberry County in the South Carolina House of Representatives from 1868 to 1876. Walter B. Edgar, ed., *Biographical Directory of the South Carolina House of Representatives*, vol. 1 (Columbia: University of South Carolina Press, 1986); Thompson, *Blacks, Carpetbaggers, and Scalawags*, 194. Sawyer later attended Allen University Law School and was admitted to the bar in 1885. See Roll of Attorneys, November 10, 1875. Sperry was from Georgetown and was a teacher before he enrolled in the law school. In 1880 Sperry was a carpenter in Georgetown. See United States Census, 1870 and 1880, Population, S.C.,

Georgetown County, available at ancestry.com. The Register of South Carolina College for the Reorganization of the University, 1873 (SCL) lists Mishow only as an undergraduate and does not list Miller or Myers as students. Miller and Myers are mentioned in the Scott letter. While Myers is not listed in the register, he is listed as a student in the university's catalog for 1876. Mishow is listed as a law student in the Report of the Chairman of the Faculty of the University of South Carolina (1875), USC Archives. Mishow was a free person of color whose father, Joshua Mishow, supported the family as a carpenter. See United States Census, 1860, S.C., Charleston County, available at ancestry.com. Mishow had attended Avery Institute in Charleston; after leaving USC, he moved to Washington, D.C., and became a physician. Drago, *Initiative, Paternalism, and Race Relations*, 98.

65. See Robert Stevens, "Two Cheers for 1870: The American Law School," in Donald Fleming and Bernard Bailyn, eds., *Law in American History* (Boston: Little, Brown, 1971). Also see Lawrence M. Friedman, *A History of American Law* (New York: Simon & Schuster, 1973), 525–38; Dennis R. Nolan, *Readings in the History of the American Legal Profession* (Charlottesville, Va.: Michie, 1980), 197–258.

66. In 1872 Dean Melton "reported that only four out of the ten students in the law school submitted to daily recitations and examinations." Rogers, *Generations of Lawyers*, 56.

67. See Lou Falkner Williams, *The Great South Carolina Ku Klux Klan Trials, 1871–1872* (Athens: University of Georgia Press, 1996), 89.

68. South Carolina College, chartered in 1801, became the University of South Carolina in 1865. See Hollis, *University of South Carolina, vol.* 2, for a discussion of the various permutations of the university's name from 1801 forward.

69. *Columbia Directory*, 1875–76.

70. *Catalogue, University of South Carolina* (1873), 11, 5, USC Archives.

71. *Catalogue of the University of South Carolina* (1869) 38, USC Archives.

72. *Catalogue, University of South Carolina, 1875–76*, 16–17, USC Archives.

73. William Shepard McAninch, "Petigru College," *South Carolina Law Review* 49 (1998): 531.

74. See United States Census, 1800, S.C., Sumter County, Slave Schedule, SCDAH.

75. *Catalogue, University of South Carolina*, 1875–76, 15.

76. *Recent Election in South Carolina*, 417.

77. W. Lewis Burke, "The Radical Law School," in Underwood and Burke, *At Freedom's Door*, 105–6.

78. Ibid., 93–94.

79. Ibid., 94–98.

80. "University Exhibition," *Columbia Daily Union*, March 13, 1874.

81. Burke, "Radical Law School," 95–96.

82. State A&M College was located on the campus of the Methodist-affiliated Claflin College. In 1896 it was separated from the private school and became the Colored Normal, Industrial, Agricultural, and Mechanical College of South Carolina. In 1954 the college was renamed South Carolina State College.

83. Burke, "Radical Law School," 96–97.

84. Ibid., 96.

85. Ibid., 97–98.

86. Ibid., 98–110.

87. "Edgefield Again—Letter from Senator Cain," *Columbia Daily Union Herald*, January 28, 1875, 1.

88. Burke, "Radical Law School," 99–100.

89. Peggy Lamson, *The Glorious Failure: Black Congressman Robert Brown Elliott and Reconstruction in South Carolina* (New York: Norton, 1973), 215.

90. "Report of the Secretary of State," *Reports and Resolutions of the General Assembly of the State of South Carolina* (1871–72) (Columbia: Republican Printing Co., 1871), 193.

91. For a full biography of Greener, see Michael Robert Mounter, "Richard Theodore Greener: The Idealist, Statesman, Scholar, and South Carolinian" (PhD diss., University of South Carolina, 2002). Also see Michael Robert Mounter, "Richard Theodore Greener and the African American Individual in a Black and White World," in Underwood and Burke, *At Freedom's Door*, 166.

92. "Cuffee in the Courts," *Atlanta Daily Constitution*, November 4, 1877.

93. *South Carolina in 1876*, 1:604–8.

94. See sketch of Styles Linton Hutchins in Burke, "Radical Law School," 105–6.

95. "Cuffee in the Courts," *Atlanta Daily Constitution*, November 4, 1877; W. N. Hartshorn, ed., *An Era of Progress and Promise* (Boston: Priscilla, 1910), 64.

96. Smith, *Emancipation*, 342.

97. Burke, "Radical Law School," 107–8.

98. "Negro Educator Dies in Columbia," *(Columbia) State*, September 14, 1913, 3.

99. "The Next General Assembly," *(Abbeville) Press and Banner*, November 25, 1874, 3; "Arrest of Niles G. Parker, Ex-Treasurer," *Anderson Intelligencer*, April 29, 1875; "Impeachment of Judge Montgomery Moses," *Anderson Intelligencer*, February 24, 1876.

100. See Gov. Hampton, *Abstracts of Letter* (1877), 265, SCDAH, noting the receipt of a letter from W. A. Warren notifying the governor of the closing of the university and the disposition of the keys and books.

101. Gergel and Gergel, "Vindicate the Cause," 51–64.

102. "Deferred Editorials," *Edgefield Advertiser*, October 23, 1873.

103. William J. Simmons, ed., *Men of Mark, Eminent, Progressive and Rising* (Cleveland: G. M. Rewell, 1887). Simmons included J. W. Morris, E. L. Cardozo, T. McCants Stewart, and Richard T. Greener.

104. William J. Cooper, *The Conservative Regime* (Baltimore: Johns Hopkins *University* Press, 1968), 84–115.

105. Dorothy Sterling, ed., *The Trouble They Seen* (Garden City, N.Y.: Doubleday, 1976), 346. Stewart was enrolled in January 1874. Report to Faculty, January 7, 1874, USC Archives.

106. Cooper, *Conservative Regime*, 10–11.

107. *University of South Carolina School of Law Alumni Directory* (White Plains, N.Y.: Harris, 1989), v.

108. Green, *History of the University of South Carolina*, 409–15.

CHAPTER 4. Law Practice in Reconstruction

1. The sixteen counties were Barnwell, Beaufort, Charleston, Clarendon, Colleton, Darlington, Edgefield, Fairfield, Georgetown, Kershaw, Marlborough, Newberry, Orangeburg, Sumter, Richland, and Williamsburg Counties. Records survive from Edgefield (Aiken), Barnwell, Beaufort, Charleston, Georgetown, Marlborough, Newberry, Orangeburg, and Williamsburg Counties.

2. A man named A. R. Watson (possibly A. W. Watson) was identified as a "colored lawyer" in "Alleged Till Tapping," *Edgefield Advertiser*, October 16, 1873. Paris Simkins and Lawrence Cain never practiced. See W. Lewis Burke, "The Radical Law School," in James L. Underwood and W. Lewis Burke, eds., *At Freedom's Door: African American Founding Fathers in Reconstruction South Carolina* (Columbia: University of South Carolina Press, 2005), *99–100, 110.*

3. Aiken County was formed in 1871 from portions of Barnwell, Edgefield, Lexington, and Orangeburg Counties. See Chris Ceasar, "Aiken County History" (2000), http://www.aikencountysc.gov/achistory/ (accessed September 1, 2016).

4. "Town and County News," *(Aiken) Tribune*, December 6, 1873, 2.

5. See Court of Common Pleas of Aiken County, Calendars No. 1, No. 2, No. 3, No. 5, and No. 6, 1873–1877, SCDAH.

6. See Eliza Henley v. Walter Henley (September Term 1873), Calendar No. 1, and James Glover v. Emma Glover (September Term 1874), "Order dissolving bonds of matrimony 19 September 1874," Calendar No. 6, Court of Common Pleas of Aiken County, 1873–1877, SCDAH.

7. *Joseph Tognesi v. Hiram Jordan, Sheriff* (September Term 1875), Calendar No. 1, Court of Common Pleas of Aiken County, 1873–1877, SCDAH.

8. *State v. Robert McEvoy*, Court of General Sessions Aiken Cnty. Bar Dockets (May 5, 1876), SCDAH.

9. *State v. Henry Sparnick*, Court of General Sessions Aiken Cnty. Bar Dockets, (May 8 & 9, 1876), SCDAH.

10. Petition to Gov. D. H. Chamberlain, October 30, 1876, Governor's Papers, SCDAH.

11. Eric Foner, *Freedom's Lawmakers: A Directory of Black Officeholders during Reconstruction* (Baton Rouge: Louisiana State University Press, 1996), 21.

12. "Town and County News," *Aiken Tribune*, December 6, 1873, and July 11, 1874.

13. Peggy Lamson, *The Glorious Failure: Black Congressman Robert Brown Elliott and the Reconstruction in South Carolina* (New York: Norton, 1973), 76–77. See also Clerk of Court Sessions Journal, Barnwell County, 1857–71, SCDAH; "Court Day in Blackville," Charleston News, September 1, 1869.

14. Clerk of Court Sessions Journal, Barnwell County, 1857–71, 201, SCDAH; Kate Woodward, WPA Project, 65–33–118, Barnwell County (1936), SCDAH.

15. Clerk of Court Sessions Journal, Barnwell County, 1857–71, 269.

16. "Court of Common Pleas," (*Beaufort) Republican and Sea Island Chronicle*, March 7, 1872, 2. In eighteen of twenty cases reported, there were no black lawyers.

17. "The Treasurer Again Enjoined," *(Beaufort) Republican and Sea Island Chronicle*, June 6, 1872.

18. "Court of Sessions," *Port Royal Commercial and Beaufort County Republican*, February 6, 1873.

19. "Habeas Corpus Case," *Port Royal Commercial and Beaufort County Republican*, January 1, 1874.

20. "Habeas Corpus Case," *Port Royal Commercial and Beaufort County Republican*, November 20, 1873.

21. Papers of Governor D. H. Chamberlain, 1874–1877, Container 9, Folder 7, Item 1, SCDAH.

22. "Court Proceedings," *(Beaufort) Republican and Sea Island Chronicle*, October 16, 1873. Whipper moved the admission of Wheeler's practice in the circuit courts on certificate of the Supreme Court of the District of Columbia.

23. On Whipper as co-counsel with younger lawyers, see "Court of General Sessions," *(Beaufort) Republican and Sea Island Chronicle*, February 10 and 17, 1876.

24. "Court of General Sessions," *Port Royal Standard and Commercial*, June 8, 1876.

25. "Court of General Sessions," *Port Royal Standard and Commercial*, June 29, 1876. T. B. Jones was acquitted. "Great excitement prevalent and threats of bodily injury were expressed against Judge Maher and the prisoner's counsel William J. Whipper, Esq. The jury was composed of 11 whites and 1 black. . . . Mr. Whipper's plea was a masterly effort so effectively delivered as to draw tears from both spectators and jurors."

26. "Court of Sessions," *(Beaufort) Republican and Sea Island Chronicle*, February 6, 1873; "Court of General Sessions," *Port Royal Standard and Commercial*, June 5, 1873, February 17, 1876, June 8, 1876, and June 29, 1876.

27. "Court of General Sessions," *Port Royal Standard and Commercial*, February 17, 1876, June 8, 1876, June 22, 1876, and August 17, 1876.

28. "Too Much Bradley," *(Columbia) Daily Phoenix*, April 17, 1873, 4; Ellis Merton Coulter, *Negro Legislators in Georgia during the Reconstruction Period* (Athens: Georgia Historical Quarterly, 1968), 114–15. For accounts of A. A. Bradley's career in politics in Georgia, see Edmund L. Drago, *Black Politicians and Reconstruction in Georgia: A Splendid Failure* (Athens: University of Georgia Press, 1982), 41–43; Coulter, *Negro Legislators in Georgia*, 37–38.

29. "Court of General Sessions," *Port Royal Standard and Commercial*, February 17, 1876.

30. "Court of General Sessions," *Port Royal Standard and Commercial*, July 27, 1876; "An Attorney Whipped," *Port Royal Standard and Commercial*, August 3, 1876.

31. "T. B. Jones," *Port Royal Standard and Commercial*, June 29, 1876.

32. "Court of General Sessions," *Beaufort Tribune and Port Royal Commercial*, February 8, 1877.

33. "Colored Lawyer," *Charleston Daily News*, February 6, 1869.

34. Thad C. Jowitt, *Jowitt's Illustrated Charleston City Directory and Business Register, 1869–70* (Charleston: Walker, Evans & Cogswell, 1869), 32. Attorney listing at p. 32 includes Whipper, Elliott, and Allen, 91 Broad Street.

35. See Roll of Attorneys, South Carolina Supreme Court, 1868 (on file with South Carolina Supreme Court, Columbia, South Carolina).

36. See Roll of Attorneys, South Carolina Supreme Court, 1876 (on file with South

Carolina Supreme Court, Columbia, South Carolina). See also Lamson, *Glorious Failure*, 49, reporting that Elliott lived in Charleston while representing Edgefield.

37. See George Evans, comp., *Hooper's Directory, Trade Index and Shippers' Guide for Charleston S.C., 1874–75* (Charleston: George W. Hooper, 1874), 49. The listing read as follows: "Macon B. Allen (c) Judge criminal court res 91 Broad St."

38. See *Charleston City Directory 1872–73* (Charleston: Walker, Evans & Cogswell, 1872), 7.

39. Court of Common Pleas, Charleston County Civil Journal, December 2, 1869, SCDAH.

40. See Court of Common Pleas of Charleston County, Calendars, April Term 1876, 131, Cause 213 Flora Ann Boone, Admin. v. Anthony Boone, M. B. Allen & L. J. Taylor for Plaintiff and J. B. Cohen & J. H. Fordham for Defendant (no action noted); Court of Common Pleas of Charleston County, Calendars, June Term, 150, cause 183, Term 2, Boone v. Boone, M. B. Allen struck thru and L. J. Taylor and M. T. Dooley for Plaintiff and J. B. Cohen & J. H. Fordham for Defendant, SCDAH.

41. See Court of Common Pleas of Charleston County, 1867–1877, SCDAH.

42. See Eli Alan Poliakoff, *Against the Grain in the Palmetto State: The Improbable Political Influence of Organized Labor in Charleston County, South Carolina* (BA thesis, Harvard University, 2000), 48.

43. See *Charleston City Directory for 1867–68* (Charleston: Jno. Orwin Lea, 1868), 182, U.S. Attorney D. T. Corbin; *Jowitt's Illustrated Charleston City Directory and Business Register, 1869–70* (Charleston: Walker, Evans & Cogswell, 1869), 32, D. T. Corbin U.S. Attorney; *Jowitt's Illustrated Charleston City Directory and Business Register, 1872–1873* (Charleston: Walker, Evans & Cogswell, 1872), 53, D. T. Corbin, U.S. Attorney, and 291, D. T. Corbin City Attorney; Evans, *Hooper's Directory, 1874–75*, 15, D. T. Corbin, U.S. Attorney. Court of Common Pleas of Charleston County, Calendars, 1872–1876 (SCDAH) lists Corbin and Stone representing both the county and the city and D. H. Chamberlain representing the county treasurer. Charleston City Directory, 1875, 76, C. W. Buttz, circuit solicitor. Directory available at ancestry.com.

44. See Court of Common Pleas of Charleston County, Calendars, 1872–1876, SCDAH.

45. "City Affairs," *Charleston Daily News*, March 14, 1872. See 1872 S.C. Acts 187–89. The court was granted exclusive criminal jurisdiction except in capital cases; however, the state supreme court declared the exclusive jurisdiction provision unconstitutional in *State v. Simmons*, 4 S.C. 72 (1872). See "Death of Judge George Lee," *Columbia Daily Union*, February 20, 1873, and "Crumbs," *Charleston Daily News, June 23, 1870*, for Lee's admission and Wright serving as his mentor. *Journal of the House of Representatives of the State of South Carolina, 1871–72* (Columbia: Republican Printing, 1872), 645.

46. "City Affairs," *Charleston Daily News*, July 17, 1872; "McLaughlin Case," *Charleston Daily News*, July 17, 1872.

47. Court of Common Pleas Journal, Charleston County, 1872, SCDAH.

48. See Charleston County Journal (S.C. Ct. Com. Pl., February 12, 1872–April 13, 1874), 139–40, SCDAH.

49. Charleston County Journal (S.C. Ct. Com. Pl., May 21, 1874–October 18, 1875), 10, 40, SCDAH.

50. See Charleston County Bar Docket (S.C. Ct. Gen. Sess., 1873–1875), SCDAH, which is actually the docket for the Charleston criminal court.

51. See the *Charleston City Directory for 1875–76* (Charleston: Walker, Evans & Cogswell, 1875), 321.

52. *The Recent Election in South Carolina*, Testimony Taken by the Select Committee on the Recent Election in South Carolina, 44th Cong. 2d Sess., Part 3., 212–13 (January 12, 1877).

53. Lawrence was later admitted by the supreme court in 1882. See Roll of Attorneys, South Carolina Supreme Court, 1882.

54. Advertisements, *(Orangeburg) Free Citizen*, November 20, 1875.

55. Court of Common Pleas Civil Journal, Charleston County (November 1, 1875–July 10, 1877), 30, 96, SCDAH.

56. Volumes 2, Bar Dockets for the Charleston County Court of General Sessions. January Term 1873 through 1875, SCDAH.

57. In his article "Black Politicians in Reconstruction Charleston, South Carolina: A Collective Study," William Hine said, "There were other black Democrats who switched political affiliations. L. J. Taylor was secretary of the South Carolina Democratic Conservative Club in 1868, but in 1872 he was a Republican delegate to the county convention." "Black Politicians in Reconstruction Charleston, South Carolina: A Collective Study," *Journal of Southern History* 49, no. 4 (November 1983): 566. See also "The South Carolina Colored Conservative Club," *Charleston News*, November 9, 1869. The *New York Times* identified Taylor as "one of the black lights of the Bar" in an article about the Fourth of July celebration in the city in 1874. "The Fourth in Charleston," *New York Times*, July 10, 1874. As to Benjamin Byas, see "South Carolina in 1878," *Report of the United States Senate Committee to Inquire into Alleged Frauds and Violence in the Elections of 1878*, Vol. II, 45th Cong., 3d sess. (Washington, D.C.: Government Printing Office, 1879). He was a delegate to the 1868 Constitutional Convention and served in the 1870–71 South Carolina House of Representatives.

58. "Court of General Sessions," *Charleston Daily News*, September 30, 1870.

59. Brian Kelly, "Black Laborers, the Republican Party, and the Crisis of Reconstruction in Low Country South Carolina," *International Institute of Social History* 51, no. 3 (2006): 399n59.

60. "Court in Edgefield," *Charleston Daily News*, October 12, 1869.

61. "South Carolina in 1876," *Testimony as to the Denial of the Elective Franchise in South Carolina at the Elections of 1875 and 1876, Taken under the Resolution of the Senate of December 5, 1876* (Washington, D.C.: Government Printing Office, 1877), 627–28.

62. "Alleged Till Tapping," *Edgefield Advertiser*, October 16, 1873.

63. *Ham v. McArn*, Georgetown County Civil Journal (S.C. Ct. Com. Pl., June 28, 1869), SCDAH.

64. *State v. Fraser*, Georgetown County Criminal Docket (Ct. Gen. Sess., June 1869), SCDAH.

65. Charleston County Journal (S.C. Ct. Com. Pl., February 12, 1872–April 13, 1874), 142, SCDAH.

66. Kate Clifford Larson, *Bound for the Promised Land* (New York: Ballantine, 2004), 88–90, 106, 237, 337n13.

67. *State v. Vanderhorst*, Georgetown Cnty. Criminal Docket (Ct. Gen. Sess., June 1874), SCDAH.

68. *State v. Boone,* Georgetown County Criminal Docket (Ct. Gen. Sess., June 1874 and June 1875), SCDAH.

69. United States Census, 1880, Population, S.C., Georgetown County, available at ancestry.com.

70. "Ex-Congressman Bowen Arrested for Instigating a Murder," *New York Times*, April 30, 1875, 7.

71. "Not Guilty," *(Columbia) Daily Phoenix*, June 26, 1875.

72. *State v. Grimes and Bowen* and *State v. Reed and Grant*, Georgetown County Criminal Docket (Ct. Gen. Sess. June 1875).

73. John Patterson Green, *Fact Stranger than Fiction: Seventy-Five Years of a Busy Life with Reminiscences of Many Great and Good Men and Women* (Cleveland: Riehl, 1920), 136–37.

74. See various calendars of the Court of Common Pleas for Marlboro County, SCDAH.

75. *State v. Charles Goodwin*, not guilty of grand larceny, January 19, 1871, General Sessions Journal, Marlboro County; *State v. Milly McIntyre*, discharged on charge of accessory after the fact of murder, January 17, 1871, General Sessions Journal, Marlboro County (January Term 1871); *State v. Irene McRae*, not guilty of murder, May 16, 1871; *State v. Kelly M. Dote*, discharged for failure to indict on grand larceny, May 16, 1871, General Sessions Journal, Marlboro County (May Term 1871), all available at SCDAH.

76. Green, *Fact Stranger than Fiction*, 138–39.

77. *State v. Franklin Cook*, General Sessions Journal, Marlboro County (January Term 1872), SCDAH; Green, *Fact Stranger than Fiction*, 139.

78. *State v. Tristan McRae*, General Sessions Journal, Marlboro County (May Term 1872, May 22, 1872), SCDAH.

79. Green, *Fact Stranger than Fiction*, 141–45. Also see letter from E. J. Sawyer to Green, in which Sawyer refers to Maxwell as "your bigoted and jealous oppose." E. J. Sawyer to John Patterson Green, August 18, 1887, John Patterson Green Papers, Western Reserve Historical Society.

80. See A. E. Patterson, ed., *The Possibilities of the American Negro* (Cairo, Ill.: Cairo Standard Publishing, 1903), 248; J. L. Nichols and William Crogman, *Progress of a Race* (Naperville, Ill.: J. L. Nichols, 1925), 376–77; Joseph J. Boris, ed., *Who's Who in Colored America* (New York: Who's Who in Colored America, 1927), 79.

81. Elsie Taylor Goins, Honorable Henry J. Maxwell, Sr., 1837–1906, typescript paper in author's possession. Ms. Goins is a descendant of Maxwell. The official records of the court list his admission as November 1871, but his certificate of admission is dated March 6, 1871 (copy in author's possession).

82. *State v. Henry J. Maxwell*, General Sessions Journal, Marlboro County (May Term 1871), SCDAH.

83. *State v. Alexander Williams*, not guilty of murder; *State v. Thomas David*, mistrial

on grand larceny, General Sessions Journal, Marlboro County (September Term 1872), SCDAH.

84. W. Lewis Burke, "Reconstruction Corruption and the Redeemers' Prosecution of Francis Lewis Cardozo," *American Nineteenth Century History* 2, no. 3 (Autumn 2001): 73.

85. Twelfth United States Census, 1900, Population, S.C., Sumter County, available at ancestry.com. Also see E. Louise, *Reflections: A Pictorial History of Certain People of South Carolina, 1840s–1940s* (Orangeburg, S.C.: Cecil Williams Publishing for Phoenix Publishers, 2009), 215.

86. *The State v. Pink Hardy* (January 12, 1875), Thomas as associate counsel for the state; *The State v. Wade Hampton* (March 25, 1875), Thomas for defendant; *State v. Milton Irby* (April 3, 1875), Thomas for defendant; *State v. Binckney Phillips* (January 11, 1876), Thomas for defendant; *State v. Charles L. Gary* (January 12, 1876), Thomas for defendant; *State v. David Shepper* (January 12, 1876), Boston for defendant; *State v. Hamp Rutherford* (January 13, 1876), Thomas for defendant; *State v. Scot Roberson* (January 21, 1876), Thomas for defendant; *State v. David Shepper* (May 3, 1876), defendant's attorneys, Boston and Thomas; *State v. Fortune Satterwhite* (May 4, 1876), Thomas for defendant; *State v. Rosannah Robertson* (May 8, 1876), Thomas for the defendant; *State v. George Washington* (May 8, 1876), burglary, not guilty, Boston; *State v. Rosannah Robertson* (May 8, 1876), Thomas for defendant; *State v. Charles L. Gary* (May 9, 1876), Thomas for defendant; *State v. Joshua Davenport* (May 10, 1876), Boston and Thomas for defendant; *State v. Rueben Carter* (May 10, 1876), Thomas for defendant; *State v. Richard Davenport* (May 10, 1876), Boston and Thomas for defendant; *State v. Minerva Griffin* (May 16, 1876), Boston for defendant; *State v. Minerva Griffin* (May 16, 1876), Boston for defendant; *State v. Alex Edwards* (May 16, 1876), Thomas for defendant. Newberry County General Sessions Journal, SCDAH.

87. According to Thomas Pope, Boston was admitted by Judge [Montgomery] Moses on July 20, 1875. See Thomas H. Pope, *History of Newberry County, South Carolina* (Columbia: University of South Carolina Press, 1973), 64, citing *Newberry Herald*, July 28, 1875.

88. "Death of an Ex-Legislator," *Newberry Herald*, February 11, 1880, 21.

89. John David Smith, *Black Judas: William Hannibal Thomas and the American Negro* (Athens: University of Georgia Press, 2001), 93–126.

90. See *Statistics of the Population of the U.S. at the Tenth Census*, vol. 1 (Washington, D.C.: Government Printing Office, 1880), 407.

91. "A New Law Firm," *Orangeburg News*, April 4, 1874.

92. "Three Members of the Bar," *Orangeburg News*, May 11, 1872, 3.

93. "Town Crier," (*Orangeburg) Free Citizen*, March 20, 1875, 2.

94. See Court of Common Pleas of Orangeburg County, Abstracts of Judgments, 1865–1903, SCDAH.

95. "Town Crier," *(Orangeburg) Free Citizen*, November 16, 1875.

96. Humbert was convicted in January 1875. "Court," *Orangeburg News*, January 23, 1875.

97. "Three Members of the Bar," *Orangeburg News*, March 11, 1872, 3.

98. "Local Items," *Orangeburg News*, March 27, 1869; "Communicated," *Orangeburg News*, February 25, 1871.

99. Lamson, *Glorious Failure*, 205, 271.

100. "Against the County," *Orangeburg News and Times*, April 22, 1876, 3.

101. See Robert J. Swan, "Thomas McCants Stewart and the Failure of the Mission of the Talented Tenth in Black America, 1880–1923" (PhD diss., New York University, 1990), 34. Also see *State v. Nerland*, 7 S.C. 241 (1876), in which Elliott, Dunbar, and Stewart are listed as counsel for the appellant.

102. *Columbia South Carolina City Directory, 1875–1876* (Columbia: Beasley & Emerson, 1875), 44.

103. "Charge of Rape," *(Columbia) Union-Herald*, July 18, 1876, 1; "Examination of Bateman," *(Columbia) Union-Herald*, August 3, 1876, 1 (arson); "Important Case," *(Columbia) Union-Herald*, September 1, 1876, 1 (assault and battery); "Acquitted," *(Columbia) Union-Herald*, September 2, 1876, 1 (acquittal in assault and battery case).

104. William Willis Boddie, *History of Williamsburg: Something about the People of Williamsburg County, South Carolina, from the First Settlement by Europeans about 1705 until 1923* (Columbia: State, 1923), 327, 363, 460.

105. *C. K. Lane v. Anthony Kinder* (Special July Term 1875), Court of Common Pleas of Williamsburg County, Calendar No. 2 1872–1909, SCDAH.

106. See Bar Dockets, 1872–1909, Court of General Sessions, Williamsburg County, SCDAH.

107. See correspondence of Hirsch and copies of deeds in the author's possession, supplied by William E. Jenkinson III, Collection of Samuel E. McIntosh.

108. *State v. Grimes and Bowen*, Georgetown County Criminal Docket (Ct. Gen. Sess., June 1875), SCDAH.

109. Joel Williamson, *After Slavery: The Negro in South Carolina during Reconstruction, 1861–1877* (Chapel Hill: University of North Carolina Press, 1967), 334, citing *New York Times*, June 14, 1869.

110. A prime example of this was noted in "Attorney Whipped in Lawtonville," *(Beaufort) Tribune and Port Royal Commercial*, August 3, 1876. "On the 22nd Thos. E. Miller was employed to defend two colored men whose family has been persecuted for the last 2 years by W. N. Ellis & sons. Miller spoke very plain; called things by their right names, denounced that portion of whites who take advantage of the ignorant negro and attempt to break him up by lawing him to poverty and want."

CHAPTER 5. The End of Reconstruction

1. See generally Walter Edgar, *South Carolina: A History* (Columbia: University of South Carolina Press, 1998), 398–406; Richard Zuczek, *State of Rebellion: Reconstruction in South Carolina* (Columbia: University of South Carolina Press, 1996).

2. *Annual Report of the Secretary of State to the General Assembly of South Carolina at Regular Session, 1876–77*, (Columbia: Republican Printing, 1877), 206–9.

3. Walter B. Edgar and N. Louise Bailey, eds., *Biographical Directory of the South Carolina House of Representatives, Session List*, vol. 1 (Columbia: University of South

Carolina Press, 1974), 425; N. Louise Bailey, Mary L. Morgan, and Carolyn R. Taylor, *Biographical Directory of the South Carolina Senate, 1776–1985*, vol. 2 (Columbia: University of South Carolina Press, 1986), 1081 (Maxwell), 1185 (Myers), 1571 (Swails).

4. Edgar and Bailey, *Biographical Directory of the South Carolina House of Representatives*, 1:426, 427. See also John David Smith, *Black Judas: William Hannibal Thomas and the American Negro* (Athens: University of Georgia Press, 2000), 123–24.

5. "Annual Report of the Secretary of State to the General Assembly of South Carolina," *Reports and Resolutions of the General Assembly of the State of South Carolina at the Regular Session, 1878* (Columbia: Calvo & Patton, 1878), 428. Frederick received 4,081 votes to Straker's 2,616 votes.

6. Edgar, *South Carolina*, 413.

7. Quoted in Robert M. Goldman, *A Free Ballot and a Fair Count: The Department of Justice and the Enforcement of Voting Rights in the South, 1877–1893* (New York: Fordham University Press, 2001), 65–66.

8. "*South Carolina in 1878*," Report of the United States Senate Committee to Inquire into the Alleged Frauds and Violence in the Elections of 1878. Testimony and Documentary Evidence, South Carolina and Mississippi, 45th Cong., 3d Sess., vol. 2 (Washington, D.C.: Government Printing Office, 1879), 122–34, 319–27, 631–38, 641–48, 510–17 (hereafter cited as "South Carolina in 1878").

9. Edgar and Bailey, *Biographical Directory of the South Carolina House of Representatives*, 1:424, 429, 458 (Miller), 443 (Miller and Washington), 447 (Washington); Bailey, Morgan, and Taylor, *Biographical Directory of the South Carolina Senate*, 3:1906 (Miller), 1910 (Reynolds). W. F. Myers of Colleton County was a lawyer who served in the legislature through 1878, but he had been elected in 1874. Bailey, Morgan, and Taylor, *Biographical Directory of the South Carolina Senate*, 3:1902.

10. "The General Assembly," *(Beaufort) Tribune and Port Royal Commercial*, May 17, 1877.

11. "The General Assembly," *(Beaufort) Tribune and Port Royal Commercial*, May 31, 1877.

12. Richard Gergel and Belinda Gergel, "To Vindicate the Cause of the Downtrodden," in James L. Underwood and W. Lewis Burke, eds., *At Freedom's Door: African American Founding Fathers in Reconstruction South Carolina* (Columbia: University of South Carolina Press, 2005), 65, 66.

13. "Concurrent Resolution to Appoint Joint Committee of Investigation," *Journal of the Senate of the State of South Carolina, Extra Session* (Columbia: Republican Printing, 1877), 407–9.

14. W. Lewis Burke, "Post-Reconstruction Justice: The Prosecution and Trial of Francis Lewis Cardozo," *South Carolina Law Review* 53 (2002): 361; W. Lewis Burke, "Reconstruction Corruption and the Redeemers' Prosecution of Francis Lewis Cardozo," *American Nineteenth Century History* 2, no. 3 (September 2001): 67–106.

15. "Cardozo Caught at Last," *(Charleston) News and Courier*, July 23, 1877, 1.

16. "The Trial of Cardozo," Columbia Register, *November 2, 1877.*

17. "J. W.," *(Charleston) News and Courier*, July 31, 1877.

18. "The Trial of Cardozo," Columbia Register, *November 2, 1877.*

19. Burke, "Post-Reconstruction Justice," 387–88.

20. "The Trial of Cardozo," *(Charleston) News and Courier*, November 3, 1877.

21. "Trial of Ex-Treasurer Cardozo," *Yorkville Enquirer*, November 8, 1877.

22. "The Trial of Cardozo," *(Charleston) News and Courier*, November 3, 1877.

23. Burke, "Post-Reconstruction Justice," 393.

24. "The Trial of Cardozo," *Columbia Daily Register*, November 6, 1877.

25. "The Trial of Cardozo," *Yorkville Enquirer*, November 15, 1877.

26. House of Representatives, *Smalls v. Tillman: Testimony and Papers in the Contested Election Case of Robert Smalls vs. George D. Tillman from the Fifth Congressional District of South Carolina*, 47th Cong. 1st Sess., House Misc. Doc. 20 (Washington, D.C.: Government Printing Office, 1881), 490.

27. W. Lewis Burke, "The Radical Law School," in Underwood and Burke, *At Freedom's Door*, 109–10.

28. For example, see M. H. Bryce, *Grand Rally of Republicans Held at Walhalla, Oconee County, S.C., November 1, 1888* (Des Moines, Iowa: Register Printing House, 1889), 4–5 (available at Hayes Presidential Center).

29. "Under Hampton's Rule," *New York Times*, October 21, 1878, 1.

30. "End of Southern Republicanism," *New York Times*, November 28, 1877, 1.

31. See M. J. Hirsch to S. A. Swails, May 26, 1877, supplied by William E. Jenkinson III from Collection of Samuel E. McIntosh.

32. Edgar and Bailey, *Biographical Directory of the South Carolina House of Representatives*, 1:423; "Conciliated South," *New York Times*, January 12, 1878.

33. Samuel W. Maurice to Governor Wade Hampton, April 6, 1878, Papers of Governor Wade Hampton, SCDAH.

34. "South Carolina in 1878," 2:399–483. See "Annual Report of the Secretary of State to the General Assembly of South Carolina," *Reports and Resolutions of the General Assembly of South Carolina*, 434. Swails was defeated by S. W. Maurice by a vote of 3,012 to 2,183.

35. "South Carolina in 1878," 2:400.

36. "Hampton's Bull-Dozers," *New York Times*, October 16, 1878, 2.

37. See Stephen A. Swails to Wade Hampton, October 7, 1878, supplied by William E. Jenkinson III in Collection of Samuel E. McIntosh, and Wade Hampton in reply to Swails, October 24, 1878, Papers of Governor Wade Hampton, SCDAH. Also see "Wade Hampton's Excuse," *New York Times*, October 31, 1878, 3.

38. See statement of E. W. Pinckney reciting the Resolution adopted by Democrats of Williamsburg County, S.C., October 8, 1878, in author's possession, supplied by William E. Jenkinson III, Collection of Samuel E. McIntosh.

39. "South Carolina in 1878," 2:400–401.

40. See Report of M. J. Hirsch to Governor Hampton, October 31, 1878, Governor Wade Hampton Papers, SCDAH.

41. "South Carolina in 1878," 2:408–9.

42. "A Walkover for Smalls," *Anderson Intelligencer*, March 13, 1884.

43. "S. A. Swails," *(Sumter) Watchman and Southron*, February 26, 1884, 2; "Black District Nominating Convention," *(Sumter) Watchman and Southron*, March 11, 1884, 3.

44. "Smalls Gets the Nomination," *(Orangeburg) Times and Democrat*, September 30, 1886, 4.

45. "Personal," *(Washington) National Tribune*, March 4, 1886, 4.

46. "South Carolina Republican State Executive Committee," *(Sumter) Watchman and Southron*, March 7, 1888, 2.

47. U.S. Government Printing Office, "Official Register of the United States 1891," https://www.gpo.gov/fdsys/pkg/GOVPUB-CS1-c06280c12aba381eb4c70f7b6de8bd70/pdf/GOVPUB-CS1- (accessed September 19, 2016).

48. "Death of S. A. Swails," *(Kingstree) County Record*, May 20, 1900, 1.

49. Bailey, Morgan, and Taylor, *Biographical Directory of the South Carolina Senate*, 2:1081.

50. John Oldfield, "The African American Bar in South Carolina, 1877–1915," in Underwood and Burke, *At Freedom's Door*, 116–29.

51. Burke, "Radical Law School," 106–7.

52. Mark Curriden and Leroy Phillips Jr., *Contempt of Court: The Turn-of-the-Century Lynching That Launched a Hundred Years of Federalism* (New York: Faber & Faber, 1999).

53. Thirteenth United States Census, 1910, Population, Ill., Peoria County, and Fourteenth United States Census, 1920, Population, Ill., Henry County, available at ancestry.com; Death Certificate of Styles Hutchins, State of Illinois Death Index, 1916–1950. Styles Hutchins died on September 9, 1950, in Coles County, Illinois. http://www.sos.state.il.us/GenealogyMWeb/IDPHDDeathServlet (last accessed March 8, 2005).

54. Eric Foner, *Freedom's Lawmakers* (Baton Rouge: Louisiana State University Press, 1996), 87.

55. District of Columbia, Select Deaths and Burials, 1840–1964, available at ancestry.com. Gleaves died on November 8, 1907, and was buried in Washington, D.C.

56. "Report of the Secretary of State to the General Assembly of South Carolina," *Reports and Resolutions to the General Assembly of South Carolina, 1882* (Columbia: Republican Printing Company, 1882), 1732; "Annual Report of the Secretary of State to the General Assembly of South Carolina," *Reports and Resolutions to the General Assembly of South Carolina*, vol. 2 (Columbia: Charles A. Calvo Jr., 1884), 791; Minutes of the State Board of Canvassers of the State of South Carolina, 228 (SCDAH), recording William Whipper as elected probate judge (November 19, 1886); Minutes of the State Board of Canvassers of the State of South Carolina, 258 (SCDAH), reporting that Thos. Talbird had defeated W. J. Whipper 852 to 613 (November 23, 1888).

57. See W. J. Whipper, *An Account of the Beaufort County Election of November 6, 1888* (Beaufort, S.C.: Sea Island News Office, 1889), 12, 9; Minutes of the State Board of Canvassers of the State of South Carolina (1888), 258, SCDAH.

58. *In re Whipper*, 32 S.C. 5, 10 S.E. 579, 580 (1890).

59. "Clinging to the Office," *New York Times*, January 30, 1889, 3.

60. In re Whipper, 32 S.C. 5.

61. Court of General Sessions Georgetown County Criminal Dockets, vol. 2 (1892–1908), SCDAH.

62. "Incendiarism," *Georgetown Times*, June 13, 1894, 2; "Murder, Robbery or Acci-

dent," *Georgetown Times*, June 16, 1894, 2; "The Murder Case," *Georgetown Times*, July 4, 1894, 2; "The General Sessions," *Georgetown Times*, November 10, 1894, 1; "Prisoners in the Soup," *Georgetown Times*, November 14, 1894, 1.

63. "Appeal to Uncle Sam," *(Columbia) State*, July 11, 1895, 1.

64. See order of Judge W. C. Benet, December 14, 1896, Court of General Sessions Georgetown County (November Term 1896), SCDAH.

65. See Return of Z. D. Greene, Judge of Probate to Rule by Judge W. C. Benet, November 21, 1896, Court of General Sessions Georgetown County (November Term 1896), SCDAH.

66. "The Notorious Green," *(Columbia) State*, May 16, 1897.

67. *State v. Greene*, 52 S.C. 520 (1898).

68. "Z. D. Greene," *Tampa Tribune*, January 2, 1989; Nancy A. Hewitt, *Southern Discomfort: Women's Activism in Tampa, Florida, 1880s–1920s* (Urbana: University of Illinois Press, 2001), 155–56.

69. Peggy Lamson, *The Glorious Failure: Black Congressman Robert Brown Elliott and the Reconstruction in South Carolina* (New York: Norton, 1973), 282–83, 288 (quotation).

70. "Doings of the Race," *New York Globe*, December 8, 1883.

71. Lamson, *Glorious Failure*, 288.

72. Burke, "Radical Law School," 104–5. Also see Michael Robert Mounter, "Richard Theodore Greener: The Idealist, Statesman, Scholar and South Carolinian" (PhD diss., University of South Carolina, 2002).

73. Thomas Holt, *Black over White: Negro Political Leadership in South Carolina during Reconstruction* (Chicago: University of Illinois Press, 1977), 218; Burke, "Radical Law School"; "Death of Ex-Legislator," *Newberry Herald*, February 11, 1880; *Biographical Directory of the United States Congress, 1774–2005* (Washington, D.C.: Government Printing Office, 2005).

CHAPTER 6. New Lawyers

1. D. A. Straker, *The New South Investigated* (Detroit: Ferguson, 1888), 143, 145.

2. "Report of the Commissioner of Education for the Year 1883–84," *Report of the Secretary of the Interior, 48th Cong., 2d Sess.* (Washington, D.C.: Government Printing Office, 1885), clxxi.

3. See Willard Hurst, "Changing Responsibilities of the Law School: 1868–1968," *Wisconsin Law Review* 2 (1968): 336; Robert Stevens, *Law School Legal Education in America from the 1850s to the 1980s* (Chapel Hill: University of North Carolina Press, 1983).

4. "Atty. N. J. Frederick, a Lawyer and Newspaper Editor Passes," *Palmetto Leader*, September 10, 1938, 1.

5. "Court of General Sessions," *Beaufort Tribune and Port Royal Commercial*, February 8, 1877, 2.

6. Demps Whipper Powell, "A Providential Revelation, Relationship with the Whipper Family," Whipper Papers, Manuscript Department, Moorland-Spingarn Research Center, Howard University, Washington, D.C.

7. "Probate Judge Whipper Acquitted," *Washington Bee*, June 11, 1887, 1.

8. Langley was convicted and jailed with Alfred Williams for election fraud in a congressional race in 1870. See Contested Election, Christopher Brown v. Robert DeLarge, 1525 H.Misc. Doc. 37 at 415–17, United States Congressional Serial Set.

9. Alrutheus Ambush Taylor, *The Negro in South Carolina during the Reconstruction* (Washington, D.C.: Association for the Study of Negro Life and History, 1924), 295.

10. See Roger Lane, *William Dorsey's Philadelphia and Ours* (New York: Oxford University Press, 1991), 45, 105, 167, 250; U.S. City Directories, Philadelphia, 1889, 1890, 1891, and 1904, available at ancestry.com.

11. "Death of Attorney J. I. Washington," *Beaufort Gazette*, January 17, 1938, 8.

12. "New Limbs of the Law," *(Columbia) State*, December 16, 1893, 8.

13. On Bowen, see "Limbs of the Law," *(Charleston) News and Courier*, December 14, 1881. On Sasportas, see A. B. Caldwell, ed., *History of the American Negro, South Carolina Edition*, vol. 3 (Atlanta: A. B. Caldwell, 1919), 703.

14. Death Certificate of T. St. M. Sasportas, October 12, 1937, File No. 14799, State of South Carolina.

15. Lee was the leading black lawyer in Charleston at the time of Browne's admission. However, Browne practiced with John M. Freeman, who had been admitted in 1875.

16. *Charleston City Directory, 1902–1903* (Charleston, S.C.), 326; Death Certificate for R. C. Browne, July 31, 1915, File No. 13240, State of South Carolina. Both available at ancestry.com.

17. Act. No. 442, 1878 S.C. Acts 471.

18. Edwin L. Green, *A History of the University of South Carolina* (Columbia: State, 1916), 100, 107. The law school reopened with ten students in 1883. "Reports of the Board of Trustees of the University of South Carolina and of the President of Claflin College," *Reports to the General Assembly of the State of South Carolina, 1884* (Columbia: Charles A. Calvo Jr., 1884), 837, 844. "Annual Report of the Secretary of State to the General Assembly of South Carolina," *Reports and Resolutions to the General Assembly of South Carolina*, vol. 2 (Columbia: Charles A. Calvo Jr., 1884), 791.

19. See *Report on the Population of the United States at the Eleventh Census*, vol. 2 (Washington, D.C.: Government Printing Office, 1890), 606; *Twelfth Census of the United States Taken in the Year 1900, Population Part 1*, Vol. 13 (Washington, D.C.: U.S. Census Office 1901), 382.

20. N. Louise Bailey, Mary L. Morgan, and Carolyn R. Taylor, *Biographical Directory of the South Carolina Senate, 1776–1985*, vol. 3 (Columbia: University of South Carolina Press, 1986), 1786.

21. "Annual Report of the Secretary of State," *Reports and Resolutions of the General Assembly of the State of South Carolina at the Regular Session 1871–72* (Columbia: State Printer, 1872), 114–15.

22. E. Horace Fitchett, "The Role of Claflin College in Negro Life in South Carolina," *Journal of Negro Education* 12, no. 1 (Winter 1943): 50.

23. Ibid., 49.

24. See John F. Marszalek, *Court Martial: A Black Man in America* (New York: Scribner, 1972), 256–57.

25. See E. Horace Fitchett, "Traditions of the Free Negro in South Carolina," *Journal of Negro History* 25, no. 2 (April 1940): 147n33; Fitchett, "Role of Claflin," 49.

26. Catalogue of Allen University (Columbia, S.C.) 1890–91 (Columbia: Bryan, 1891), 3, 447; "Rev. James C. Waters," in Benjamin W. Arnett, ed., *The Budget: Containing Biographical Sketches, Quadrennial and Annual Reports of the General Officers of the African Methodist Episcopal Church of the United States of America* (Dayton, Ohio: Christian Publishing House, 1884), 19.

27. Straker, *New South Investigated*, 48.

28. Bureau of Education, *Report of the Secretary of the Interior, 47th Cong., 2d Sess.* (Washington, D.C.: Government Printing Office, 1884), lii.

29. Ibid., 448.

30. A similar phenomenon was present at Howard University in Washington. In 1885 its law school had more students than the university's undergraduate college. Education Report, Report of the Secretary of the Interior, 53d Cong., 2d Sess. (Washington, D.C.: Government Printing Office, 1895), 1554.

31. Straker, *New South Investigated*, 53.

32. "Address of the President of the Association of American Law Schools by Henry Wade Rogers," *Report of the 29th Annual Meeting of the American Bar Association Part 2* (Philadelphia: Dando, 1906), 155.

33. The most successful black law school in the South was begun in 1888 by Shaw University in Raleigh, North Carolina. This black Baptist school had fifty-four graduates between 1888 and 1914. It closed in 1916. See J. Clay Smith, *Emancipation: The Making of the Black Lawyer, 1844–1944* (Philadelphia: University of Pennsylvania Press, 1993), 59.

34. William J. Simmons, ed., *Men of Mark: Eminent, Progressive and Rising* (Cleveland: G. M. Rewell, 1887), 163.

35. Report of the Secretary of the Interior, Report of the Commissioner, 49th Cong., 1st sess. (Washington, D.C.: Government Printing Office, 1886), 653.

36. Education Report (1895), 1566.

37. *Catalogue of Allen University, 1890–1891* (Columbia: Bryan, 1891), 40.

38. D. Augustus Straker quoted in G. F. Richings, *Evidences of Progress among the Colored People* (Philadelphia: Geo. S. Ferguson, 1896), 288.

39. R. A. Smith, comp., *South Carolina State Gazetteer for 1880–81* (Charleston: R. A. Smith, 1880–81), 680.

40. S. C. Armstrong, *Hampton Normal and Agricultural Institute* (Hampton, Va.: Normal School Press, 1891), 136.

41. "Protection," *Wichita Eagle*, July 12, 1888, 5.

42. Register of the South Carolina College, School of Law 1874–75, USC Archives; Roll of Attorneys, South Carolina Supreme Court, 1885 (on file with South Carolina Supreme Court, Columbia).

43. *Catalogue of Allen University, 1890–1891* (Columbia: n.p., n.d.), 40.

44. *Catalogue of Allen University, 1908–1910* (Columbia: Bryan, 1910), 73.

45. See Judith Kilpatrick, *Arkansas' Early African American Lawyers: A History*

(Fayetteville: University of Arkansas School of Law, 2003), 11, 24. Jamison taught at Allen and moved to Little Rock, Arkansas, where he taught and then worked for the U.S. Post Office. See "Trouble at Allen," *(Columbia) State*, January 12, 1893; *Catalogue of Allen University, 1910* (Columbia, S.C.); Twelfth United States Census, Population, Ark., Pulaski County, Little Rock, 1900, and Thirteenth United States Census, Population, Ark., Pulaski County, Little Rock, 1910, both available at ancestry.com.

46. From 1891 until 1903, more than fifty articles appeared about Hampton's state fair. See, for example, "The State's Survey," *(Columbia) State*, November 23, 1893.

47. "Report of the Commissioner of Education" in Report of the Secretary of the Interior (49th Cong. 2d Sess. 1887), 547.

48. "Report of the Secretary of State to the General Assembly of South Carolina," *Reports and Resolutions of the General Assembly 1888* (Columbia: James H. Woodrow, 1888), 779.

49. "The News in Tampa Ten Years Ago Today," *Tampa Tribune*, May 9, 1909, 6.

50. Caldwell, *History of the American Negro*, 3:316–19.

51. "Stole the Guard's Clothes," *(Columbia) State*, May 17, 1897; Twelfth United States Census, 1900, Population, S.C., Fairfield County, and Thirteenth United States Census, 1910, Population, S.C., Richland County, both available at ancestry.com.

52. May C. Nerney to Butler Nance, July 1, 1915, Papers of the NAACP, Part 12, Selected Branch Files, 1913–1939, Series A, The South, reel 18–19, Columbia Branch (hereafter cited as NAACP Papers).

53. Walton may have farmed or became a teacher. See Twelfth United States Census, 1900, Population, S.C., Richland County, and Population, S.C., Beaufort County, available at ancestry.com.

54. Report of 1890, p. 1181.

55. "The Colored Lawyers of Allen," *(Columbia) State*, May 29, 1891, 8.

56. "The Faculty," *(Columbia) State*, November 9, 1891, 9; "The Close at Allen," *(Columbia) State*, June 9, 1893.

57. *Catalogue of Allen University, 1910*.

58. "Colored Law Graduates," *(Columbia) State*, May 28, 1892.

59. *Catalogue of Allen University*, 1908–1910, 77–78.

60. *Wm. McElhose v. Samuel Faber* (October Term 1901, February Term 1902), Court of Common Pleas of Berkeley County, Bar Calendar No. 2, SCDAH.

61. "Allen's Trouble Settled," *(Columbia) State*, January 13, 1893.

62. Education Report, 1566.

63. "Allen's Commencement," *(Columbia) State*, June 8, 1893.

64. Education Report, 1566.

65. "Close of Commencement, Morris Will Not Be Back as President of Allen," *(Columbia) State*, June 7, 1894.

66. The catalog included the following on the curriculum and admissions process:

> A knowledge of the Latin language is a great help in the study of Law, and a course in liberal studies is recommended. All applications should be filed, and all arrangements should be perfected with the Dean, before the opening of the Department.

Junior Year.

FIRST TERM.—Federal Constitution; Constitution of South Carolina, with Black's Constitutional Law, six Lectures; Smith's Elementary Law; Brown's Blackstone, ten Lectures; Brown's Kent, eight Lectures.

SECOND TERM.—Bradner on Evidence, four Lectures; Jones' Evidence in Civil Cases, six Lectures; Clark on Contracts, five Lectures; Norton on Notes and Bills, five Lectures; Warlie on Elements of Real Property, four Lectures; Cooley on Torts, three Lectures.

Senior Year.

FIRST TERM.—Hale on Damages, three Lectures; Equity, Fetler's, six Lectures; Shipman's Common Law Pleading, six Lectures; Clark's Criminal Law and Criminal Procedure, six Lectures; Boone on Mortgages and Code Pleading, with the Code of South Carolina, six Lectures; General Statutes of South Carolina; Rules of the State Courts.

67. *Catalogue of Allen University, 1899 and 1900* (*Columbia*, S.C.), 27.

68. Frank Lincoln Mather, *Who's Who of the Colored Race: A General Biographical Dictionary of Men and Women of African Descent* (Chicago: F. L. Mather, 1915), 194.

69. "Allen's Commencement," *(Columbia) State*, June 3, 1896.

70. See Thirteenth United States Census, 1910, Population, Ga., Camden County, and Fourteenth United States Census, 1920, Population, Ga., Camden County, available at ancestry.com. Also see *Brown v. State*, 10 Ga. App. 457 (1912), where Brinkins was listed as counsel, but see *Brinkins v. State*, 29 Ga. App. 189 (1922), where he was a criminal defendant.

71. "Fifteen New Ones," *(Columbia) State*, December 13, 1895, 8; "Want to Be Lawyers," *(Columbia) State*, May 21, 1896, 8; "Eleven New Lawyers," *(Columbia) State*, May 22, 1896, 2.

72. "Mr. A. L. Tucker," *(Savannah) Colored Tribune*, December 19, 1891.

73. See Twelfth United States Census, 1900, Population, Ga., Chatham County, Savannah; Thirteenth United States Census, 1910, Population, Ga., Chatham County, Savannah; Fourteenth United States Census, 1920, Population, Ga., Chatham County; Fifteenth United States Census, 1930, Population, Pa., Philadelphia County, Philadelphia, available at ancestry.com.

Also see *Charity Hospital and Training School for Nurses v. Taylor, et al*, 25 S.E. 519 (1920), in which Tucker was counsel for one of the parties.

74. *Catalogue of Allen University, 1908–1910* (*Columbia*, S.C.), 83.

75. See Roll of Attorneys, 1898.

76. "Address of the President of the Association of American Law Schools," 155.

77. Robert Sobel, ed., *Biographical Directory of the United States Executive Branch, 1774–1977* (Westport, Conn.: Greenwood, 1977), 266, 387.

78. Education Report, 1551.

79. The state superintendent of education and the president of Claflin reported on the operations of the school during the period, but no mention of the law school or Jonathan Jasper Wright can be found. See *Reports to the General Assembly of the State of South Carolina* (Columbia: State Printer, 1883), 536, 575–79; *Reports to the General Assembly of the State of South Carolina* (Columbia: Charles A. Calvo Jr., 1884), 848–51;

Reports to the General Assembly of the State of South Carolina (Columbia: Charles A. Calvo Jr., 1885), 796–98.

80. Act No. 272, 1886 S.C. Acts 521.

81. Report of the Sec. of the Interior (50th Cong., 1st Sess., 1887), 751;

82. Roll of Attorneys, South Carolina Supreme Court, 1868–98 (on file with South Carolina Supreme Court, Columbia, South Carolina); Report of the Sec. of the Interior (51st Cong., 1st Sess., 1891), 1181.

83. *Catalogue of Allen University, 1890* (Columbia, S.C.), 30.

84. Extracts from the "Report of the Committee on Legal Education and Admissions to the Bar, to the American Bar Association, in 1906," *American Law Review* 41 (1907): 594.

85. Education Report, 1551.

86. "Columbia Notes," *Christian Recorder*, May 14, 1891.

87. "Allen University Burned," *(Columbia) State*, February 21, 1895.

88. Harold R. Washington, "*History and Role of Black Law Schools*," Howard Law Journal 18 (1974), quoting Rev. J. W. Witherspoon, who was working on a history of the school (396).

89. "Address of the President of the Association of American Law Schools by Henry Wade Rogers," *Report of the 29th Annual Meeting of the American Bar Association Part 2* (Philadelphia: Dando, 1906), 148, 155.

90. "Address of the President of the Association of American Law Schools," *Yale Law Journal* 16 (1907): 550–51.

91. See *Catalogues of Allen University*, 1890–1891, 1896–1897, 1899–1900, and 1911–1912 (*Columbia*, S.C.). The 1911/12 catalog lists the following alumni: 1885—J. B. Edwards, LLB, attorney, Charleston; T. R. Holmes (deceased); P. F. R. Oliver (deceased); R. A. Stewart, LLB, attorney, Washington, D.C.; 1886—E. J. Sawyer, editor, Bennettsville, S.C.; E. C. Washington, LLB (deceased); B. Watson, LLB, Washington, D.C.; 1887—A. J. Jamison, Little Rock, Ark.; T. A. Saxton, S.C.; A. E. Hampton, LLB, attorney, Columbia, S.C.; Z. D. Greene, Tampa, Fla.; 1890—Charles Brown, merchant/teacher, Horatio, S.C.; James L. Bumgardner (deceased); C. G. Garrett, LLB, Prof. Allen University; Walton T. Williams, LLB (deceased); Butler Nance, LLB, railway mail clerk, Columbia, S.C.; 1891—Thomas Williams (deceased); N. Edwards, LLB (deceased); Thomas T. Hilton, LLB (deceased); 1892—James W. Goudlock, LLB, Rock Hill, S.C.; Eugene R. Hayne, attorney, New York City; Dock Jordan, LLB, President of Kittrell College, admitted May 19, 1892; S. Simons, LLB, Georgetown District, AME Church, Charleston; 1896—Edmund R. Anderson, LLB, pastor, Greenville; E. Woodbury Brinkins, LLB, teacher, Waycross, Georgia; 1897—Abraham L. Tucker, attorney, Savannah, Ga.; 1898—Green Jackson, LLB, editor, Columbia; L. M. Rice, LLB (deceased); E. R. Anderson, LLB, pastor, Greenwood, S.C. Julius Mitchell of Moncks Corner claimed to have graduated in 1894. See Mather, *Who's Who of the Colored Race,* 194.

92. See Roll of Attorneys.

93. Charles Brown of the class of 1890, S. Simons of the class of 1892, Edmund R. Anderson of the class of 1896, and E. R. Anderson of the class of 1898.

94. "The Close at Allen," (*Columbia) State*, June 9, 1893, reports the election of

Bumgardner (law class of 1891) to the Allen faculty. A "James M. Bumgardner" appears listed as a professor in the Twelfth United States Census, 1910, Population, S.C., Richland County, Columbia, available at ancestry.com.

95. Education Report, 866.

96. Caldwell, *History of the American Negro*, 3:444–45.

97. Report of the Secretary of the Interior 1891–1892, 868.

98. Ibid., 869.

99. "Howard University Law School," *Albany Law Journal* 49 (January 13, 1894): 31.

100. Education Report, 1565.

101. Washington, "*History and Role of Black Law Schools*," 392–95.

102. Education Report, 1565. In a Note in the *Michigan Law Review*, it was reported that Wilberforce opened its law school in 1872. H. L. Wilgus, "Legal Education in the United States," *Michigan Law Review* 6 (1907): 647, 656. However, J. Clay Smith says the school never had any graduates. *Emancipation*, 57.

103. Shaw Law Department bulletins, Shaw University Archives, Raleigh, North Carolina. Also see Twelfth United States Census, 1900, Population, Va., Danville, available at ancestry.com.

104. See *Thirty-Third[–Thirty-]Fourth Annual Catalogue of the Officers and Students, Shaw University Raleigh, N.C.* (Raleigh: Edwards & Broughton, 1910), 76; "On Motion," *(Columbia) State*, May 13, 1897, 3.

105. See Washington, "History and Role of Black Law Schools," 385.

106. Frederick D. Wilkinson, ed., *Directory of Graduates, Howard University, 1870–1963* (Washington, D.C.: Howard University, 1965), 512, 514; Roll of Attorneys, 1884.

107. Thirteenth United States Census, 1910, Population, S.C., Colleton County, available at ancestry.com.

CHAPTER 7. Law Practice and Politics in the Gilded Age

1. See Mark Twain and Charles Dudley Warner, *The Gilded Age: A Tale of Today* (Hartford, Conn.: American Publishing Company, 1873).

2. J. R. Oldfield, "A High and Honorable Calling: Black Lawyers in South Carolina, 1868–1915," *Journal of American Studies* 23, no. 2 (December 1989): 395–406.

3. See "Court of Sessions," (*Charleston*) *News and Courier*, June 4, 1878. He tried one case in the first term of court in Charleston after the overthrow of the Republican government.

4. "The Tripe Row Murder," (*Charleston*) *News and Courier*, June 8, 1878, 1.

5. *State v. Lizzie Johnson* (Ct. Gen. Sess., February Term 1882), guilty of manslaughter; *State v. Bill Brown* (Ct. Gen. Sess., February Term 1883), guilty of manslaughter; *State v. John Grant* (Ct. Gen. Sess., June Term 1883), guilty of manslaughter; *State v. James Anderson* (Ct. Gen. Sess., February Term 1890), guilty of manslaughter; *State v. Thomas Wright* (Ct. Gen. Sess., June Term 1888), guilty of murder; *State v. Caesar Fraser alias Wm. Fraser alias Berkeley and Ned Criss* (Ct. Gen. Sess., February Term 1889), S. J. Lee for Fraser, guilty of murder. Charleston County Criminal Docket, SCDAH.

6. *State v. Jane Deas* (Ct. Gen. Sess., November Term 1884), not guilty; *State v. Paul*

Smith (Ct. Gen. Sess., November Term 1884), mistrial; *State v. Robert Gibbes* (Ct. Gen. Sess., June Term 1888), not guilty; *State v. Willie Baber [or Baker]* (Ct. Gen. Sess., June Term 1890), not guilty; *State v. Alexander Noisette* (Ct. Gen. Sess., November Term 1890), not guilty; *State v. Jesse Evans* (Ct. Gen. Sess., February Term 1892), not guilty; *State v. Warley Edgefield* (Ct. Gen. Sess., Nov Term 1892), not guilty. Charleston County Criminal Docket, SCDAH.

7. Charleston County Court of General Sessions Dockets, 1882–1893, SCDAH.

8. Berkeley County Court of General Sessions Dockets, 1883 and 1884, SCDAH.

9. *U.S. v. Mallard*, 40 F. 151 (D.S.C. 1889); *U.S. v. Brown*, 40 F. 457 (E.D.S.C. 1889); *U.S. v. Stewart* 44 F. 483 (E.D.S.C. 1891); *U.S. v. Wilson*, 44 F. 593 (E.D.S.C. 1891); *U.S. v. Reynolds*, 48 F. 215 (D.S.C. 1891); *U.S. v. Reynolds*, 48 F 721 (E.D.S.C. 1892); *U.S. v. Delany*, 55 F. 475 (C.C.D.S.C. 1893).

10. See Court of Common Pleas of Berkeley County, Calendars 1, 2, and 3, 1883–1895, SCDAH.

11. These were not courts of record, and consequently, there are no docket books or other records from these courts in the state archives.

12. Won: *State v. Gathers*, 15 S.C. 370 (1881); *State v. Smalls*, 17 S.C. 62 (1882); *State v. Haines*, 23 S.C. 170 (1885); *State v. Brown*, 24 S.C. 224 (1886); *State v. Ezekiel*, 33 S.C. 115 (1890); *State v. Grant*, 34 S.C. 109 (1891); *State v. Williams*, 40 S.C. 373 (1894); *City Council of Charleston v. Brown*, 42 S.C. 184 (1894); *State v. Larkins*, 44 S.C. 362 (1895). Lost: *Campbell v. Sanders*, 42 S.C. 522 (1894); *State v. Bright*, 14 S.C. 7 (1880); *State v. Collins*, 15 S.C. 373 (1881); *State v. Bowen*, 17 S.C. 58 (1882); *State v. Beadon*, 17 S.C. 55 (1882); *State v. Minton*, 19 S.C. 280 (1883); *State v. Huckie*, 22 S.C. 298 (1885); *State v. Evans*, 23 S.C. 209 (1885); *State v. Bee*, 29 S.C. 81 (1888); *State v. Talbert*, 41 S.C. 526 (1894).

13. *City Council of Charleston v. Brown*, 42 S.C. 184 (1894); *State v. Larkins*, 44 S.C. 362 (1895).

14. Won: *Brown v. Buttz*, 15 S.C. 488 (1881); *Moultrie v. Dixon*, 26 S.C. 296 (1887); *Liberian Exodus Joint-Stock SS Co. v. Rodgers*, 21 S.C. 27 (1884). Lost: *Buttz v. Charleston County*, 17 S.C. 585 (1882); *Buttz v. Charleston County*, 17 S.C. 586 (1882); *Sanders v. Etiwan Phosphate Co.*, 19 S.C. 510 (1883); *Dingle v. Mitchell*, 20 S.C. 202 (1883); *State ex rel Maxwell v. Lewis*, 21 S.C. 598 (1884); *Talbird v. Whipper*, 31 S.C. 600 (1889); *Ex parte Whipper*, 32 S.C. 5 (1890); *Whipper v. Talbird*, 32 S.C. 1 (1890); *Hargrove v. Washington*, 32 S.C. 584 (1890); *Connor v. Edwards*, 36 S.C. 563 (1892); *Campbell v. Sanders*, 42 S.C. 522 (1894).

15. "The Lynchers in Central," *Keowee (Walhalla) Courier*, January 12, 1888; "Court at Pickens," *Keowee (Walhalla) Courier*, January 26, 1888; Bruce Baker, "Lynch Law Reversed: The Rape of Lula Sherman, the Lynching of Manse Waldrop, and the Debate over Lynching in the 1880s," *American Nineteenth Century History* 6, no. 3 (September 2005): 273.

16. "The Murray-Moise Contest," *(Columbia) State*, November 26, 1892, 8.

17. "A Political Sensation," *(Columbia) State*, November 27, 1892, 1.

18. John Oldfield, "The African American Bar in South Carolina, 1877–1915," in James L. Underwood and William Lewis Burke, eds., *At Freedom's Door: African American Founding Fathers in Reconstruction South Carolina* (Columbia: University of

South Carolina Press, 2005), 123, citing "Genl. Sam Lee Dead," *(Charleston) News and Observer*, April 2, 1895.

19. *State v. Bill Brown*, Charleston County, Case No. 37 (S.C. Ct. Gen. Sess., February Term 1883), SCDAH. Tried February 26, 1883, convicted of manslaughter; Berkeley County Criminal Docket (S.C. Ct. Gen. Sess., June Term 1883), SCDAH.

20. *State v. R. L. Smith and J. R. McKnight*, Case 10, Charleston County (S.C. Ct of Gen. Sess., June Term 1884), SCDAH.

21. Richard Gergel and Belinda Gergel, "To Vindicate the Cause of the Downtrodden," in Underwood and Burke, *At Freedom's Door*, 69.

22. "Court of General Sessions," *(Beaufort) Tribune and Port Royal Commercial*, February 15, 1877; "Local Items," *(Beaufort) Tribune and Port Royal Commercial*, June 21, 1877.

23. See *Charleston City Directory* (Livonia, Mich.: R. L. Polk, 1884); "South Carolina News," *Yorkville Enquirer*, May 16, 1888.

24. "The Central Lynchers," *Anderson Intelligencer*, March 14, 1889, 2. His services were not needed as local white lawyers represented the men.

25. *Welch v. Gleason*, 28 S.C. 247 (1888).

26. *D. T. Pope, M.D. v. F. W. Reid*, Case no. 42, Berkeley County (Ct. of Common Pleas, June Term 1889); *James Meachem v. Jas. B. v. Wiggins*, Case no. 29 (Ct. of Common Pleas, June Term 1890). *Meachem* continued in 1891, 1892, 1893, 1894, and 1895 (SCDAH).

27. "The Ballot in Berkeley," *(Charleston) News & Courier*, November 10, 1886, 8.

28. Robert Smalls and Freeman to President Benjamin Harrison, December 10, 1881, Benjamin Harrison Papers, microfilm, Library of Congress, Washington, D.C.

29. "From a Federal Standpoint," *Anderson Intelligencer*, January 11, 1893, 1; Certificate of Death, John M. Freeman, May 30, 1892, Health Department, City of Charleston, available at ancestry.com.

30. "Death of Sam Dickerson," *(Charleston) News and Courier*, April 12, 1885, 8.

31. "The Court of Sessions," *(Charleston) News and Courier*, February 29, 1876, 4.

32. "Negro Legislators," *(Columbia) State*, February 23, 1903, reprinting from *New York Times*, February 8, 1903; "Sam Dickerson," *(Columbia) State*, May 26, 1918.

33. Certificate of Death, Joshua Williams Polite, September 29, 1895, Health Department, City of Charleston, available at ancestry.com.

34. *State v. Vari*, 35 S.C. 175 (1892); *State v. Washington*, 26 S.C. 604 (1887); *Smith v. McFall*, 19 S.C. 607 (1883); *Christopher v. Christopher*, 18 S.C. 600 (1882).

35. House of Representatives, *Papers in the Case of Mackey* v. *O'Connor, Second Congressional District of South Carolina*, 46th Cong., 2nd Sess., House Misc. Doc. 40, pt. 2 (Washington, D.C.: Government Printing Office, 1880).

36. John Marszalek, *Assault at West Point: The Court Martial of Johnson Whittaker* (New York: Collier / Macmillan, 1994), 28, 241.

37. "Sumter," *Columbia Daily Register*, February 24, 1887.

38. Robert N. C. Nix Sr., *South Carolina State College: A History*, Reference and Serials Center, Miller F. Whittaker Library, South Carolina State University, Orangeburg, South Carolina.

39. He began practice in Sumter with J. C. Whittaker in 1887. "Sumter," *Columbia Daily Register*, February 24, 1887.

40. *State v. Washington*, 55 S.C. 372 (1899); *Roberts v. Herron*, 78 S.C. 115 (1907); *Singleton v. Progressive Be. Ass'n.*, 77 S.C. 531 (1907); *Seabrook v. Mostowitz*, 51 S.C. 433 (1898).

41. See *Providence Business Directory, 1922–1937*, available at ancestry.com. He had ten appellate cases in the Rhode Island Supreme Court and one in Pennsylvania. *In re Howard*, 90 A. 819 (R.I. 1914); *Johnson v. Randall*, 92 A. 829 (R.I. 1915); *State v. Smith*, 93 A. 1 (R.I. 1915); *Gromada v. Mardinyan*, 94 A. 261 (R.I. 1915); *State v. Brown*, 102 A. 65 (R.I. 1917); *State v. Brown*, 119 A. 324 (R.I. 1923); *State v. Brown*, 146 A. 415 (R.I. 1929); *Ex parte Brown*, 152 A. 694 (R.I. 1930); *National Casket Co. v. Montgomery*, 158 A. 723 (1932); *Newport Trust Co. v. Johnson*, 167 A. 128 (R.I. 1933); *Dickerson v. Midvale Beneficial Association*, 107 A. 778 (1919).

42. Frank Lincoln Mather, *Who's Who of the Colored Race: A General Biographical Dictionary of Men and Women of African Descent* (Chicago: F. L. Mather, 1915), 194.

43. Court of Common Pleas of Berkeley County, Bar Calendars 1, 2, and 3 (SCDAH) record the following numbers of civil cases with or without co-counsel on the docket in Berkeley County: 1897, Polite & Mitchell 1, Mitchell, 1, Mitchell & Edwards 1; 1898, Mitchell and Culler 8, Polite & Mitchell 1, Mitchell & Edwards 1, Mitchell 1; 1899, Mitchell & Culler 6, Polite & Mitchell 1, Mitchell & Culler 2, Mitchell 1; 1900, Mitchell & Culler 3, Polite & Mitchell 1, Mitchell 2; 1901, Polite & Mitchell 1, Mitchell 2, Mitchell & Culler 1; 1902, Mitchell 1; 1903, Mitchell 4; 1904, Mitchell 6; 1905, Mitchell 6; 1906, Mitchell 5; 1907, Mitchell 2.

44. See Georgetown County Criminal Dockets (1899–1901), SCDAH.

45. "A Miscarriage of Justice," *Georgetown Semi-Weekly Times*, November 18, 1899, 1.

46. Court of Common Pleas of Berkeley County, Bar Calendar 1 (SCDAH): 1900, Mitchell and Edwards 5, Mitchell 4; 1901, Mitchell & Edwards 3, Mitchell 3; 1902, Mitchell & Edwards 1, Mitchell v. Edwards 1, Mitchell 3; 1903, Mitchell 3, Mitchell v. Edwards 1; 1904, Mitchell 2; 1905, Mitchell 1.

47. See *Providence Business Directory, 1914*, available at ancestry.com.

48. *State v. Smith*, 93 A. 1 (R.I. 1915); *State v. Smith*, 93 A. 353 (R.I. 1915).

49. *Calvary Baptist Church v. Dart*, 68 S.C. 221 (1904); *Lee v. Methodist Episcopal Church in the U.S.*, 78 N.E. 646 (Mass. 1906); *Battle v. Robinson*, 65 A. 273 (R.I. 1906); *State ex. Inf. Fletcher v. Gaines*, 68 A. 1119 (R.I. 1907); *Metropolitan Life Ins. Co. v. Armstrong*, 70 A. 1103 (R.I. 1908); *Adelson v. Keller*, 70 A. 1103 (R.I. 1908); *Dousette v. Pawtucket Gas Co.*, 69 A. 847 (R.I. 1908); *Krikorian v. Rhode Island Co.*, 71 A. 369 (R.I. 1908); *Hart v. Superior Court*, 71 A. 513 (R.I. 1909); *State v. Robinson*, 79 A. 580 (R.I. 1911); *In re Howard*, 90 A. 819 (R.I. 1914); *People ex rel. v. African Wesleyan Episcopal Church*, 177 N.Y. S. 393, 394 (1913); *Dixon v. Dixon*, 177 N.Y.S. 63 (Sup. Ct. 1919).

50. "News Briefs of Brooklyn," *New York Amsterdam News*, December 8, 1926, 8.

51. Twelfth United States Census, 1900, Population, S.C., Charleston County, Charleston, available at ancestry.com. Hayne probably practiced in Charleston for a time, and he and Alonzo Twine had cases in Berkeley County in 1901 and 1902. See chapter 6.

52. See *New York City Directory 1903*, available at ancestry.com.

53. "A Plain Statement," *(Columbia) State*, May 5, 1900, 4; "Whipper Counsels Lawbreaking," *(Columbia) State*, March 9, 1904, 1; "South Carolina Supreme Court," *(Columbia) State*, August 23, 1907.

54. "The Stafford's Cross Roads Case," *(Beaufort) Tribune and Port Royal Commercial*, June 28, 1877.

55. "Stafford's X Roads Case," *(Beaufort) Tribune and Port Royal Commercial*, June 14, 1877.

56. "Supreme Court," *(Columbia) State*, December 2, 1897.

57. *Wyman v. Hoover*, 10 S.C. 135 (1878); *Rollin v. Whipper*, 17 S.C. 32 (1882); *Alston v. Franz*, 19 S.C. 603 (1883); *Gibbes v. Town of Beaufort*, 20 S.C. 213 (1883); *State v. Thompson*, 24 S.C. (1886); *Town Council of Beaufort v. Ohlandt*, 24 S.C. 158 (1886); *Rhodes v. Burkart*, 28 S.C. 154 (1888); *State v. Grant*, 34 S.C. 109 (1891); *State v. Brownfield*, 60 S.C. 509 (1901).

58. Carole Ione, *Pride of Family: Four Generations of American Women of Color* (New York: Summit, 1991), 189–90.

59. "Judge Whipper's Defense," *Washington Bee*, May 14, 1887, 2. Also see "A Colored Judge Arrested," *Washington Bee*, May 7, 1887, 2.

60. "Whipper Behind the Bars," *Washington Bee*, May 28, 1887, 2.

61. "Probate Judge Whipper Acquitted," *Washington Bee*, June 11, 1887, 1.

62. Smalls also had been upset by the fact that the Republican Party had chosen Thomas Miller to run for Congress instead of him. Lewis H. Reece IV, "Pure Despotism: South Carolina's Route to Disfranchisement, 1867–1895" (PhD diss., Bowling Green State University, 2001), 196.

63. A. A. Bradley was listed by a business directory as having a law office in Beaufort in 1880 and 1881, but according to one historian, Bradley had moved to Saint Louis, Missouri, in 1880. *The South State Gazetteer and Business Directory for 1880–81* (Charleston: R. A. Smith, 1881), 676; E. Merton Coulter, *Negro Legislators in Georgia during the Reconstruction Period* (Atlanta: Georgia Historical Quarterly, 1968), 118–19.

64. See "Notice to Liquor Dealers," *(Beaufort) Tribune and Port Royal Commercial*, June 28, 1877; "Beaufort County Vote," *(Beaufort) Tribune and Port Royal Commercial*, November 15, 1876; letter of T. H. Wheeler to President Benjamin Harrison, March 2, 1889, Benjamin Harrison Papers.

65. "Judge Whipper's Defense," *Washington Bee*, May 14, 1887.

66. Letters, March 2, 1889, and May 2, 1889, Benjamin Harrison Papers.

67. "A Novel Brief," *Washington Bee*, October 3, 1891, 1.

68. See *Miller v. Elliott* in Chester Rowell, *A Historical and Legal Digest of Contested Election Cases in the House of Representatives of the U.S. from the First to the Fifty-Sixth Congress* (Washington, D.C.: Government Printing Office, 1901), 461.

69. "A Novel Brief," *Washington Bee*, October 3, 1891, 1.

70. "Final Figures on the Vote for Governor and on the Convention," *(Sumter) Watchman and Southron*, November 28, 1894, 2.

71. See *Murray v. Elliott* in Rowell, *Historical and Legal Digest*, 543.

72. *Washington City, District of Columbia, City Directory*, 1896, available at ancestry .com.

73. See Roger Lane, *William Dorsey's Philadelphia and Ours* (New York: Oxford University Press, 1991), 171–73; Death Certificate of T. H. Wheeler, July 27, 1903, Index No. 1854605, State of Pennsylvania.

74. *South State Gazetteer*, 678; Thomas Miller to President Benjamin Harrison, January 7, 1889, Benjamin Harrison Papers.

75. *United States v. Polite*, 35 F. 58 (D.S.C. 1888); *United States v. Durant*, 46 F. 753 (E.D.S.C. 1891).

76. "Hon. Thomas Miller of S.C. Has Swelled Head," *Cleveland Gazette*, October 25, 1890, 2; Thomas Miller to President Benjamin Harrison, March 2, 1889, March 22, 1889, and May 1, 1889, Benjamin Harrison Papers.

77. William C. Hine, "Thomas E. Miller and the Early Years of South Carolina State University," *Carologue* 12 (Winter 1996): 4.

78. George Brown Tindall, *South Carolina Negroes, 1877–1900* (Columbia: University of South Carolina Press, 2002), 73.

79. "Tom Miller Checkmated," *(Columbia) State*, April 14, 1891.

80. Tindall, *South Carolina Negroes*, 56.

81. I. Garland Penn, *The Afro-American Press and Its Editors* (Springfield, Mass.: Wiley, 1891), 205.

82. "List of Known African-American Postmasters, 1800s," United States Postal Service, http://about.usps.com/who-we-are/postal-history/african-american-postmasters-19th-2010.htm (accessed July 17, 2012).

83. Penn, *Afro-American Press and Its Editors*, 205.

84. "S. J. Bampfield," *Colored American*, January 20, 1900, 9.

85. Powell worked in the Charleston Navy Yard in the 1890s. In 1922 he moved to Washington, D.C., and died at age 101 in 1952. See Employee Bulletin, United States Civil Service Commission, July 31, 1952, Whipper Papers, Moorland-Spingarn Research Center, Howard University, Washington, D.C.

86. A. A. Taylor, *The Negro in South Carolina during the Reconstruction* (Washington, D.C.: Association for the Study of Negro Life and History, 1924), 295.

87. *Grayson v. Harris*, 37 S.C. 606 (1892).

88. *United States v. Reynolds*, 48 F. 215 (D.S.C. 1891).

89. *United States v. Reynolds*, 48 F. 721 (E.D.S.C. 1892).

90. Bailey, Morgan, and Taylor, *Biographical Directory of the South Carolina Senate*, 2:1353.

91. Edgefield County Minute Session Journal (Ct. Com. Pl., 1868–1879) (SCDAH), admission of Mardenborough by Judge R. B. Carpenter. See Senate, *Miscellaneous Documents of the Senate of the United States for the 2nd Session of the Forty-Fourth Congress: South Carolina in 1876, Testimony as to the Denial of the Elective Franchise in South Carolina at the Elections of 1875 and 1876*, 44th Cong., 2nd Sess. (Washington, D.C.: Government Printing Office, 1877), 623, 627, 743; House of Representatives, *Papers in the Case of Tillman v. Smalls, Fifth District of South Carolina*, 45th Congress, 1st Sess., House Misc. Doc. 11 (Washington, D.C.: Government Printing Office, 1877), 247; testimony of Mardenborough in *Smalls v. Elliott*, at 19 (1888); Langley's employment at Report of the Secretary of War, 47th Cong. (Washington, D.C.: Government Printing Office, 1881).

92. *Lincoln University College and Theological Seminary Biographical Catalogue* (Lancaster, Pa.: New Era, 1918), 20. Also see *Proceedings of the Trustees of the John F. Slater Fund for the Education of Freedmen* (Baltimore: Press of William K. Boyle & Son, 1888), 10. Find a Grave records his death as January 19, 1912. http://www.findagrave.com/cgi-bin/fg.cgi?page=gr&GRid=74667885 (accessed September 1, 2016).

93. "Probate Judge Whipper Acquitted," *Washington Bee*, June 11, 1887, 1.

94. *Grayson v. Harris*, 37 S.C. 606 (1892); "Election Results," *(Columbia) State*, November 23, 1892.

95. *State v. Ezekiel*, 33 S.C. 115, 11 S.E. 635 (1890); "Lawyer Gets Limit," *(Sumter) Watchman and Southron*, October 24, 1906.

96. Death Certificate of A. H. Ezekiel, November 12, 1926, File no. 26242, State of Georgia, available at ancestry.com.

97. Twelfth United States Census, 1900, Population, D.C., Washington; Washington, D.C. City Directory, 1902; Sixteenth United States Census, 1940, Population, D.C., Washington, available at ancestry.com.

98. "Death of Attorney J. I. Washington," *Beaufort Gazette*, January 17, 1938, 8.

99. Caldwell, *History of the American Negro*, 3:512–13.

100. "Death of Attorney J. I. Washington," *Beaufort Gazette*, January 17, 1938, 8.

101. See the following articles from the *(Columbia) State*: "Eighteen Mortal Hours," April 21, 1892; "A Ghastly Assembly," September 30, 1892; "Plans of the Enemy," February 13, 1895; "The City by the Sea," October 14, 1896; "An Appeal to Caesar," May 19, 1893; "Quay asked to Come," October 2, 1896; "Second District Republicans," October 15, 1896; "Protests Heard," November 24, 1896; "All about Aiken," November 29, 1896; "Planned by G. W. Murray," May 17, 1897; "Seymour Smith Goes to Try His Old Pull," April 12, 1900; "Death of Well Known Lawyer," January 27, 1907.

102. *State v. John Bacon, Frank Brown and John Jones* (Ct. Gen. Sess., April Term 1886), Aiken County Criminal Docket, SCDAH.

103. *State v. Fleming Watkins* (Ct. Gen. Sess., April Term 1887); *State v. Stephen Wigfall* (Ct. Gen. Sess., June Term 1887); *State v. William King* (Ct. Gen. Sess., September Term 1887), Aiken County Criminal Docket, SCDAH.

104. *State v. Johnson Carroll* (Ct. Gen. Sess., April Term 1888); *State v. Sanford Arnold et al.* (Ct. Gen. Sess., April Term 1888); *State v. Sam Cummings* (Ct. Gen. Sess., April Term 1888); *State v. Lewis Brown* (Ct. Gen. Sess., April Term 1891); *State v. Sam Oliver* (Ct. Gen. Sess., April Term 1891); *State v. Charles Morgan* (Ct. Gen. Sess., September term 1892); *State v. George Washington* (Ct. Gen. Sess., April Term 1893); *State v. Dickey Branch* (Ct. Gen. Sess., April Term 1894); *State v. Milledge Price* (Ct. Gen. Sess., April Term 1894); *State v. Sandy Jackson* (Ct. Gen. Sess., June Term 1895); *State v. John Stewart, John Small and Britton Madison* (Ct. Gen. Sess., April Term 1896) (nol pros of Small and Madison and not guilty for John Stewart); *State v. Henry Coker* (Ct. Gen. Sess., February Term 1897); *State v. Lucius Ivey* (Ct. Gen. Sess., October Term 1898); *State v. John Cuthberton* (Ct. Gen. Sess., February Term 1902) (not guilty); *State v. Henry Scott* (Ct. Gen. Sess., June Term 1902); and *State v. Willie Thomas* (Ct. Gen. Sess., October Term 1904), Aiken County Criminal Docket, SCDAH.

105. *Maria Williams v. George Ealey* (Ct. Com. Pl., April Term 1891); *Samuel Spen-*

cer v. Octavia Spencer (Ct. Com. Pl., September Term 1891); *Otis & John Chaffee Copartners as Chaffee Bros. v. Solomon Lockhart* (Ct. Com. Pl., October Term 1906–April Term 1907); *Sophia Dickerson v. Henry Bronson* (Ct. Com. Pl., November Term 1905–April Term 1907), Aiken County Civil Journal, SCDAH.

106. "An Appeal to Caesar," *(Columbia) State*, May 19, 1893.

107. *State v. Johnson Carroll* (Ct. Gen. Sess., April Term 1888); *State v. Shannon Walton* (Ct. Gen. Sess., September Term 1891); *State v. James Stephens* (Ct. Gen. Sess., April Term 1894); *State v. Linus Woodward* (Ct. Gen. Sess., April Term 1894); *State v. Henry Coker* (Ct. Gen. Sess., February Term 1897); *State v. Lucius Ivey* (Ct. Gen. Sess., October Term 1898), Aiken County Criminal Docket, SCDAH.

108. "A Ghastly Assemblage," *(Columbia) State*, September 30, 1892.

109. "Seymour Smith Goes to Try His Old Pull," *(Columbia) State*, April 12, 1900. He lost that position in 1910. See "Charleston News Gathered," *(Columbia) State*, April 16, 1910.

110. *Charleston City Directory* (Livonia, Mich.: R. L. Polk, 1900, 1910, and 1919).

111. "Town Crier," *Orangeburg) Times and Democrat*, April 4, 1874; "Taylor, Fordham and Lawrence," *(Orangeburg) Free Citizen*, November 20, 1875.

112. *State v. Robert Green*, Orangeburg County Journal No. 5, 1890–1895 (S.C. Ct. Gen. Sess., September 17, 1894), SCDAH; *Sophia Dickerson v. Henry Bronson*, Aiken County Civil Journal (S.C. Ct. Com. Pl., November Term 1905–April Term 1907), SCDAH.

113. "Court," *Orangeburg Democrat*, May 7 and 14, 1880. He had represented the county in a case in the spring of 1876. See "Against the County," *Orangeburg News and Times*, April 22, 1876.

114. "General News," *Georgetown Enquirer*, January 19, 1881.

115. Terence Finnegan, "Lynching and Political Power in Mississippi and South Carolina," in W. Fitzhugh Brundage, ed., *Under Sentence of Death: Lynching in the South* (Chapel Hill: University of North Carolina Press, 1997), 189.

116. "Local Items," *Georgetown Enquirer*, February 16, 1881, 3.

117. Tindall, *South Carolina Negroes*, 43.

118. He had one civil case on the Lexington County docket in 1885 and 1886. See *Simeon Thomas v. Preston Thomas*, Lexington County Bar Calendar, vol. 2 (S.C. Ct. Com. Pl., February Term 1885 and September Term 1886), SCDAH; *Ruff v. Doty*, 20 S.C. 173 (1887) (Fairfield County case).

119. His accent was reportedly helpful to him in Detroit with Irish immigrants. J. W. Gibson and W. H. Croghan, eds., *Progress of a Race* (Naperville, Ill.: J. L. Nichols, 1912), 630.

120. Grant v. Grant, 12 S.C. 29 (1879). The divorce action was brought on the grounds of adultery on December 12, 1878, eight days before the approval of the act of December 20, 1878 (16 Stat. 719), repealing all laws of South Carolina relating to the granting of divorces. Kershaw circuit judge Thomson dismissed the action, ruling that he could not proceed to consider an action taken under a repealed act. The supreme court upheld the dismissal.

121. W. Lewis Burke, "From Barristers to Corporate Lawyers," *American Journal of*

Legal History 37 (1993): 51–52, citing “The Murder Case,” *(Columbia) Daily Register*, April 5, 1883.

122. See Dorothy Drinkard Hawkshare, “David Augustus Straker” (PhD diss., Catholic University, 1974), 56–74, 54.

123. McGowan to unnamed judge, February 25, 1884, SCL; *State v. Shuler*, 19 S.C. 140 (1883); *Green v. Spann*, 25 S.C. 273 (1886).

124. “Court,” *Orangeburg Democrat*, May 7, 1880.

125. “Court of General Sessions,” *Columbia Daily Register*, July 4, 1883.

126. D. A. Straker, *The New South Investigated* (Detroit: Ferguson, 1888), 62, 72–73; Hawkshare, “David Augustus Straker,” 62.

127. See *Report on the Population of the United States at the Eleventh Census, 1890*, vol. 1 (Washington, D.C.: Government Printing Office, 1890), table 15 on 427. Out of 49,393 people in Orangeburg County, 33,738 were black. In Richland County, out of 38,821 people, 24,885 were black.

128. Conrad Harper, “Some Black Lawyers in the Post–Civil War South,” *Litigation* 3 (Spring 1977): 41, quoting *Columbia Daily Register*.

129. Gibson and Croghan, *Progress of a Race*, 630.

130. “Thou Art the Man,” *Columbia Daily Register*, January 8, 1887; “A Card from Lawyer Straker,” *Columbia Daily Register*, July 7, 1883.

131. Hawkshare, “David Augustus Straker,” 82. Also see “Political Independence,” *Detroit Free Press*, August 10, 1888, in which a letter writer asserts that Straker claimed to have left under a “twenty-four hour” command.

132. “Personals,” *Wichita Eagle*, July 12, 1888, 5.

133. “Protection,” *Wichita Eagle*, July 18, 1888, 5.

134. His political activities were noted several times in the *Wichita Eagle*: “Protection,” July 18, 1888; “Republican Rally,” November 4, 1888; “The Hon. Fred Douglass,” November 17, 1889; “Colored Mass Meeting,” March 12, 1889, 5; “Colored Mass Meeting,” August 3, 1889, 5. His legal work in defense of a young boy for stealing a newspaper was his only case noted in the press. “That Paper Theft Case,” *Wichita Eagle*, January 17, 1889, 5.

135. “The Black Territory,” *(Columbia) State*, September 17, 1894, 7; “It Will Be a Pretty Black State,” *(New York) Sun*, August 5, 1894, 14.

136. “Died in Oklahoma,” *(Columbia) State*, November 29, 1895, 5.

137. “The Negro Aroused,” *(Columbia) State*, April 27, 1893. Other activities included “Emancipation Day,” *(Columbia) State*, December 26, 1892, 5; “The Hampton Colored Fair,” *(Columbia) State*, February 3, 1893, 8; “Hampton’s Colored Fair Again,” September 17, 1893, 8; “An Appeal to Caesar,” *(Columbia) State*, May 19, 1893. Washington was in attendance at a Republican ward meeting in Columbia in January 1896. “Republicans Organize,” *(Columbia) State*, January 16, 1896.

138. See Thirteenth United States Census, 1910, S.C., Richland County, available at ancestry.com.

139. “The Radical Convention,” *(Sumter) Watchman and Southron*, September 24, 1890, 1; “News from Union,” *(Columbia) State*, April 9, 1892, 3; “Report of the Secretary of State,” *Reports and Resolutions to the General Assembly of the State of South Carolina* (Columbia, S.C.: James A. Woodrow, 1888), 1557–58.

140. "The Old Line Republicans," *(Columbia) State*, March 22, 1892, 8.

141. "Will Prosecute Now," *(Columbia) State*, March 14, 1895.

142. A. B. Caldwell, "Casper George Garrett," in Caldwell, ed., *History of the American Negro, vol. 3* (Atlanta: A. B. Caldwell, 1919), 316–19.

143. See "South Carolina Delegation to the 1928 Republican National Convention," http://politicalgraveyard.com/parties/R/1928/SC.html (accessed July 12, 2011).

144. May C. Nerney to Butler Nance, July 1, 1915, NAACP Papers.

145. See "Edward James Sawyer," in Caldwell, *History of the American Negro*, 3:265; John Troy McQueen, Edward James Sawyer pamphlet, 1996, in Thomas Cooper Library, University of South Carolina; Roll of Attorneys, 1885.

146. Letter of Sawyer to John Patterson Green, August 18, 1887, John Patterson Green Papers, Western Reserve Historical Society.

147. John P. Green, *Fact Stranger than Fiction: Seventy-five Years of a Busy Life with Reminiscences of Many Great and Good Men and Women (Cleveland: Riehl, 1920)*, 136.

148. John Troy McQueen, *Edward James Sawyer*, Thomas Cooper Library, University of South Carolina (1996).

149. See articles from *(Columbia) State*: "A Ghastly Assemblage," September 30, 1892; "The Eve of the Battle," November 8, 1892; "Marlboro," November 9, 1892, "Election Results," November 23, 1892; "Republican Delegates," March 19, 1896; "Republicans Meet Week After Next," September 5, 1922; Sawyer to John Patterson Green, April 24, 1896, John Patterson Green Papers, Western Reserve Historical Society. He served as an alternate to the national convention in 1912. "South Carolina Delegation," politicalgraveyard.com (n. 153).

150. "Marlboro's Forty Calls," *(Columbia) State*, March 13, 1895.

151. "A Pair of Macs," *(Columbia) State*, March 20, 1895.

152. "The Pee Dee Colored Leader," *(Columbia) State*, June 5, 1895.

153. "Marlboro Matters," *(Columbia) State*, August 20, 1895.

154. "Matters in Marlboro," *(Columbia) State*, May 21, 1892; "The Pee Dee Colored Leader," *(Columbia) State*, June 5, 1895.

155. "As to Lynchings," *(Columbia) State*, August 11, 1897.

156. See articles from *(Columbia) State*: "J. E. Sawyer [*sic*]," May 11, 1929; "Negro Farmers Organize," August 17, 1910; "Colored State Fair," November 5, 1911; "State Colored Fair Association," October 3, 1914. See also articles from *Palmetto Leader*: "Colored State Fair," August 13, 1927; "Seventh Conclave," October 22, 1927; "Masonic Grand Lodge Buys Stock," December 24, 1927.

157. "J. E. Sawyer [*sic*]," *(Columbia) State*, May 11, 1929.

158. O. Vernon Burton, *In My Father's House Are Many Mansions: Family and Community in Edgefield, South Carolina* (Chapel Hill: University of North Carolina Press, 1987). He was on the state party executive committee in 1888. "The South Carolina Republican State" *(Sumter) Watchman and Southron*, March 7, 1888.

159. *Grand Rally of Republicans held at Walhalla, Oconee County, S.C., November 1, 1888* (Des Moines, Iowa: Register Printing House, 1889), 4–5 (Hayes Presidential Center Library, Fremont, Ohio).

160. See John C. Blythe, "Paris Simkins Home," National Register of Historic Places—Nomination Form (n.d., in the author's possession), citing interview with C. Bruce Bailey (January 18, 1984).

161. See Felicia Flemming-McCall, *African Americans of Chesterfield County* (Mount Pleasant, S.C.: Arcadia, 2008), 13; Thirteenth United States Census, 1910, Population, S.C., Chesterfield County; Fourteenth United States Census, 1920, Population, S.C., Chesterfield County, available at ancestry.com; "Chesterfield," *(Columbia) State*, September 15, 1898.

162. Death Certificate of Major McFarlan, No. 2274, State of South Carolina, County of Chesterfield, February 6, 1923.

163. House of Representatives, *Miller vs. Elliott*, 51st Cong., 1st Sess., June 20, 1890, House Rep. No. 2502, 17.

164. See *Proceedings and Returns of the State Board of Canvassers, 1868–1929*, November 1, 1890, vol. 1, 314, SCDAH.

165. *Hill v. Garrett*, 83 S.C. 572 (1909); *Huguenin v. Cont'l Cas. Co.*, 94 S.C. 138 (1913).

166. S. C. Armstrong, *Hampton Normal and Agricultural Institute* (Hampton, Va.: Normal School Press, 1891), 136.

167. "To Be Africanized," *Manning Times*, August 4, 1897.

168. Armstrong, *Hampton Normal and Agricultural Institute*, 136.

169. "Court," *Manning Times*, March 9, 1898 (his client was convicted of housebreaking, larceny, and arson in a trial that drew the interest of both white and black citizens); Twelfth United States Census, 1900, Population, S.C., Clarendon County, available at ancestry.com; *Report of M. R. Cooper, Secretary of State to the General Assembly of South Carolina for the Fiscal Year Beginning January 1, 1900 and Ending December 31, 1900* (Columbia: State, 1901), 798.

170. *Twenty-Fifth Annual Report of the United States Civil Service Commission for the Year Ended June 30, 1908* (Washington, D.C: Government Printing Office, 1909), 142.

171. Fifteenth United States Census, 1930, Population, Washington, D.C., available at ancestry.com.

172. "Eleven New Lawyers," *(Columbia) State*, May 22, 1896.

173. "The Colored Preachers," *(Orangeburg) Times and Democrat*, December 13, 1905, 8; "Claflin University," *(Orangeburg) Times and Democrat*, April 24, 1908, 8; "Colored Preachers," *(Orangeburg) Times and Democrat*, December 3, 1910, 1; "Summer School for Negro Teachers," *(Sumter) Watchman and Southron*, June 19, 1901, 1. See also Mather, *Who's Who of the Colored Race*, 52.

174. "For Unregistered Negroes," *(Columbia) State*, March 25, 1895; "Advised to Scatter," *(Columbia) State*, January 12, 1896, 3.

175. "Double Republicans," *Anderson Intelligencer*, September 23, 1896, 2.

176. "As to Lynchings," *(Columbia) State*, August 11, 1897.

177. See, e.g., "Intemperance and the Negro," *(Columbia) State*, January 26, 1907. See Death Certificate of E. B. Burroughs, June 16, 1919, Certificate No. 11167, State of South Carolina, available at ancestry.com.

178. Straker, *New South Investigated*, 58–61, 72 (quotation), 66, 87, 64.

CHAPTER 8. A Last Stand

1. See generally *The Election of 1880 in South Carolina: Address of the State Executive Committee of the Union Republican Party of South Carolina* (Charleston: J. W. Hammond, 1880) (describing widespread violence against black and Republican voters during 1880 elections); "South Carolina in 1878," *Report of the United States Senate Committee to Inquire into Alleged Frauds and Violence in the Elections of 1878*, Vol. II, 45th Cong., 3d sess. (Washington, D.C.: Government Printing Office, 1879) (collecting testimony of fraud and violence during the 1878 elections).

2. Lou Falkner Williams, *The Great South Carolina Ku Klux Klan Trials* (Athens: University of Georgia Press, 1996), 144–45; 1884 S.C. Att'y Gen. Rep. 562.

3. Act No. 229, 1883 S.C. Acts 360, 365.

4. Williams, *Great South Carolina Ku Klux Klan Trials,* 145.

5. Edward McCrady Jr., *The Necessity of Raising the Standard of Citizenship and the Right of the General Assembly of the State of South Carolina to Impose Qualifications upon Electors* (Charleston: Walker, Evans & Cogswell, 1881), 38.

6. See generally George Brown Tindall, *South Carolina Negroes, 1877–1900* (Columbia: University of South Carolina Press, 2002), 68–91.

7. Act No. 717, 1882 S.C. Acts 1110, 1111–12; Walter Edgar, *South Carolina: A History* (Columbia: University of South Carolina Press, 1998), 414.

8. Act No. 717, 1882 S.C. Acts 1113.

9. *An Act to Raise Supplies and Make Appropriations for the Fiscal Year Commencing November 1, 1878*, 1878 S.C. Acts 793, 797.

10. Tindall, *South Carolina Negroes,* 69.

11. Act No. 717, 1882 S.C. Acts 1113.

12. Edgar, *South Carolina,* 413. For examples of altered precincts, see Act No. 171, 1879 S.C Acts 169; Act No. 177, 1879 S.C. Acts 174; Act No. 242, 1880 S.C. Acts 285.

13. Tindall, *South Carolina Negroes,* 69; Edgar, *South Carolina,* 414.

14. Act No. 9, 1888 S.C. Acts 10; *Rules for Governing the Membership of Democratic Clubs, the Qualification of Voters and Conduct of Primary Elections of the Democratic Party of South Carolina* (Columbia: Charles A. Calvo Jr., 1892).

15. *Rules for Governing the Membership of Democratic Clubs,* 1.

16. Tindall, *South Carolina Negroes,* 72; see generally Letters Received by the Department of Justice from South Carolina, 1871–1884 (describing ongoing Department of Justice efforts) and Letters Sent by the Department of Justice: Instructions to U.S. Attorney Generals and Marshals, 1867–1904, Publication 701, microform, National Archives Microfilm Publications (1967).

17. *Ex parte Mackey,* 15 S.C. 322 (1881); *Ex parte Elliott,* 33 S.C. 602 (1890).

18. Tindall, *South Carolina Negroes,* 73.

19. House of Representatives, *Recent Election in South Carolina*, 44th Cong., 2nd Sess., House Misc. Doc. 44–31 (Washington, D.C.: Government Printing Office, 1877). These lawyers were Macon B. Allen, S. J. Bampfield, James Bowley, Laurence Cain, R. B. Elliott, John Humbert, Henry Johnson, W. R. Jones, Samuel J. Lee, John Mardenborough, Thomas Miller, W. F. Myers, Paris Simkins, D. A. Straker, and J. J. Wright.

20. Chester H. Rowell, *A Historical and Legal Digest of All the Contested Election Cases in the House of Representatives of the United States from the First to the Fifty-sixth Congress, 1789–1901* (Westport, Conn.: Greenwood, 1976), 381–87.

21. This was the first standing committee created by the House. It was charged with examining and reporting on the certificates of election and other credentials of the members. *Annals of the Congress of the United States*, 1st Cong., 1st Sess., 1789, 122.

22. Rowell, *Historical and Legal Digest*, 381.

23. Also in 1888, black lawyer Seymour E. Smith ran against Democrat George D. Tillman for Congress in the Fifth Congressional District and contested his defeat on the grounds that the registration laws effectively disenfranchised black voters. See "Smith to Contest," *Manning Times*, November 21, 1888, 4. Apparently his contest was abandoned.

24. Rowell, *Historical and Legal Digest*, 461, 464. The overwhelming vote was the result of a boycott by the Democrats.

25. Minutes of the State Board of Canvassers of the State of South Carolina (hereafter cited as MSBC), November 1, 1890, vol. 1, 300, SCDAH. Miller's lawyers in this contest were two white Republicans, Abial Lathrop and John Wingate.

26. MSBC, 1:321, 318–19.

27. *Ex parte Elliott*, 33 S.C. 602 (1890).

28. Rowell, *Historical and Legal Digest*, 480–82.

29. "The Murray Moise Contest," *(Columbia) State*, November 26, 1892.

30. "A Political Sensation," *(Columbia) State*, November 27, 1892.

31. Tindall, *South Carolina Negroes*, 57.

32. Marszalek, *A Black Congressman in the Age of Jim Crow: South Carolina's George Washington Murray* (Gainesville: University Press of Florida, 2006), 48–50.

33. MSBC, 1:498.

34. Minutes of Board of Canvassers for Federal Election, November 13, 1894, Election Commission State Board of Canvassers, Protests of Elections 1868–1962, p. 1894, SCDAH.

35. "The Final Figures on the Vote," *(Sumter) Watchman and Southron*, November 28, 1894; "The Board at Work," *(Columbia) State*, November 22, 1894.

36. Rowell, *Historical and Legal Digest*, 543.

37. MSBC, 1:495.

38. Rowell, *Historical and Legal Digest*, 542.

39. MSBC, 1:498.

40. "Contest from Seventh Congressional District," *(Sumter) Watchman and Southron*, October 20, 1897.

41. Rowell, *Historical and Legal Digest*, 531.

42. Tindall, *South Carolina Negroes*, 62–63.

43. Thomas Wheeler, James Wigg, and A. S. Bascomb served as commissioner in Beaufort, and G. E. Herriott served as Georgetown's school head until 1902. See Minutes of the State Board of Canvassers, 1:502, 505.

44. Ibid., 1:384, 410, 502, 581, 595.

45. John Marszalek, *Black Congressman*, 35–38.

46. See Francis Butler Simkins, *Pitchfork Ben Tillman* (Columbia: University of

South Carolina Press, 2002), 151–68. See also Stephen Kantrowitz, *Ben Tillman and the Reconstruction of White Supremacy* (Chapel Hill: University of North Carolina Press, 2000), 162, where the author describes a Tillman campaign in which he boasted of having murdered black Republicans.

47. Kantrowitz, *Ben Tillman,* 198.

48. Tindall, *South Carolina Negroes,* 73–74.

49. Joint Resolution No. 9 (December 19, 1892), 21 S.C. Acts 6.

50. Tindall, *South Carolina Negroes,* 73–74.

51. "A Ghastly Assemblage," *(Columbia) State*, September 30, 1892.

52. These were S. E. Smith, R. A. Stewart, W. F. Myers, Paris Simkins, Z. D. Greene, C. G. Garrett, J. H. Fordham, and J. W. Morris.

53. "An Appeal to Caesar," *(Columbia) State*, May 19, 1893. These lawyers included E. J. Dickerson, R. A. Stewart, T. A. Saxon, J. H. Fordham, J. W. Morris, and E. C. C. Washington.

54. No. 717 Sec. 3, Statutes at Large of S.C. 1882.

55. "The Southern Problem," *(New York) Sun*, January 6, 1883.

56. *Ex parte Lumsden*, 41 S.C. 553, 554 (1894). The three plaintiffs' racial identification is based on the census. See Twelfth United States Census, 1900, South Carolina, Richland County, Columbia Ward 3 (stating the race of Lawrence P. Mills) and South Carolina, Richland County, Ward 4 (identifying Cormack as white). The only Lumsden in the census is a Joshua Lumsden in the 1860 census who was listed as a white slave owner. See U.S. Census, 1860, South Carolina, Richland, 29. See also U.S. Census, 1860, Slave Schedule, Columbia, Richland County, 9, available at ancestry.com.

57. *Ex parte Lumsden.*

58. See *Ex parte Wade* in 1894 S.C. Att'y Gen. Rep. 531.

59. See *Ex parte Isaac Hall* in 1894 S.C. Att'y Gen. Rep. 531; *State ex rel. Henry Y. Arnett vs. W. W. Mason, Supervisor of Registration for Richland County; State ex rel. Henry Hopkins vs. W. W. Mason, Supervisor of Registration for Richland County* in 1894 S.C. Att'y Gen. Rep. 531. Arnett's racial identification is based on his photograph and the fact that he was a professor at Allen University. See Richard R. Wright Jr., ed., *Encyclopedia African Methodist Episcopal Church* (1916), 27, available in African American Biographical Database, http://aabd.chadwyck.com. Hopkins was a farmer. See Twelfth United States Census, 1900, Schedule 1, Population, S.C., Richland County, Lower Township, 13B, available at ancestry.com.

60. Tindall, *South Carolina Negroes,* 75–76.

61. "Message of the Governor," *Journal of the Senate of the State of South Carolina* (Columbia: Charles Calvo, 1893), 35.

62. 1894 S.C. Acts 802.

63. "The State's Survey," *(Columbia) State*, March 8, 1895.

64. "A Pair of Macs," *(Columbia) State*, March 20, 1895.

65. "The State's Survey," *(Columbia) State*, March 8, 1895.

66. "Will Prosecute Now," *(Columbia) State*, March 14, 1895.

67. "Another Notary Removed," *(Columbia) State*, March 11, 1895.

68. "A Preacher's Turn," *(Columbia) State*, March 15, 1895.

69. "Will Prosecute Now," *(Columbia) State*, March 14, 1895. Also see "Further Removal of Notaries," *(Sumter) Watchman and Southron*, March 20, 1895.

70. "For Unregistered Negroes," *(Columbia) State*, March 25, 1895.

71. William J. Gaboury, "George Washington Murray and the Fight for Political Democracy in South Carolina," *Journal of Negro History* 62 (July 1977): 258.

72. "What the Negroes Will Do," *(Columbia) State*, March 23, 1895.

73. "The Canary to the Blackbird," *(Columbia) State*, April 1, 1895.

74. John Marszalek, *Black Congressman*, 89.

75. Murray to Whitefield McKinlay, May 3, 1894, quoted in Tindall, *South Carolina Negroes*, 58.

76. "An Unwarranted Appeal," *(Columbia) State*, April 19, 1895.

77. *Mills v. Green*, 67 F. 818, at 833 (C.C.D.S.C. 1895), rev'd, 69 F. 852 (4th Cir. 1895), appeal dismissed, 159 U.S. 651 (1895).

78. *Mills v. Green*, 67 F. 818, at 830.

79. Ibid., 830, 826–29. Judge Goff began with a discussion of the "institution of slavery" and summed up with the observation that "the right of suffrage" should be "exempt from discrimination."

80. *Mills v. Green*, 67 F. at 818, *rev'd*, 69 F. at 852, *appeal dismissed*, 159 U.S. at 651 (quotation).

81. MSBC, 1:527–32.

82. *(Columbia) State*, October 23, 1895, cited in James Lowell Underwood, *The Constitution of South Carolina*, Volume 4: *The Struggle for Political Equality* (Columbia: University of South Carolina Press, 1994), 79–80.

83. "Address of Robert Aldrich on September 10, 1895," *Journal of the Constitutional Convention of the State of South Carolina* (Columbia: Charles A. Calvo Jr., 1895), 2 (hereafter cited parenthetically).

84. Underwood, *Constitution of South Carolina*, 4:68–69.

85. See Krystal J. Williams, "Criminal Disenfranchisement: Taking a Closer Look at Fifteenth Amendment Remediation," *Human Rights and Globalization Law Review* 2 (2008–2009): 75–76.

86. S.C. Const. of 1895, art. II, §6.

87. S.C. Const. of 1868, art. VIII, §8; Edgar, *South Carolina*, 417.

88. Laughlin McDonald, "An Aristocracy of Voters: The Disenfranchisement of Blacks in South Carolina," *South Carolina Law Review* 37 (1986): 557.

89. I. A. Newby, *Black Carolinians: A History of Blacks in South Carolina from 1895 to 1968* (Columbia: University of South Carolina Press, 1973), 30.

90. S.C. Const. of 1895, art. II, §4(d).

91. Newby, *Black Carolinians*, 89.

92. "The State's Survey," *(Columbia) State*, September 24, 1895.

93. See Leon F. Litwack, *Trouble in Mind: Black Southerners in the Age of Jim Crow* (New York: Vintage, 1999), 223–25, 227. In fact, it succeeded in other southern states. Alabama promulgated a new constitution with a literacy test in 1901. Despite being presented with the evidence of the Alabama constitutional convention's racist intent, the U.S. Supreme Court, in an opinion written by Oliver Wendell Holmes, refused

to declare the plan unconstitutional. See *Giles v. Harris*, 189 U.S. 475 (1903). As to the racist intent of the Alabama convention, see the comment on day two of the convention by John Knox, chairman of the convention. See Alabama Legislature, "Constitutional Convention Journals of 1901," Day 2, 8–10, http://www.legislature.state.al.us/aliswww/history/constitutions/1901/journal/NavigationPage.html (accessed September 20, 2016). With the *Giles* decision, the federal role in enforcing black voting rights was more or less extinguished, since Congress had already repealed virtually every provision of the three enforcement acts it had passed in 1870 and 1871 to combat Klan violence and intimidation against black voters. Ch. 25, 28 Stat. 36 (1894).

94. "Negroes Protest," *(Columbia) State*, October 12, 1895, cited in Underwood, *Constitution of South Carolina*, 78.

95. "Smalls and Whipper," *(Columbia) State*, October 27, 1895.

96. Underwood, *Constitution of South Carolina*, IV, 85, 87.

97. Ibid., 86.

98. "Suffrage Problem," *Richmond Dispatch*, October 27, 1895.

99. Underwood, *Constitution of South Carolina*, 4:79 (quotation), 82.

100. Ibid., 89.

101. "The Convention at Work," *Marlboro Democrat*, September 25, 1895.

102. S.C. Const. of 1895, art. II, §10.

103. A 1903 statute provided that a party primary voter had to have registered with the party under its rules. Act No. 8, 1903 S.C. Acts 9.

104. See S.C. Const. of 1895, art. I, §9 and art. II.

105. Edgar, *South Carolina*, 446.

106. See cases reprinted in Rowell, *Historical and Legal Digest*, 381–87, 461–64, 530–34.

107. Ibid., 461–64.

108. MSBC, 1:579.

109. See Tindall, *South Carolina Negroes*, 89–90.

110. MSBC, 1:578.

111. Ibid., 1:583, 2:22, 73, 135, 208, 253.

112. The county was 77 percent black in the 1900 Census. See Twelfth United States Census, 1900, Population, Part 1, S.C., Georgetown County, available at ancestry.com.

113. MSBC, 1:581, 2:20, 13, 70, 133, 206, 2.

114. See *Report of the Population of the U.S. at the Eleventh Census, 1890*, Vol. 1 (Washington, D.C.: Government Printing Office, 1891), 38; *Twelfth Census of the U.S. Taken in the Year 1900, Population, Part 1* (Washington, D.C.: U.S. Census Office, 1901), 555; *Thirteenth Census of the U.S., General Reports and Analysis, Vol. 1* (Washington, D.C.: Government Printing Office, 1913), 242. With a peak population of 35,495 in 1900, the county had declined to 22,269 in 1920. All of the decline was in the black population.

115. Minutes of the State Board of Canvassers of the State of South Carolina, Contested, Results of the Election of November 3, 1896, 542–73, SCDAH.

116. MSBC, 1:554–55. Also see "All About Aiken," *(Columbia) State*, November 29, 1896; "The Final Figures," *Abbeville Press and Banner*, December 2, 1896.

117. MSBC, 1:547. (Edwards and Sasportas on behalf of G. W. Murray in the First Con-

gressional District protesting the reopening of the counting of ballots after the result had been certified, November 10, 1896.)

118. MSBC, 1:554–73.

119. *New York Times*, "The South Carolina Vote," February 7, 1897, 1.

120. *Butler v. Ellerbe*, 44 S.C. 256, 281 (1895).

121. *Sproule v. Fredericks*, 11 So. 472, 475 (1892).

122. Rowell, *Historical and Legal Digest*, 540–41.

123. There is no record of these candidates appealing their cases to the congressional committees. They all lost before the state Board of Canvassers.

124. *Reports and Resolutions to the South Carolina General Assembly*, part 1 (Columbia: Bryan, 1899), 252.

125. MSBC, 2:15, 6–12.

126. *Reports and Resolutions to the South Carolina General Assembly*, part 1, 255.

127. MSBC, 2:86.

128. *Reports and Resolutions to the South Carolina General Assembly*, vol. 2 (Columbia: State, 1901), 798.

129. See generally, Merrill Moores, coll., *A Historical and Legal Digest of All the Contested Election Cases in the House of Representatives of the United States from the Fifty-Seventh to and Including the Sixty-Fourth Congress, 1901–1917* (Washington, D.C.: Government Printing Office, 1917) (reporting contested cases in Congress, 1901–17); Rowell, *Historical and Legal Digest* (reporting several contested cases in the Fifty-Sixth Congress, 1899–1901).

130. MSBC, 2:524.

131. *Reports and Resolutions to the South Carolina General Assembly* (Columbia: State, 1903), 1372.

132. Ibid., 80, 82, 85.

133. "Colored Congressmen Contesting for Seats," *(Washington, D.C.) Colored American*, January 23, 1904.

134. S.C. Election Commission Protests and Appeals of Elections, 1904, File S155019, SCDAH.

135. The March 18, 1904, House of Representatives Report Number 1740 was cited in this report. H.R. Rep. No. 4781, at 1–3 (1906).

136. March 18, 1904, House of Representatives Report Number 1740 as a precedent: *Isaac Myers v. J. O. Patterson* (Second Congressional District, November 8, 1904).

137. MSBC, 2:248.

138. S.C. Election Commission Protests and Appeals of Elections, November 3, 1908.

139. See Brief of Defendant in Error, *Brownfield v. South Carolina*, 189 U.S. 426 (1903).

140. Moores, *Historical and Legal Digest*, 25–27.

141. Moorer cases: House Committee on Elections, *Contest of Isaac Myers v. James O'H. Patterson, South Carolina: Hearings on H.R. 4780*, 59th Cong., 1st sess., 1906, 1–4 (Second Congressional District); House Committee on Elections, *Contest of Alexander D. Dantzler v. Asbury F. Lever, South Carolina: Hearings on H.R. 1817*, 60th Cong., 2nd sess., 1909, 1–4 (Seventh Congressional District, November 6, 1906); House Committee on Elections, *Contest of Isaac Myers v. J. O. Patterson, South Carolina: Hearings*

on H.R. 1819, 60th Cong., 2nd sess., 1909, 1–5 (Second Congressional District, November 6, 1906); House Committee on Elections, *Contested Election of R. H. Richardson v. Asbury F. Lever, South Carolina: H.R. 1638,* 61st Cong., 2nd sess., 1910, 1–7 (Seventh Congressional District, November 3, 1908); House Committee on Elections, *Contested Election of Isaac Myers v. J. O. Patterson, South Carolina: Hearings on H.R. 1640,* 61st Cong., 2nd sess., 1910, 1–4 (Second Congressional District, November 3, 1908). Moorer argued *Myers v. Patterson* and *Richardson v. Lever* from the 1908 election cases before the House committee in 1910.

142. Moores, *Historical and Legal Digest,* 92.

143. MSBC, 2:516.

144. "All Amendments Given 'Yea' Vote," *(Columbia) Record,* November 17, 1920.

145. For example, in 1916 black Republican Isaac Myers ran in the Second Congressional District, and black Republican I. S. Leevy ran in the Seventh Congressional District. But the elections were not contested. See Records of the Election Commission, vol. 2, supra note 138, at 459. In 1918 black Republican R. H. Richardson ran in the Seventh Congressional District and lost but did not contest the election. Ibid., 481. In 1924 black Republican Jesse E. Beard lost in the First Congressional District but did not contest the election. Ibid., 556–57. In 1944 black Progressive Democrat Osceola McKaine ran against Olin D. Johnston for the U.S. Senate and filed no appeal from his loss. See Supplemental Report of the Secretary of State, Election November 7, 1944, 10–13; see also Miles S. Richards, "Osceola E. McKaine and the Struggle for Black Civil Rights, 1917–1946" (PhD diss., University of South Carolina, 1994), 169, 192–204. And in 1946 black Republican I. S. Leevy ran for Congress in the Second Congressional District, and black candidate James E. Prioleau ran in the Sixth Congressional District. Neither contested their election. Supplemental Report of the Secretary of State, Election November 5, 1946, in *Reports and Resolutions of South Carolina to the General Assembly* (Columbia: Joint Committee of Printing, n.d.), 5–7.

CHAPTER 9. From the Great Migration to the Great Depression

1. Act No. 63, 1896 S.C. Acts 171.

2. S.C. Const. of 1895, art. III, §33. Criminal Code, Chap. XV sec. 385.

3. Act No. 483, 1898 S.C. Acts 777.

4. XXI secs. 672–74 and Chap. XII sec. 315.

5. Act No. 52, 1906 S.C. Acts 76; Civ. C. sec. 3266, 1912.

6. I. A. Newby, *Black Carolinians: A History of Blacks in South Carolina from 1895 to 1968* (Columbia: University of South Carolina Press, 1973), 47, 46.

7. Act No. 69, 1915 S.C. Acts 79.

8. Act No. 20, 1917 S.C. Acts 48.

9. Act No. 893, 1934 S.C. Acts 1536.

10. S.C. Code 1924 (33) 895.

11. Act No. 110, 1911 S.C. Acts 169; Act No. 246, 1900 S.C. Acts 443.

12. S.C. Const. of 1895, art. II, §10.

13. Act No. 25, 1896 S.C. Acts 56; Act No. 105, 1896 S.C. Acts 223; Act No. 438, 1898

S.C. Acts 702; Act No. 211, 1900 S.C. Acts 375; Act No. 348, 1901 S.C. Acts 612; Act No. 8, 1903 S.C. Acts 9; Act No. 73, 1903 S.C. Acts 112–13.

14. George Brown Tindall, *South Carolina Negroes, 1877–1900* (Columbia: University of South Carolina Press, 2002), 256–58.

15. "Mistrial Resulted," *(Columbia) State*, April 23, 1899.

16. "Severe Arrangements," *(Columbia) State*, April 20, 1899.

17. Newby, *Black Carolinians*, 53–59, 192.

18. Leon F. Litwack, *Trouble in Mind: Black Southerners in the Age of Jim Crow* (New York: Vintage, 1999), xiv.

19. Peter F. Lau, *Democracy Rising: South Carolina and the Fight for Black Equality since 1865* (Lexington: University of Kentucky Press, 2006), 16–17.

20. David Duncan Wallace, *The History of South Carolina*, vol. 3 (New York: American Historical Society, 1935), 400n15.

21. Act No. 514, 1898 S.C. Acts 812. Also see *State v. Napier*, 63 S.C. 60, 41 SE 13 (1902); *State v. Bates*, 101 SE 651 (S.C. 1919); *State v. Reeves*, 112 S.C. 383, 99 SE 841 (1919).

22. Lau, *Democracy Rising*, 26.

23. *State v. Brownfield*, 60 S.C. 509 (1901), *aff'd sub nom. Brownfield v. State of S.C.*, 189 U.S. 426 (1903).

24. "Plain Statement," *(Columbia) State*, May 3, 1900.

25. "Thomas Convicted," *(Columbia) State*, June 1, 1900.

26. "Death of a Cultured Colored Woman," *(Columbia) State*, October 19, 1901.

27. "Whipper Counsels Lawbreaking," *(Columbia) State*, March 9, 1902.

28. "South Carolina Supreme Court," *(Columbia) State*, August 23, 1907.

29. *State v. Mack*, 77 S.C. 388 (1907).

30. Demps Whipper Powell, "A Providential Revelation, Relationship with the Whipper Family," March 1, 1940, Leigh Whipper Papers, Moorland-Spingarn Research Center, Howard University, Washington, D.C.

31. A. B. Caldwell, ed., *History of the American Negro, South Carolina Edition*, vol. 3 (Atlanta: A. B. Caldwell, 1919), 512–13.

32. *Ex parte District Grand Lodge, No. 13, G.U.O.O.F. et al. v. People Federation Bank, et al.*, 147 S.C. 103 (1928).

33. "Death of Attorney, J. I. Washington," *Beaufort Gazette*, January 17, 1938.

34. U.S. Social Security Death Index, September 1967, available at ancestry.com.

35. "Notes from Beaufort," *Palmetto Leader*, May 2, 1925.

36. "Beaufort Lawyer Points to Record," *Palmetto Leader*, March 28, 1925.

37. N. Louis Bailey, Mary L. Morgan, and Carolyn R. Taylor, eds., *Biographical Directory of the South Carolina Senate*, vol. 2 (Columbia: University of South Carolina Press, 1986), 1185.

38. He was co-counsel with J. H. Fordham, J. C. Whittaker, J. L. Mitchell, and John H. Ostendorf. "Contests from Seventh Congressional District," *(Sumter) Watchman and Southron*, October 20, 1897.

39. Chester Rowell, *A Historical and Legal Digest of Contested Election Cases in the House of Representatives of the U.S. from the First to the Fifty-Sixth Congress* (Washington, D.C.: Government Printing Office, 1901), 530–34.

40. "South Carolina News and Gossip," (Columbia) *State,* April 11, 1903; "Delegates Elected to Republican Convention," *Keowee Courier,* March 9, 1904; "Capers on Deck," *Marlboro Democrat,* August 17, 1906; "Republicans Row," (Columbia) *State,* April 29, 1908.

41. "Negro Business Men," (Columbia) *State,* July 4, 1910; "Emancipation Day," (Columbia) *State,* December 31, 1913.

42. *Biographical Directory of the South Carolina Senate,* 2:1185.

43. *Huguenin v. Continental Casualty Co.,* 94 S.C. 138 (1913); *Hill v. Garrett,* 83 S.C. 572 (1909).

44. William C. Hine, "South Carolina State University," in Walter Edgar, ed., *The South Carolina Encyclopedia* (Columbia: University of South Carolina Press, 2006), 905. Because of the racial designation as well as the convoluted name, the school became known as "State College."

45. E. J. E. Wallace to Whitefield McKinley, October 2, 1910, NAACP Papers.

46. Miller to Frances Blascoer, December 5, 1910, NAACP Papers.

47. *Wall v. Chelsea Plantation Club,* 88 S.C. 434 (1911).

48. Miller to Blascoer, January 31, 1911, NAACP Papers.

49. See *State v. Ferebee,* 109 S.C. 117 (1918); *State v. Ferebee,* 115 S.C. 235 (1920); *State v. Ferebee,* 115 S.C. 235 (1920); *Slave Narratives: A Folk History of Slavery in the United States from Interviews with Former Slaves,* State of South Carolina, Interviewee: Miller, T. E., Works Project Administration, Federal Writers Project, available at ancestry.com.

50. Newby, *Black Carolinians,* 158–59.

51. William C. Hine, "Thomas Ezekiel Miller," in Edgar, *South Carolina Encyclopedia,* 636. Also see Standard Certificate of Death, State of South Carolina, File No. 5053, April 9, 1938, available at ancestry.com.

52. On Aiken County Criminal Docket (SCDAH): *State v. Johnson Carroll* (Ct. Gen. Sess., April Term 1888); *State v. Sanford Arnold* (Ct. Gen. Sess., April Term 1888); *State v. Sam Cummings* (Ct. Gen. Sess., April Term 1888); *State v. Lewis Brown* (Ct. Gen. Sess., April Term 1891); *State v. Sam Oliver* (Ct. Gen. Sess., April Term 1891); *State v. Charles Morgan* (Ct. Gen. Sess., September Term 1892); *State v. George Washington* (Ct. Gen. Sess., April Term 1893); *State v. Dickey Branch* (Ct. Gen. Sess., April Term 1894); *State v. Milledge Price* (Ct. Gen. Sess., April Term 1894); *State v. Sandy Jackson* (Ct. Gen. Sess., June Term 1895); *State v. John Stewart, John Small and Britton Madison* (Ct. Gen. Sess., April Term 1896) (nol pros of Small and Madison and not guilty for John Stewart); *State v. Henry Coker* (Ct. Gen. Sess., February Term 1897); *State v. Lucius Ivey* (Ct. Gen. Sess., October Term 1898); *State v. John Cuthberton* (Ct. Gen. Sess., February Term 1902) (not guilty); *State v. Henry Scott* (Ct. Gen. Sess., June Term 1902); *State v. Willie Thomas* (Ct. Gen. Sess., October Term 1904). Aiken County Civil Journal (SCDAH): *Maria Williams v. George Ealey* (Ct. Com. Pl., April Term 1891); *Samuel Spencer v. Octavia Spencer* (Ct. Com. Pl., September Term 1891); *Otis & John Chafee Copartners as Chaffee Bros. v. Solomon Lockhart* (Ct. Com. Pl., October Term 1906–April Term 1907); *Sophia Dickerson v. Henry Bronson* (Ct. Com. Pl., November Term 1905–April Term 1907).

53. "All About Aiken," *(Columbia) State*, November 29, 1896; "On the Black List," *(Columbia) State*, August 2, 1897.

54. "The Carolina Contests," *(Columbia) State*, December 16, 1897.

55. "Negroes Rule Republican Party," *(Columbia) State*, October 4, 1900.

56. "Death of Well Known Negro," *(Columbia) State*, January 27, 1907.

57. *Charleston City Directory* (Livonia, Mich.: R. L. Polk, 1902); Death Certificate of R. C. Browne, July 31, 1915, File No. 13240, State of South Carolina.

58. *Charleston City Directory* (Livonia, Mich.: R. L. Polk, 1898).

59. Caldwell, *History of the American Negro*, 3:704–5. See also Thirteenth United States Census, 1910, Population, S.C., Georgetown County, available at ancestry.com.

60. Georgetown County Criminal Dockets and Civil Journal (1901–1908), SCDAH.

61. *Charleston City Directory* (Livonia, Mich.: R. L. Polk, 1915).

62. *Seabrook v. Mostowitz*, 51 S.C. 433 (1898); *State v. Washington*, 55 S.C. 372 (1899); *Easton v. Woodburry*, 71 S.C. 250 (1905); *Pyross v. Fraser*, 82 S.C. 498 (1909); *State v. Lucas*, 88 520 (1911); *State v. Baxter*, 88 S.C. 545 (1911); *Jackson v. S.C. Colored State Fair*, 109 S.C. 283 (1918); *Peets v. Wright*, 117 S.C. 409 (1921); *Roberts v. Drayton*, 121 S.C. 124 (1922); *Ex parte Mercer*, 129 S.C. 531 (1924); *People's Federation Bank v. English*, 133 S.C. 129 (1925).

63. "File Two Protests," *(Columbia) State*, November 13, 1920.

64. *Charleston City Directory* (Livonia, Mich.: R. L. Polk, 1934).

65. Death Certificate of Thaddeus St. Mark Sasportas, October 12, 1937, File No. 14799, Charleston County, State of South Carolina.

66. Twelfth United States Census, 1900, Population, Pa., Philadelphia County, Philadelphia, available at ancestry.com.

67. *New York City Directory for Manhattan and Bronx* (1903), 775, available at ancestry.com.

68. Twelfth United States Census, 1900, Population, N.C., Wake County, Raleigh, available at ancestry.com.

In 1910 he was employed as a letter carrier. Thirteenth United States Census, 1910, Population, N.C., Wake County, Raleigh, available at ancestry.com.

69. *Singleton v. Progressive Ben. Assn.*, 77 S.C. 531 (1907).

70. See Ct. of Common Pleas (Berkeley County) Bar Calendar No. 1, Vol. 2, 1906–1918; *(Columbia) State*, September 7, 1904; *State v. Dalby*, 86 S.C. 367 (1910); *State v. Davis*, 86 S.C. 208 (1910); *State v. Cokley*, 83 S.C. 197 (1910).

71. Louis Venters, "'Most Great Reconstruction'": The Baha'i Faith in Jim Crow South Carolina, 1898–1965" (PhD diss., University of South Carolina, 2010).

72. *State v. Glover*, 90 S.C. 166 (1911).

73. See Court of Common Pleas of Berkeley County, Bar Calendar no. 2 1883–1922; *State v. Kenney*, 77 S.C. 236 (1907); "New Trial Refuesed [*sic*] Kenny [*sic*]," *(Sumter) Watchman and Southron*, July 3, 1907.

74. "Charleston News Gathered," *(Columbia) State*, December 14, 1909.

75. *State v. Glover*, 91 S.C. 562 (1912).

76. Certificate of Death, State of S.C., County of Dorchester, #4441 (April 1, 1915).

77. "Stole the Guard's Clothes," *(Columbia) State*, May 17, 1897; Twelfth United States Census, 1900, Population, S.C., Fairfield County; Thirteenth United States Census, 1910, Population, S.C., Richland County, Columbia, available at ancestry.com.

78. May C. Nereny to Butler Nance, July 1, 1915, NAACP Papers.

79. See Butler Nance to John R. Shillady, January 24, 1919, NAACP Papers.

80. Butler Nance to Moorfield Story, May 9, 1919, NAACP Papers.

81. Memorandum, on Butler Nance letterhead from the Columbia Branch, May 20, 1919, NAACP Papers.

82. "Negroes Appeal to County Court," *(Columbia) State*, September 16, 1920.

83. A number of his cases required legal notices to be published in the newspaper. See *(Columbia) State*, (n.t.), February 11, 1919, June 20, 1920, September 2, 1920, December 14, 1920, November 13, 1921, and July 19, 1922.

84. *Peets v. Wright*, 117 S.C. 409 (1921); *Frederick, et al. v. Brown et al.*, 115 S.C. 415 (1921); *Jackson v. South Carolina Colored State Fair Association, et al.*, 109 S.C. 283 (May 14, 1918).

85. See handwritten note from R. W. Jackson, Secretary of the Local Branch of the NAACP, NAACP Papers (received February 21, 1923).

86. Frank Lincoln Mather, *Who's Who of the Colored Race: A General Biographical Dictionary of Men and Women of African Descent* (Chicago: F. L. Mather, 1915), 10.

87. Letter to W. E. B. DuBois, October 26, 1916, NAACP Papers.

88. "A New Negro Paper," *(Sumter) Watchman and Southron*, October 23, 1903; "Summer Schools for the Negroes," *(Columbia) State*, June 22, 1899; "Board of Education Meeting," *(Sumter) Watchman and Southron*, September 19, 1900; "Realty Company Forming," *(Columbia) State*, February 14, 1914. As to real estate transactions, see "Real Estate Transfers" column in *(Sumter) Watchman and Southron*, March 12, May 14, May 21, and June 1, 1910; February 15, 1911; November 5, 1913; and February 3, 1915. Two other references to Andrews's real estate came when his property was damaged by fire. *"Newspaper Plant Burned to Ground," (Columbia) State*, June 19, 1921; "News of Sumter," (Columbia) State, January 6, 1922; "Change of Business," *(Sumter) Watchman and Southron*, May 6, 1896; "New Enterprises," *(Columbia) State*, October 1, 1912. See also Mather, *Who's Who of the Colored Race*, 10.

89. *Andrews v. Willson*, 87 S.C. 301 (1910); Reynolds v. Price, 88 S.C. 525 (1911); *Osteen v. Bultman*, 94 S.C. 496 (1913).

90. "See Here, Ye 'Ultras'!" *(Columbia) State*, March 8, 1895.

91. "Negroes Protest," *(Columbia) State*, October 12, 1895.

92. (n.t.), *(Sumter) Watchman and Southron*, April 26, 1905; "Race Conference," *(Columbia) State*, January 23, 1907; "Negro Race Conference," January 28, 1911; "Race Conference Begins," *(Columbia) State*, February 5, 1917; (n.t.), *Seattle Republican*, June 7, 1907.

93. "Negro Grand Lodge," *(Columbia) State*, July 30, 1914; "The Colored Masons," *(Columbia) State*, June 25, 1901; "Want Real Reformatory," *(Sumter) Watchman and Southron*, January 29, 1916.

94. "Seventh District Delegates," *(Columbia) State*, April 28, 1908; "South Carolina Promises to Help Col. Roosevelt," *Washington Times*, April 19, 1912.

95. "Washington Again Elected," *(Columbia) State*, August 20, 1911.

96. "Booker Washington's Visit," *(Sumter) Watchman and Southron*, March 13, 1909.

97. "Negro Lawyers Organize," *(Columbia) State*, August 18, 1911.

98. W. T. Andrews to Chapin Brinsmade, July 23, 1914, and August 15, 1914, NAACP Papers.

99. W. T. Andrews to Roy Nash, November 21, 1916, NAACP Papers.

100. "Race Conference Begins," *(Columbia) State*, February 5, 1917.

101. Lester C. Lamon, "W. T. Andrews Explains the Causes of Black Migration from the South," *Journal of Negro History* 63 (1978): 366.

102. "Subscription from Baltimore," *(Sumter) Watchman and Southron*, April 17, 1918; "Colored Officers and the Regular Army," *(Chicago) Broadax*, May 17, 1919.

103. Professional Card listing in *(Charleston) Afro-American Citizen*, January 17, 1900.

104. *McWhite v. The Atlantic Coast Line Railroad Co.* and *Couser v. The Atlantic Coast Line Railroad*, Sumter County Pleadings and Judgments Book 1 (Ct. Com. Pl.), 369–72, SCDAH.

105. *Pooler v. Smith*, 73 S.C. 102 (1905); *Kiddell v. Bristow*, 67 S.C. 175 (1903).

106. "Colored Cotton Mill," *(Columbia) State*, October 29, 1897; "Citizens Furniture Co. Opens," *Palmetto Leader*, August 6, 1927; "Editor Green Jackson," *(Columbia) State*, May 20, 1904. See also "Editor Jackson Gets Bail," *(Sumter) Watchman and Southron*, October 28, 1908, as to his dispute with W. T. Andrews from an editorial by Jackson.

107. "The Colored Voters," *(Columbia) State*, March 24, 1894; "Republicans Organize," *(Columbia) State*, January 16, 1896; "Richland's Lily Whites," *(Columbia) State*, April 14, 1896; "Judson Lyons at Allen University," *(Columbia) State*, June 6, 1906; "The Colored State Fair," *(Columbia) State*, November 6, 1913; "The A.M.E. Church," *(Columbia) State*, November 16, 1913; "K. of P.'s Meet in Winnsboro," *Palmetto Leader*, July 9, 1927; "The Local Negro Business League," *Palmetto Leader*, April 30, 1927; "Allen University Notes," *Palmetto Leader*, April 24, 1926; *Jackson v. South Carolina State Colored Fair*, 109 S.C. 283 (1918). His role as administrator of an estate was found in a legal notice. See "Master's Sale," *(Columbia) State*, July 24, 1905.

108. Memorandum, Butler Nance to NAACP, May 20, 1919.

109. *Columbia City Directory* (Richmond, Va.: Hill Directory Co., 1929, 1934); Fifteenth United States Census, 1930, Population, S.C., Richland County, available at ancestry.com.

110. "Local News Paragraphed," *(Sumter) Watchman and Southron*, September 17, 1902.

111. Roll of Attorneys, South Carolina Supreme Court, 1903 (on file with South Carolina Supreme Court, Columbia).

112. "Marion J. Frederick," in Caldwell, *History of the American Negro*, 3:520.

113. "Roster of Cases," *(Sumter) Watchman and Southron*, April 10, 1907.

114. See the following from *(Sumter) Watchman and Southron*: "Roster of Court," April 11, 1906 (1); "Roster of Cases," October 16, 1907 (2); "Roster of Cases," April 1, 1908 (2); "Roster of Cases," October 23, 1912 (1); "Roster of Cases," March 18, 1914 (1); "Roster of Cases," October 31, 1914 (1); "Roster of Cases," March 13, 1915 (1); "Roster of Cases," October 30, 1915 (1); "Roster of Cases," March 15, 1916 (2); "Roster of Cases," March 17, 1917 (1); "Roster of Cases," November 8, 1919 (1); "Roster of Cases," October 10, 1920 (1); "Roster of Cases," July 20, 1921 (2); "Roster of Cases," November 5, 1921 (2); "Roster of

Cases," May 3, 1922; "Roster of Cases," January 7, 1922; "Roster of Cases," November 19, 1919.

115. "Blind Tiger Given the Limit," *(Sumter) Watchman and Southron,* March 5, 1910; "In the Police Court," *(Sumter) Watchman and Southron,* April 22, 1911.

116. *State v. Anderson*, 109 S.C. 211 (1918); *Frederick v. Culler*, 118 S.C. 102 (1921); *Williams v. Wannamaker*, 122 S.C. 368 (1923); *Barley v. Davis*, 123 S.C. 228 (1923).

117. See the following from *(Sumter) Watchman and Southron:* "Sheriff's Sales," October 7, 1908; "Real Estate Transfers," April 24, 1912 (paid $3,450 for a building and lot); "Real Estate Transfers," November 20, 1912 (sold a lot); "Master's Sales," January 10, 1914; "Sales Day Transfers," January 10, 1917.

118. "Several New Concerns," *(Columbia) State,* July 13, 1905 (Sumter Dry Goods Co.); "Booker Washington Day," *(Sumter) Watchman and Southron,* March 20, 1909.

119. "Gin Company," *(Sumter) Watchman and Southron*, May 5, 1920; "New Enterprises," *(Columbia) State*, October 21, 1905.

120. See the following from *(Sumter) Watchman and Southron*: "Men's Day Services," September 11, 1915; "Would Reduce Acreage," October 10, 1914; "Colored Safety Committee," April 18, 1917; "Colored Y.M.C.A. Drive," July 23, 1919; "Annual Clean-Up Week," April 5, 1922; "Afro-American Improvement Association," November 30, 1904. See also "Form New Enterprises," *(Columbia) State*, May 28, 1919.

121. "Negroes Rule the Republican Party," *(Columbia) State*, October 4, 1900; "Roosevelt Endorsed," *(Orangeburg) Times and Democrat*, February 21, 1904; "Much Bickering in Convention," *(Columbia) State*, September 30, 1914; "Republican Delegates Elected," *(Sumter) Watchman and Southron,* February 24, 1912; "Black and Tan Republican Convention," *(Sumter) Watchman and Southron,* September 22, 1922.

122. See Myron Ferguson, Death Certificate 37338, Cuyahoga County, June 20, 1936 (Ohio, Death Certificate). This certificate is supplemented by an affidavit of Marion T. Frederick, son of Marion J. Frederick, to the effect that his father had used the name "Myron Ferguson to conceal his identity" (August 20, 1936).

123. See Roll of Attorneys, 1905; Twelfth United States Census, 1900, Population, S.C., Richland County, available at ancestry.com.

124. "Arthur Wright Given Ten Years," *(Columbia) State,* June 9, 1906.

125. "Abram Davis Acquitted," *(Columbia) State,* September 13, 1907.

126. "Goes to the Pen," *Times and Democrat*, January 21, 1908.

127. *State v. Samuel Gantt,* Fairfield County Criminal Docket (Ct. Gen. Sess., February 1908 Term), SCDAH.

128. J. Clay Smith, *Emancipation: The Making of the Black Lawyer, 1844–1944* (Philadelphia: University of Pennsylvania Press, 1993), 481n171. Adams was admitted to the Washington bar between April 1, 1911, and April 1, 1912. See *Washington Reports* 65 (1912): v.

129. Smith, *Emancipation*, 465.

130. See George James Fleming and Christian E. Burckel, *Who's Who in Colored America* (New York: C. E. Burckel, 1950), 3. Adams lived until 1961. See Nebraska Bar Association, "Proceedings, 1961," *Nebraska Law Review* 42 (1962): 350.

131. Thirteenth United States Census, 1910, Population, S.C., Orangeburg County,

Orangeburg, available at ancestry.com; Roll of Attorneys, 1896; death certificate of Jacob Moorer, State of South Carolina, SCDAH.

132. See Thomas Miller to Francis Blascoer, October 10, 1910, NAACP Papers; "Grand Lodge Officers of South Carolina Pythians," in Clement Richardson, ed., *National Cyclopedia of the Colored Race* (Montgomery, Ala.: National Publishing Co., 1919), 440; Proceedings and Returns of the State Board of Canvassers, 1868–1897, 586, SCDAH.

133. *State v. Perry,* 74 S.C. 551, 556 (1906); *State v. Franklin,* 80 S.C. 332 (1908); *State v. Haigler,* 90 S.C. 319 (1912); *State v. Glover,* 91 S.C. 562 (1912); *In re Williams' Estate,* 98 S.C. 211 (1914); *Fairey v. Haynes,* 101 S.C. 499 (1915) (won); *Fairey v. Haynes,* 107 S.C. 115 (1917) (won); *Little v. Henry,* 108 S.C. 230 (1917); *Conner v. Grand Lodge of Pythias of S.C.,* 107 S.C. 308 (1917); *Fairey v. Haynes,* 111 S.C. 132 (1918); *State v. Walton,* 107 S.C. 353 (1917); *Bellamy v. Grand Lodge,* 110 S.C. 315 (1918); *State v. Danelly,* 116 S.C. 113 (1921) (won); *Cusack v. Sou.R.Co,* 116 S.C. 143 (1921) (won); *Bamberg Banking Co. v. Matthews,* 118 S.C. 83 (1921) (won); *Frederick v. Culler,* 118 S.C. 102 (1921); *Williams v. Wannamaker,* 122 S.C. 368 (1923); *Sandel v. Crum,* 130 S.C. 317 (1924); *Dantzler v. Funderburg,* 129 S.C. 79 (1924); *Simpson v. Antley,* 137 S.C. 380 (1926).

134. See Proceedings and Returns of the State Board of Canvassers, 1898–1929, SCDAH.

135. "Contest Papers Served on Lever," *(Columbia) State,* December 16, 1906, 1.

136. Mamie Garvin Fields and Karen Fields, *Lemon Swamp and Other Places: A Carolina Memoir* (New York: Free Press, 1983), 101–3.

137. Lizelia Augusta Jenkins Moorer, *Prejudice Unveiled* (Boston: Roxburgh, 1907), reprinted in Joan R. Sherman, ed., *Collected Black Women's Poetry* (New York: Oxford University Press, 1988).

138. Sherman, *Collected Black Women's Poetry,* xxxii.

139. See Roll of Attorneys, 1913. Frederick was also admitted in Ohio in 1920 and Michigan in 1924. See Supreme Court of Ohio certificate of admission dated June 15, 1920, and Certificate of the Board of Law Examiners of the State of Michigan, dated January 16, 1924. Copies of these documents were supplied to the author by Natalie Williams, Frederick's granddaughter.

140. *Columbia City Directory* (Richmond, Va.: Hill Directory Co., 1915).

141. "Atty. N. J. Frederick," *Palmetto Leader,* September 10, 1938.

142. See *Palmetto Leader,* January 26, 1926, to January 4, 1930; Joseph J. Boris, ed., *Who's Who in Colored America* (New York: Who's Who in Colored America Corp., 1927), 70.

143. Kerstyn M. Haram, "The Palmetto Leader's Mission to End Lynching in South Carolina: Black Agency and the Black Press in Columbia, 1925–1940," *South Carolina Historical Magazine* 107 (2006): 308.

144. See the following articles from the *Palmetto Leader:* "The Sweets with Bagnall," January 23, 1926 (Ossian Sweet case); "N.A.A.C.P. Branches to Fight Anti-intermarriage Bill," February 6, 1926); "Thirty Years of Lynching," February 27, 1926; "'Birth of A Nation'" Film Barred in Ohio," March 27, 1926; "Mayor Favors Segregation," April 3, 1926; "Sweet Case at Rest," May 15, 1926; "Henry Sweet Acquitted," May 22, 1926; "The Supreme Court's Decision," June 5, 1926; "Sounds Gavel for Citizenship," July 3, 1926;

"Norfolk Branch NAACP Fights Segregation Ordinance," July 17, 1926; "Qualified White Electors Only," August 21, 1926; "Survey of Negro Schools," August 28, 1926; "Three Lynched," October 16, 1926; "And Still They Lynch," November 20, 1926; "Moorfield Story Argued Case," December 4, 1926; "NAACP Opposes Connecticut Law," January 29, 1927; "Grand Jury Finds No Bill," February 5, 1927; February 12, 1927 (five front-page articles about NAACP); "NAACP Wins White Primary Case," March 12, 1927; "NAACP Commended for Victory," March 19, 1927; "Clarence Darrow Addresses D.C. NAACP," March 26, 1927; "New York Police Involved," April 2, 1927; "Procured by L. G. Southard," April 9, 1927; "Colored Citizens Barred from Training Camps," April 16, 1927.

145. "He Is Still Appreciated," *Palmetto Leader*, August 26, 1939.

146. *State v. Sanders*, 103 S.C. 216 (1916).

147. "White Man Was Badly Wounded," *(Columbia) State*, May 26, 1915.

148. "Important Ruling by Judge Townsend," *(Columbia) State*, May 27, 1919.

149. Richland County Court, Judgment Rolls 17676 to 20650 (1926–1930), Richland County Clerk of Court, Columbia, S.C. Frederick had nineteen judgments in those four years.

150. *Richards v. Trezvant*, 185 S.C. 489 (1937); *Floyd v. Victory Sav. Bank*, 185 S.C. 87 (1937); *Leevy v. N.C. Mutual Life Ins. Co.*, 184 S.C. 111 (1937); *Floyd v. Victory Sav. Bank*, 182 S.C. 357 (1937); *Perry v. N.C. Mutual Life Ins. Co.*, 180 S.C. 72 (1936); *State v. Floyd*, 174 S.C. 288 (1934); *In re Brazman's Will*, 172 S.C. 188 (1934); *Derrick v. N.C. Mutual Life Ins. Co.*, 167 S.C. 434 (932); *Edwards v. Grand Lodge, K.P of S.C.*, 166 S.C. 445 (1932); *Washington v. King*, 159 S.C. 431 (1931); *Lemon v. Lemon*, 158 S.C. 71 (1930); *Carolina-Portland Cement Co. v. Calhoun*, 158 S.C. 362 (1930); *Anderson v. Southern Railway Co.*, 157 S.C. 518 (1930); *Guignard Brick Works v. Allen University*, 155 S.C. 507 (1930); *Ex parte Bess*, 152 S.C. 410 (1929); *Roberts v. National Ben. Life Ins. Co. of Washington, D.C.*, 150 S.C. 326 (1929); *Hall v. Grand Lodge, K.P of S.C.*, 148 S.C. 506 (1929); *State v. Lowman*, 134 S.C. 485 (1926); *Robinson v. Grand Lodge, Knights of Pythias of the State of S.C.*, 134 S.C. 86 (1926); *Deadwyler v. Grand Lodge, K.P of S.C.*, 131 S.C. 335 (1925); *Dent v. Bolar*, 125 S.C. 63 (1923); *Williams v. Wannamaker*, 122 S.C. 368 (1923); *Bushardt v. United Inv. Co.*, 121 S.C. 324 (1922); *Bailey v. Free and Accepted Masons of S.C.*, 116 S.C. 263 (1921); *Frederick v. Brown*, 115 S.C. 415 (1921); *Freeman v. Chavis*, 113 S.C. 326 (1920); *Penn v. Atlantic Coast Line R. Co.*, 111 S.C. 499 (1919); *Mimnaugh v. Baker*, 111 S.C. 490 (1919); *Jackson v. S.C. Colored State Fair Ass'n*, 109 S.C. 283 (1918); *McNair v. Alex*, 105 S.C. 445 (1916); *Wesley M.E. Church v. City of Columbia*, 105 S.C. 303 (1916); *State v. Sanders*, 103 S.C. 216 (1916); *Vant v. Grand Lodge, Knights of Pythias of S.C.*, 102 S.C. 413 (1915).

151. The discrepancy in his winning percentages is because he represented the appellee in one case and won.

152. *State v. Floyd*, 174 S.C. 288 (1934); *State v. Lowman*, 134 S.C. 485 (1926); *Ex parte Bess*, 152 S.C. 410 (1929); *State v. Sanders*, 103 S.C. 216 (1916).

153. *State v. Sanders*, 103 S.C. 216 (1916).

154. *State v. Lowman*, 134 S.C. 485 (1926).

155. See undated statement of N. J. Frederick and Walter White to Governor T. G. McLeod, October 26, 1926, NAACP Administrative File, Lynching (chronicling his investigation of the Lowman lynchings), NAACP Papers.

156. See Kenneth Campbell, "A Miserable Miscarriage of Justice: R. Charlton Wright and the (Columbia) Record's Editorial Crusade in the Aiken, S.C., Triple Lynching," presented to History Division, Southeast Colloquium, Association for Education in Journalism and Mass Communications (March 8, 2002, Gulfport, Mississippi), 1.

157. Director of Branches of the NAACP to N. J. Frederick, December 4, 1926, NAACP Correspondence file, congratulating him on taking over the task of reorganizing the Columbia chapter. NAACP Papers.

158. For an excellent account of the Bess case see Janet G. Hudson, "Ben Bess and the Dictates of White Supremacy: The Unpardonable Crime?" *Proceedings of the South Carolina Historical Association* (1999): 15.

159. "Pardon Revoked," *New York Amsterdam News,* July 25, 1928.

160. *Ex parte Bess,* 152 S.C. 410 (1929).

161. See Frederick to W. T. Andrews, July 27, 1928, and Frederick to National NAACP, October 16, 1929, NAACP Correspondence file, NAACP Papers.

162. *State v. Floyd,* 174 S.C. 288 (1934).

163. "Lexington Has Heavy Docket," *(Columbia) State*, September 11, 1933.

164. "Columbia Girl," *(Columbia) State*, August 11, 1933.

165. Transcript of Record, *State v. Floyd,* 174 S.C. 288 (1934) (No. 13951).

166. "Jury Convicts Clarence Floyd," *(Columbia) State,* September 16, 1933.

167. Points and Authorities of the State at 2, *State v. Floyd,* 174 S.C. 288 (1934) (No. 13951).

168. "Lexington Negro Seeks New Trial," *(Columbia) State*, June 13, 1934; *State v. Floyd*, 174 S.C. 288.

169. *Darby v. S. Ry. Co.*, 194 S.C. 421 (1940). See *State v. Adams*, 78 S.C. 523 (1906) for the first use in a criminal case.

170. *Jenkins v. Atlantic Coast Line R. Co.*, 84 S.C. 343 (1909).

171. *State v. Floyd,* 174 S.C. 288.

172. Cases rejected, 1919–1939, NAACP Papers. These files have no record of Frederick or anyone else seeking assistance for Floyd.

173. "Clarence Floyd Pays with Life," *(Columbia) State*, January 5, 1935.

174. "Convicted Negro May Beat Chair," *(Columbia) State*, June 12, 1937.

175. "Pneumonia Beats Electric Chair," *(Columbia) State*, June 13, 1937.

176. "Editorial," *Southern Indicator*, April 11, 1914; "NAACP Wins White Primary Case," *Palmetto Leader,* March 12, 1927.

177. Roy Nash to N. J. Frederick, February 19, 1917, NAACP Papers.

178. *E. A. Adams et al v. Board of Commissioners of Elections of Columbia*, Complaint in the Court of Common Pleas in the county of Richland, April 22, 1932, NAACP Papers.

179. See Frederick to Walter White, May 7, 1932, and Frederick to James Marshall, July 2, 1932, NAACP Papers.

180. "3 Brilliant Lawyers," *Palmetto Leader*, July 9, 1932.

181. See Walter White to Arthur Spingarn, June 3, 1932, NAACP Papers.

182. See press releases of July 1, 1932, and July 8, 1932, NAACP Papers.

183. "N. J. Frederick Bar Director," *(Columbia) State*, November 2, 1935.

184. See *Frederick v. Southern Fidelity Mutual Insurance Co.*, 221 N.C. 409 (1942) (court declared his estate insolvent).

185. "Noted Criminal Lawyer Dies," *New York Amsterdam News*, September 17, 1938.

186. Smith, *Emancipation*, 151, 183; *Roberts v. Drayton*, 121 S.C. 124, 128 (1922). (Court notes that Dart had "removed to Atlantic City.") Also see Fifteenth United States Census, 1930, and Sixteenth United States Census, 1940, Population, N.J., Atlantic County, Atlantic City, available at ancestry.com. Dart practiced law in New Jersey.

187. *Roberts v. Drayton*, 113 S.E. 365 (1922).

188. Sadie T. M. Alexander, ed., *Who's Who Among Negro Lawyers* (National Bar Association, 1945), 12.

189. "Are Licensed as Lawyers," *Keowee Courier*, November 15, 1922.

190. "Negro Lawyer Sworn in," *(Columbia) State*, November 19, 1922.

191. "Republicans Hold State Convention," *(Columbia) State*, September 20, 1922.

192. "Negroes Released and Again Jailed," *(Columbia) State*, July 29, 1925; "Burden of Proof Lies with State," *(Columbia) State*, October 15, 1926.

193. A Herbert McGirt was killed in Gary, Indiana, in 1927. See "Whistling Killer Is Sought," *(Zanesville, Ohio) Times Recorder*, July 8, 1927. The only witness to the robbery/murder was his wife. In the 1930 census, a four-year-old Herbert McGirt is living with his mother in Camden, South Carolina. Fifteenth United States Census, 1930, Population, S.C., Kershaw County, Camden, available at ancestry.com.

194. Platt's law school graduation was confirmed by the Boston University Registrar's Office. Bill Eutis, e-mail correspondence with author, June 10, 2003.

195. Booker T. Smith is listed as a lawyer in *Simms' Bluebook and National Negro Business and Professional Directory* (Chicago: James M. Simms, 1923), 274, and in *Hill's Spartanburg Directory* (Richmond, Va., 1929), 376. However, there is no record of Smith having been admitted to the bar.

196. *Foster v. N.C. Mutual Ins. Co.*, 150 S.C. 482 (1929); *Hawkins v. N.C. Mutual Life Ins. Co.*, 170 S.C. 478 (1933); *Kerr v. Cleveland*, 182 S.C. 29 (1936) (with J. C. Wrightson as co-counsel); *Bank v. N.C. Mutual Ins. Co.*, 186 S.C. 394 (1938) (with C. Y. Brown as co-counsel).

197. Interview with Matthew J. Perry. See W. Lewis Burke and William C. Hine, "The South Carolina State College Law School," in W. Lewis Burke and Belinda F. Gergel, eds., *Matthew J. Perry: The Man, His Times, and His Legacy* (Columbia: University of South Carolina Press, 2004), 20.

198. *Hill's Spartanburg Directory*, 376; Fifteenth United States Census, 1930, Population, S.C., Spartanburg County, available at ancestry.com.

199. See Correspondence, Jim Davis file, Group I, box D-55, NAACP Papers.

200. Arthur Platt to Thomas B. Dyett, January 13, 1927, NAACP Papers.

201. Letter to Walter White, January 15, 1927, NAACP Papers.

202. Damon L. Fordham, *Voices of Black South Carolina* (Charleston: History Press, 2009), 143–44.

203. Burke and Hine, "State College Law School," 20.

204. Eric Foner, *Freedom's Lawmakers* (Baton Rouge: Louisiana State University Press, 1996), 154.

205. Orangeburg County Civil Calendars 1925–1939 and Orangeburg Criminal Dockets 1925–1942, SCDAH; *State v. Wright*, 228 S.C. 432 (1955); *Owens v. North Carolina Mutual Life Insurance Co.*, 175 S.C. 37 (1935).

206. For example, Morgan was contacted by Marshall about an Orangeburg County jail inmate who had filed a petition for writ of habeas corpus. Morgan visited the prisoner in the jail and advised Marshall that he thought the petitioner was guilty and that there was no reason for the NAACP to become involved. See Morgan to Marshall, April 8, 1939, Cases rejected, 1919–1939, NAACP Papers.

207. Burke and Hine, "State College Law School," 21.

208. *Thompson v. Gibbes*, 60 F. Supp. 872 (E.D.S.C. 1945).

209. Atty. S. Morgan, Find a Grave index on ancestry.com.

210. *Columbia City Directory* (Richmond, Va.: Hill Directory Co., 1925), 596.

211. Miles S. Richards, "Osceola McKaine and the Struggle for Black Civil Rights, 1917–1946" (PhD diss., University of South Carolina, 1994), 6.

212. *Federal Land Bank of Columbia v. Wells*, 172 S.C. 1 (1934).

213. *Wrighten v. Board of Trustees of the University of South Carolina*, 72 F. Supp. 948 (E.D.S.C. 1947).

214. *Carolina Housing and Mortgage Corp. v. Orange Hill A.M.E. Church, et al.*, 230 S.C. 498 (1957).

215. Walter Edgar, *South Carolina: A History* (Columbia: University of South Carolina Press, 1998), 483.

216. Newby, *Black Carolinians*, 192.

217. Edgar, *South* Carolina, 484, 481 (quotation), 200, 490.

CHAPTER 10. All-White Juries and the Continuing Struggle for Voting Rights

1. "Orders Sanders to Death Chair," *(Columbia) State*, June 13, 1915.

2. *Carter v. State of Texas*, 177 U.S. 442 (1900), 448.

3. For a fuller account of the Brownfield trial and its implications, *see* Tom Rubillo, *Trial and Error: The Case of John Brownfield and Race Relations in Georgetown, South Carolina* (Charleston: History Press, 2005), 140.

4. "South Carolina News and Gossip," *(Columbia) State, March 18, 1903*. See Transcript of Record of *Brownfield v. State of S.C.*, 189 U.S. 426 (1903) (No. 172), 7.

5. "All Laws Set at Defiance," *Georgetown Semi-Weekly Times*, October 3, 1900.

6. George Rogers, *The History of Georgetown County, South Carolina* (Columbia: University of South Carolina Press, 1970), 481–82.

7. "The Mayor's Court," *Georgetown Semi-Weekly Times*, October 10, 1900.

8. "Brownfield to Be Hanged," (*Charleston) News and Courier*, November 21, 1900, 6.

9. "Editor Doar's Condition Still Quite Serious," *(Columbia) State*, October 5, 1900, 2. Also see the editor's reflections on the incident in *Georgetown Semi-Weekly Times*, March 14, 1903, 1.

10. "A Miscarriage of Justice," *Georgetown Semi-Weekly Times*, November 18, 1899, 1.

11. Georgetown County Gen. Sess. Journal (S.C. Ct. Gen. Sess., 1895–1916), 201–2, SCDAH.

12. Rogers, *History of Georgetown County*, 481–82.

13. Stephen Kantrowitz, *Ben Tillman and the Reconstruction of White Supremacy* (Chapel Hill: University of North Carolina Press, 2000), 92–94. Matthew Gary was so popular that a steamship built for use on the rivers of Georgetown County was named for Gary. See Ronald Bridwell, *Gem of the Atlantic Seaboard* (Georgetown, S.C.: Georgetown Times, 1991), 36.

14. David Duncan Wallace, *The History of South Carolina*, vol. 3 (New York: American Historical Society, 1935), 461, citing (Charleston) *News and Courier*, October 27, 1903.

15. "John Brownfield Guilty of Murder," *(Columbia) State*, November 17, 1900, 1.

16. U. R. Brooks, *South Carolina Bench and Bar* (Columbia: State, 1908), 306–7.

17. N. Louise Bailey, Mary C. Morgan, and Carolyn R. Taylor, eds., *Biographical Directory of the South Carolina Senate*, vol. 3 (Columbia: University of South Carolina Press, 1986), 1658.

18. "Commending the Soldiers," *Georgetown Semi-Weekly Times*, November 17, 1900, 1.

19. Georgetown County Gen. Sess. Journal (Ct. Gen. Sess., 1895–1916), 201–2, SCDAH.

20. "Commending the Soldiers," *Georgetown Semi-Weekly Times*, November 17, 1900, 1.

21. Georgetown County Gen. Sess. Journal (Ct. Gen. Sess., 1895–1916), 201–2, SCDAH.

22. "John Brownfield Guilty of Murder," *(Columbia) State*, November 17, 1900, 1.

23. Georgetown County Gen. Sess. Journal (Ct. Gen. Sess., 1895–1916), 201–2 (SCDAH).

24. "Court Calendar," *Georgetown Semi-Weekly Times*, November 21, 1900, 4.

25. "Noose Will Soon Be About His Neck," *(Columbia) State*, April 10, 1903, 4.

26. "Court Calendar," *Georgetown Semi-Weekly Times*, November 21, 1900, 4.

27. Rubillo, *Trial and Error*, 140.

28. *State v. Brownfield*, 60 S.C. 509, 511 (1901).

29. Transcript of Record, *State v. Brownfield*, 60 S.C. 509, 511 (1901), 3–4.

30. "Negro's Appeal Fails," *New York Times*, March 10, 1903, 2.

31. *Brownfield*, 60 S.C. at 513.

32. *Brownfield v. State of S.C.*, 189 U.S. 426 (1903).

33. Georgetown County Gen. Sess. Journal (Ct. Gen. Sess., 1900), 201–2 (SCDAH).

34. "Noose Will Soon Be About His Neck," *(Columbia) State*, April 10, 1903, 4.

35. Undated Letter, Gov. McSweeney, General Correspondence (Georgetown County, 1899–1903) in Papers of Governor Miles B. McSweeney, SCDAH.

36. "Noose Will Soon Be About His Neck," *(Columbia) State*, April 10, 1903.

37. "John Brownfield, Convicted Murder," *Georgetown Semi-Weekly Times*, March 14, 1903; "The Courthouse and the City Hall," *Georgetown Semi-Weekly Times*, March 21, 1903.

38. Papers of Governor Miles B. McSweeney, SCDAH.

39. "Good Work of Sessions Court," *Georgetown Semi-Weekly Times*, June 17, 1903, 1.

40. Rubillo, *Trial and Error*, 171, quoting *(Georgetown) Sunday Outlook*, June 20, 1903.

41. "Good Work of Sessions Court," *Georgetown Semi-Weekly Times*, June 17, 1903, 1.

42. "Poison Ends Life of Famed Prisoner," *(Columbia) State*, June 24, 1903, 1.

43. "The Murderer Escapes," *Georgetown Semi-Weekly Times*, June 24, 1903, 1.

44. "Poison Ends Life of Famed Prisoner," *(Columbia) State*, June 24, 1903, 1.

45. See Rubillo, *Trial and Error*, 161–83.

46. Lizelia Augusta Jenkins Moorer, "The Peonage System," in *Prejudice Unveiled* (Boston: Roxburgh, 1907), 17.

47. See Theodore Rosengarten, *All God's Dangers* (New York: Random House, 1974), for a description of the tasks of farm laborers as well as information about diet, housing, and cotton farming.

48. A fuller account of the *Franklin* case can be found at W. Lewis Burke, "Pink Franklin v. South Carolina: The NAACP's First Case," *Journal of American Legal History* 54 (2014): 265.

49. "Valentine's Inquest Held," (*Charleston) News and Courier*, August 4, 1907, 1-A; "Got Him Safe," *(Orangeburg) Times and Democrat*, August 8, 1907, 8. "Franklin said that he was under contract with Mr. Thomas, and that he left him on May 20 and started to move his things to Mr. Spires' place, but that Mr. Thomas wouldn't let him take them away. 'I didn't even have a bed to sleep on and just had to sleep on the floor.'"

50. Act No. 243, 1904 S.C. Acts 428–429.

51. *Ex parte Drayton*, 153 F. 986, 997 (D.S.C. 1907).

52. "AGAINST LABOR LAW—Judge Brawley declares the State Statute Null and Void," (*Orangeburg) Times and Democrat*, May 30, 1907.

53. "Contract Labor Law Unconstitutional," *(Charleston) News and Courier*, May 24, 1907.

54. Transcript of Record of *Franklin v. State of South Carolina*, 218 U.S. 161 (1910) (No. 164), 2 (filed May 18, 1908); "Constable at Cope Shot This Morning," *Orangeburg Evening News*, July 29, 1907, 1; Transcript of Record, *Franklin v. State*, testimony of Sol Spires, 30–33.

55. "The Injured Man Dies from Wounds," *Orangeburg Evening News*, July 30, 1907, 1A. Also see Terrence Finnegan, "At the Hands of Parties Unknown" (PhD diss., University of Illinois, 1993), 71–74. Finnegan found lynchings in neighboring Dorchester and Barnwell Counties. In the Dorchester lynching the sheriff was charged with malfeasance in office for not preventing the lynching but was found not guilty by an Orangeburg County jury.

56. Jack Simpson Mullins, "Lynching in South Carolina, 1900–1914" (master's thesis, University of South Carolina, 1961), 129–30.

57. Ralph Ginzburg, *100 Years of Lynching* (New York: Lancer, 1962), 267.

58. "Pink Franklin in Penitentiary," *(Columbia) State*, August 1, 1907.

59. "Negro Feared Lynching," (*Charleston) News and Courier*, August 2, 1907, 2-A.

60. J. F. B. Coleman, *Tuskegee to Voorhees* (Columbia, S.C.: R. L. Bryan, 1922), 71.

61. Sawyer to Gonzalez, December 17, 1917, Pardon, Paroles and Commutations files, SCDAH.

62. See, for example, "Got Him Safe," *Orangeburg Evening News*, August 8, 1907.

63. "The Franklin Case," *Barnwell People Sentinel*, September 26, 1907, 4.

64. U. R. Brooks, *South Carolina Bench and Bar* (Columbia, S.C.: R. L. Bryan, 1908), 292–95.

65. "Pink Franklin to Be Hanged," (*Charleston) News and Courier*, September 10, 1907, 1-A; "He Will Hang," (*Orangeburg) Times and Democrat*, September 12, 1907, 10.

66. "Report of the Secretary of State," *Reports and Resolutions to the South Carolina General Assembly* (Columbia: State, 1901), 802.

67. "Pink Franklin to Be Hanged," (*Charleston) News and Courier*, September 10, 1907, 1-A.

68. "Will Come Here for Franklin," *(Columbia) State*, September 7, 1907, 1.

69. "Pink Franklin to Be Hanged," (*Charleston) News and Courier*, September 10, 1907, 1-A.

70. Transcript of Record, *Franklin v. South Carolina*, 18, 21, 24, 28, 30, 33, 35, 38, 49, 39–41.

71. *State v. Wimbush*, 9 S.C. 309 (1878).

72. *State v. Byrd*, 72 S.C. 104, 107 (1905); *State v. Brooks*, 79 S.C. 144, 149 (1908); *State v. Bodie*, 33 S.C. 117, 131 (1890).

73. Transcript of Record, *Franklin v. State of South Carolina*, 34.

74. "Pink Franklin to Hang," *(Columbia) State*, September 7, 1910, 1.

75. "He Will Hang," (*Orangeburg) Times and Democrat*, September 12, 1907, 10.

76. Brooks, *South Carolina Bench and Bar*; *Journal of the Constitutional Convention of the State of South Carolina* (Columbia, S.C.: Charles A. Calvo Jr., 1895).

77. See Barry Edmond Hambright, "The South Carolina Supreme Court" (PhD diss., University of South Carolina, 1981), 79–81.

78. *Ex parte Hollman*, 79 S.C. 9 (1908).

79. *Orangeburg Evening News*, March 17, 1908.

80. *State v. Franklin*, 80 S.C. 332 (1908).

81. "Case Interests Southerners," (*Charleston) News and Courier*, April 6, 1910, 1-A.

82. See "Mary White Ovington and William Edward Burghardt (W. E. B.) DuBois," http://www.pointsoflight.org/programs/recognition/extra-mile/mary-white-ovington-and-william-edward-burghardt-web-dubois (accessed September 1, 2016); Dickson D. Bruce Jr., *Archibald Grimke: Portrait of a Black Independent* (Baton Rouge: Louisiana State University Press, 1993), 147–58.

83. John E. Milholland to Oswald Garrison Villard, February 25, 1901, Papers of the NAACP, Part 8 Discrimination in Criminal Justice, 1910–1955, Series A, Legal Department and Central Records Office, Franklin, Pink, Trial, Litigation, 1910–1911, 1914–1919 (hereafter cited as Pink Franklin NAACP Papers). Supposedly, the Baltimore lawyer and grandnephew of Napoleon Bonaparte was paid $1,000 for his services. Ed. J. Wallace to Whitefield McKinlay, October 2, 1910, Pink Franklin NAACP Papers.

84. Transcript of Record, *Franklin v. State of South Carolina*, 166–67.

85. Ibid., 170–71.

86. "Pink Franklin Will Die," *(Columbia) State*, September 7, 1910, 1.

87. Judge J. C. Klugh to Governor Ansel, December 20, 1910; Solicitor P. T. Hildebrand to Gov. Ansel, August 10, 1910, SCDAH.

88. See "Late Returns," *(Columbia) State*, September 14, 1910; "Cole Blease's Majority," *(Columbia) State*, September 15, 1910.

89. "May Make Further Move in Pink Franklin Case," *(Columbia) State*, November 10, 1910.

90. "Some Talk About Town," *(Columbia) State*, June 29, 1910.

91. Thomas E. Miller to William English Walling, July 29, 1910, Pink Franklin NAACP Papers.

92. Miller to Blascoer, October 27, 1910, Pink Franklin NAACP Papers.

93. Bonaparte to Frances Blascoer, July 30, 1910, NAACP Papers.

94. Ansel to Taft, September 7, 1910, and Taft to Villard, September 10, 1910, NAACP Papers.

95. "Pink Franklin's Reprieve," *The Crisis*, February 1911, 15; DuBois to Adams and Moorer, October 13, 1910, NAACP Papers.

96. Affidavit of Franklin dated November 8, 1910, NAACP Papers.

97. Blascoer to Villard, November 4, 1910, NAACP Papers.

98. Walter Edgar, *South Carolina: A History* (Columbia: University of South Carolina Press, 1998), 468.

99. "The Pink Franklin Case," (Charleston) *News and Courier*, December 5, 1910.

100. Miller to Blascoer, December 5, 1910, NAACP Papers.

101. Franklin to Blascoer, February 14, 1915, NAACP Papers.

102. I must thank genealogists Cindy and Mike Gillis for having the skill and patience to find Pink Franklin. According to the 1920 and 1930 censuses, Mack Rockingham was living with Patsy Rockingham, Pink Rockingham, and Nolan Rockingham in Blackville Township in Barnwell County. Not only did Mack Rockingham have a wife and children with the same names as Pink Franklin's wife and children, Rockingham was the same age and skin color as Franklin. Fourteenth United States Census, 1920, Population, S.C., Barnwell County, and Fifteenth United States Census, 1930, Population, S.C., Barnwell County, available at ancestry.com.

103. Standard Certificate of Death, Division of Vital Statistics, of Mack Rockingham, August 12, 1949, File No. 49–007955, State of South Carolina, available at ancestry.com. The cause of death is listed as prostate and liver cancer. In both censuses Rockingham is listed as a farmer. Neither record shows whether he owned land, but the 1920 census does record that he was farming "on account" or sharecropping. His death certificate simply says he did "farm work." Penciled in on the death certificate is the last name of "Franklin."

104. "Shot in the Back," *(Columbia) Record*, May 27, 1915.

105. "Negro and Wife Placed on Trial," *(Columbia) Record*, June 11, 1915.

106. See *State v. Sanders*, 103 S.C. 216, 217 (1916).

107. Notes of Judge Rice, Pardons, Paroles, and Commutations File, 1919–1922, Papers of Governor Robert A. Cooper, 3, SCDAH.

108. "Convicted Negro Tries to End Life," *(Columbia) State*, June 13, 1915.

109. Ibid.

110. State v. *Sanders*, 218 (quoting the first exception of the appeal).

111. Ibid.

112. "Trial of Sanders Has Begun with New Features," *(Columbia) Record*, June 10, 1915, 2.

113. *Neal v. Delaware*, 103 U.S. 370 (1880), in which the Delaware judge opined that blacks lacked the qualifications to be jurors.

114. State v. *Sanders*, 220.

115. "Bogus Sanders on Trial Again," *(Columbia) State*, May 25, 1916, 6.

116. "Sanders Was Given Life in Prison; Jury Merciful," *(Columbia) Record*, May 28, 1916, 28.

117. *Petition for Clemency dated November 13, 1920, Letter of Mendel L. Smith, Trial Judge, dated December 13, 1920, and petition signed by nine jurors*, Papers of Governor Robert A. Cooper, Pardons, Paroles, and Commutations (1919–1922), SCDAH.

118. "Negro Leaders Call Conference," *(Columbia) Record*, June 7, 1915, 3.

119. Butler Nance to W. E. B. DuBois, June 5, 1915, microform, NAACP Papers.

120. NAACP to Butler Nance, July 1, 1915, and Roy Nash to N. J. Frederick, February 19, 1917, microform, NAACP Papers.

121. Butler Nance to Walter F. White, September 14, 1920, microform, NAACP Papers.

122. Butler Nance to Morefield Storey, April 14, 1919, microform, NAACP Papers.

123. NAACP to Nance, April 29, 1919; Nance to Storey, May 9, 1919; NAACP to C. L. Henderson, May 12, 1919; C. L. Henderson to Walter White, May 17, 1919; NAACP Office Secretary to Henderson, May 21, 1919, microform, NAACP Papers.

124. William Pickens, "The Woman Voter Hits the Color Line," *The Nation*, October 6, 1920, 372–73.

125. Butler Nance to Walter White, September 12, 1920, microform, NAACP Papers.

126. "Negroes Appeal to County Court," *(Columbia) State*, September 16, 1920.

127. "Sixteen Negroes Appeal to Court," *(Columbia) State*, October 12, 1920, 15; *Ellen Bookman v. Richland County Board of Registration*, 1920 S.C. Att'y Gen. Rep. 13. In Reports of State Officers, Boards and Committees to the General Assembly of South Carolina, vol. 1 (Columbia: Gonzales and Bryan, 1921).

128. "Congressman Stevenson Wrong," *Palmetto Leader*, January 29, 1927, 4.

129. "Race Barred from Democratic Primary," *Palmetto Leader*, August 21, 1926.

130. "Negroes Barred from the Democratic Primary in South Carolina," *Palmetto Leader*, August 21, 1926, 4.

131. "Three Lynched," *Palmetto Leader*, October 16, 1926, 1.

132. "To Revive Local Branch of N.A.A.C.P.," *Palmetto Leader*, December 4, 1926, 4.

133. William T. Andrews to L. G. Southard, May 22, 1928, and May 28, 1928, microform, NAACP Papers.

134. *Nixon v. Condon*, 286 U.S. 73 (1932).

135. See Complaint, *Adams vs. Board of Commissioners*, April 22, 1932, microform, NAACP Papers; Letter of N. J. Frederick to Walter White, May 5, 1932, and Frederick to James Marshall, July 2, 1932, microform, NAACP Papers.

136. Frederick to James Marshall, July 2, 1932, microform, NAACP Papers.

137. "3 Brilliant Lawyers Join N.A.A.C.P. Nat'l Legal Committee," *Palmetto Leader*, July 9, 1932, 6.

138. See W. Lewis Burke and William C. Hine, "The South Carolina State College Law School," in W. Lewis Burke and Belinda F. Gergel, eds., *Matthew J. Perry: The Man, His Times, and His Legacy* (Columbia: University of South Carolina Press, 2004), table 1 and table 2, 40–41.

139. Ibid., 26. See also "Atty. N. J. Frederick," *Palmetto Leader*, September 9, 1938; as to his financial well-being, see *In re: The Estate of N. J. Frederick, deceased, Corinne*

Frederick, Executrix, in Probate Court of Richland County, South Carolina, Box 491, Package No. 12,783; *see also Frederick v. Southern Fidelity Mutual Insurance Co.*, 221 N.C. 409 (1942) (court ordering Mrs. Frederick to return the only monies in the estate to an insurance company).

140. See Burke and Hine, "State College Law School," table 1 and table 2, 40–41.

141. *Rogers v. State of Alabama*, 192 U.S. 226 (1904).

142. See, for example, *Martin v. State of Texas*, 200 U.S. 316 (1906), and *Thomas v. State of Texas*, 212 U.S. 278 (1909).

143. *Norris v. State of Alabama,* 294 U.S. 587 (1935).

CHAPTER 11. The 1940s and the Civil Rights Era

1. Edwin D. Hoffman, "The Genesis of the Modern Movement for Equal Rights in South Carolina, 1930–1939," *Journal of Negro History* 44 (1959): 346.

2. Peter Lau, *Democracy Rising* (Lexington: University Press of Kentucky, 2006), 96.

3. I. A. Newby, *Black Carolinians: A History of Blacks in South Carolina from 1895 to 1968* (Columbia: University of South Carolina Press, 1973), 234.

4. Peter Lau, "Mr. NAACP: Levi G. Byrd and the Re-Making of the NAACP in State and Nation, 1917–1960," in Winfred B. Moore Jr. and Orville Vernon Burton, eds., *Toward the Meeting of the Waters: Currents in the Civil Rights Movement of South Carolina during the Twentieth Century* (Columbia: University of South Carolina Press, 2008), 146.

5. R. Scott Baker, *Paradoxes of Desegregation: African American Struggles for Educational Equity in Charleston, South Carolina, 1926–1972* (Columbia: University of South Carolina Press, 2006), 30–31.

6. *Murray v. Maryland*, 169 Md. 478, 182 A.590 (1936).

7. For more on the Murray and Gaines cases, see Richard Kluger, *Simple Justice: The History of Brown v. Board of Education and Black America's Struggle for Equality* (New York: Random House, 1975), 188–94, 202–5, 212–13; Mark V. Tushnet, *The NAACP Legal Strategy against Segregated Education, 1925–1950* (Chapel Hill: University of North Carolina Press, 1987), 70–74.

8. H. C. Byrd to L. T. Baker, February 4, 1936, Law School Folder, Office of the President, 1935–36, SCL.

9. J. Nelson Frierson to Leonard T. Baker, February 14, 1936, Law School Folder, Office of the President, 1935–36, SCL.

10. Bailey to University of South Carolina, referencing a letter of April 27, 1938, to the dean of USC School of Law, May 18, 1938, NAACP correspondence file, NAACP Papers.

11. Jack Irby Hayes Jr. briefly discusses Bailey's case and the creation of the law school at South Carolina State in *South Carolina and the New Deal* (Columbia: University of South Carolina Press, 2002), 181.

12. Charles B. Bailey to Walter White, April 6, 1938; Charles H. Houston to Charles B. Bailey, April 11, 1938, Legal Department and Central Office Records, 1913–1940, NAACP Papers. Nineteen black men attended the law program at the University of South Carolina between 1873 and 1877. Eleven of them received degrees. See W. Lewis Burke, "The Radical Law School: The University of South Carolina School of Law and Its African

American Graduates, 1873–1877," in James L. Underwood and W. Lewis Burke, *At Freedom's Door* (Columbia: University of South Carolina Press, 2005), 90–115.

13. Charles B. Bailey to President J. Rion McKissick, May 18, 1938, NAACP Papers. Bailey indicated in this letter that he had written to Frierson in April and had received no response. Charles B. Bailey to Board of Trustees, June 27, 1938, NAACP Papers.

14. Solomon Blatt to Charles B. Bailey, July 19, 1938, and January 2, 1939, NAACP Papers.

15. Press release, "Solomon Blatt Declares USC to Keep Status," August 28, 1938, Papers of the NAACP, Part 3, The Campaign for Educational Equality: Legal Department and Central Office Records, 1913–1950 (hereafter cited as NAACP Campaign for Education Equality).

16. NAACP General Education Board Records, Rockefeller Archive Center, North Tarrytown, New York.

17. "Bill for Negro Law School Dead for Year," *(Columbia) State*, June 18, 1939; *Journal of the Senate, First Session of the 83rd General Assembly of the State of South Carolina* (Columbia: Joint Committee of Printing, 1939), 445, 566, 720.

18. C. B. Bailey, interview by W. Lewis Burke, November 11, 1997.

19. In the 1944 election, black candidates I. S. Leevy and J. B. Lewie, ran unsuccessfully against the Democratic Party candidates for state representatives in Richland County. See Supplemental Report of the Secretary of State, Election November 7, 1944, in *Reports and Resolutions of South Carolina to the General Assembly* (Columbia: Joint Committee of Printing, n.d.), 27. In 1946 black candidates ran in the First Congressional District (A. Dingle), the Second Congressional District (I. S. Leevy), the Sixth Congressional District (James E. Prioleau), and the local races in Beaufort, Fairfield, Florence, Georgetown, Orangeburg, and Richland Counties. See *Supplemental Report of the Secretary of State, Election November 5, 1946* (Columbia: Joint Committee of Printing, n.d.), 5–7, 19–29.

20. *United States v. Ellis*, 43 F. Supp. 321 (W.D.S.C. 1942); Roy Wilkins to Robert H. Jackson, U.S. Attorney General, August 28, 1940, NAACP Campaign for Education Equality.

21. "Board Acquitted," *Gaffney Ledger*, March 17, 1942, 4; "School Board Fires Teacher for Trying to Register, Vote," *(Columbia) Lighthouse and Informer*, June 28, 1942; Thurgood Marshall to Lottie P. Gaffney, July 27, 1942, The Campaign for Educational Equality, NAACP Papers.

22. Baker, *Paradoxes of Desegregation*, 30.

23. Wim Roefs, "The Impact of 1940s Civil Rights Activism on the State's 1960s Civil Rights Scene," in Moore and Burton, *Toward a Meeting of the Waters*, 159–60.

24. See Richards, "Osceola E. McKaine and the Struggle for Black Civil Rights: 1917–1946" (PhD diss., University of South Carolina, 1994), 119–20.

25. See "Judge Harold Stevens, 83, Dies," *New York Times*, November 11, 1990.

26. Report by Robinson on the election of officers on December 15, 1947, December 17, 1947, The Campaign for Educational Equality, NAACP Papers.

27. Minutes, Seventh Annual Meeting for the S.C. Conference for the NAACP, Modjeska Simkins Papers, SCL.

28. Roll of Attorneys, South Carolina Supreme Court, 1941.

29. See Maxwell to Prentice Thomas, Assistant General Counsel, July 6, 1942, NAACP Campaign for Education Equality.

30. "Local Woman First Black Female Attorney," *(Orangeburg) Times and Democrat*, February 27, 2000. See cases such as *Norwood v. Robie*, 102 Ga. App. 206 (1960) and *Howell v. Cataldi*, 464 F.2d 272 (3d Cir. 1972).

31. Obituary, September 5, 1974, Cassandra Maxwell Birnie Collection, Miller F. Whittaker Library, South Carolina State University, Orangeburg, South Carolina.

32. *State v. Grant*, 199 S.C. 412 (1941).

33. *Grant v. Richardson*, 129 F.2d 105 (4th Cir. 1942); see deathpenaltyusa.org/usa1/date/1942.htm (accessed July 9, 2015).

34. Baker, *Paradoxes of Desegregation*, 53–54.

35. "Judge's Decision Opens Way for Further Suits," *Florence Morning News*, February 15, 1944, 3.

36. "Civil Liberties Cases Held at the National Archives at Atlanta," National Archives, http://www.archives.gov/atlanta/finding-aids/civil-liberties-cases.html (accessed February 4, 2013).

37. National Archives and Records Administration, "U.S. World War II Army Enlistment Records, 1938–1946," available at ancestry.com. Another teacher pay case was not heard until 1945. See James Hinton to Thurgood Marshall, September 21, 1942; Thurgood Marshall to Hinton, November 18, 1942; Harold Boulware to Thurgood Marshall, December 6, 1943; and James Hinton to Thurgood Marshall, March 3, 1944, NAACP Campaign for Education Equality.

38. *Thompson v. Gibbes*, 60 F. Supp. 872 (E.D.S.C. 1945).

39. *Smith v. Allwright*, 321 U.S. 649, 660 (1944).

40. See Richards, "Osceola E. McKaine," 164–65.

41. *Elmore v. Rice*, 72 F. Supp. 516, 520 (E.D.S.C. 1947).

42. *Elmore v. Rice*, 72 F. Supp. 516, 519, 528 (E.D.S.C. 1947), aff'd, 165 F.2d 387 (4th Cir. 1947), cert. denied, 333 U.S. 875 (1948).

43. *Rice v. Elmore*, 165 F.2d 387 (4th Cir. 1947), *cert. denied* 333 U.S. 875 (1948).

44. *Baskin v. Brown*, 174 F.2d 391, 392 (4th Cir. 1949).

45. *Brown v. Baskin*, 78 F. Supp. 933, 940–41 (E.D.S.C. 1948).

46. *Brown v. Baskin*, 80 F. Supp. 1017, 1019 (E.D.S.C. 1948).

47. *Baskin*, 174 F.2d at 391.

48. *Wrighten v. Bd. of Trustees of Univ. of S.C.*, 72 F. Supp. 948 (E.D.S.C. 1947).

49. Harold Boulware, interview by Dr. Grace Jordan McFadden, n.d., USC Film Archives.

50. In his letter to Siebels, Wrighten declared that "on or about the 6th day of July, 1946, I received a letter from President Norman H. Smith of the University of South Carolina informing me that the University was unable to act favorably upon my application and has refused me admission solely on account of my race and color." Wrighten asked that the board overrule the president. John H. Wrighten to the Dean of the Law School, June 30, 1946, and John H. Wrighten to E. G. Siebels, Chairman, Board of Trustees, University of South Carolina, August 17, 1946, NAACP Campaign for Education Equality. John Wrighten, telephone interview by William C. Hine, June 6, 1989, cited in

W. Lewis Burke and William C. Hine, "The South Carolina State College Law School," in W. Lewis Burke and Belinda F. Gergel, eds., *Matthew J. Perry: The Man, His Times, and His Legacy* (Columbia: University of South Carolina Press, 2004), 30.

51. See Summons and Complaint, Civil Action No. 1670 in the District Court of the United States for the Eastern District of South Carolina (January 8, 1947) (National Archives, Southeast Region). Also see *Wrighten v. Bd. of Trustees*, 72 F. Supp. 949 (E.D.S.C. 1947).

52. *Wrighten v. Bd. of Trustees*, 953.

53. Jay Bender, "One Week That Changed the State," *South Carolina Lawyer* 11 (1999): 32.

54. Miller F. Whittaker to J. B. Felton, May 27, 1947, Department of Education Folder, President's Papers (S.C. State). The stress of presiding over the college through the Depression and World War II combined with the difficulty of attempting to satisfy white leadership and the black community simultaneously may have been too much for Whittaker. He died of a heart attack in November 1949 at age fifty-six.

55. Transcript of Record at 28–30, 34, *Wrighten v. Bd. of Trustees*, 949. Also see "Negro Avers No SC Law School for Race Exists," *(Columbia) State*, June 6–7, 1947. The General Assembly had appropriated $545,000 to South Carolina State for the fiscal year beginning July 1, 1947, with the stipulation that the college offer courses in law, medicine, pharmacology, and other disciplines in higher education.

56. *Wrighten v. Bd. of Trustees*, 948, 952; "State Must Provide Law Training for Race," *(Columbia) State*, July 13, 1947.

57. C. F. Brooks to Miller F. Whittaker, July 28, 1947, Trustees Folder, President's Papers, Historical Collection, South Carolina State University (hereafter cited as SCSU).

58. Report of Attorney Harold R. Boulware to the NAACP, October 1, 1947, NAACP Campaign for Education Equality.

59. Memorandum to Mr. Harrington from Legal Department for Press Release, November 6, 1947, NAACP Campaign for Education Equality.

60. Thurgood Marshall to John Wrighten, September 29, 1947, NAACP Campaign for Education Equality.

61. John H. Wrighten to J. M. Hinton, October 8, 1947; Harold R. Boulware to Edward Dudley, October 13, 1947; Thurgood Marshall to Harold R. Boulware, March 3, 1948, NAACP Campaign for Education Equality. Wrighten further enraged Marshall when he wrote a letter to Judge Waring's wife in 1949 asking for financial assistance to attend the S.C. State Law School. John Wrighten to Mrs. J. Waties Waring, February 6, 1949; J. Waties Waring to Thurgood Marshall, February 8, 1949; Thurgood Marshall to John Wrighten, February 21, 1949, NAACP Campaign for Education Equality. Marshall informed Wrighten that his letter to Mrs. Waring was "in extremely bad taste."

62. See appendix A.

63. Richard Kluger, *Simple Justice: The History of Brown v. Board of Education and Black America's Struggle for Equality* (New York: Knopf, 1976), 15–16.

64. Peter F. Lau, "From the Periphery to the Center," in Peter F. Lau, ed., *From the Grassroots to the Supreme Court: Brown v. Board of Education and American Democracy* (Durham, N.C.: Duke University Press, 2004), 106–7.

65. Ophelia DeLaine Gona, *Dawn of Desegregation: J. A. DeLaine and Briggs v. Elliott* (Columbia: University of South Carolina Press, 2011), 45.

66. Lau, "From the Periphery to the Center," 117.

67. Gona, *Dawn of Desegregation*, 118–19, 123 (quotation).

68. Ibid., 73.

69. Ibid., 12.

70. Ibid., 136.

71. Robert J. Cottrell, Raymond T. Diamond, and Leland B. Ware, *Brown v. Board of Education: Caste, Culture, and the Constitution* (Lawrence: University Press of Kansas, 2003), 121.

72. Ibid., 126, 127.

73. "Counties Sued in Lynching," *Brownsville (Tex.) Herald*, February 27, 1949.

74. See Peter W. Bardaglio, "Rape and the Law in the Old South: 'Calculated to Excite Indignation in Every Heart,'" *Journal of Southern History* 60 (November 1994): 756n23.

75. Charles Franklin Beall Jr., "With Malicious Intent: John McCray, Willie Tolbert and the Struggle for Equal Justice in South Carolina" (bachelor's thesis, University of Virginia, April 20, 1987), 26.

76. "Greenwood Negro Gets Death Sentence," *(Columbia) State*, September 14, 1949.

77. "Jury Convicts," *Florence Morning News*, September 14, 1949.

78. "Greenwood Negro Gets Death Sentence," *(Columbia) State*, September 14, 1949.

79. John McCray, "Lawyer Boulware," The Way It Was, February 12, 1983, McCray Papers, SCL. The author knew Judge Boulware and was told by him that he was put in the trunk of the highway patrolman's car.

80. Beall, "With Malicious Intent," 41, 50.

81. But McCray's troubles were not over. A condition of his probation prohibited him from "leaving the state," and McCray, supposedly believing that the term meant "permanently leaving the state," had traveled to Illinois and North Carolina for speaking engagements. McCray was embroiled in a divorce and custody fight with his wife, whose lawyer reported McCray's out-of-state trips to the state parole board. McCray did not avoid jail this time and was sentenced to sixty days on the chain gang. Ibid., 54, 57. McCray's actual probation condition read "Remain within the State of S.C. (unless given permission by the S.C. Probation and Parole Board)." *State v. McCray*, 222 S.C., 391, 393 (1952).

82. McCray to Thurgood Marshall, June 5, 1950, John Henry McCray Papers, SCL.

83. Beall, "With Malicious Intent," 40, 67.

84. When the trial began before the three-judge federal court in Charleston in May 1951, Boulware was prominently mentioned in press reports. See "Segregation Suit Begins," *Florence Morning News*, May 28, 1951.

85. See Arthur Clement Letter, September 28, 1981, A. J. Clement Papers, SCL.

86. See Boulware to James Hinton, January 29, 1957, Modjeska Simkins Papers, SCL.

87. *State v. Jamison*, 221 S.C. 312 (1952); *State v. Waitus*, 226 S.C. 44 (1954); *State v. Green*, 227 S.C. 1 (1955); *State v. Cavers*, 236 S.C. 305 (1960).

88. Between 1951 and 1955 he had thirty-four cases on the dockets of the Richland County Court. See L40145, Richland County Court, Civil Calendar (1950–1955), SCDAH.

89. Boulware ran for the South Carolina House of Representatives in 1966. See Boulware announcement, Modjeska Simkins Papers, SCL.

90. "Family Court Judge," *(Columbia) State*, September 21, 1974.

91. "A Pioneer Retires," *(Columbia) State*, September 4, 1982; "Harold R. Boulware," *(Columbia) State*, February 2, 1983.

92. William B. James Papers, SCL.

93. Editorial, "William B. James: A Giant of Sumter," *(Sumter) Item*, February 8, 1989; "W. B. James, Sumter Lawyer, Civic Leader," *(Columbia) State*, February 8, 1989.

94. Roll of Attorneys, South Carolina Supreme Court, 1900.

95. Judge Robert Fields, interview by W. Lewis Burke, June 21, 2013.

96. *Charleston City Directory* (Livonia, Mich.: R. L. Polk, 1948); Roll of Attorneys, South Carolina Supreme Court, 1948; Sandra K. McKinney, ed., *South Carolina Legislative Manual, 74th ed. (1993), 303.*

97. *State v. Green*, 227 S.C. 1 (1955); *State v. Jamison*, 221 S.C. 312 (1952).

98. "Negro Teachers Test State Law," *Florence Morning News*, September 11, 1956; James L. Felder, *Civil Rights in South Carolina: From Peaceful Protests to Groundbreaking Rulings* (Charleston: History Press, 2012), 21.

99. *Nash v. Sharper*, 229 S.C. 451 (1955).

100. "Negro Teachers Test State Law," *Florence Morning News*, September 11, 1956; Felder, *Civil Rights in South Carolina*, 21.

101. "Clarendon Negroes Aren't Sure," *Florence Morning News*, August 22, 1958; "Clarendon Negroes File Integration Petitions," *Florence Morning News*, September 1, 1959; "District Rejects Negroes' Request," *Florence Morning News*, October 14, 1959.

102. "NAACP Sets Sunday Rally at Manning," *Florence Morning News*, November 11, 1959; Randall L. Kennedy, "Introduction: Matthew J. Perry, a Lawyer with a Cause," in Burke and Gergel, *Matthew J. Perry*, 6.

103. "Negro Lawyers Appeal," *Florence Morning News*, November 14, 1961.

104. "Judge Gives Temporary Race Ruling," *Florence Morning News*, February 18, 1961.

105. "Judge Also Orders Segregation in State's Public Parks Be Ended," *(Appleton, Wis.) Post Crescent*, July 11, 1963; "Another Victory in Rights Battle," *(Benton Harbor, Mich.) News Palladium*, July 11, 1963.

106. "State Parks Ordered Closed Down," *Florence Morning News*, August 21, 1963.

107. *Clark v. Flory*, 237 F.2d 597 (4th Cir. 1956).

108. Robert J. Moore, "Matthew J. Perry's Preparation," in Burke and Gergel, *Matthew J. Perry*, 162.

109. "Judge Jenkins Dies," *(Columbia) State*, May 15, 1986.

CHAPTER 12. The Modern Civil Rights Era

1. See W. Lewis Burke and William C. Hine, "The South Carolina State College Law School: Its Roots, Creation and Legacy," in W. Lewis Burke and Belinda F. Gergel, eds., *Matthew J. Perry: The Man, His Times, and His Legacy* (Columbia: University of South Carolina Press, 2004), 34–36.

2. Miller F. Whittaker to Solomon Blatt, May 2, 1947. The same letter was sent to the Orangeburg legislative delegation, including James Brailsford, Hugo Sims Jr., Charlton B. Hoger, and Marshall Williams. President's Papers, SCSU. 1948. Act No. 851.

3. *State Agricultural and Mechanical College.* In Announcements for 1950–51, 126 (Orangeburg, S.C., 1950), and Franklin R. DeWitt, *A History of the School of Law of South Carolina State College*, 145 (Orangeburg: Franklin R. DeWitt, 1999).

4. John G. Hervey, American Bar Association, to President Benner C. Turner, March 18, 1955; Turner to Hervey, March 22, 1955, School of Law file, President's Papers, SCSU.

5. Information on the faculty and deans is derived from the bulletins and catalogs of State Agricultural and Mechanical College and South Carolina State College between 1947–48 and 1966–68. (In 1954 the legal name of the institution was changed from the Colored Normal, Industrial, Agricultural and Mechanical College of South Carolina to South Carolina State College.) The information on Paul A. Simmons is from http://www.jtbf.org/article_iii_judges/simmons_p.htm (accessed August 5, 2014; page no longer available).

6. There are few reported cases that were handled by S.C. State faculty. None of these involved civil rights. See *Bultman v. Barber*, 277 S.C. 5 (1981); *Houston v. International Paper Co.*, 233 F.2d 69 (4th Cir. 1956) (cases of Professor Blinzy Gore); *Isaacson v. Penn Community Services, Inc.*, 450 F.2d 1306 (4th Cir. 1971); *State v. Bostick*, 253 S.C. 205, 169 S.E.2d 608 (1969); *Bostick v. State*, 247 S.C. 22, 145 S.E.2d 439 (1965) and U.S. v. 1,534 *Acres of Land More or Less, in Beaufort* County S.C., 141 F. Supp. 720 (E.D.S.C. 1956); and cases of Professor Charles Washington. However, Professor LeMarquis Marmon did handle civil rights litigation in North Carolina. For example, see *Chambers v. Hendersonville City Bd. of Ed.*, 245 E. Supp. 759 (W.D.N.C. 1965).

7. No system of tenure existed to protect the academic freedom of faculty. For more on race in South Carolina in the 1950s, see Howard H. Quint, *Profile in Black and White: A Frank Portrait of South Carolina* (Washington: Public Affairs Press, 1958), 104.

8. "Negro Teachers Test State Law," *Florence Morning News*, September 11, 1956; "Case against NAACP Goes Back to S.C.," *(Burlington, N.C.) Daily Times-News*, January 24, 1957.

9. For example, in 1959 approximately forty lawyers convened on the campus in connection with a meeting of the Southeastern Lawyers Association to discuss "Problems and Techniques of Estate Planning for Small Estates." *Annual Report of South Carolina State College,* October 1958–May 1959, 17; Law School Alumni File; *School of Law Announcements for 1965–66* (Orangeburg, S.C., 1965), SCSU, 17.

10. Burke and Hine, "State College Law School," 38.

11. Julius Williams was in the school's first class. While admitted by the diploma privilege to the South Carolina Bar, Williams returned to Savannah, Georgia, his home, where he passed the bar exam. He struggled to make a living practicing law but did work for the NAACP. Williams was married to Strom Thurmond's daughter, Essie Mae Washington. They moved to California in 1953 but Williams never practiced there. In 1961 he returned to Savannah and practiced again, but he died in 1964. See Essie Mae Washington Williams and William Stadiem, *Dear Senator: A Memoir by the Daughter*

of Strom Thurmond (New York: Harper Collins, 2005), 158, 160, 177–78, 183. James B. McQuirter of the class of 1956 returned to Chicago, where he became a teacher. *"Air Force Captain to See Dad for 1st Time," Chicago Defender*, March 31, 1965. Orangeburg native Paul R. Webber III practiced for a time in Columbia but moved to Washington, D.C., where he became a superior court judge. Talmadge Bartell joined the army and served in the Judge Advocate General's Corps. While he passed the South Carolina bar, Ned Felder joined the army and rose to the rank of colonel serving in the Judge Advocate General's Corps. Mack Davis was admitted to the South Carolina bar but moved to Washington, D.C., and practiced there. See, for example, *Holmes v. U.S.*, 615 A.2d 555 (D.C. Ct. App. 1992). Alphonso W. Pendergrass practiced in Beaufort with Charles Washington and then moved to Washington, D.C., to practice. John J. Rodgers graduated in 1954 and was admitted to the bar but never practiced in the state. Two graduates practiced law overseas: Bassey Mbrey Bassey in Nigeria and Allen A. Christian in Frederiksted in the U.S. Virgin Islands. Ralph Waldo Sparks became a housing court judge in New York City. Laura A. Ponds, the only female graduate of the law school, moved to New Jersey. James Jackson returned to Florida. Charles Benton returned to Columbus, Georgia, and passed the state bar but died before he could practice a day. Robert Knight moved to Georgia but never practiced law. William C. Hall moved to California and went into the insurance business. Joe Louis Black left the state and may have moved to Colorado. Robert K. Wright returned to Florida. Father Rupert F. Taylor never was admitted to the bar but remained an Episcopal priest. Zack Townsend, interview by author, August 19, 2013.

Significant civil rights litigation includes primarily cases recorded in the Federal Reporters or in the South Carolina Reports. The South Carolina Reports include only appellate cases. Thus other graduates may have handled tried cases in state court at the trial level or at the federal trial at the state level, or in federal court, level since where many federal cases do not result in reported opinions. For a complete list of this significant litigation, see Burke and Hine, "State College Law School," 44–49.

12. On Albert A. Kennedy, see Burke and Hine, "State College Law School," 36. On W. Newton Pough, for example, see *State v. Fields*, 242 S.C. 357, 131 S.E.2d 91 (163). Pough handled at least ten other reported appellate cases. On Frank E. Cain, for example, see *State v. Hamm*, 256 S.C. 1, 180 S.E.2d 628 (1971). (A civil rights worker was charged with drug possession.) On John Wrighten, see, for example, see *Clark v. Flory*, 237 F.2d 597 (4th Cir. 1956). (Unsuccessful effort to desegregate Edisto Beach State Park. The case was mooted by the closure of the park by the state.) Even as late as the 1970s, before he went on the bench, Ernest A. Finney was still handling civil rights cases. See *Ellison v. Rock Hill Printing and Finishing Co.*, 64 F.R.D. 415 (D.S.C. 1974) (wage discrimination case). Willie T. Smith Jr.'s first reported case was *Mackey v. Chandler*, 152 F. Supp. 579 (W.D.S.C. 1957) (warrantless search case). William Bennett handled five reported cases. His earliest was a sit-in case, *State* v. *Randolph*, 239 S.C. 79, 121 S.E.2d 349 (1961). Russell Brown was counsel in six reported cases. His first was *City of Charleston v. Mitchell*, 239 S.C. 376, 123 S.E.2d 512 (1961). On Ruben L. Gray, see *State of South Carolina v. Davidman*, 250 F. Supp. 989 (D.S.C. 1966). (Civil rights workers charged with contributing to the delinquency of a minor.) Zack E. Townsend handled seven cases. His first was a

desegregation case. *Adams v. School District No. 5, Orangeburg County, S.C.*, 232 F. Supp. 692 (E.D.S.C. 1964). On George A. Payton, see *State v. Stallings*, 252 S.C. 451, 171 S.E.2d 588 (1969) (challenged exclusion of women from jury).

13. Townsend interview by author.

14. Phylicia Fleming-McCall, *Images of America: African-Americans in Chesterfield County* (Mount Pleasant, S.C.: Arcadia Publishing, 2008), 15.

15. Burke and Hine, "State College Law School," 47–49.

16. Ernest A. Finney, "Chief Counsel," in Burke and Gergel, *Matthew J. Perry*, 118–19.

17. R. Scott Baker, *Paradoxes of Desegregation: African American Struggles for Educational Equity in Charleston, South Carolina, 1926–1972* (Columbia: University of South Carolina Press, 2006), 30. In 1938 Perry's principal, J. Andrew Simmons, had encouraged Charles Bailey to apply to the University of South Carolina School of Law.

18. Robert J. Moore, "Matthew J. Perry's Preparation," in Burke and Gergel, *Matthew J. Perry*, 67.

19. Matthew J. Perry interview, April 2, 2003, in Burke and Hine, "State College Law School," 37.

20. Sec. 313 of the S.C. Code Ann. 1942 provided the diploma privilege. The diploma privilege was then revoked on July 1, 1950, by Act 808, Acts and Joint Resolutions of the General Assembly of the State of South Carolina. Also see R. Scott Baker, "A New Racial Order in Education: South Carolina's Response to the African American Struggle for Equity and Access, 1945–1975," unpublished paper, Citadel Conference of Civil Rights, March 2003, 7–8.

21. Matthew J. Perry, interview by author, June 10, 2010.

22. Ibid.

23. Cameron McGowan Currie, "Before Rosa Parks: The Case of Sarah Mae Flemming," in Burke and Gergel, *Matthew J. Perry*, 81; Virginia L. Vroegop, "A Postscript: Flemming's Role in Matthew J. Perry's Civil Rights Career," in Burke and Gergel, *Matthew J. Perry*, 95.

24. *Edwards v. South Carolina*, 372 U.S. 229 (1962).

25. NAACP Statement quoted in *(Columbia) State*, March 4, 1961.

26. "State House March Lands 189 in Jail," *(Columbia) State*, March 3, 1961.

27. "Convictions of Negroes Are Upheld," *(Columbia) State*, December 6, 1961.

28. *Edwards v. South Carolina*, 230–35, 239–43.

29. 370 U.S. 935 (1962).

30. In addition to Peterson and Edwards, see *Mitchell v. City of Charleston*, 378 U.S. 551 (1964); *Hamm v. City of Rock Hill*, 377 U.S. 988 (1964); *Henry v. City of Rock Hill*, 376 U.S. 776 (1964); *Barr v. City of Columbia*, 374 U.S. 804 (1963); *Bouie v. City of Columbia*, 374 U.S. 805 (1963).

31. *Brown v. School District No. 20, Charleston, South Carolina*, 328 F.2d 618 (4th Cir. 1964) affirming 226 F. Supp. 819 (E.D.S.C. 1963).

32. *Randall v. Sumter School District No. 2*, 232 F. Supp. 692 (E.D.S.C. 1964); *Adams v. School District No. 5, Orangeburg County*, 232 F. Supp. 692 (E.D.S.C. 1964); *Brunson v. Board of Trustees of School Dist. No. 1 Clarendon County*, 244 F. Supp. 859 (E.D.S.C. 1964).

33. *Miller v. School District No. 2 of Clarendon County*, 253 F. Supp. 552 (D.S.C. 1966).

34. *Green v. County School Board of New Kent County*, 391 U.S. 430 (1968); *Alexander v. Holmes County Board of Education*, 396 U.S. 19 (1969).

35. *Stanley v. Darlington County School District*, 424 F.2d 195 (4th Cir. 1970).

36. *Swann v. Mecklenburg Board of Education*, 402 U.S. 1 (1970); *Adams v. School District No. 5, Orangeburg County*, 44 F.2d 99 (4th Cir. 1971).

37. Robert J. Moore, "The Civil Rights Advocate," in Burke and Gergel, *Matthew J. Perry*, 171.

38. See Eric L. Mueller, "The Legal Defense Fund's Capital Punishment Campaign: The Distorting Influence of Death," *Yale Law and Policy Review* 15 (1985): 158.

39. "Dishwasher's .22 Pistol Verified as Weapon," *Florence Morning News*, August 10, 1958.

40. "Bullock Ordered Held in Dillon Slaying," *(Columbia) State*, August 23, 1958.

41. "Negro Admits Dillon Slaying," *(Columbia) State*, August 9, 1958.

42. "Fatal Bullets Came from Negro's Pistol," *(Columbia) State*, August 10, 1958.

43. "Bullock Ordered Held in Dillon Slaying," *(Columbia) State*, August 23, 1958.

44. See articles from *Florence Morning News*: "Dishwasher's .22 Pistol Verified as Weapon," August 10, 1958; "Bullock Leads Dillon Officers," August 12, 1958; "Full Moon Big Motive in Killing," August 13, 1958; "Confessed Slayer Boasted of Living Straight Life," August 21, 1958; "She Must Have Lost Control," September 1, 1958.

45. "Negro Admits Dillon Slaying," *(Columbia) State*, August 9, 1958; "Bullock Says State Forced Confession," *(Columbia) State*, January 10, 1961.

46. "State Rest Case against Bullock," *Florence Morning News*, October 25, 1958.

47. "Bullock Found Guilty Faces Electric Chair," *(Columbia) State*, October 26, 1958.

48. "Bullock Sentenced to Die," *Florence Morning News*, October 26, 1958.

49. See *State v. Bullock*, 235 S.C. 356 (1959); S.C. Briefs and Records, 235 S.C. 356.

50. "Bullock's Appeal Heads for S.C.'s High Court," *(Columbia) State*, October 5, 1959.

51. "Chair-Bound Bullock Loses Another Round," *(Columbia) State*, November 17, 1959.

52. "Court Won't Change Verdict on Bullock," *Florence Morning News*, February 21, 1961.

53. *State v. Bullock*, 365 U.S. 292 (1961).

54. "Frightened Negro Dies in S.C.'s Chair," *(Columbia) State*, April 29, 1961.

55. See Moore, "Civil Rights Advocate," 77; http://genealogytrails.com/scar/executions1.htm (accessed September 30, 2013).

56. In 1977 this campaign culminated with the U.S. Supreme Court declaring the death penalty unconstitutional in rape cases. See *Coker v. Georgia*, 433 U.S. 584 (1977).

57. Jack Greenburg, *Crusaders in the Courts: How a Dedicated Band of Lawyers Fought for the Civil Rights Revolution (New York: Basic Books, 1994)*, 440.

58. "Escapee Is Sought after Two Women Attacked in Motel," *(Columbia) State*, November 29, 1961.

59. "Search Widens for Negro Man Wanted in Rape," *(Columbia) State*, December 1, 1961.

60. "Negro, 19, Arrested in Assault," *(Columbia) State*, December 2, 1961.

61. "Heavy Court Docket Set in Kingstree," *(Columbia) State,* February 22, 1962; "Rape Trial Set Thursday at Kingstree," *(Columbia) State,* February 28, 1962.

62. "Two Women Take Stand in Kingstree," *(Columbia) State,* March 2, 1962; "In Rape of Two Women," *(Columbia) State*, March 3, 1962.

63. "High Court Review Asked," *(Columbia) State,* May 23, 1963.

64. *(Columbia) State v. White*, 243 S.C. 238, 240–241 (1963).

65. "Kingstree Rape Trail Set Again," *(Columbia) State,* February 25, 1964.

66. "Testimony Is Delayed," *(Columbia) State,* February 26, 1964; "Kingstree Rape Case Continues," *(Columbia) State,* February 27, 1964.

67. *State v. White*, 246 S.C. 502, 144 S.E.2d 481 (1965).

68. "The Week in Review," *(Columbia) State,* March 1, 1964.

69. "White Granted a Third Trial," *(Columbia) State,* October 14, 1965.

70. "Twelve Wait to Meet Fate," *(Columbia) State,* December 4, 1966.

71. See http://www.deathpenaltyinfo.org/executions-us-1608-2002-espy-file (accessed September 1, 2016).

72. "Court to Hear Jasper Sheriff Slayer's Appeal," *(Columbia) State,* May 7, 1963.

73. Ibid.

74. "Youth Sentenced to Die in Slaying of Sheriff," *(Columbia) State*, March 1, 1962.

75. "Court Told Condemned Negro Got Fair Trial," *(Columbia) State,* May 14, 1963.

76. *State v. Bostick*, 243 S.C. 14 (1963).

77. "Bostick Is Granted Stay," *(Columbia) State,* August 15, 1963.

78. *Bostick v. State*, 247 S.C. 22 (1965).

79. "Condemned Man Denied New Trial," *(Columbia) State,* July 10, 1964; *Bostick v. State*, 247 S.C. 22 (1965).

80. Brief for Petitioner, *Bostick v. South Carolina*, 386 U.S. 479 (1967) (No. 647), 5–6. Judge Johnson had thrown out a drunk driving charge when a white attorney, John Bolt Culbertson, challenged the makeup of a Jasper County jury. In that case, when Clerk of Court R. L. Sensenbach was asked if he had excluded blacks from the jury list, he invoked his Fifth Amendment right not to incriminate himself and refused to answer the question. "Jasper County Sees Tiff in Jury Legality," *Columbia State,* February 25, 1954. Johnson's ruling was influenced by the recent state supreme court ruling in *State v. Waitus*, 224 S.C. 12 (1953), which overturned a Georgetown County murder conviction because of the systematic exclusion of blacks from jury service.

81. Brief for Petitioner, *Bostick v. South Carolina,* 66. Also see "New Trial for Bostick Is Promised," *(Columbia) State,* March 30, 1967.

82. Brief for Petitioner, *Bostick v. South Carolina*, 76, 82, 88, 66–72.

83. "Bostick Appeal Lost in S.C. High Court," *(Columbia) State,* December 1, 1965.

84. "Bostick Granted Hearing," *(Columbia) State,* October 11, 1966.

85. *Whitus v. State of Ga.*, 385 U.S. 545, 551 (1967).

86. *State v. Bostick,* 386 U.S. 479 (1967).

87. "New Trial for Bostick Is Promised," *(Columbia) State,* March 30, 1967. Also see *State v. Bostick*, 253 S.C. 205 (1969).

88. "Jury Gives Life Verdict in 2nd Trial," *(Columbia) State,* March 1, 1968.

89. "Armed Students Occupy Building at Voorhees," *(Columbia) State*, April 29, 1969.

90. "Voorhees Rebels Vacate Buildings," *(Columbia) State*, April 30, 1969. Also see *State v. Albert*, 257 S.C. 131 (1971).

91. Interviews with Fred Henderson Moore by author, February 4, 11, 17, 24, March 3, and 17, 2014. Unless otherwise noted, all of the Moore material is from these interviews. Also see Robert Goldstein, *Political Repression in Modern America, 1870–1976* (Urbana: University of Illinois Press, 2001), 521.

92. *State v. Albert,* 257 S.C. 131 (1971) cert. denied 409 U.S. 966 (1972); *State v. Raysor,* 257 S.C. 265 (1971), cert. denied 407 U.S. 916 (1972).

93. *Adams v. School District No. 5, Orangeburg County,* 232 F. Supp. 692 (E.D.S.C. 1964).

94. *Rackley v. School District No. 5, Orangeburg County*, 258 F. Supp. 676 (D.S.C. 1966).

95. *Rackley v. Board of Trustees of the Orangeburg Regional Hospital*, 238 F. Supp. 512 (E.D.S.C. 1965).

96. *Henry v. Greenville Airport Commission*, 191 F. Supp. 146 (W.D.S.C. 1961).

97. *Stevenson v. West,* 413 U.S. 902 (1973). His co-counsel in the case included Fred Henderson Moore, George Payton, Bernard Fielding, Armand Derfner, and Nathaniel Jones.

98. Timothy J. Minchin, "Making Best Use of the New Laws: The NAACP and the Fight for Civil Rights in the South, 1965–1975," *Journal of Southern History* 74, no. 3 (2008): 694.

99. Moore, "Civil Rights Advocate," 175.

100. News Release of South Carolina State University, June 17, 2014, http://www.scsu.edu/news_article.aspx?news_id=1719 (accessed September 1, 2016).

101. "14 Candidates Seek Six Posts on NAACP Board," Chicago Defender, November 26, 1966, 28; "NAACP problem: Finding Spottswood's Successor," *Washington Afro-American,* December 24, 1974, 4.

102. See Robert W. Foster to Matthew J. Perry, June 20, 1972, Matthew J. Perry File, Former Faculty Files, University of South Carolina School of Law Archives.

103. "M. J. Perry Jr., Legal Pioneer Dies at 89," *New York Times,* August 5, 2011.

104. "Rep. Spence Re-Elected," *(Columbia) State*, November 6, 1974.

105. "M. J. Perry Jr., Legal Pioneer Dies at 89," *New York Times,* August 5, 2011.

106. Interview by author with Langdon D. Long, May 6, 2014.

107. See table 6 in Burke and Hine, "State College Law School," 47–49.

108. Interview by author with Ernest J. Finney and Frances Davenport Finney, July 2013. Also see George C. Rogers Jr., *Generations of Lawyers: A History of the South Carolina Bar* (Columbia: South Carolina Bar Foundation, 1992), 230.

109. "Lawyers Seek Attorneys' Fees," *Florence Morning News*, October 7, 1966.

110. For example, see "425 Negro Protestors Jailed," *(Columbia) State*, March 16, 1960; "Rock Hill Has New Counter Demonstration," June 12, 1960; "Another Is Convicted in Rock Hill Sitin," July 15, 1960.

111. *Henry v. City of Rock Hill*, 241 S.C. 427, vacated 375 U.S. 6 (1962); *Henry v. City of Rock Hill*, 244 S.C. 74, rev'd 376 U.S. 776 (1964); *Hamm v. City of Rock Hill*, 241 S.C. 420, rev'd 377 U.S. 988 (1964).

112. *City of Sumter v. McAllister*, South Carolina Supreme Court Brief and Records, 241 S.C. 409 (1962); *City of Sumter v. Gregg*, 241 S.C. 409 (1962).

113. "Attorneys Seek $29,000 to Free Jailed Negroes," *Sumter Daily Item*, October 15, 1963, 2.

114. "Sumter Lawyer for Negroes Holds Parley," *(Columbia) State*, February 24, 1961.

115. "Dorchester District Faces Court Suits," *Florence Morning News*, August 27, 1965.

116. *Randall v. Sumter School District No. 2*, 232 F.Supp.786 (E.D.S.C. 1964); *Stanley v. Darlington County School District*, 424 F. 2d 195 (4th Cir., 1970); *DeLee v. School District Number 3, Dorchester County, S.C.*, 306 F. Supp. 905 (D.S.C. 1965); *Whittenberg v. Greenville County School District*, 298 F. Supp. 784 (D.S.C. 1969); *Miller v. School District Number 2 Clarendon County, S.C.*, 256 F. Supp. 370 (D.S.C. 1966).

117. *James v. Carnegie Public Library*, 235 F. Supp. (E.D.S.C. 1964).

118. *Brown v. South Carolina State Forestry Commission*, 226 F. Supp. 646 (E.D.S.C. 1963); *Brown v. South Carolina State Board of Education*, 296 F. Supp. 199 (D.S.C. 1968).

119. "Timmerman, Finney Got Write-Ins," *Florence Morning News*, November 14, 1964.

120. "Negroes Seek Legislative Seats in Area Counties," *Florence Morning News*, March 22, 1966.

121. "State Civil Rights Group Appeals to LBJ," *Florence Morning News*, April 6, 1968.

122. Sylvia W. Orange, ed., *South Carolina Legislative Manual*, 55th ed. (1974), 76.

123. "Invincibles Clipped," *Florence Morning News*, September 1, 1972.

124. *South Carolina Legislative Manual* (1974), 76.

125. William Whipper was elected to a circuit judgeship in 1875, but Governor Chamberlain withheld his commission and Whipper never served as a circuit court judge.

126. 335 S.C. 58 (1995).

127. Interview with Ernest A. Finney Jr. and Frances Davenport Finney by author on June 27, 2013.

128. *Hill's Columbia City Directory* (Richmond, Va.: Hill Directory Co., 1951), 1006.

129. His only reported case was a probation revocation appeal in federal court, which he lost. See *U.S. v. Leevy*, 371 F. 2d 912 (4th Cir. 1967).

130. Interview with Hemphill Pride II by the author on June 24, 2013.

131. *In the matter of Albert A. Kennedy*, 254 S.C. 463, 465 (1970).

132. *Clark v. Flory*, 230 F.2d 597 (4th Cir. 1956); *Clark v. Flory*, 141 F. Supp. 240 (E.D.S.C. 1956); Robert J. Moore, "Civil Rights Advocate," 160.

133. "Jury to Get Orangeburg Shooting Case," *(Columbia) State*, January 14, 1966.

134. "Jury Still Out in Murder Case," *(Columbia) State*, January 15, 1966.

135. "Orangeburg Man Sentenced to Death," *(Columbia) State*, September 24, 1966.

136. *State v. Richburg*, 250 S.C. 451 (1968).

137. "Orangeburg Case Is Tried for Third Time," *(Columbia) State*, April 22, 1969.

138. "Richburg Verdict Is Manslaughter," *(Columbia) State*, April 24, 1969.

139. Interview with Zach Townsend. Also see *State v. Richburg*, 253 S.C. 458 (1969).

140. "A Service of loving memory of attorney W. Newton Pough," Friday, September 1, 2006, Trinity United Methodist Church, Orangeburg, South Carolina. (Funeral bulletin in possession of author.)

141. *City of Sumter v. Gregg*, 241 S.C. 409 (1962); *City of Sumter v. Lewis*, 241 S.C. 364 (1962); *City of Sumter v. McAllister*, 241 S.C. 355 (1962); *City of Florence v. George*, 241 S.C. 77 (1962).

142. "Seek Mixing in Florence Schools," *Florence Morning News*, June 30, 1955.

143. "Trials for 48 Negroes," *Florence Morning News*, March 26, 1960.

144. "Motions Delay Students' Trials," *(Columbia) State*, March 17, 1960.

145. "Legal Notice," *Florence Morning News*, April 1, 1954, and March 30, 1969. More than fifty notices appeared.

146. "Two 'Erroneous Rulings' Caused Loss, Negro Says," *(Columbia) State*, March 18, 1965; "County by County Runoff Results," June 26, 1968.

147. "Bennett Rites Wednesday," *(Columbia) State*, July 15, 1969.

148. State v. Hamm, 256 S.C. 1, at 12 (1971).

149. *State v. Hamm*, 409 U.S. 524 (1973).

150. "Ham Sentenced in Florence," *(Columbia) State*, January 26, 1973.

151. *South Carolina Bar Lawyers Desk Book* (Columbia: South Carolina Bar, 2013–14), 125.

152. *Maryland Casualty Company v. Connor*, 200 F. Supp. 647 (D.S.C. 1961).

153. Interview with Judge Ruben Gray by author, July 18, 2013.

154. See U.S. Veterans Gravesites, ca. 1775–2006, available at ancestry.com. Bunch's birth date is listed as March 15, 1922, and his death date is March 9, 2002. He was buried in Holly Hill, South Carolina.

155. Edmund L. Drago, *Charleston's Avery Center: From Education and Civil Rights to Preserving the African American Experience*, rev. ed. by W. Marvin Dulaney (Charleston: History Press, 2006), 251, 256–57.

156. *Charleston v. Mitchell*, 239 S.C. 376 (1961).

157. *Mitchell v. City of Charleston*, 378 U.S. 551 (1964).

158. *Clark v. Flory*, 141 F. Supp. 248 (E.D.S.C. 1956) and 237 F.2d 597 (4th Cir. 1956).

159. *State v. White*, 246 S.C. 502 (1965).

160. *Porter v. News & Courier Co.*, 237 S.C. 102 (1960); *U.S. v. Brown*, 296 F.2d 565 (4th Cir. 1961); *United States v. Grisby*, 335 F.2d 652 (4th Cir. 1964); *Moorer v. South Carolina*, 379 U.S. 860 (1964); *Betterson v. Stewart*, 245 S.C. 296 (1965); *Miller v. Lee*, 241 F. Supp. 19 (D.S.C. 1965); *Chestnut v. Chestnut*, 247 S.C. 332 (1966); *State v. Jenkins*, 249 S.C. 570 (1967); *State v. Nelson*, 250 S.C. 6 (1967); *Brown v. Ford Motor Company*, 287 F. Supp. 906 (D.S.C. 1968); *State v. Stallings*, 253 S.C. 451 (1969).

161. *In re Wrighten*, 257 S.C. 184 (1971).

162. Felicia Fleming-McCall, *Images of America: African-Americans in Chesterfield County* (Charleston: Arcadia, 2008), 15.

163. *State v. Funderburke*, 251 S.C. 536 (1968).

164. "City Issues 3 New Business Licenses," *(Columbia) State*, January 14, 1961; Interview by author with I. S. Leevy Johnson, June 12, 2013; South Carolina, Find a Grave Index, 1729–2012, available at ancestry.com.

165. "Horry Negro Registration Grown to 2,000," *(Columbia) State*, September 27, 1963.

166. "Motions Delay Students' Trials," *(Columbia) State*, March 17, 1960.

167. *In re Wrighten*, 257 S.C. 184 (1971).

168. "Woomer's Lawyers Wanted to Avoid Death Penalty," *(Columbia) State*, July 23, 1979; "Mistrial Is Declared in Beach Ambush Case," *(Columbia) State*, October 25, 1979.

169. *Matter of Stevens*, 298 S.C. 74 (1989).

170. "Obituary," *(Columbia) State*, October 25, 2004.

171. *Mackie v. Chandler*, 152 F. Supp. 579 (W.D.S.C. 1957).

172. Richard Henry was represented in his suit in federal district court by Jack Greenberg and Lincoln Jenkins. They lost initially but won in the Fourth Circuit Court of Appeals. See *Henry v. Greenville Airport*, 175 F.Supp. 343 (1959), rev'd 279 F.2d 751 (4th Cir. 1960).

173. Stephen O'Neill, "Memory, History, and the Desegregation of Greenville, South Carolina," in Winfred B. Moore Jr. and Orville Vernon Burton, eds., *Toward the Meeting of the Waters: Currents in the Civil Rights Movement of South Carolina during the Twentieth Century* (Columbia: University of South Carolina Press, 2008), 289–90.

174. *City of Greenville v. Peterson*, 239 S.C. 298 (1961); *Henry v. City of Rock Hill*, 376 U.S. 776 (1964); *Hamm v. City of Rock Hill*, 377 U.S. 988 (1964).

175. O'Neill, "Memory, History," 291.

176. *Peterson v. Greenville*, 373 U.S. 244 (1963).

177. *Gantt v. Clemson Agricultural College of South Carolina*, 208 F. Sup. 416 (W.D.S.C. 1962).

178. See footnote 12.

179. Drago, *Charleston's Avery Center*, 260.

180. *Tracy v. Robbins*, 40 F.R.D. 108 (D.S.C. 1966); *City of Charleston v. Mitchell*, 239 S.C. 376 (1961); *Abernathy v. Conroy*, 429 F. 2d 1170 (4th Cir. 1970).

181. *State v. Moorer*, 241 S.C. 487 (1963); *Moorer v. State*, 244 S.C. 102 (1964).

182. *In the Matter of Russell Brown*, 356 S.C. 10 (2003).

183. Interview of Judge Ruben Gray by author.

184. Ibid.

185. Zack E. Townsend, "A Remembrance of a Cooperating Attorney," in Burke and Gergel, *Matthew J. Perry*, 122.

186. Interview with Zack E. Townsend by author, June 13, 2013.

187. *State v. Allen*, 266 S.C. 175 (1976).

188. *State v. Rogers*, 270 S.C. 285 (1978).

189. DeWitt died March 22, 2008. Social Security Death Index, 1935–current, available at ancestry.com.

190. City Code Section 31–195 provided that "No permit shall be granted under this subdivision for a parade to convene before 8:00 A.M. or terminate after 8:00 P.M."

191. The state authorities subsequently reduced the bail for each plaintiff to $5,000. 429 F.2d 1170 (4th Cir. 1970).

192. *Abernathy v. Conroy*, 429 F.2d 1170 (4th Cir. 1970).

193. "Abernathy Released," *(Columbia) State*, May 3, 1969. Also see Philip S. Foner, *Organized Labor and the Black Worker, 1619–1973* (New York: Praeger, 1974), 386–96.

194. *Counts v. Voorhees College*, 312 F. Sup. 598 (D.S.C. 1970), aff'd 439 Fed.2d723 (4th Cir. 1971).

195. See *State v. Rouse*, 262 S.C. 581 (1974); *State v. Smith*, 259 S.C. 496 (1972); *State v. Wiggins*, 257 S.C. 167 (1971); *State v. Stallings*, 253 S.C. 451 (1969).

196. "George Payton Jr. Slain in His Office," *(Charleston) News and Courier*, March 19, 1975.

197. "Second Orangeburg March Follows Mayor's Warning," *(Columbia) State*, October 2, 1963.

198. "Anderson Elected to Staff Office," *Aiken Standard*, January 19, 1976. Also see James Felder, *Civil Rights in South Carolina: From Peaceful Protests to Groundbreaking Rulings* (Charleston: History Press, 2012), 37.

199. "Charges Dismissed against Bus Driver," *Aiken Standard*, December 22, 1970; "Court," *Aiken Standard*, May 11, 1971.

200. See "George A. Anderson," http://www.lawyers.com/aiken/south-carolina/George-A-Anderson-1580084-a/ (accessed August 5, 2014).

201. "Voorhees Group to Hear Black House Hopefuls," *(Columbia) State*, October 20, 1972.

202. "Notice of Death," *Charleston Post and Courier*, February 18, 2008.

203. "Legal Notices," *(Columbia) State*, January 17, 1976; "Legal Notices," *Marietta Daily Journal*, May 27, 1983. Also see "George Marion Crawford," *(Columbia) State*, April 13, 2006; South Carolina, Find a Grave Index, 1729–2012, available at ancestry.com.

204. See *Brown v. Ford Motor Company*, 287 F. Supp. 906 (D.S.C. 1968); *Graham v. Charleston County School Bd.*, 262 S.C. 314 (1974).

205. *Fielding v. South Carolina Election Commission*, 305 S.C. 313 (1991).

206. *Winters v. Fiddie*, 394 S.C. 629 (2011).

207. Thurgood Marshall to William R. King, October 2, 1947, in NAACP Campaign for Education Equality.

208. Richard L. Abel, *American Lawyers* (New York: Oxford University Press, 1989), 100.

209. The University of Arkansas and Louisiana State University desegregated in the late 1940s and early 1950s but had few students. See Judith Kilpatrick, "Desegregating the University of Arkansas School of Law: L. Clifford Davis and the Six Pioneers," *Arkansas Historical Quarterly* 68 (2009): 123; W. Lee Hargrave, *L.S.U. Law: The Louisiana State University School of Law from 1906 to 1977* (Baton Rouge: Louisiana State University Press, 2004), 151–53.

210. Annual Report, October 1965–1966, South Carolina State College, 30. In contrast, a huge controversy erupted in Tallahassee when the Florida A&M Law School was closed in 1968. See Larry O. Rivers, *Florida Agricultural and Mechanical University: School of Law (1949–2000)* (Tallahassee: Larry O. Rivers, 2000), 35–51.

CHAPTER 13. A New Generation

1. For additional information on Washington, see chapter 12. After the law school closed in 1966, he practiced in Beaufort until his death in 1972.

2. See *School District of Greenville County v. Whittenberg*, 397 U.S. 1066 (1970);

State v. Edwards, 239 S.C. 339 (1961); *City of Rock Hill v. Hamm*, 241 S.C. 420 (1962); *Gantt v. Clemson Agricultural College of S.C.*, 320 F.2d 611 (1963). Also see *State v. Randolph*, 239 S.C. 79 (1961); *City of Rock Hill v. Henry*, 244 S.C. 74 (1963).

3. *Walker v. Shaw*, 209 F. Supp. 569 (W.D.S.C. 1962).

4. *Mackey v. Chandler*, 152 F. Supp. 579 (W.D.S.C. 1957).

5. Briefs and Records, *State v. Brooks*, 235 S.C. 344 (1959) (No. 17580).

6. *State v. Bullock*, 235 S.C. 356 (1959).

7. *State v. Gist*, 237 S.C. 262 (1960).

8. "Greenville 'White Block' Law Is Voided by Eppes," *Greenville News*, January 16, 1963.

9. Stephen O'Neill, "Memory, History, and Desegregation of Greenville, South Carolina," in Winfred B. Moore Jr. and Orville Vernon Burton, eds., *Toward the Meeting of the Waters: Currents in the Civil Rights Movement of South Carolina during the Twentieth Century* (Columbia: University of South Carolina Press, 2008), 286.

10. "Donald James Sampson," *Greenville News*, May 30, 2001.

11. Fourteenth United States Census, 1920, Population, S.C., Darlington County, available at ancestry.com; "1,800 Degrees Make Record at Harvard," *New York Times*, June 24, 1927.

12. *Muskogee (Oklahoma) City Directory 1928, 1930, 1932, and 1934*, "U.S. City Directories, 1821–1989," available at ancestry.com; *Bruce v. Bruce*, 141 Okla. 160 (1930); *Smith v. Gibson*, 150 Okla. 101 (1931); *Wesley v. Chandler*, 152 Okla. 22 (1931); *Anderson v. Malone*, 154 Okla. 4 (1932); *Brown v. Dixon*, 156 Okla. 11 (1932); *Brown v. State Nat'l Bank of Shawnee*, 167 Okla. 366 (1934); *Ingram v. Wesley*, 169 Okla. 248 (1934); *In re Buffington's Estate*, 169 Okla. 487 (1934); *Ingram v. Lewis*, 37 F.2d 259 (1930); *Ingram v. Wesley*, 37 F.2d 201 (1930); *Jackson v. Harris*, 43 F.2d 513 (1930); *Ingram v. Jones*, 47 F. 2d 135 (1931); *Ingram v. Mandler*, 56 F.2d 994 (1932); *Lewis v. Ingram*, 57 F. 2d 463 (1932).

13. See testimony of Water S. Steele regarding communist activities in the United States in hearings before the Committee on Un-American Activities, House of Representatives, 80th Congress, First Session on H.R. 1884 and H.R. 2122, Bills to Curb or Outlaw the Communist Party in the United States, Public Law 601, July 21, 1947, printed for the use of the Committee on Un-American Activities (Washington, D.C.: Government Printing Office, 1947), 113. The camp was operated by a cooperative, which Steele viewed as especially sinister.

14. *Graves v. Dubose*, 229 S.C. 123 (1956); *Belin v. Stikeleather*, 232 S.C. 116 (1957); *Turbeville v. Gordon*, 233 S.C. 75 (1958); *Williams v. Marion County Bd. of Ed.*, 234 S.C. 273 (1959); *Singleton v. Mullins Lumber Co.*, 234 S.C. 330 (1959); *Jackson v. Hobbs*, 234 S.C. 497 (1959); *Turbeville v. Gordon*, 236 S.C. 57 (1960); *Bennett v. Floyd*, 237 S.C. 64 (1960); *Stanley v. Gary*, 237 S.C. 237 (1960); *State v. McIver*, 238 S.C. 401 (1961); *Betterson v. Stewart*, 238 S.C. 574 (1961); *City of Darlington v. Stanley*, 239 S.C. 139 (1961); *Jackson v. Powe*, 241 S.C. 35 (1962).

15. "Negro Aide Wins on Segregation," *New York Times*, February 29, 1956.

16. Transcript of Record, *City of Darlington v. Stanley*, 239 S.C. 139 (1961), p. 5, Cases Heard and Submitted, Supreme Court of South Carolina; *City of Darlington v. Stanley*, 239 S.C. 139 (1961).

17. See Thomas J. Bynum, NAACP *Youth and the Fight for Black Freedom, 1936–1965* (Knoxville: University of Tennessee Press, 2013), 107; John W. White, "The White Citizens' Councils of Orangeburg County, South Carolina," in Moore and Burton, *Toward the Meeting of the Waters*, 261.

18. *Byrd v. Gary*, 184 F. Supp. 388 (E.D.S.C. 1960).

19. *Stanley v. Gary*, 237 S.C. 237 (1960).

20. "Elliott Turnage, Negro Attorney, Dies at Darlington," *Florence Morning News*, July 27, 1962.

21. "Alabama Sheriff Draws Pickets in Charleston," *(Columbia) State*, July 19, 1966.

22. "NAACP Plans Voting Suit," *(Columbia) State*, October 11, 1968.

23. See record in *Stevenson v. West*, 413 U.S. 902 (1972).

24. Matthew J. Perry, "Voices from the Civil Rights Movement," in Moore and Burton, *Toward the Meeting of the Waters*, 349.

25. *Fielding v. South Carolina Election Commission*, 305 S.C. 313 (1991).

26. See *Charleston City Directory, Colored Resident Directory* (Livonia, Mich.: R. L. Polk, 1955), 27; interview with Judge Richard Fields by author on June 21, 2013. Also see *California Death Index, June 13, 1976*, available at ancestry.com.

27. Obituary, Digital Library of Georgia, http://funeral.galileo.usg.edu/funeral/view?docId=funeral/hinton19980131-001.xml (accessed September 16, 2016).

28. Fred Henderson Moore interview by author, March 17, 2014. Also see "Helping People Is Reward for Magistrate Harvey," *(Charleston) News and Courier*, April 26, 1970.

29. "Law Day 1990 A Black Perspective on the S.C. Judiciary," *(Columbia) State*, April 29, 1990; *South Carolina Legal Directory for 1988* (Dallas: Legal Directories, 1988), 113.

30. Ruth Williams Cupp, *Portia Steps Up to the Bar* (Raleigh, N.C.: Ivy House, 2003): 124–25.

31. "Suzanna Blackwell, 94, Dies; Founder of Business College," *Washington Post*, February 19, 1983. She was a realtor and owned a business college. See *Blackwell College of Business v. Attorney General*, 454 F.2d 928 (D.C. Cir. 1971).

32. W. Lewis Burke and William C. Hine, "The South Carolina State College Law School," in W. Lewis Burke and Belinda F. Gergel, eds., *Matthew J. Perry: The Man, His Times, and His Legacy* (Columbia: University of South Carolina Press, 2004), 35.

33. Arthur J. H. Clement III and Leroy Nesbit were admitted to the bar in 1960 but never practiced in the state. Clement had a long career with the North Carolina Mutual Life Insurance Company in Durham, North Carolina. Richard Fields, interview with author, June 21, 2013. Also see *S.C. Bar Lawyers Desk Book, 2013–2014* (Columbia: South Carolina Bar, n.d. [2013–14]), 139. Nesbit practiced in Washington, D.C., until his death in 1998. See "Defense Lawyer Leroy Nesbitt Dies," *Washington Post*, November 24, 1998.

34. See Journal of the House of Representatives, South Carolina General Assembly, 109th Session, 1991–1992, January 31, 1991.

35. See *Whittenberg v. Greenville County School District*, 298 F. Supp. 784 (D.S.C. 1969); *DeLee v. School District No. Three, Dorchester County, S.C.*, 306 F. Supp. 905 (D.S.C. 1969); *Stanley v. Darlington County School District*, 424 F.2d 195 (1970), reh'g denied, 424 F.2d 197 (1970), cert. denied, 397 U.S. 1066 (1970).

36. "Hamm Sentenced in Florence," *(Columbia) State*, January 26, 1973; "Court Ruling Upheld against Florence Man," *Florence Morning News*, May 13, 1973.

37. "NAACP Suit 'Highly Likely,'" *(Columbia) State*, February 17, 1980.

38. *Simkins v. Gressette*, 631 F. 2d 287 (4th Cir. 1980).

39. Jack Bass, "Blacks to Gain Senate Seats in South Carolina," *Southern Changes: Journal of the Southern Regional Council* 5, no. 3 (1983): 3–4.

40. "Profile Detail—Mordecai Christopher Johnson," *Who's Who in American Law (Chicago: Marquis, 198), 269*. As to the Southern Regional Council, see *The New Georgia Encyclopedia*, http://www.georgiaencyclopedia.org/articles/government-politics/southern-regional-council (accessed September 22, 2016).

41. "UCP Nominates City Candidate," *Florence Morning News*, September 13, 1970; "UCP Candidates Here," *Florence Morning News*, October 18, 1972.

42. "Council Candidates Elected Unopposed," *Florence Morning News*, May 4, 1977.

43. "Deaths Last Week," *Chicago Tribune*, April 24, 1994; "Mordecai C. Johnson," *Orlando Sentinel*, April 21, 1994.

44. "Florence Civil Rights Activist, NAACP Lawyer Johnson Dies," *(Columbia) State*, April 19, 1994.

45. Interviews with Fred Henderson Moore by author, February 4, 11, 17, 24, March 3 and 17, 2014. Unless otherwise noted, all of the Moore material is from these interviews.

46. Moore interview by author, February 17, 2014.

47. Edmund Drago, *Charleston's Avery Center: From Education and Civil Rights to Preserving the African American Experience*, rev. ed. by W. Marvin Dulaney (Charleston: History Press, 2006), 252.

48. Cleveland Sellers with Robert Terrell, *The River of No Return* (Jackson: University Press of Mississippi, 1990).

49. Moore interviews by author. The next year, Matthew Perry, Lincoln Jenkins, and Moore represented armed Voorhees College students who took over a school building and were charged with riot.

50. *State v. Sellers*, 257 S.C. 35 (1971).

51. Jack Bass and Jack Nelson, *The Orangeburg Massacre* (Macon, Ga.: Mercer University Press, 1984). Also see Cleveland L. Sellers Jr., "The Orangeburg Massacre," in Moore and Burton, *Toward the Meeting of the Waters*, 364. Sellers was pardoned in 1993 and would become a faculty member at the University of South Carolina and president of Voorhees College.

52. See *Abernathy v. Conroy*, 429 F.2d 1170 (4th Cir. 1970).

53. "Armed Students Occupy Buildings at Voorhees," *(Columbia) State*, April 29, 1969.

54. "Voorhees Rebels Vacate Buildings," *(Columbia) State*, April 30, 1969. Also see *State v. Albert*, 257 S.C. 131 (1971).

55. Moore interviews by author; Robert Goldstein, *Political Repression in Modern America from 1870 to 1976* (Urbana: University of Illinois Press, 2001), 521.

56. *State v. Albert*, 257 S.C. 131 (1971), cert. denied, 409 U.S. 966 (1972); *State v. Raysor*, 257 S.C. 265 (1971), cert. denied, 407 U.S. 916 (1972).

57. "Voorhees Forced to Close," *(Columbia) State*, February 21, 1970.

58. "Voorhees to Start Classes on Monday," *(Columbia) State*, March 19, 1970.

59. *Counts v. Voorhees College*, 312 F. Supp. 598 (D.S.C. 1970); *Counts v. Voorhees College*, 439 F. 2d 723 (4th Cir. 1971).

60. *Richardson v. McFadden*, 563 F.2d 1130 (4th Cir. 1977), cert. denied, 435 U.S. 968 (1978).

61. R. Scott Baker, "Schooling and White Supremacy," in Moore and Burton, *Toward the Meeting of the Waters*, 301.

62. *Richardson v. McFadden*, 540 F.2d 744 (1976).

63. *Richardson v. McFadden*, 563 F.2d 1130 (4th Cir. 1977), cert. denied, 435 U.S. 968 (1978).

64. *Gordon V. Executive Committee of Democratic Party of City Charleston*, 335 F. Supp. 166 (D.S.C. 1971); Record, *Stevenson v. West*, 413 U.S. 902 (1972).

65. *Simkins v. Gressette*, 631 F.2d 287 (4th Cir. 1980).

66. *State v. Smith*, 259 S.C. 496 (1971); *State v. Nelson*, 250 S.C. 6 (1967); *State v. Jenkins*, 249 S.C. 570 (1967); *U.S. v. Harris*, 409 F.2d 77 (4th Cir. 1969); *Broughton v. Jaffee*, 275 S.C. 541 (1981); *Brown v. State Farm Mutual Ins. Co.*, 275 S.C. 276 (1980); *Lance v. Bell*, 125 F.3d 848 (4th Cir. 1997); *Scott v. First Family Financial Services*, 57 F.3d 1067 (4th Cir. 1995); *Blake v. Waccamaw Regional Planning and Development Council of Georgetown County, S.C.*, 45 F.3d 425 (4th Cir. 1994); *Priest v. City of Myrtle Beach, S.C.*, 7 F.3d 225 (4th Cir. 1993); *Green v. K-Mart*, 986 F.2d 1413 (4th Cir. 1993); *Devine v. Thalhimers*, 977 F.2d 572 (4th Cir. 1992); *Mack v. Mobay Corp., Inc.*, 972 F.2d 341 (4th Cir. 1992); *Allen v. Fidelity and Deposit Co. of Maryland*, 515 F.Supp. 1185 (D.S.C. 1981); *State v. Burroughs*, 328 S.C. 489 (Ct. App. 1997); *State v. Singleton*, 319 S.C. (1995); *State v. Creech*, 314 S.C. 76 (1993); *U.S. v. Bright*, 14 F.3d 597 (4th Cir. 1993); *U.S. v. Smalls*, 8 F.3d 822 (4th Cir. 1993).

67. *In re Moore*, 342 S.C. 1, 5 (2000); *Matter of Moore*, 275 S.C. 280 (1980).

68. Moore interviews by author.

69. *Matter of Moore*, 280 S.C. 178 (1984); *Matter of Moore*, 298 S.C. 13 (1989).

70. *In re Moore*, 342 S.C. 1 (2000).

71. Moore interviews by author.

72. Moore interview by author, February 17, 2014.

73. "S.C. Lawyer in Aldermanic Race," *Chicago Defender*, March 16, 1963.

74. *Moorer v. State of S.C.*, 347 F.2d 502 (4th Cir. 1965); *Moorer v. MacDougall*, 245 S.C. 633 (1965); *Moorer v. State of S.C*, 240 F. Supp. 529 (E.D.S.C. 1964); *Moorer v. State*, 244 S.C. 102 (1964); *Moorer v. State of S.C*, 239 F. Supp. 180 (E.D.S.C. 1965).

75. Moore interviews by author.

76. See *Whittenberg v. Greenville County School District*, 298 F. Supp. 784 (D.S.C. 1969).

77. See *Martindale-Hubbell Law Directory*, vol. 5 (Summit, N.J.: Martindale-Hubbell, 1977), 48. Cook died in July 1975. See *U.S. Social Security Death Index, 1935*, available at ancestry.com.

78. *Newman v. Piggie Park Enterprises*, 389 U.S. 815 (1967). See "Trial under Civil Rights Act Begins in Aiken Court," *(Columbia) State*, April 5, 1966.

79. Pride interview by author. This was before *Batson v. Kentucky*, 476 U.S. 79 (1986).

80. See articles about the trial in *(Columbia) State*, October 14, 1975, October 18, 1975,

October 20, 1975, October 21, 1975, October 24, 1975, October 25, 1975, October 27, 1975, and November 24, 1975.

81. *Holt v. Yonce*, 370 F. Supp. 374 (D.S.C. 1973), aff'd, 415 U.S. 969 (1974).

82. "Pride Submits Innocence Plea," *(Columbia) State*, August 20, 1977.

83. "Justice Department Probing Allegations by Hemphill Pride," *(Columbia) State*, March 21, 1980.

84. Editorial, "Black Leaders Off in Pre-Trial Statement," *(Columbia) State*, December 20, 1977.

85. "Pride Is Convicted of Funds Misuse," *(Columbia) State*, December 17, 1977.

86. *In the matter of Hemphill P. Pride*, 11, 276 S.C. 363 (1981).

87. "11 Negroes Running for State Posts," *Florence Morning News*, March 30, 1968.

88. "Candidate Makes Charges against Police," *Florence Morning News*, May 10, 1968.

89. *In the matter of Dorothy V. Sampson*, 259 S.C. 471 (1972).

90. Pride interview by author.

91. Senate Resolution, S. 193, S.C. Gen. Ass., 116th Sess. (January 12, 2005).

92. *Green v. Coffin*, 379 F. Supp. 361 (D.S.C. 1974).

93. *U.S. ex rel. Chaparro v. Resor*, 412 F.2d 443 (4th Cir. 1969); *Dash v. The Commanding General, Fort Jackson, S.C.*, 307 F. Supp. 849 (D.S.C. 1969). See also *McWhirter v. Froehlke*, 351 F. Supp. 1098 (D.S.C. 1972); "Court Recesses Pending Decision on Jurisdiction," *(Columbia) State*, April 23, 1969.

94. "Eight Voices of Dissent in Uniform," *(Columbia) State*, April 16, 2000.

95. A Senate Resolution, adopted January 12, 2005, S.C. General Assembly, 116th Session, 2005–2006.

96. *In the matter of James L. Felder*, 265 S.C. 192 (1975).

97. *In the matter of John Lake, Jr.*, 269 S.C. 170 (1977).

98. Jasper Cureton interview by author, June 19, 2013.

99. *U.S. v. Poston*, 312 F. Supp. 587 (D.S.C. 1970).

100. *Chavous v. Brown*, 299 S.C. 398 (Ct. App. 1989), rev'd, 302 S.C. 308, 312 (1990).

101. *Chavous v. Brown*, cert. granted, judgment vacated, 501 U.S. 1202 (1991) and aff'd, 305 S.C. 387 (1991). See *Edmonson v. Leesville*, 500 U.S. 614 (1990), which applied *Batson v. Kentucky*, 476 U.S. 79 (1985) to civil trials. In *Batson* the court had held that prosecutors could not use peremptory strikes to exclude black jurors without citing a nondiscriminatory reason.

102. See, for example, *State v. Whatley*, 407 S.C. 460 (2014). Opinion by Cureton issued March 19, 2014.

103. Unless otherwise noted, the information on Johnson is from author's interview of I. S. Leevy Johnson on June 12, 2013.

104. "Wife, Children Now on Trial in Man's Death," *(Orangeburg) Times and Democrat*, May 5, 1987, 1B.

105. "Jury Finds Family Innocent of Murder," *(Orangeburg) Times and Democrat*, May 6, 1987, 1.

106. "Black Legislators to Be Forceful," *(Columbia) State*, November 15, 1979; "Blacks to Meet with Civiletti on Senate Reapportionment," *(Columbia) State*, February 5, 1980; "Legislators Urged to Work for Voting Restrictions End," *(Columbia) State*, July 7, 1972.

107. See articles from *(Columbia) State*: "Single Member Council Districts to Be Sought in Suit—Johnson," July 21, 1977; "City Seeks City Council Remapping," September 7, 1977; "Lawsuit Could Make City Vote Moot," December 18, 1979; "Columbia City Council Hears Redistrict Plan," January 11, 1980. Also see *Washington v. Finlay*, 664 F.2d 913 (4th Cir. 1981).

108. See *NAACP v. City of Columbia*, 850 F. Supp. 404 (D.S.C. 1994), aff'd, 33 F.3d 52 (4th Cir. 1994).

109. Doward Harvin, "The History of Blacks in the South Carolina Bar 'I. S. Leevy Johnson'" (unpublished student paper submitted to the author, April 24, 2008).

110. See George Rogers, *Generations of Lawyers* (Columbia: South Carolina Bar Foundation, 1992), 268–69.

CONCLUSION

1. "Negro Lawyers Note Tremendous Improvement," *(Charleston) News and Courier*, July 21, 1968.

2. Ibid.

3. "Marion J. Frederick," in A. B. Caldwell, ed., *History of the American Negro, South Carolina Edition*, vol. 3 (Atlanta: A. B. Caldwell, 1919), 520.

4. Twenty-eight out of 127 lawyers were black. See Roll of Attorneys, South Carolina Supreme Court, 1868–77.

5. "State House: Law School Flap," *(Columbia) State*, 2–A, March 7, 1973.

6. Charles F. Reid, ed., *2013 South Carolina Legislative Manual*, 94th ed. (Columbia: General Assembly of South Carolina, 2013).

7. U.S. Census Bureau; EEO Detailed Census Occupation by Sex and Race/Ethnicity for Residence Geography; Lawyers, and Judges, Magistrates, and other Judicial Workers, 210. http://factfinder.census.gov/faces/tableservices/jsf/pages/productview.xhtml?src=bkmk (accessed September 26, 2016).

INDEX

Printed in the United States
By Bookmasters